CRITICAL SURVEY OF POETRY
German Poets

Editor

Rosemary M. Canfield Reisman
Charleston Southern University

SALEM PRESS
A Division of EBSCO Publishing, Ipswich, Massachusetts

Cover photo:
Bertolt Brecht (© Alfredo Dagli Orti/The Art Archive/Corbis)

Copyright © 2012, by Salem Press, A Division of EBSCO Publishing, Inc.
All rights in this book are reserved. No part of this work may be used or reproduced in any manner whatsoever or transmitted in any form or by any means, electronic or mechanical, including photocopy, recording, or any information storage and retrieval system, without written permission from the copyright owner except in the case of brief quotations embodied in critical articles and reviews or in the copying of images deemed to be freely licensed or in the public domain. For information address the publisher, Salem Press, at csr@salempress.com.

ISBN: 978-1-42983-659-3

CONTENTS

Contributors iv

German Poetry to 1800 1
German Poetry: 1800 to Reunification 22

Rose Ausländer 47
Gottfried Benn 55
Johannes Bobrowski 63
Bertolt Brecht 70
Joseph von Eichendorff 81
Stefan George 92
Johann Wolfgang von Goethe 102
Eugen Gomringer 116
Gottfried von Strassburg 124
Hartmann von Aue 129
Heinrich Heine 138
Hermann Hesse 149
Friedrich Hölderlin 159
Christian Morgenstern 170
Eduard Mörike 179
Lisel Mueller 185
Novalis 192
Rainer Maria Rilke 205
Nelly Sachs 216
Friedrich Schiller 225
Walther von der Vogelweide 237
Wolfram von Eschenbach 248

Checklist for Explicating a Poem 257
Bibliography 260
Guide to Online Resources 263
Category Index 266
Subject Index 269

CONTRIBUTORS

Robert Acker
University of Montana

Lowell A. Bangerter
University of Wyoming

Desiree Dreeuws
Sunland, California

Jack Ewing
Boise, Idaho

Donald P. Haase
Wayne State University

Todd C. Hanlin
University of Arkansas

Rebecca Kuzins
Pasadena, California

R. C. Lutz
CII Group

Laurence W. Mazzeno
Alvernia College

David J. Parent
Normal, Illinois

Margaret T. Peischl
Virginia Commonwealth University

Helene M. Kastinger Riley
Clemson University

Joachim Scholz
Washington College

Nancy E. Sherrod
Georgia Southern University

Jean M. Snook
Memorial University of Newfoundland

Richard Spuler
Rice University

Klaus Weissenberger
Rice University

GERMAN POETRY TO 1800

Poetry as a pleasant distraction from life, as a conventional ornament for social occasions, as linguistic play or experiment, even as the sincere expression of heartfelt emotions, belongs to comparatively recent times. In its beginnings, humankind used the magical power of patterned, rhythmic speech to impose meaning and order on the world. Through poetry, humankind hoped to gain mastery of both the natural and the social environment. Certainly this was true of the Germanic tribes: The first writer to mention Germanic poetry, the Roman historian Tacitus (c. 55-120 C.E.), expressly refers to the Germanic custom of celebrating gods and heroes in song. Religion (humanity's relation to God) and history (humanity's relation to the community in time) were to remain poetry's central domain for centuries to come. Thus, the historical and cultural context can never become a matter of indifference to those who care for poetry. What might appear to later generations as mere background was related strictly to the purpose and theme of poetry in its own day. In ancient times, few deeds were unaccompanied by the poetic word, and fewer still would be remembered were it not for poetry.

Germanic tribes lived on the shores of the North and Baltic seas as early as 2000 B.C.E. Some time after 500 B.C.E., when climatic changes forced most of them to migrate south, they divided into three distinct groups. The North Germanic tribes (Normans, Danes, Jutes) were those that stayed behind; the East Germanic tribes (Goths, Vandals, Burgundians) slowly drifted southward into present-day Hungary, Romania, and Bulgaria; and the West Germanic tribes (Saxons, Franks, Angles, Swabians, Alemanni) moved into the middle of Europe, present-day Germany, northern France, Belgium, and the Netherlands.

The Germanic tribes had barely settled in their new environment when the Huns, a fierce Mongolian people, swept into Europe around 400 C.E. The impact of the Hunnish invasion was most directly felt by the East Germanic tribes. Pushed forward by the relentlessly advancing Huns, the Germanic tribes fell on an already tottering Roman civilization, gaining and losing power over the nations in their path with spectacular speed. The Vandals established kingdoms in Italy, Spain, and North Africa; the Goths, in Italy and Spain; the Burgundians, on the Rhine.

ORIGINS TO ELEVENTH CENTURY

Two hundred years later, these tribes had all but disappeared, exhausted and decimated by their heroic exploits, absorbed by the cultures and people they had overrun, yet they disappeared only after leaving behind a lasting record of their remarkable feats. If history demands patterned, poetic order, it certainly demanded it here, in the face of the splendid achievements and the tragic end of the East Germanic tribes. Soon, the scop, the warrior-poet, sang in the lord's hall of heroic courage and loyalty, of betrayal and revenge, of inscrutable fate and man's fortitude when confronted with its cruel decrees. For centuries, this oral poetry informed and stimulated the imagination of the Germanic tribes until, several hundred years later, some accounts were finally given literary form.

Though naturally influenced by the tumultuous events around them, the West Germanic tribes underwent a gradual development. The most notable migratory action was that of the Angles and some of the Saxons, who, after the Roman forces had pulled out of Britain, began to settle there in the fifth and sixth centuries. On the Continent, historical progress took place under the steady ascendancy of the Franks. Clovis I (481-511) united all major West Germanic tribes, with the exception of the Continental Saxons, under Frankish leadership. When Clovis converted to Roman Catholicism, Latin culture quickly accompanied Christianity on its missionary journeys. The ensuing political and cultural unification was underscored by a growing linguistic unity among the tribes. Starting among the Alemanni of Germany's southern highlands, a consonant shift spread through the West Germanic tribes, differentiating their language from that of their North Germanic neighbors as well as that of the Angles and Saxons. This language, Old High German, is considered the first distinct forerunner of modern German.

The unity of the West Germanic tribes reached its culmination under the rule of Charlemagne (768-814). Charlemagne was not only a brilliant political leader but also a farsighted patron of the arts; the earliest extant literary fragments in the vernacular date from his reign. Baptismal vows, creeds, and prayers give evidence of the importance that church and state placed on the vernacular in their concerted effort to convert the Germanic peoples to Christianity. Nevertheless, cultural life under Charlemagne and his Carolingian successors proceeded mostly in Latin. Of lyric poetry in Old High German, only two fragments of poems have survived. Both are religious in nature, though secular poetry did exist, as is indicated by an ecclesiastical injunction against the writing or sending of *Winileodos* (songs of friendship). The "Wessobrunner Gebet" (c. 780; "Wessobrunn Prayer") contains in twenty-eight lines a fragmentary account of creation, while the "Muspilli" (c. 830), almost four times as long, describes the Day of Judgment.

The most important poetic work of the ninth century, however, is an epic, the religious epic *Der Heliand* (c. 840; *The Heliand*, 1966). In its six thousand lines of dramatic alliterative verse, Christ has been transformed into a magnanimous Germanic lord and his apostles into retainers who, moving with him from castle to castle, believe in his mission with unflinching loyalty. Unfortunately, the epic did not have its deserved impact on German literature, because it was not written in Old High German, but in Old Low German (Old Saxon), a Germanic dialect as yet unassimilated by the developing German language. Thus, it was quickly forgotten and not rediscovered until, in the sixteenth century, the Protestant Reformation searched high and low for a historical tradition.

Charlemagne's liberal cultural policies also encouraged a collection of heroic songs reaching back into the pre-Christian days of the Great Migrations. This collection is said to have been burned by Charlemagne's son, the weak and bigoted Louis the Pious. A glimpse of what such a collection might have contained is provided by a brief fragment, the sixty-eight lines of the *Hildebrandslied* (c. 800; *The Song of Hildebrand*, 1957). It commemorates in a terse and somber style the tragic conflict which pits Hildebrand's loyalty to his liege against his affection for his son, who, with an equally fervent loyalty, has embraced the cause of Hildebrand's sworn enemies. Though the poem breaks off before the issue is decided, it is clear that Hildebrand's ideals of heroic conduct will force him to kill his son rather than forsake his lord in battle.

The future of German poetry did not lie with *The Heliand* or with *The Song of Hildebrand*, but with Otfrid von Weissenburg's *Krist* (c. 865; Christ). An Alsatian monk, the first German poet whose name is known, Otfrid incorporated a most promising metrical innovation into his otherwise lackluster disquisitions into the life of Christ. Influenced by the style of Latin church hymns, Otfrid decided to rhyme his poetry. With his work, rhyme—until the ninth century essentially foreign to the alliterative verse of the Germanic tribes—was to establish a hold over German poetry that would not be relinquished until the twentieth century.

Whatever promise Old High German poetry might have held, historical changes brought it to a most ignoble end. Charlemagne's vision of a politically, culturally, and linguistically unified Europe disintegrated in the dynastic feuds of his grandsons. Scarcely thirty years after his death, his empire divided along lines that foreshadowed the borders between the future states of Germany and France. The political split was ratified by a linguistic one: The oaths confirming the Frankish division were no longer sworn in one Frankish language, but in two: Old High German and Romance, the ancestor of modern French.

During the declining years of the Carolingian Empire, the religious unity of Western Europe provided the only force against the centrifugal tendencies of the Germanic tribes. With the growing influence of the Church, Latin inhibited the development of German poetry. This situation became even more serious following the accession of the dukes of Saxony to the throne of what by then had become Germany. With forceful single-mindedness, the Saxon emperors achieved a degree of political and administrative unity that allowed Germany to dominate European politics for more than two centuries. On the other hand, these emperors had neither the time nor the inclination for poetry. Moreover, Saxon—as has been mentioned before—was the only major West Germanic dialect on the Continent that had not yet adopted the consonant shift of Old High German. It was only to be expected that a house of Saxons would have no particular interest or stake in the advance of an Old High German language or literature. The results are certainly striking: Not a single poem in German is extant from a period of some one hundred and fifty years. During these dark ages of neglect, Old High German starved to death. It was only after further linguistic changes, which led to the new language patterns of Middle High German, that German poetry received a second chance.

Eleventh to fourteenth century

In an effort to weaken tribal independence in their realm, the Saxon emperors had relied increasingly on the prelates of the Church for the administration of the country. Unmarried, the higher clergy would obviously be less likely to form dynastic interests of their own and would be more inclined to give their unreserved loyalty to the man who had invested them with their office. In the course of a century, the Church in Germany had thus been transformed into an effective branch of imperial government. Under the Frankish line of the Salians, which followed that of the Saxons, this practice had finally overtaken Rome itself. Henry III (1039-1056) considered it simply one of his personal responsibilities to install and depose popes as he saw fit. Against this glaring political abuse of the Church, the Burgundian monastery of Cluny started a campaign that struck at the heart of the German Empire. The battle cry of Cluny was that all further lay interference in appointments to high ecclesiastical office should cease. Henry IV (1056-1106), politically dependent on a Church hierarchy willing to do his bidding, had no choice but to defy this religious reform. The confrontation lasted for about fifty years and ended in a devastating defeat of the imperial cause, resulting in a dramatic loss of German power without and German unity within.

The effect of the rigorously ascetic revival on poetry proved, at least immediately, no less intimidating. Heavily dogmatic and didactic poetry dominated the second half of the eleventh century. However, it was the very same religious enthusiasm of Cluny that made another spiritual call possible, a spiritual call that was soon to overwhelm Cluny's monastic objectives with a renewed worldliness. Unforeseen adventures arose from the fervent appeal to free the Holy Land from the Saracens, to organize a Crusade. For almost two centuries—the First Crusade began in 1096, the last ended in 1270—the European imagination was captivated by the ideal and the reality of the Crusades as nothing had captivated it since the Great Migrations half a millennium before. The joys of the world quickly crept back into poetry. Narrative poems were told for the sheer fun of telling tall tales of exotic lands. What these poems still lacked, however, was some organizing principle that would lift their episodic style to the level of a unified theme and ethos. This vacuum was soon to be filled by the new, ideal man of the Crusades, the Christian knight.

Knighthood, or chivalry, could trace its origins most directly to the political and economic conditions during and after the Great Germanic Migrations. At a time of rapid tribal expansion and in the absence of the necessary logistical means for the operation of large-scale armies, the tribal lord stood in need of a highly mobile and well-equipped fighting elite. To maintain this force and to gain its unswerving loyalty, the lord rewarded its members by granting them land, the surplus of which would support them and their military craft befittingly. When not called up to serve his lord, the vassal administered his land. He would also be free to grant land to some of his retainers on similar conditions. In this way, there arose over the centuries a whole pyramid of intricate dependencies—the system of feudalism.

Feudalism, however, had slowly begun to deteriorate. The property which the lord had lent to those who had served him faithfully tended to become hereditary. As tribal expansion within the limits of Western Europe could not go on forever, the lords found themselves increasingly hard put to reward those they needed for the exercise of their power, while at the same time and for the same reason, many young noblemen saw themselves excluded from the lifestyle of their fathers.

In this deepening crisis, the Crusades provided European society with a momentary easing of its social and economic dilemmas. Through the Crusades, the inevitable decline of the feudal system was delayed. Knighthood received a reprieve during which it rose to heights of artistic splendor and ethical idealism that were to dazzle the people of Europe long after knighthood itself had lost its historical relevance.

What was new about the ideal of the Christian knight was that, for the first time, Germanic political and social realities were sanctioned by Christian idealism. The perfect knight was to strike a balance between the primarily Germanic virtues of courage, loyalty, and honor and a more tempered set of Christian values such as moderation, chastity, generosity, and mercy. Self-interest, class-interest, and Christian idealism joined forces, allowing the knight to prove himself, through endless adventures, worthy before God and the world.

France was the first nation in which the ideals of chivalry gained a firm hold on literature and life. In Germany, it was only during the rule of Frederick I (1152-1190) of the Swabian house of the Hohenstaufen that chivalry was accepted as an indigenous element of Germanic culture. An extraordinarily brilliant period of German poetry was soon to follow. In the short span of merely two decades (1190 to 1210), several poetic masterpieces were produced which not even the great works of German Romanticism can be said to have surpassed.

NIBELUNGENLIED

The *Nibelungenlied* (c. 1200; English translation, 1848), an epic composed by an unknown Austrian monk, is built on specifically Germanic conceptions in its effort to explore the true values of knighthood. At least two Germanic oral traditions—the Frankish legend of Siegfried and the narrative of the downfall of the Burgundians (or Nibelungs) under the onslaught of the Huns in 437 C.E.—are here combined to create the German national epic. It tells the story of Siegfried, the perfect knight, at the court of the Burgundians and of Kriemhild, his wife, a Burgundian princess, who swears revenge on her kinsmen when she learns that they killed Siegfried—jealous of his unequaled prowess. For thirteen years, she has brooded on the wrong done to her, when Attila offers her his hand in marriage. She accepts and another thirteen years later lures the nobles of her homeland to the court of Attila, where they are slaughtered in a bloodbath which finally engulfs even the vengeful queen. Behind a veneer of courtly decorum and Christian morality, there arises before the listener the most profound image of the heroic age in the German language. A world holds sway in which the joys and sorrows of life are experienced with stark intensity, in which the virtues and vices of men are as bold as the actions they engender, but also a world in which fate, not the deeds of heroes, ultimately determines the course of all events.

Romance

More directly indebted to French influence and the newly established ideals of chivalry are the court epics of Hartmann von Aue (c. 1160-1165 to c. 1210-1220), Wolfram von Eschenbach (c. 1170-c. 1217), and Gottfried von Strassburg (fl. c. 1210). In contrast to the heroic epic, the court epic, or romance (so called because of its origins in the Romance languages), does not restrict itself to the praise of national heroes. Even great men of classical antiquity such as Aeneas and Alexander become heroes of courtly epics. Neither are the fates of nations the concern of romances. Instead, the romance is focused on an individual knight whose valor is tested against the temptations and afflictions of the world. To make these tests as representative as possible, a romance will prefer ideal knights in ideal settings to anything that might smack of mere reality.

The most famous and most popular locale of the German romance is the legendary court of King Arthur and his Knights of the Round Table. Hartmann von Aue introduced the Arthurian theme into the German language. His two Arthurian romances, *Erek* (c. 1190; *Erec*, 1982) and *Iwein* (c. 1190-1205; *Iwein: The Knight with the Lion*, 1979), closely follow court epics of the French poet Chrétien de Troyes in their devotion to the typical preoccupation of the French romance: the discussion and exemplification of ethical conflicts arising within the knightly code of values. Erec neglects his duties as a knight for love of his wife; Iwein neglects his wife for love of knightly adventures. In both cases, harmony is reestablished as soon as the knights have learned the lesson of the golden mean.

The discussion of these neatly, dialectically arranged conflicts proved to be more French than German. The two greatest masters of the German court epic moved away from such delicate planning to pursue the very limits of all courtly conventions. Wolfram, much less learned than Hartmann, proceeded in his *Parzival* (c. 1200-1210; English translation, 1894) with a decidedly unconventional style and theme. Highly individualistic, often obscure in his use of metaphors, he created a world of daring and immoderate yearnings. The story is that of Parzival's vicissitudes on the way to an understanding of life, suffering, and death. During this journey, King Arthur's Round Table is recognized as little more than a stage on the long and narrow path to perfection. Only by abandoning the security of all previous values—not merely by balancing them in an aesthetically pleasing order—only by a complete change of heart does Parzival finally discover the source of all inner peace in the total submission to the will of God. For Wolfram, perfect knighthood is nothing less than sainthood.

It is hard to believe that two works of such contrasting styles and themes as Wolfram's *Parzival* and Gottfried's *Tristan und Isolde* (c. 1210; *Tristan and Isolde*, 1899) were written in the span of less than a decade. What they obviously have in common is their determination to follow courtly ideals beyond all courtly conventions. However, where Wolfram was consciously obscure and other-worldly, Gottfried wanted to be consciously lucid and human. *Tristan and Isolde* is also an epic of immoderation: It speaks of the earthly, sensual passion that Tristan and Isolde feel for each other. Tristan is a vassal of King Mark of Cornwall and Isolde is Mark's young wife, yet Tristan and Isolde persist in their love and build an illicit relationship through long adventures of deceit and subterfuge. The willful, often mocking breach of the knightly ideal of chastity was in itself nothing new for courtly poetry. What was new was the total seriousness, the total lack of frivolity with which Gottfried treated this adulterous union as a troubling human predicament.

Lyric poetry

Lyric poetry, too, experienced an amazing surge of creativity under the auspices of the chivalric ethos. It was poetry devoted primarily to an extremely stylized, extremely idealized form of loving adoration of the "fair sex," a love which in German was to be known as *Minne*, the practitioners of which would become known as *Minnesänger*. This lyric poetry reached its most elaborate form in the song of the troubadour, the *canso d'amor* (love song) of southern France. With ever new variations, the poet describes in his song the typical stages through which he courts a lady who is almost always of a higher station than himself and married to another man. Arduous periods of wooing and pleading are often rewarded by shows of the lady's favor. These shows of favor—smiles, acknowledgments, the wearing of the knight's colors (sexual favors are granted only rarely)—are, nevertheless, constantly jeopardized by malevolent friends and cold conventions, frequently by the fickle or obdurate heart of the lady herself. Thus, brief moments of bliss are usually followed by long spells of mournful longing and dejection. Though a poet's love did at times stray from the elevated plane of these platonic feelings, *Minne* was not incompatible with marriage and should not be misunderstood as an actual challenge to the harsh and dreary marriage conventions of the day. More often than not, *Minnelieder* (songs of *Minne*) were barely more than a fashionable parlor game. In spite of the assumed intimacy of the confessional style, little of what is expressed in them should be taken for more than the polite gallantry of a professional singer in his attempt to gain the protection of a powerful lady at court.

Walther von der Vogelweide

Walther von der Vogelweide (c. 1170-c. 1230) gave the conventions of the troubadours their most creative adaptation in the German language. His strong and unabashed zest for life filled his *Minnelieder* with a surprising vitality. It was this zest for life which convinced Walther that *Minne* cannot be bound to social station, that it can be felt toward any woman, and that true nobility of heart is found more often outside rather than inside the nobility of rank. There, too, love seems so much freer to give itself to the beloved. Walther refused to consider a *Minne* that is predicated on the notion of its remaining unfulfilled anything but a false and inhuman emotion.

In a similar vein, Walther's spontaneous appreciation of nature enlivened the many threadbare metaphors inherited from the troubadours. Even the tradition of the troubadour's *sirventes* (poems exploring political and moral questions) assumed in Walther's hands an unusual urgency. Fights between emperor and pope had erupted again; civil war had returned to Germany; and the lyricist of fervent love threw himself into the partisan struggle with political verse of equal ardor. Walther was undoubtedly not only the greatest but also the most versatile poet of the Middle Ages. Love, nature, politics, and religion were themes for his inspiration, creating an unmatched lyric summa of medieval culture on the eve of that culture's collapse.

Fourteenth to sixteenth century

With the execution of the last of the Hohenstaufens at the hands of his enemies in Italy (1268), the fabric of medieval politics in Germany unraveled rapidly. The election of Rudolph of Habsburg (1273) ushered in an era in which imperial power forsook its claim to European leadership and restricted itself to the politics of dynastic self-aggrandizement. Of even greater importance for the future of medieval culture was the glaring failure of the Crusades in 1270. European nobility in all of its heroic posturing saw itself confronted initially with a serious loss of face and ultimately with an even more serious loss of legitimacy.

While knighthood had weakened itself in seven Crusades, its adventures in the East had helped another class to gather unforeseen strength. As it turned out, the Crusades had opened wider horizons not only for the idealistic imagination of chivalry but also for the decidedly materialistic imagination of the middle class. Trade was flourishing, and so were the cities of Germany. A money economy, originating in Italy, replaced the complex relations of loyalty with the simple cash nexus. Armies of loyal knights gave way to armies of mercenaries; light infantry and gunpowder relegated the heavily armored knight to eventual obsolescence. Even where the knights did manage to redirect their crusading spirit—as did the Knights of the Teutonic Order when they declared the conversion and colonization of Prussia to be a new goal—their efforts could no longer be sustained without the ever more obtrusive money of the burghers. The Middle Ages had entered a period of complex yet obvious transition. The effects of this transition on poetry were equally complex but not nearly as obvious.

The demands of the changing times were felt in the nobility itself. In search of novel themes and renewed vitality, *Minnelieder* strove to combine, rather incongruously, the overwrought ideals of *Minne* with intentionally crude peasant settings. Much of this lyric poetry reads like a deliberate satire of itself. Didactic poems, on the other hand, tried desperately to explain chivalric ideals to a less and less receptive audience. Furthermore, the court epic, sensing the need for a closer grasp of reality, admitted historical events and characters into the never-never land of romance. Soon, the peasant epic evolved to debunk the whole conceited glitter of courtly perfection. *Meier Helmbrecht* (c. 1250; peasant Helmbrecht), the most famous peasant epic in the German language, tells the story of a young man who, seduced by social ambition and the airs of chivalry, joins a band of robber barons. At the end of a short life of tragic illusions and suffering, he is turned away by his own father and finally hanged by the people of his own village.

Social and economic power shifted from the knightly courts to the towns and their burghers. The rising middle class, however, was slow to realize a class consciousness of its own. The cultural vacuum that arose as a result of this hesitation was not easily filled. Instead of creating values appropriate to its interests and aspirations, the middle class felt that its socioeconomic power entitled it at long last to the values of its erstwhile betters. The resulting disparity between the anachronistic idealism of what was believed and the materialism of what was practiced led to a whole culture of satire, a culture castigating itself for its lack of authenticity.

The pretensions of the court epic were lampooned in the mock epic, while the excitement of knightly adventures gave way to stories about the pranks with which clever rogues exploited the vanity of others. The animal fable, derived from Greek and Oriental sources, finally broadened the social critique to include all classes of society. *Reynke de Vos* (1498; Reynard the fox) no longer poked fun at the nobility, but at all the social climbers who, like their archetype, the cunning and unprincipled fox, spare no effort on their way into the antechambers of the king. The international best seller of late medieval satire was Sebastian Brant's *Das Narrenschiff* (1494; *The Ship of Fools*, 1509), a poem whose author viewed his own times with an utterly jaundiced eye. Brant, who is considered one of Germany's earliest Humanists, was in fact no reformer. He favored no trend or class and offered no prospect of any solution. More than one hundred follies and vices are paraded around and soundly thrashed by an impartially venomous tongue, leaving a vivid picture of the cultural uncertainty that gripped the waning Middle Ages.

The curious inability of the middle class to move beyond the cultural values of a society whose economic and social restrictions it had long left behind is evidenced in the appropriation by sturdy and conscientious burghers of the courtly *Minnelieder.* From a wide variety of *Minnelieder*, which they carefully collected and studied, artisans in the towns culled a system of twelve rigid patterns. These they proceeded to employ, with slavish adherence, for their own songs on moral and didactic themes. *Minnesänger* had turned into *Meistersänger* (master singers), well-intentioned craftspeople who made up for their lack of imagination by a display of pedantic learning and a bizarre ingenuity in the arrangement of their metrical schemes. Inventiveness reached fantastical heights when it was felt that only those singers could be declared *Meistersänger* who had added at least one original "tone" (verse arrangement) to their guild's stock in trade. In his middle-class smugness and with his matter-of-fact imagination, the cobbler Hans Sachs (1494-1576)—one of the last and certainly the most accomplished of the *Meistersänger*—assumed an almost patriarchal stature in German literature. Nine years before his death, he proudly counted among his numerous literary works no fewer than 4,275 *Meistersänge* (master songs) in 275 strophic forms, 13 of which he had invented himself.

The *Volkslied* (folk song)—to the modern sensibility, the most appealing poetic achievement of the fourteenth and fifteenth centuries—occupied a very marginal place in the literary world of its day. It, too, had its origins in the *Minnelied*, but, in contrast to the *Meistersäng*, the *Volkslied* refused to live up to the formality of its courtly predecessor and instead infused the conventional themes of love and longing with the simplicity of experience. In simple rhymes, repetitive images, and catchy refrains, the *Volkslied* deals with typical situations of easily identifiable classes of people: hunters, millers, students, soldiers, and so on. Over the centuries, many of the *Volkslieder* were overlaid with the patina of a garbled text, a naïve nonsense which, if anything, seems to have added to their perennial charm.

In spite of its popularity, the *Volkslied* did not possess the formative power to fill the cultural void that the receding chivalric society had left behind. Other forces had to originate to fashion a new image of world, humans, and society. When these forces arrived on the scene, they were not particularly related to poetry, nor were they particularly productive of it. The origins of modern humans were accompanied by a tremendous loss of the power of poetry. The culture of knighthood had been an unmistakably poetic one; prose virtually did not exist as a literary form. The new society arose almost in the absence of poetic formulation and evolved a decidedly prosaic culture.

Like the eleventh century, the fourteenth century was marked by a wave of religious fervor. In contrast to the earlier revival, however, this religious enthusiasm championed no ecclesiastical cause. The secular power of the Church had reached its high point at the end of the thirteenth century when, with almost no transition, it found itself embroiled in every imaginable ecclesiastical and political trouble. The Babylonian Captivity of the Papacy in southern France (1309-1377) and the following forty years of schism—in which two, then three popes stood against one another—had driven the religious aspirations of the people upon themselves and into the arms of mysticism. Mysticism, a form of religious individualism which strives for a direct union with God through contemplation, found its most creative expression in the philosophical sermons of Meister Eckhart (died 1327). The imaginative prose style used to explain his difficult and often highly paradoxical thoughts greatly extended the scope of the German language.

At a time when northern Europe developed in mysticism a religious version of individualistic self-reliance, the Italian city-states—for once uninhibited by the presence of either pope or emperor—advanced a strictly secular counterpart. Believing themselves the rightful heirs of classical Rome, the Italians accepted it as their duty to resurrect the classical ideal of a human perfection to be achieved without interference of church or state. Faith in a rebirth (renaissance) of classical antiquity soon spread to other parts of Europe. What the Humanists of the German Renaissance lacked in natural links to the classical spirit, they eagerly compensated for by a meticulous adherence to its letter. Preoccupied with the editing and translating of classical texts, German Humanism quickly degenerated from a rebirth of humanity to a mere rebirth of philology. It is true that with the image of the *poeta doctus* (poet-scholar), Humanism gave the poet a fresh and lofty mission. As a learned educator, he was no longer to be subservient to anything outside the demands of his chosen profession. At the same time, however, Humanism clipped the wings of German poets by insisting that Humanist poetry could only succeed in the clarity of Latin, not in the murky barbarisms of the German language. The rich harvest of Latin poetry produced by German poets during the Renaissance yielded some impressive fruit. Nevertheless, it has remained a harvest unclaimed, a literature relegated to the limbo of unread and forgotten books.

As admirable as the goals and values of the German Humanists in all of their balanced sanity might have been, no cultural reform is likely to succeed that sets itself up in opposition to the imaginative propensities of the people it wants to educate. Humanism was destined to remain the ideal of a small elite of literati. It was quickly swept away by a reform that did speak to the imagination of the people, Martin Luther's Protestant Reformation.

SIXTEENTH TO EIGHTEENTH CENTURY

When Martin Luther (1483-1546) posted his ninety-five theses against indulgences on a church door in Wittenberg, nobody, least of all Luther, could have predicted the repercussions this act would have for him and his country. Despair about the prevailing corruption of the Church was general, and there was nothing in Luther's theses that had not been said before. Still, the object of his attack was chosen with the instinct of a true rebel.

In the granting of indulgences, the Church had given itself the power to remit some of the punishment a sinner had to expect after death even for those sins that had been forgiven in the sacrament of penance. This remittance of future punishment for past sins was usually tied to some spiritual or material sacrifice on the part of the sinner: fasting, praying, almsgiving, pilgrimages, and so on. In the fifteenth century, a financially strapped Papacy had made monetary "sacrifices" by the sinner—to be paid into the Papacy's always empty coffers—the center of its dealings with indulgences and a regular item in its fiscal planning. Soon, unscrupulous monks roamed the countryside, promising nothing short of salvation to those willing and able to pay for it. The poor, who of all classes were most dependent on the hereafter for any hope of a happier life, felt excluded from the spiritual benefits of these transactions. The selling of indulgences represented simply too much of what people in Germany had hated for so long: the Church's heavy-handed interference in people's most personal affairs, its greedy exploitation of foreign countries, and its un-Christian preference for the rich. Thus, a devotional practice which had existed in the Church for a long time galvanized the discontented masses of Germany almost overnight.

The initial strength of a movement is rarely a reliable indication of its staying power. What made Luther's reforms survive was that Luther himself, appalled by the widespread anarchy he had caused, directed his reform into the rigid channels of a new ecclesiastical organization. Excommunicated by the pope and under imperial ban, he turned for support to the only authority that could still profit from his cause: the power of Germany's territorial princes. Lured by the promise of the confiscation of Church property, they were only too willing to become Luther's *Notbischöfe* (emergency bishops). When the emperor finally found the time and means to intervene, he saw himself confronted by a well-entrenched state church. Reluctantly, he accepted its existence in the Peace of Augsburg (1555).

It remains astounding that the sixteenth century, which stirred so many political, social, and religious emotions, produced almost no poetry. It is less surprising that the important contributions that were made came during the first two decades of the Reformation and were the work of Luther himself.

Luther's greatest literary achievement was his extraordinarily successful translation of the Bible. It is hard to think of any book in the German language that has influenced German literature more than has the *Lutherbibel* (1522, 1534). For more than a century, Middle High German had been in transition. The imperial chancery had long attempted to arrive at a uniform German language for its own legal and diplomatic affairs. Whatever effort may have gone before, Modern High German came alive only when Luther, through his ingenious use of dialect and idiom, transformed the German of the chanceries into a language that could serve all people for all purposes. Luther's language spread even faster than his Reformation. By the end of his life, more than 100,000 copies of the *Lutherbibel*—an amazing number for those days—were in circulation. For the first time in its history, Germany had a standard written language.

Luther contributed most directly to poetry through his composition of thirty-six hymns, the only lasting poetic creations of the whole of the sixteenth century in Germany. Spiritual songs had certainly existed before, often as converted versions of popular secular songs. What distinguishes Luther's hymns—one has only to think of the rousing "Ein feste Burg ist unser Gott" ("A Mighty Fortress Is Our God")—is that they express not only the communing of an individual with his God but also the common faith of the whole congregation. Luther's *Geistliche Lieder* (1524; *Spiritual Songs*, 1853) started a tradition of hymnal poetry in Germany which was to remain creative well into the nineteenth century.

It must have seemed clear from the beginning that the Peace of Augsburg had been arranged as little more than a truce between the warring parties. By the early seventeenth century, Catholic and Protestant princes began to arm and organize their hatred in opposing leagues. The bloody Thirty Years' War (1618-1648) started in Prague when the Protestant nobility of Bohemia refused to acknowledge the accession of the Catholic emperor, Ferdinand II, to the throne of Bohemia. With the help of the Catholic League, Ferdinand proved victorious in 1620, and the war appeared to have come to a quick end. Too much, though, rode on the Protestant cause. Alarmed by the Catholics' easy victory and their brutal reprisals, the Protestant princes, under the leadership of Danish King Christian, resolved to try for another outcome. Once again, Ferdinand prevailed in 1626, this time with the help of his celebrated general Albrecht von Wallenstein. The next Protestant willing to try improving Protestant fortunes was Swedish King Gustavus, and under him—not without the financial support of Catholic France—the Protestant cause finally triumphed, though Gustavus himself was killed in the decisive battle in 1632. With the death of Gustavus and the murder of Wallenstein in 1634, it looked as if the war had spent itself, yet as no one seemed satisfied with the resulting stalemate, hostilities were resumed on an even larger scale. France entered the war on the side of the Protestants, while Spain fought for the imperial and Catholic party. In 1635, chastened by seventeen years of grueling war and appalled by its widening dimensions, the Protestant princes arranged a peace with Ferdinand. The task of ridding themselves of their former allies, however, proved to be a lengthy and frustrating affair. None of these friends wanted to leave Germany without having something to show for his pains. War and negotiations dragged on for another thirteen years, until the Peace of Westphalia, in 1648, ratified the total exhaustion and despoiling of Germany.

About half of the German population died as a result of the Thirty Years' War. Agriculture almost ground to a halt as hundreds of villages simply ceased to exist. Trade had been interrupted for too long to be resumed without great delay; neither was there any capital to restart even the most essential industries. The country had been bled white. Only political systems, the most parasitic of all human organizations, increased and multiplied with prodigious fertility. By 1648, Germany had disintegrated into eighteen hundred independent territories, fifteen hundred of them averaging a population of about three hundred people. Even among the remaining territories, barely a handful could be classified as states. The nobility survived the war nearly intact, and the reconstruction of Germany proceeded under its leadership and on its terms, delaying the assertion of a middle-class consciousness for more than a century.

In the context of this momentous national decline, German literature tried belatedly to absorb the Humanism of the Italian Renaissance into the vernacular. For guidance and inspiration, poets and critics turned to France, the country in which such an assimilation of the Italian Renaissance had been accomplished most successfully. What the French poet and aesthetician Joachim du Bellay had done for France with his *La Défense et illustration de la langue française* (1549; *The Defence and Illustration of the French Language*, 1939), Martin Opitz wanted to do for his compatriots seventy-five years later.

Martin Opitz

Das Buch von der deutschen Poeterey (1624; book on German poetry), by Martin Opitz (1597-1639), although a very slim volume by the standards of German scholarship, became the most influential treatise on German poetry for more than a century. Its program was as simple as it was practical. For the Renaissance, poetry was a branch of rhetoric, a rhymed form of oratory whose ultimate aim lay not within itself, but in the pleasing instruction and persuasion of its reader. Since Aristotle's treatment of the subject, rhetoric had always been thought to follow objective, teachable rules. All that needed to be stated more explicitly was simply how German poets could profit from these rules in their efforts to construct more persuasive poems. First, Opitz suggested, rhetorical poetry, like any other argument, needs to be organized rationally, avoiding everything that might startle or confuse. Second, rhetorical poetry ought to be elegant, employing the fitting word while never offending with even the semblance of crudity. Finally, rhetorical poetry must be dignified, a goal to be achieved by borrowing as many lofty metaphors from the ancients as can reasonably be accommodated by the text.

In his poetry—very mediocre stuff—Opitz conformed to the letter of his own law. It is poetry in which virtuosity of form and coldness of feeling stand in direct proportion to each other. As with the classical Sophists, who prided themselves on the fact that they could argue with equal conviction on both sides of any issue, Opitz's poetic persuasiveness comes across as strangely opportunistic, even indifferent to the ostensible purpose for all of his rhetorical posturing: the themes of his poetry. The vanity of all earthly things, the praise of love, the inconstancies of fortune, the sorrows of war, and the longing for peace are all treated with an equally detached expediency.

Baroque poetry

Soon, however, the frightening insecurities of life, made so obvious by the horrors of the Thirty Years' War, asked more from poetry than Opitz's rationalistic disdain and stoic equanimity. Life could no longer be treated as a mere occasion for the making of good poetry. The resulting seriousness about subject matter also placed greater demands on the rhetorical form, straining it to the breaking point in the service of a poem's passionate pleading. The period characterized by this new strain, this contorted urgency, is called the Baroque (a word of Portuguese origin describing the contorted shape of irregular pearls).

Andreas Gryphius

The poet most often identified with German Baroque poetry is Andreas Gryphius (1616-1664). Having experienced the brutalities of war in a traumatic childhood that left him an orphan at an early age, Gryphius became obsessed with the Christian message of humanity's utterly fallen state. In contrast to Opitz, Gryphius was a man of unshakable conviction, and it was the strength of this conviction which made his rhetoric so Baroque, so forced in its effort to persuade at all costs. At no point did it occur to Gryphius that the direct expression of his personal experiences might be the most appropriate theme for his poetry. The rhetoric of the Renaissance valued the persuasiveness of the representative, not the individualistic or existential. Gryphius, therefore, clothed his fears and pains in the verbal pomp of grandiose metaphors, expanding, recapitulating, polishing his unvarying message in an endless drive for more perfect rhetorical strategies.

If in Gryphius's poetry representative rhetoric and existential message still fused in a creative though distorted vision, by the end of the seventeenth century, the power of rhetoric overwhelmed even the most serious subjects and finally disentangled itself from all of them. Opitz had not been very particular about his themes, but at least the comparative simplicity of his rhetoric had allowed no jarring disparity between elaborate form and superficial content. By the end of the seventeenth century, however, rhetoric resolved to disguise the absence of original themes by a most ornate extravagance in its treatment of traditional ones. This trend toward rhetorical affectation was by no means peculiar to German poetry; Italian and Spanish poets had set the example of virtuosity for its own sake.

CHRISTIAN HOFMANN VON HOFMANNSWALDAU

In Germany, the leading exponent of ultimate refinement and the mastery of all technical skills was Christian Hofmann von Hofmannswaldau (1617-1679). Hofmannswaldau's cherished subject was the vanity of all earthly joys, particularly the futility of erotic pleasure, yet his painstaking search for the most exquisite epithet, the most luxuriously sensuous metaphor, the most sensational analogy seemed to circumvent rather than to promote his somber faith. The feverish obsession with which Hofmannswaldau dwelled on the erotic pleasures he condemned betrayed him for what he really was: an eroticist with a bad conscience. In this respect, Hofmannswaldau was quite typical of Baroque culture at the end of the seventeenth century. Those espousing this culture no longer were convinced of what it said yet lived under the compulsion to say it ever more vehemently, as if repeating its faltering beliefs might rouse them to their former vigor. Instead, a less troubled generation started to react to the whole phantasmagoric display of the Baroque with swift retribution. At the turn of the eighteenth century, middle-class rationality still prided itself on its own good conscience and felt absolutely no qualms about dismissing the bad conscience that had preceded it.

EIGHTEENTH CENTURY

The politics of continental Europe in the eighteenth century—until the French Revolution of 1789—were taken up with a series of dynastic struggles that led to several international wars: the War of the Spanish Succession (1701-1714), the War of the Polish Succession (1733-1735), the War of the Austrian Succession (1740-1748), and the War of the Bavarian Succession (1778-1779). The absolute control which royal and princely families exercised over their states transformed any dynastic haggling among the intricately related ruling houses of Europe into an immediate and serious international power struggle. If these prolonged family feuds had a common concern, it was their desire to let no upstart join their illustrious ranks and thus destroy whatever balance of power they had orchestrated. However, it was the rapid rise of just such an upstart house and nation that provided Germany with its most important political development of the century. Prussia under the rule of the Hohenzollerns was the last state in Europe to emerge as one of its leading powers. Not even a kingdom before 1701, Prussia had become, under the hands of frugal and disciplined rulers, a power that half a century later was able to hold its own against the combined forces of Austria, France, and Russia.

Oddly enough, these dramatic political events did not influence German culture significantly. While the nobility had reserved for itself the theater of international politics, it had, at the same time and by an unspoken agreement, granted the middle class a considerable degree of private security and peace. After the hardships of the Thirty Years' War, the middle class was eager to accept such a bargain, at least until it would be able to rebuild its economic stamina. Thus, the eighteenth century presents the picture of a Germany in which the nobility was responsible for matters of politics and the middle class was responsible for everything else.

In the running of its affairs, the middle class was greatly helped by the spirit of rationalism and empiricism. Rationalism had become the philosophy of the bourgeoisie in France since René Descartes had declared reason, rather than tradition or precedent, as the sole authority in the management of human conduct. Empiricism, an elaboration of rationalism developed in England by John Locke (1632-1704), specified that reason needs to be based on experience and that no rational judgment ought to be made without prolonged observation of the facts. French rationalism and English empiricism combined to inspire the Age of Enlightenment. The middle class, which had nothing to lose by the abolition of a tradition that kept it out of power and had everything to gain from the rational observation of political, social, and economic facts, embraced the Enlightenment as its most sacred mission.

To the poets of the Enlightenment, the contorted rhetoric of the Baroque appeared neither rational nor based on facts. A first reaction against Baroque poetry had occurred in France, where Nicolas Boileau-Despréaux, in his *L'Art poétique* (1674; *The Art of Poetry*, 1683), had insisted on the sober standards of truthfulness, naturalness, and reasonableness in the writing of poetry. In 1730, Johann Christoph Gottsched (1700-1766) presented his countrymen with a German version of Boileau's creed in his *Versuch einer critischen Dichtkunst vor die Deutschen* (1730; attempt at a critical art of poetry for Germans). How quickly, though, attitudes were beginning to change in Germany is evident from the fact that Gottsched and his theories of rational poetry turned into the laughingstock of German poets in less than twenty years.

The reaction against Gottsched was led by two Swiss professors, Johann Jakob Bodmer (1698-1783) and Johann Jakob Breitinger (1701-1776). Both men were admirers of the English scene and favored its literature over that of the French. In typically empiricist fashion, they suggested that it might prove more profitable to deduce a good poetic theory from the study of good poetry, rather than to hope for good poetry to be written in accordance with some preconceived poetic theory. In short, the theory of poetry must follow, not precede, the practice of poetry. Looking at poems without prejudicial expectations, Bodmer and Breitinger discovered that a good poem is, above all, imaginative and that reason played a very secondary role in its creation. The ensuing fight between the two camps ended with the total defeat of Gottsched and of the French influence over German poetry. In the end, what turned the tide in the acrimonious squabbles was the fact that Bodmer and Breitinger could point to a young poet who substantiated and justified all of their claims, while Gottsched, as hard as he tried, could not.

FRIEDRICH GOTTLIEB KLOPSTOCK

This young, amazingly original poet was Friedrich Gottlieb Klopstock (1724-1803). Klopstock's poetry, with its outbursts of feeling and its flights of the imagination, caught the reading public totally by surprise. Klopstock made it his personal responsibility to restore to poetry the honorable function which it once had exercised within the Germanic tribes: to guide and express humanity's relation to God, nature, and society. As the prophet of an all-powerful poetry, he naturally felt no inhibition to dismiss what small-minded academicians had laid down as poetic law. Language, Klopstock believed, belongs to poets, and only they can determine its possibilities. In incomplete sentences, in irregular syntax, often in free rhythms, Klopstock stammered in awe before the grandeur of his themes (God, nature, love, patriotism) as much as before the sublime emotions these themes evoked in him.

It was Klopstock's faith in the power of poetry that impelled him to write in the genre in which poetry had exercised its power over society most forcefully: He set out to write an epic. Klopstock's genius, unfortunately, was lyric rather than epic, and his *Der Messias* (1748-1773), which swelled to twenty thousand lines, has remained one of the most monotonous and unreadable epics of all time. The passion which gave Klopstock's shorter poems their distinction could not be sustained over the course of twenty-five years; his emotions turned flat and belabored, exhausting and finally grating on the sensibilities of the reader.

Not even Klopstock's lyric poems withstood the test of time as well as one might have expected. In spite of his emotionalism, Klopstock abided by the basic principles of rhetorical poetry: His feelings did not spontaneously transform themselves into words. To create a poetic effect, it was not enough for Klopstock to relate his experience poetically. That experience, however personal, needed to be made representative of all experiences under similar conditions. To arrive at this representative quality, the poet had to generalize the intimacy of what he felt until the feeling became comprehensible, not to say reasonable, to the reader. Klopstock, who was a very emotional poet, almost never lets the reader share in the immediacy of his emotions. Even when Klopstock seems to have been sincerely overwhelmed, one almost always senses the rational scaffolding that supports the poetic expression of his ecstasies.

In the second half of the eighteenth century, faith in human experience as representative and rational received a mighty jolt when it became clear that experiences are neither shared nor accessible to reason. On the contrary, each person's experiences create a unique world—a strictly individualistic world and therefore (as one needs a point of reference outside oneself for rationality) beyond the power of reason.

JOHANN GOTTFRIED HERDER

From these disturbing insights, the philosopher and critic Johann Gottfried Herder (1744-1803) drew some surprisingly fruitful conclusions for poetry. As language originally was meant to express the emotional responses to experiences, and as these emotional responses are as individualistic and irrational as the experiences which caused them, the most primordial form of language could not have been rational prose but must have been irrational poetry. Poetry is the mother tongue of the human race, because it is in poetry that humanity's first and only appropriate interpretations of the world occurred.

Most existing poetry, sadly enough for Herder, served as pleasing ornament or rhetorical confirmation of an already charted human environment. This trend needed to be reversed; poetry needed to reassume its primary function. Above all, it had to regain access to basic human experiences within the tradition to which it wanted to speak. Attempts to rejuvenate German poetry in accordance with the standards of Greece, Rome, or France were doomed to fail. Instead, a conscious effort was necessary to enable German poetry to reestablish its ties to the life of the German people. To this end, the poetic language would have to cleanse itself of all artificiality and return to the simplicity and spontaneity exemplified in the creations of folk poetry.

JOHANN WOLFGANG VON GOETHE

The success of Herder's ideas was not, as has often been claimed, immediate or sweeping. Of the young poets of the time, only one showed himself deeply affected, yet one poet was all Herder needed for his theory to triumph, for this young man was Johann Wolfgang von Goethe (1749-1832).

Goethe met Herder in 1770, and one year later Goethe's poems usually designated as *Sesenheimer Liederbuch* (1775-1789, 1854; *Sesenheim Songs*, 1853) made Herder's program come true. The twenty-two-year-old poet speaks of his love for the pastor's daughter at Sesenheim in tones of boundless joy, as if such love had never existed before and would never exist again. With a relaxed innocence, he trusts the poetic quality of all that is natural and recovers for the language of poetry, without the slightest tinge of embarrassment, love and heart, flowers and kisses, the sun, the moon, the air, and the clouds.

Still, for Herder, the poet was not merely an innocent participant in the world's harmony. As a creator, the poet also carried grave responsibilities for the state of human affairs. In a series of forceful odes, Goethe explored the challenges of any creative response to earthly existence. Through a study of great prototypes (Prometheus, Mohammed, Ganymede) and their rhythms of life, Goethe felt confirmed in his belief that equal creativity is required for rebellion against and submission to the flow of things in this world. A poet can prefer one of these attitudes to the other only at the expense of constraining his or her most vital gifts, an infinite capacity for experience.

Goethe's career as an administrator at the court of Weimar (1775-1786) demanded a firmer, more realistic response from the poet. In view of humanity's innumerable limitations, moderation had the last word. Emotional introspection was replaced by objective overview, as the typical rather than the extraordinary in life received Goethe's attention. Only in an occasional lyric sigh for release—as in Germany's most famous poem, the weightless, dreamlike "Über allen Gipfeln ist Ruh" ("Over All the Hilltops It Is Still")—could Goethe admit to himself the strain which his search for order and objectivity had placed on him.

Emotional release in the midst of order and objectivity became Goethe's great discovery on his journey through Italy (1786-1788). Goethe lived and celebrated this release upon his return to Weimar in his cycle of *Römische Elegien* (1793; *Roman Elegies*, 1876). The unashamed eroticism of the classical age is praised here in the strict order of classical meters. Emphasizing the sensual, often outright licentious foundations of antiquity's formal achievements, Goethe freely mocked his compatriots' prudishly ideal conception of classical perfection. Almost a quarter of a century later, Goethe would reaffirm his faith in sensuality as a precondition of great art—this time encouraged by his discovery of Persian poetry—in a similar cycle of poems, his *Westöstlicher Divan* (1819; *West-Eastern Divan*, 1877).

Goethe's lyric poetry reached its last peak in the eighteenth century between 1797 and 1798 when, in friendly competition with Friedrich Schiller, Goethe wrote several of his finest ballads.

Friedrich Schiller

Friedrich Schiller (1759-1805), the greatest dramatist of the eighteenth century, was a primarily speculative mind, and his poetry rarely achieves the confessional intimacy which so often makes Goethe's poems read like fragments of an autobiography. Schiller philosophized in his poems on the painful antagonism between what is and what ought to be, between the innate freedom of humans and the acquired constraints of a person's conventional mind and heart.

These differences of poetic perspective also distinguish Goethe's and Schiller's ballads. The ballads of Goethe remain close to their popular roots; they focus on the inexplicable omnipresence of demonic powers, as in the well-known "Der Zauberlehrling" ("The Sorcerer's Apprentice"). Schiller's ballads, by contrast, dramatize ethical or philosophical conflicts: The downfall of pride is the theme of "Der Taucher" ("The Diver"); the jealousy of the gods, that of "Der Ring des Polykrates" ("The Ring of Polycrates"); and "Die Bürgschaft" ("The Pledge") proclaims the invincible power of friendship. With their easy combination of dramatic narrative and didactic intent, Schiller's ballads enjoyed an unparalleled popularity throughout the nineteenth century; in modern times, they are often unjustly dismissed.

Friedrich Hölderlin

Schiller's poetry of ideas and Goethe's poetry of experience were fused at the beginning of the nineteenth century by Friedrich Hölderlin (1770-1843). Hölderlin wrestled for a few intense years with such apparent abstractions as freedom, love, fatherland, divinity, and fate in intensely existential, at times opaque poems until the onset of a severe mental illness at the age of thirty-three broke up his creative struggle.

Classical Greece was Hölderlin's model of a harmonious society, and the French Revolution raised his hopes for a reconstitution of such a society even in his own country. Hölderlin wanted to be the prophet of this great advent. To be a worthy prophet, he was ready to bridge the gulf between future and present, ideal and reality, knowing full well that this would mean to be exiled from both, to exist as a lonely wanderer in time, a victim of his own promises. His having been exiled by God and humanity—expressed in poems such as "Die Heimat" ("Homeland") and "Abendphantasie" ("Evening Fantasy")—Hölderlin considered a great suffering and a great distinction, the suffering and distinction of a heroic fate. Hölderlin's only fear was that he might not be equal to the demands of this calling. His unquestioning faith in the power of poetry he shared with the Romantics of his era, while the humility with which he lived his vocation foreshadowed a much more modern sensibility.

Bibliography

Becker-Cantarino, Barbara, ed. *German Literature of the Eighteenth Century: The Enlightenment and Sensibility.* Rochester, N.Y.: Camden House, 2005. Essays ranging from historical contexts to dominant ideas in the works of major writers. Bibliography and index.

Beiser, Frederick C. *The Romantic Imperative: The Concept of Early German Romanticism.* Cambridge, Mass.: Harvard University Press, 2003. Explains how early German romanticism differed from later romanticism. One chapter defines "Romantic Poetry," which the writer insists dominates and defines the Romantic movement. An important reinterpretation.

Classen, Albrecht, ed. and trans. *Late-Medieval German Women's Poetry: Secular and Religious Songs*. Rochester, N.Y.: D. S. Brewer, 2004. Through intensive research, the writer has discovered and identified a number of German women who wrote lyric poetry in the fifteenth and sixteenth century and undoubtedly will be added to the literary canon. An important contribution to medieval studies. Introduction, notes, and interpretive essay by the editor.

Cocalis, Susan L., ed. *German Feminist Poems from the Middle Ages to the Present: A Bilingual Anthology*. New York: Feminist Press, City University of New York, 1986. Introduces and rediscovers German women poets dating back to the thirteenth century.

Dobozy, Maria. *Re-membering the Present: the Medieval German Poet-Minstrel in Cultural Context*. Turnhout, Belgium: Brepois, 2005. Examines performance art from 1170 to 1400, pointing out both how the fact of performance influenced the poet's techniques and how the poet-performer used his art to mold his society. Bibliography and index.

Gentry, Francis G., et al., eds. *German Epic Poetry*. New York: Continuum, 1995. Heroic poetry from the great epics of German literature, including *Jungere Hildebrandslied*, *The Battle of Ravenna*, *Bitterolf and Dietlieb*, and *The Rose Garden*.

Haymes, Edward R., and Susann T. Samples. *Heroic Legends of the North: An Introduction to the Nibelung and Dietrich Cycles*. New York: Garland, 1996. Traces the origins of epic tales in the Dark Ages and follows their spread throughout medieval literature. Surveys the medieval literary versions: the hero, heroic poetry, and the Heroic Age.

Hutchinson, Peter, ed. *Landmarks in German Poetry*. New York: Peter Lang, 2000. Examines the scope of German poetry, providing critical essays and history.

Newman, Jane O. *Pastoral Conventions: Poetry, Language, and Thought in Seventeenth Century Nuremberg*. Baltimore: Johns Hopkins University Press, 1990. Traces the development of the seventeenth century Nuremberg pastoral poetry society Pegnesischer Blumenorden as a historical, interpretive community of theorists and poets, and offers a detailed analysis of their writings, through which are explored issues at the center of scholarly debate about the Renaissance and early modern period.

Resler, Michael, ed. and trans. *German Romance I*. Rochester, N.Y.: D. S. Brewer, 2003. In this first volume of a series, Middle High German versions of Arthurian romances and translations into English are presented on facing pages. Extensive notes, bibliography, and index.

Walsøe-Engel, Ingrid, ed. *German Poetry from the Beginnings to 1750*. Foreword by George C. Schoolfield. New York: Continuum, 1992. These translations into English are an excellent starting place for the study of early German poetry. Bibliography and index.

Joachim Scholz

GERMAN POETRY: 1800 TO REUNIFICATION

The French critic Hippolyte Taine (1828-1893) once wrote that between 1780 and 1830, Germany brought forth all the ideas of his age. Although somewhat hyperbolic, Taine's pronouncement should not be taken lightly. These fifty years span the period of Romanticism in German literature, art, and philosophy, and its many innovations in poetry left their mark in a pervasive, if occasionally discontinuous, tradition.

Romanticism

German Romanticism can be said to have an early and a late phase. The early period is identified chiefly with August Wilhelm von Schlegel (1767-1845), his brother Friedrich (1772-1829), Ludwig Tieck (1773-1853), Novalis (Friedrich von Hardenberg, 1772-1801), Friedrich Schiller (1759-1805), and Friedrich Schleiermacher (1768-1834). The early phase was more critical and theoretical than late Romanticism, which counted more poets among its adherents, including Achim von Arnim (1781-1831), Clemens Brentano (1778-1842), and Joseph von Eichendorff (1788-1857).

Walter Benjamin has maintained that the German Romantics confronted their times not primarily on epistemological terms, even though these were in fact significant (for example, the philosophy of Johann Gottlieb Fichte, 1762-1814), but instead primarily through the medium of art. Friedrich von Schlegel saw the potential of the new age in the spirit of poetry. His essay "Progressive Universalpoesie" ("Progressive Universal Poetry") addresses a fundamental design of early Romanticism: the universal poeticization of life. Conceptually, Romantic poetry (in the broad sense) embraces all traditional genres of literary and philosophic discourse within its totalizing system. This view radically reformulated the mimetic possibilities of nature and privileged poetic perspective in new, epoch-making ways.

Novalis once wrote:

> Romanticism is nothing other than a qualitative sublimation.... By giving the commonplace exceptional significance, the habitual an air of mystery, the familiar the dignity of the unfamiliar, the finite an infinite meaning—in so doing I romanticize.

Viewed against its cultural and sociohistorical context, a basic feature of early Romanticism is its systematic desystematization of what were perceived by the Romantics to be restrictive and rigid norms. Abhorring the profane and mourning the loss of life's poetic qualities, the Romantics were among the first to recognize and react against the modern forces of social and economic alienation. They blamed the rationalization and instrumentalization of Enlightenment ideology for having emptied life of its poetry and in contrast projected the Middle Ages as the last great harmonious historical age.

The revolutionary ideas advanced in philosophy and aesthetics have their parallel in

Novalis's collection of poems *Hymnen an die Nacht* (1800; *Hymns to the Night*, 1897, 1948). Novalis suffered greatly at the deaths of his brother and his fiancé in 1797, and in 1799, he composed these six hymns, the poetic manifestation of his encounter with death (a central experience of German Romanticism). *Hymns to the Night*, a combination of ecstatic prose and strophic hymns, asserts that true perception of the world comes only after having acquired complete knowledge of the self. This view, related to Fichte's philosophy, is pivotal, for it locates the human being at the center of comprehending the universe.

Novalis's collection recounts both personal and individual experience and, through a quasi-mystical vision, projects the situation onto the dimensions of the historical-eschatological course of humankind. The objectification of Novalis's vision reveals the central transformation of the metaphoric function of light and dark, day and night, whereby night becomes the primal force of the universe. This transvaluation of their respective ranges of meaning takes place through a foregrounding of paradox and oxymora. Evolving ultimately into myth, Novalis's *Hymns to the Night* is a classic example of Romanticism, especially along those lines where its symbolism intersects with that of Christianity.

While Novalis's work is indisputably central to any discussion of early German Romantic poetry, the fact that critics are able today to speak of a "Romantic poetry" is largely a result of other factors. One of them was the publication, in 1805, of *Des Knaben Wunderhorn* (the boy's magic horn), a collection of German folk songs compiled by Achim von Arnim and Clemens Brentano. Interest in folk literature had been generated earlier by the young Johann Wolfgang von Goethe (1749-1832) and Johann Gottfried Herder (1744-1803), who in fact coined the German word *Volkslied* (folk song) in 1775. The work of Arnim and Brentano revived this interest, a task made easier by the current of nationalism running through Germany at the time.

Nearly all writers associated with German Romanticism wrote poetry, but, in the spirit of Schlegel's "Progressive Universal Poetry," these poems generally formed part of a larger text, most often a novel (the privileged genre within Romantic aesthetics). Typically, the heroes of Romantic novels are poets, or at least lead "poetic lives," and they are prone to express their emotional states—whether joy or sorrow, exhilaration or despair—in the relatively spontaneous form of the lyric poem. These factors, then, also help define the contours of Romantic poetry.

CLEMENS BRENTANO

Clemens Brentano had a great affinity for the folk song and used its features in his own verse. (The folk-song strophe, common to much nineteenth century German verse, is easily recognized by its alternating *abab* masculine/feminine rhyme scheme.) Brentano was a diverse and creative writer with an exceptionally active imagination. Although his poems are sometimes formally inconsistent, the tenor of his work is constant:

musical, synesthetic, crafted, rich in texture. "Auf dem Rhein" ("Upon the Rhine") reveals a characteristic fascination for the macabre, manifested (from the Romantic perspective) in the eerie dimensions of the twilight. Appearance and reality become indistinguishable and effect a strikingly modern sense of disorientation. "Sprich aus der Ferne" ("Speak from Afar") uses the refrain as magic incantation. A desire to see all things as related informs this poem's lyric voice: the individual and the universe, the near and the far. The structured dimensions of casual (and causal) reality give way and flow together, presented through synesthesia and oxymora. The poem's closing rhetorical gesture reflects the universalizing tendency of Romanticism.

Joseph von Eichendorff

Joseph von Eichendorff's poetry displays a longing for unity and simplicity. He uses nature as a medium for understanding human existence and not merely as an object of imitation. Nature becomes a grand hieroglyph, and the poet's task is to render the most approximate translation. A fundamental Romantic dualism—nature as both demonic and divine—informs his work. The mood evoked by Eichendorff's landscapes often suggests impending danger, perhaps the risk of losing one's way in the dark. One critic has said of Eichendorff—who, unlike his contemporary Brentano, a late convert to Catholicism, was a devout Catholic throughout his life—that he "is not so much the poet of romantic longing as the poet of the *dangers* of romantic longing."

Patriotic Romantics

The poetry of Ernst Moritz Arndt (1769-1860), Max von Schenckendorff (1783-1817), and Karl Theodor Körner (1791-1813) represents another dimension of German Romanticism. According to E. L. Stahl,

> The patriotic verse of these soldier-poets expresses the satisfaction of an urge to share in communal life. In the same way conversion to Catholicism fulfils religious Romantic longings, Patriotic activity and traditional religiosity cause the primary Romantic impulse to abate and new attitudes to prevail. The wanderer returns home and settles down to perform his acknowledged civic and domestic tasks. The age of "bürgerlicher Realismus" [Bourgeois Realism] begins with this change in outlook which was imposed on German writers by the social developments and the political events of the post-Napoleonic era.

Biedermeier and Vormärz

Between 1830 and 1849, two distinct trends appeared within German poetry. The first, known as *Biedermeier*, was an introspective turn in response to the severe social and political repression exercised by Prince Metternich (1773-1859). The second, referred to as *Vormärz*, was an effort to politicize literature in the hope of effecting social and political reform. The public at large still preferred poetry to the popular novel, and in its various forms (verse epic, cycles, and ballads) its purpose was mainly to entertain and (from an ideological point of view) "distract." Tomes of poetry, mostly traditional and derivative, depicted a charming poetic world of tranquil harmony. Against this numerically significant backdrop, the Young Germans, idealists and political activists, advanced their theory of prose. Between 1830 and 1848, social tensions grew and the political spirit turned more radical.

Heinrich Heine (1797-1856) recognized that even the conservative patriotic verse of the Romantic poets could play into the interests of social and political liberals, since as an ideological instrument, poetry was capable of stirring great enthusiasm among the people. Interest in the "political poem" accrued because—viewed pragmatically—it was the most appropriate literary form for subversive agitation and propaganda. Heine derided the hackneyed declarations of freedom and the ponderously didactic reflections often found in the more cumbersome representatives of ostensibly political verse. Concerned with matters of immediate social and political relevance, this poetry was often subjected to the mechanisms of censorship in Metternich's control. (The reports of his spies frequently referred to the danger posed by these political "folk poems," an indication that the liberals had succeeded in part in redefining the readership of poetry as well as the genre's objectives.)

Not all poets wrote within this mainstream of events. Two of note who remained relatively aloof from political affairs are Annette von Droste-Hülshoff (1779-1848) and Eduard Mörike (1804-1875). Although they did not enjoy the recognition they deserved during their lifetimes, their poetry has come to be highly valued for its complexity and its moral intensity.

Annette von Droste-Hülshoff

Annette von Droste-Hülshoff, perceptive and intelligent, recognized the changed social conditions of her times, but family ties and the traditions of conservatism and Catholicism, coupled with a deep attachment to the countryside of her home region, Westphalia, exercised a strong authority in her poetry. Westphalia becomes the locus of her search for harmony and order between the individual and nature. In contrast to the Romantic nature imagery of forests and streams, one finds in Droste-Hülshoff for the first time in German literature the poetic treatment of the moors and heaths of her own Westphalia. The realism of her verse lies in its attention to minute detail both in nature and in human nature. The senses of sight and sound play important roles throughout her work. She felt the presence of a demoniac undercurrent in all of existence, and thus her poems are often ballads or at least balladesque. The Catholic Church provided a sanctuary for Droste-Hülshoff. She understood her role as author to be a "power by the grace of God." Her confessional poems, such as "Geistliches Jahr" ("Spiritual Year"), show her coping with the dilemma of sin and the fall from grace.

Eduard Mörike

Eduard Mörike is often called the greatest German lyric poet of the nineteenth century. His poetry shares features with that of late Romanticism, and his use of classical forms and themes shows his affinity with classicism. Some consider his work *Biedermeier* because of its introspective and unpretentious nature; still others refer to the "impressionism" of his poetry. All in all, these varying assessments give testimony to the artistic complexity of his work. His poetic technique is marked by a sensitivity for chiaroscuro and for the minutely observed symbolism of the divine within nature.

Mörike sought to reconcile the ideal with the real; his poems are accompanied by a sense of despair, helplessness, and resignation. The landscape of the country idyll provides order and security. Isolated and alienated, Mörike views love and nature in his poems with melancholy. Still, his deep Christian faith seems to have counteracted his melancholy. He always returned to the central problem of death; he preferred a life of the soul, but he failed to find the ultimate harmony he desired. Unlike his contemporary Nikolaus Lenau (1802-1850), Mörike managed to contain his despair at least enough to resist nihilism. Showing the tensions between what Sigmund Freud later described as the pleasure principle and the reality principle, Mörike's poems register important sociohistorical antagonisms of nineteenth century Germany.

Nikolaus Lenau

Nikolaus Lenau is a figure of several contradictions. At once a great Austrian revolutionary poet and a late Romantic poet of *Weltschmerz*, Lenau suffered the isolation characteristic of the bourgeois intellectual, and his works turn around a central moment of melancholy. His poetry documents both the individual's revolt against the instrumentalization of human beings and the rejection of bourgeois complacency. His early poem "Einsamkeit" ("Loneliness") best illustrates his *Weltschmerz*, bordering on existential dread. In his verse epic *Die Albigenser* (1837; the Albigensia), on the other hand, Lenau acknowledges Georg Wilhelm Friedrich Hegel's *Weltgeist*. Lenau's reworking of historical material (the fate of the Cathars, against whom Pope Innocent III waged war from 1209 to 1229) reveals his interest in the struggle for economic and political power, an interest not merely antiquarian. The poem begins: "Nicht meint das Lied auf Tote abzulenken" ("Not of the dead shall the song give pause to think").

Heinrich Heine

Probably the most fascinating and enigmatic poet of the nineteenth century, Heinrich Heine is most often identified with his first volume of poetry, *Buch der Lieder* (1827; *Book of Songs*, 1856). With these poems, it became clear that Heine was both the heir and the bane of German Romantic poetry. In the vein of Romantic poets, he could create moods and turn nature into a mirror for subjective feelings, but he no longer shared their belief in the mysterious whole. For Heine, the integrity of the whole is an illusion (even though one that is longed for), and in its place there appears a sense of disintegration, nature as a collage of signs and indicators of his own subjectivity. His Byronic irony draws on both sentiment and sharp criticism. His right hand creates a sentimental mood or atmosphere which his left hand all the while is busy undermining through critical observation, exposing its illusory dimensions, rejecting them as unrealistic. The result of this double labor is the special tension characteristic of Heine's work, the central poignancy behind his poetic voice.

Heine's attraction and aversion to German Romanticism resulted from the fact that by 1830, Romanticism was a greatly inflated commodity. Backward-looking and conservative, it no longer offered appropriate solutions for dealing with the changed conditions. Heine thus distanced himself from its ideological subtext, while on the surface employing to his own advantage its artistic conventions. Thus, the special shape of Heine's wit, a kind of "double take," is evidenced in the poem "Ein Jüngling liebt ein Mädchen" ("A Young Boy Loves a Young Girl"). Here, the final lines reaffirm the validity of feeling after exposing it to mockery. In another poem, "Ich wandle unter Blumen" ("I Amble Among Flowers"), Heine, as the critic Robert M. Browning has observed, "does not so much ridicule feeling, the 'romantic' attitude, as reveal its inappropriateness as a mode of social behavior. Such is the world and we have to accept it." In "Mein Herz, mein Herz ist traurig" ("My Heart, My Heart Does Sorrow"), the antithesis of the pleasant surroundings and the sorrowful observer/narrator suggests at first that the cause for his mood is misfortune in love (although this is not stated explicitly). Instead, the poem is a remarkable example of the more general historical conditions of despair. When contrasted with the expressed death wish of the observer in the final line, the peaceful, serene summer landscape appears as reified and proplike, testifying to Heine's alienation both as lover and vis-à-vis nature. Heine's works thus contain the central ambivalences of his time.

In "My Heart, My Heart Does Sorrow," for example, the ambivalence of the summer idyll is juxtaposed to the ambivalence of the nostalgia expressed for an unattainable restored world. On one hand, Heine indulges his *Weltschmerz*, while, on the other, he exposes it as a pose, as illusionary game playing. The characteristic result is the combination of haunting appeal to sincere emotional states and their frequent reversal through pungent intellectual stimulation. The different tone of Heine's later poetry results from its more explicit politicization. Rejecting aesthetic banality as well as profane content, such as could be found in much of the tendentious poetry of the *Vormärz*, Heine's own political poetry offers successful counterexamples, as in "Die schlesischen Weber" ("The Silesian Weavers").

A CHANGE IN STYLES

The political poetry typical of the *Vormärz* virtually disappeared with the failed revolution of 1848. Complacency, disillusionment, and a conservative patriotism prevailed. Derivative didactic poetry predominated, represented by the work of the Munich

Circle of poets, the most popular of whom was Emanuel Geibel (1815-1884). The more significant writers and poets of the genre known as Bourgeois Realism relied on the tradition of the *Erlebnislyrik*, or poetry of personal experience, such as that initiated by Goethe and practiced widely by the Romantics. This tradition, as well as that of the *Stimmungsgedicht*, or mood poem, ran its course in the period from 1850 to 1880.

Realism

It is not customary to speak of lyric poetry in terms of realism, although one can consider it from this point of view, keeping in mind that the term "realism" has a range of meanings. Gottfried Keller's (1819-1890) realism is to be found in the unpretentious experience of his *Erlebnislyrik* and in the restraint of emotion. Friedrich Hebbel (1813-1863) and Conrad Ferdinand Meyer (1825-1898) showed an exacting attention to poetic form and rejected the highly rhetorical declamatory mode of earlier lyric diction. The realism of Theodor Storm (1817-1888) resides in his affinity for the folk song and in the acoustic sensitivity of his poems. Theodor Fontane (1819-1898) used everyday speech and eschewed the predominant bombastic style of the ballad of his day. The realists sought poetic experience in a balance or harmony among the divergent forces acting upon the self and the world around them, forces of alienation and isolation. On the whole, their poems display a preference for simple motifs and rhythms, uncomplicated strophes and lines of verse. Brevity and modesty proved more conducive to a sincere personal tone. Antiquated forms, viewed as rhetorically empty, fell into disrepute. Themes of love and nature, joy and sorrow, longing and remembrance prevailed, with an underlying tone of resignation evident. With some poets, especially Storm and Meyer, one senses an aura of *Spätzeitlichkeit*, the feeling of having been born too late, a condition suggested by the increasing artistic stylization of their poetry. Meyer's symbolic imagery finally broke with the conventions of the *Erlebnisgedicht* (poem of personal experience) more completely than any of his predecessors, and he stands at the threshold of what we commonly acknowledge to be modern poetry.

Friedrich Hebbel

Friedrich Hebbel's poetry is pensive and intellectual. He rejected the tendentious poetry of his day, but his own verse sometimes suffers because of its highly intellectualized reflection, especially evident in his later sonnets and epigrams. As a postclassicist, Hebbel was drawn between the reflection and speculation characteristic of Schiller's work and the emotion and immediacy essential to Goethe's. Hebbel's imagery tends to be static, with the intellectual tension and the unnatural syntax of his poems countering the illusion of immediacy. He treats the themes of dream and night, pain and death, in a dialectic fashion. The antithesis of the individual and the universe provides a central tension at the core of his lyric ego. The poetic symbol overcomes the fundamental opposition of self and universe.

Theodor Storm

With Theodor Storm, the poetic symbol loses its comprehensive meaning and evolves into something more psychological and impressionistic, an attribute of a given mood, disposition, or atmosphere. Storm always proceeds from a single experience and then, through precise observations—particularly acoustic ones—achieves the artistic translation of this moment into compelling figurative language. Aware of the interdependency of form and content, Storm considered the brevity of the lyric poem structurally appropriate to the intense communication of states or moods. After 1848, his often sentimental lyric subjectivity gave way to a preoccupation with external reality in distinct, descriptive language. His nature poems, like those of Droste-Hülshoff, reveal close ties with his own home region, Schleswig-Holstein. Storm's later poems became more acerbic and, as with Meyer, the strong presence of death and isolation within Storm's lyric voice suggests a sense of *Spätzeitlichkeit*.

Conrad Ferdinand Meyer

Conrad Ferdinand Meyer's poetry marks a significant historical moment between the realists' reformulation of the *Erlebnisgedicht* and the Symbolism of Rainer Maria Rilke (1875-1926). Some scholars therefore speak of Meyer's poetry as "anachronistic," while others stress those features of his work which point toward the future and the predominant course of modern poetry into the twentieth century. Meyer dealt continuously and in various ways with the problem of existence. Caught in the historical currents of pessimism and the accompanying sense of the loss of values which afflicted the late nineteenth century, Meyer preached the instructive and redemptive power of poetry. His own poetry evolves toward the poetic figuration of a subjective moment. His collection of poems from 1882 evidences a new kind of language, one intent on uncovering the essence of things through objectification. Even the most personal experience undergoes a transformation that objectifies it as a symbol or an allegorical image. In contrast to the more conventional mode of the *Erlebnisgedicht*, direct speech in Meyer's poetry is rare and generally recedes entirely behind the distance of intellectuality. The formal perfection of his poems is one means of coping with suffering and death, as in, for example, "Eingelegte Ruder" (inlaid rudder) or "Im Spätboot" (in the late boat). In "Zwei Segel" (two sails), the fundamental experience of human love is transformed and objectified in a symbolically rich texture of images.

Naturalism

The publication of *Moderne Dichtercharaktere* (characters of modern poets) in 1885, an anthology showcasing the revolutionary bravado of the younger generation and its new aesthetic program, introduced naturalist poetry. Few of the original contributors, however, became significant poets, perhaps because the aesthetics of naturalism were not compatible with the conventions of lyric poetry.

Arno Holz

Arno Holz (1863-1929), an avid experimentalist, was the most accomplished poet among the German naturalist writers. His *Buch der Zeit* (1885; book of this time), a pithy, coarse, and "thoroughly modern" collection of poems, rejected the artifice and pretense of conventional poetic diction. *Phantasus* (1898, enlarged 1916, 1925, 1929, 1961) shows his indebtedness to Walt Whitman's rhythms, his pathos, and his nontraditional use of form.

Detlev von Liliencron

Although unaffiliated with any literary movement, Detlev von Liliencron (1844-1909) realized in his verse many of the objectives of naturalist aesthetics. He achieved a naturalist effect in his combination of simple and precise perceptions, a technique which could just as well be called impressionistic in several instances. (Some critics have remarked that Liliencron's poems are "impressionistic" insofar as they are snapshots of reality as viewed from the surface, evocative glimpses of life, strung together according to the principle of juxtaposition and showing disdain for conventional rules of grammar and syntax.) His poems display spontaneity, rich imagery, and sensitivity to rhythm. The evocative atmosphere of his poems creates a depth which haunts the imagination. *Adjutanternritte* (1883; rides of an adjutant), his first book of poems, proved to be his most lasting; the quality of his later work generally did not live up to its promise.

Turn of the twentieth century

While the naturalist poem per se remained more a concept than a reality, the abundance of poetry written around the turn of the twentieth century displayed a variety of forms, styles, and graces. There was the neo-Romantic balladry of Agnes Miegel (1879-1964), Börries Freiherr von Münchhausen (1874-1945), and Lulu von Strauss und Torney (1873-1956), generally traditional in form and content and conservative in ideology. There was also a revival of nature poetry in the vein of *Heimatkunst* (provincial art). At the same time, the style known as *Jugendstil*, or Art Nouveau, emerged. With its penchant for the charming and the ornate, *Jugendstil* was naturally drawn toward poetry. Some of Stefan Zweig's (1881-1942) poems can be considered representative of this style: They deal frequently with death, particularly its paradoxical relation to the centrifugal forces of life. *Jugendstil* experiences nature as a palliative for moroseness, pain, and suffering.

Around the same time, Frank Wedekind (1864-1918) and others were writing much satirical poetry, often with a political thrust, popular above all in the cabarets of large cities such as Berlin and Munich. The work of Christian Morgenstern (1871-1914) was singular in the tenor of his keen, penetrating questions of reality. Then as now, his poems have proved to be enormously popular. The work of Richard Dehmel (1863-1920) met with great success during his own lifetime, but today Dehmel's passionate vitalism is chiefly of historical interest. Erotic and sexual overtones dominate his later poems, and his equation of "poetic power" with "divine power," influenced by Friedrich Nietzsche, reveals a fundamental ideological interest of the time.

Symbolism

Of more lasting significance for modern poetry was Symbolism, which includes the works of Stefan George (1868-1933), Rilke, and Hugo von Hofmannsthal (1874-1929).

Stefan George

As Robert M. Browning has said, "modern poetry in the eminent sense begins in Germany" with Stefan George. George sought to retrieve the forces of creativity that the forces of materialism had either inhibited or destroyed. Through beauty, he sought to restore magic and majesty to art. Incorporating the tradition of Symbolism from the French poets Charles Baudelaire, Stéphane Mallarmé, and Arthur Rimbaud, George was a language purist, striving for precision and perfection in his highly sculptured works. His aesthetics of art for art's sake evolved to accommodate a view of the poet as seer and teacher. George identified himself with Dante and with Hölderlin and advocated a kind of pagan beauty and aristocratic conservatism, behind which resided an ideology of hero-worship. The manner in which George flaunted his "eccentricity"—from his homosexual Maximin cult and his antiphilistine typographical innovations to the liturgical earnestness with which he read his own verse—repelled and impressed his contemporaries, frequently both. His highly aristocratic view of poetry and his technique of pictorial stylization, whereby the meaning of life can be grasped only as an aesthetic phenomenon, reveal a debt to Nietzsche.

Hugo von Hofmannsthal

Nearly all of Hugo von Hofmannsthal's poetry was written between 1890 and 1900, between the ages of sixteen and twenty-six. His *Ein Brief* (1901; *Letter to Lord Chandos*, 1952) is a central document for understanding much of the poetry that preceded it. Here, Hofmannsthal confronts the language crisis which plagued him at the time (for a period immediately before and after the fictitious letter, he produced almost nothing). The letter envisions a way out of the dilemma—by seeking a new language, one of ciphers and symbols which allow objects to speak directly. This path was, however, to be Rilke's, not Hofmannsthal's; the latter rejected this kind of aestheticism. One of Hofmannsthal's best-known poems is the "Ballade des äusseren Lebens" (ballad of external life). While the title addresses the external life, it implies an internal—and qualitatively superior—plane of existence, which the poem reveals through an aesthetics of the moment that rescues objects and life from transitoriness and gives meaning to an otherwise meaningless existence. As such, it anticipates the magic exorcism of language as described in the Chandos letter.

RAINER MARIA RILKE

The poetry of Rainer Maria Rilke is unrivaled in its aesthetic richness and its capacity to induce new modes of vision. After reading Rilke's poetry, one simply sees the world differently from before. The best example of this transforming power can be found in "Archaischer Torso Apollos," with its thematization of art's redemptive value, as expressed in the final line: "Du musst Dein Leben ändern" ("You must change your life"). This notion of "art's redemptive value" was not new with Rilke, but it is articulated with particular force in his works. It is a notion basic to what one might term the " ideology of art" as it first developed with Romanticism: namely, that art can claim a specific visionary power not common to other forms of human activity and production. Coupled with this fundamental tenet is the assumption that art is not divorced from life, that it has real, affective functions—which is why the lyric voice in Rilke's poem on Apollo, itself a work of art, is compelled to acknowledge its "redemptive effect." Rilke's first volume, *Leben und Lieder* (1894; life and songs), was followed by five more before 1900. Much of the early work reveals that Rilke was still struggling for a distinctive poetic voice. This he found by the turn of the twentieth century, beginning with *Die frühen Gedichte* (1909; early poems), *Das Buch der Bilder* (1902, 1906; *The Book of Images*, 1994), *Das Stundenbuch* (1905; *Poems from the Book of Hours*, 1941), and culminating in his *Neue Gedichte* (1907, 1908; *New Poems*, 1964). In *The Book of Images*, he moved tentatively toward a more objective poetry. From Auguste Rodin, Rilke had learned a new definition of artistic creativity, emphasizing craftsmanship rather than inspiration. In these poems, and later ones, he sought to be as plastic as possible. *Poems from the Book of Hours* depicts a Russian monk seeking God and the essence of all things through confession and prayer. Ultimately, this search proves futile, but the prayers are from the very start imbued with an underlying sense of doubt; all of Rilke's overtly religious poetry is informed by a modern skepticism. Rilke then abandoned his search for God and concentrated on creating a type of poem known as the *Dinggedicht*, or "object poem." Instead of a conventional portrayal of the symbolic confluence of the individual and nature, Rilke sought an "objective art." "Der Panther" ("The Panther"), from *New Poems*, was the first text in which Rilke realized this technique to an absolute degree. The poem articulates no sentimentality or "human" sympathy; instead, the affective possibilities of the poem are left entirely to the dimensions of the object itself, the panther.

Rilke's later volumes of poetry, *Duineser Elegien* (1923; *Duinese Elegies*, 1931; better known as *Duino Elegies*) and *Die Sonette an Orpheus* (1923; *Sonnets to Orpheus*, 1936), written after a decade of silence, celebrate the transmutative power of feeling, a power capable of transforming the material world into spirit. By rendering the physical world "invisible," Rilke hoped to rescue it from the forces of transitoriness, to secure it forever within a dimension beyond space and time. As Browning has commented:

The world is here to be felt and we are in the world to feel it. We *can* feel it because of our awareness of transiency, i.e., because we know death. Death is therefore Rilke's theme of themes. But for the poet feeling is not enough; the poet must also say. In saying, the rest of humanity is given to understand what is to be felt. In this way, the poet's work extends our consciousness.

Expressionism

Rilke's work spans the period of German expressionism, although he should not be identified with it. The strident bravado of the new poetry of expressionism was chiefly concerned with shocking the complacent bourgeoisie. Moralistic pathos and visionary élan exploded the baser constraints on form and material, and the boldness of imagery challenged established perspectives and advocated novel and free modes of perception. Kurt Pinthus (1886-1975), editor of the influential anthology *Menschheitsdämmerung* (1920; twilight of humanity), wrote in 1915 that the new poetry surged forth "out of torment and scream, out of admiration and disdain, analysis and honor . . . toward the essential, toward the essence not only of appearance, but of Being." Expressionist poetry countered the forces which rendered language automatic and void of meaning by introducing innovative syntax and imagery, thus creating novel dimensions within the newly discovered relations of space and time and making manifest a new hermetic reality. Reality was transformed into word and sign, transfigured as cipher. Alienating meter and rhyme effected a grotesque refraction of reality, also an essential feature of expressionist poetry.

The first phase of German expressionism in particular (roughly from 1911 to 1914) discarded the "sensibility wasting in reflection" of much nineteenth century poetry and urged a sensibility animated and absorbed in construction, in presenting simultaneously the "what" and the "how" of perception. Expressionist poetry experimented with the possibilities of metaphor, substituting a fusion of image and idea for the older parallelism of image and idea. Reality and referentiality were thus made problematic. Foreign influence was also a factor. George's translation in 1901 of Baudelaire's *Les Fleurs du mal* (1857, 1861, 1868; *Flowers of Evil*, 1909) was an important contribution to the German literary scene. Whitman was introduced to the German public in 1868, but the popular edition of his poems appeared only in 1901, translated by Johannes Schlaf (1862-1941). Translations of François Villon and Rimbaud also appeared. Rimbaud's influence was chiefly in the realm of imagery, and his idea that "the Poet becomes a seer through an extended, immense and consistent disordering of all the senses" compelled Georg Trakl (1887-1914) and others to break with the concept of purely rational continuity. Filippo Tommaso Marinetti and Italian Futurism also encouraged German poets to experiment with linguistic innovations.

"Weltende" ("End of the World"), by Jakob von Hoddis (1887-1942), is typical of the apocalyptic visions manifest in early expressionist poetry; its discontinuities were intended to reflect the dissolution of civilization. After undergoing psychiatric treatment in 1915, von Hoddis was finally committed to a mental institution in the 1920's. Still, his work struck a central nerve of the time. Writing initially in the fashion of Symbolism, von Hoddis found a distinctive character in his apocalyptic projections. His compression of contemporary thought and emotion into signs and iconic formulas typified the grotesque and cynical expressions of the crisis-consciousness of these years. Similarly, "Der Gott der Stadt" ("The God of the City"), by George Heym (1887-1912), locates the source of eschatological anxiety in the modern metropolis, where Baal rules as the god of material pleasure. The poem "Morgen" ("Morning"), by Alfred Lichtenstein (1889-1914), is yet another example of the expressionist vision of the world on the brink of destruction, where failure to communicate forebodes the ultimate demise of society.

This basically imagist poetry, which privileged visionary experience over visual experience (*ex*pressionism versus *im*pressionism), resulted in a diversity of individual poetic dictions. The contours of the early years of German expressionism are marked by a sharp disdain for the bourgeois conventions of poetry and by experimentation with new techniques of montage and imagery. After 1914, as the critic and translator Michael Hamburger has written, "its craft of imagery was vulgarized and, at the same time, its mental climate became predominantly political." Behind the outrage and the utterances—sometimes cynical, sometimes grotesque—one senses the urgent longing for the "New Man."

GEORG HEYM

Despair, fear, and the presentiment of catastrophe are the constant themes of Georg Heym's poetry. Heym experienced life as a prison-house and suffered existential ennui, from which even death promised no escape. Melancholy pervades his eschatological visions; elements of Christian belief are transformed, as with Trakl's poetry, into apocalyptic images. His verse is largely paratactic, and this simple poetic syntax is supported by a predominance of iambic pentameters or rhymed tetrameters. As the poems develop, however, along simple syntactic lines, images are superimposed, one over the other, creating a density and tension that belie the surface simplicity of the discourse.

ELSE LASKER-SCHÜLER

The poetry of Else Lasker-Schüler (1876-1945) is charged with anxiety, *Weltschmerz*, and ennui. Her poems exhibit a longing for a return to the beliefs of the "fathers" and celebrate mythical origins in transparent and yet enigmatic language. Expressionism with Lasker-Schüler becomes a liberation of the imagination. Her poems exude the sense of security peculiar to dreams.

Georg Trakl

Georg Trakl viewed in his poems an "all too faithful reproduction of a godless, cursed century." Hyperaccentuated guilt and the experience of horror and degeneration inform his poems. Trakl claimed that his work was an "incomplete attempt" to expiate "guilt," both of the individual and of humankind. Nature objectifies his own inner strife and reveals the lack of harmony within Trakl's poetic world. The recurrence of a few central images in his poems has led one critic to speak of Trakl's oeuvre as "one poem." Trakl's experimentation with drugs heightened his apocalyptic visions. Remembrance, dream, and drug-induced intoxication, along with lines from Maurice Maeterlinck and Rimbaud, produce an evocative poetry, a singular accomplishment of German expressionist writing.

Hamburger maintains that Trakl best understood the nature of the crises that he and his generation faced, exploring how it is that modern men and women relate to death and to evil, whereas Heym (to cite a counterexample) avoided analysis of the crisis by projecting onto the landscapes of his text images of death and evil and suggesting their omnipresence and inexorability. Hamburger also notes that a distinction can be made between Heym's consistently dark view of nature and Trakl's more variable imagery. The effect of the latter's, even if only vague and highly mediated, is to uncover the traces of a paradise that is perhaps not forever lost.

A new freedom

Expressionism was the first literary movement in Germany that made the anticlassicist tendency a mass phenomenon, but the disruption of old realities and old poetic conventions created at the same time a new freedom, or at least the perception that freedom (and novelty) were real possibilities. From then on, every poet had to decide what to do with this potential freedom. Since the time of expressionism, there has been no authoritative norm governing the production and reception of poetry which one could manipulate in order to shock and to draw attention to the work of art ("épater les bourgeois") and to the possibility of new experiences. Expressionism broke with all norms and thereby created an utterly new situation (which, significantly, itself soon became an established and "authoritative" convention).

Ernst Stadler

Ernst Stadler (1883-1914), thoroughly versed in the European literary tradition, experienced the early years of the twentieth century less as an end than as a beginning, seeing in them not the disintegration of modern society but the promise of its transformation. Initially, he had difficulty achieving an individual tone and style. Ultimately, after experimenting with Symbolism, he adopted a dithyrambic voice of political activism—what he called a "new joyous, all-embracing world feeling." His verse espouses an ecstatic devotion to fellow human beings, a longing for freedom, and an acceptance of life's abundance. Rather than viewing the city as the locale of degenerate corruption and destruction, Stadler saw it as a cause for celebration, as the facilitator of ecstatic union.

Johannes R. Becher

The early radical poems of Johannes R. Becher (1891-1958) struck out at the bourgeois world in which he grew up. Immoderate and shrill, their forceful imagery "spits in the face" of his immediate milieu and social mores; rhetorical exposition disrupts the traditional form of these poems. With the advent of war, he sent out an urgent appeal for a "new syntax," a "catastrophic syntax" that would raze conventions: Word and deed were coterminous for Becher the political activist. Much later, his voice lost resonance; his visions largely unfulfilled, Becher wrote that "The poem cannot survive without truth."

Franz Werfel

The dithyrambic prophecies of human redemption and reconciliation found in the work of Franz Werfel (1890-1945) struck a resonant chord among his generation. As the conscience of his time, Werfel, whose poetry sought to transform feelings into music, represents a significant dimension of expressionism. Werfel celebrates the redemptive value of the poetic word and projects an optimism utterly open to the world, while at the same time humbly acknowledging the presence of God. Art and theology thus blend; political activism yields to a "Christian mission" sustained by verbal dynamism and full-toned musicality. Werfel experienced his poems acoustically and was more concerned with emotive charge than with formal consistency.

Gottfried Benn

Gottfried Benn (1886-1956) drew upon Nietzsche's philosophy of art to form his concept of artistry and perspectivism, whereby form becomes the "primary instance," taking precedence over all contextual considerations. Benn's first volume of poetry, *Morgue, und andere Gedichte* (1912; morgue, and other poems), used montage and calculated scientific jargon mixed with profane colloquialisms to achieve a shocking alienation. Benn confronted the empty prophecies and shabby progress of his time with the final reality of death. Disease, decay, and death are his themes in the early poems; humans are portrayed as helpless creatures—miserable, pitiful, despicable. The volume *Söhne* (1913; sons), the central theme of which is the characteristically expressionistic father-son conflict, reveals a futuristic aspect (again typical of expressionism) with its projection of a "New Man," an artist who will overcome death in ecstatic vision.

Alfred Lichtenstein

Alfred Lichtenstein (1887-1914) applies the grotesque to expose reality as absurd—a juxtaposition of the ridiculously banal and the sublimely tragic. His lyric voice, marked by alienation and the dislocation of images and motifs, is often compared with that of Jakob von Hoddis. Objects in Lichtenstein's poems are always distorted and displaced, always perceived from bizarre, radical, and unsettling perspectives.

AUGUST STRAMM

The poetry of August Stramm (1874-1915), characterized by a constructivist style, is not easily accessible. A tremendous diversity is evident within his modest oeuvre, and estimations of his work range from "thoroughly expressionistic" to "pretense and sham." Striving to reunite meaning and sound, Stramm dispenses with tradition in order to allow the individual word to appear in untrammeled isolation. Such deformation effects an unusual concentration of expression. In allowing the word to exercise its own effect, his poems turn programmatically from empirical reality. The resulting abstraction is charged with the currents of eros and chaos.

THE 1920'S THROUGH 1940'S

Following the strong element of subjectivity evident in the poetry of expressionism, the 1920's ushered in a new responsiveness to the factual and the objective. The human being was of such central interest to the poetry of German expressionism that nature as such found little room there. By the mid-1920's, however, nature was once again a central theme of poetry, often perceived as the only medium through which objectivity and precision of detail could be achieved. As Alfred Döblin proclaimed in 1925: "Art is boring, we want facts, facts." In part, this trend encouraged a revival of nature poetry, in German referred to as *naturmagisch*, focusing on the objective details of nature and celebrating their cosmic relevance. The particular dimensions of this cosmic order vary among poets. For Elisabeth Langgässer (1899-1950), for example, the order is largely determined by Christian ideas, while Günther Eich (1907-1972) concentrates on the parameters of language per se.

NATURE POETS

Both Langgässer and Eich worked in a circle of poets connected with a poetry journal called *Kolonne* (column), whose contributors included Peter Huchel (1903-1981), Hermann Kasack (1896-1966), and Georg von der Vring (1889-1968). In the works of these *naturmagische* poets, visible nature is considered "wondrous"; their realism is thus "magical" to the extent that their poetic diction is a kind of invocation. Lyric expression is thus an act of revelation as well as of interpretation.

PETER HUCHEL

Peter Huchel wrote nature poetry typical of the *Kolonne* group. Nature here appears not as a romantic object of poetic longing, for an elegiac tone is mixed with contemporary metaphors of struggle and warfare. Natural processes are depicted in crystalline, precise language that often reveals their underlying violence. Huchel's nature poetry never simply flees into boundless and timeless space; the poet delivers testimony as an eyewitness.

Günther Eich

Günther Eich first began writing poetry in the company of the *Kolonne* group. His early nature poems are both subjective and reflective; one can see in them the first steps toward the dispassionate stance and the extreme brevity which characterize his poems after 1945. Contemplating specific, concrete objects, such as the blue feather in "Die Häherfeder" ("Jay Feather"), Eich searches for the deeper reality behind "signs" and "omens." Still, language—at least the cognitive, rational faculties of the mind—proves unyielding, for the "sly answer" lies somewhere just beyond the dimensions of habituated thought and perception. The sudden surprise initiated by the sign is thus a central moment for Eich's work.

Wilhelm Lehmann

Wilhelm Lehmann's (1882-1968) poetry deals with nature and myth, the dual constituents of meaning and order in his universe. The individual, subjective ego of the poet recedes behind the objectivity of language, which, through precise concentration on objects, attempts to open vistas to that level of order which transcends the individual. The unreal and the dreamlike are also part of Lehmann's poetic world. There is a certain consistency within or behind Lehmann's poetic landscape, but the imagery is not static; instead, it moves as part of a larger cosmic cycle, as the passing of seasons relates to mythical signs.

Elisabeth Langgässer

Depictions of nature and the presence of myths also determine the imagination of Elisabeth Langgässer, but are used as portals through which to recognize the underlying order of Christianity. This sense of order is not always achieved in her poetry, but where it is absent one at least senses that a struggle has taken place to realize it. During the war, Langgässer held on to the "magical" qualities of reality as a vehicle for hope and for redemption in the Christian sense.

Oskar Loerke and Georg Britting

The poetry of Oskar Loerke (1884-1941) gives expression to the complete poetic universe. Balancing intellect and emotion, the static and the fluid, Loerke achieves a consistency and sense of order that extends beyond his own subjectivity. Loerke's concise observations result in a spiritualization of nature.

Georg Britting (1891-1964) was the poet of the Bavarian landscape. He stressed the idyllic and the bucolic but experienced nature as magical, disclosing it as a sign of a larger cosmic order. This combination of the sensuous and the intellectual makes Britting's poetry representative of the so-called Magical Realism.

Topical poetry

The objectivity of another group of poets, including Kurt Tucholsky (1890-1935) and Erich Kästner (1899-1974), was directed toward social conditions. Their poems read like warnings of imminent catastrophe; their efforts to awaken the public rested on a faith in the social efficacy of the poetic word. In the 1920's, this objective poetry was best represented by the song, the broadsheet, and the ballad. The work of Tucholsky falls into this category, as does that of Kästner and Bertolt Brecht (1898-1956).

The epic quality of Brecht's anti-Aristotelian theater figures in his poetry as well: It is distancing, descriptive, and critical rather than sentimental and empathetic. His poems break with the bourgeois tradition of aestheticism, nature, and confessional poetry. His description of these years as a "bad time for poetry" did not imply a rejection of poetry altogether, but rather only a rejection of the conventional forms and traditional subject matter of poetry, which were no longer adequate to the changed historical circumstances. Brecht thus tried to rejuvenate art, but not (like Rilke) exclusively through formal and aesthetic means, although he was sensitive to the historical necessity of formal experimentation. In his verse, Brecht admits to a longing for the conventional elements of lyric poetry, but since "a talk about trees is almost a crime/ because it implies silence about so many horrors," he does not indulge this desire. His vocabulary and poetic diction are strict and sober, marked by clear and unsentimental precision.

Countermovements against the new objective tone are visible in the poetry of Rudolf Alexander Schröder (1878-1962) and Hans Carossa (1878-1956), whose conservative political and aesthetic orientation drew them toward the classical heritage in both form and content. They were more interested in the timeless aspects of poetic diction than in the merely topical. With the advent of National Socialism, their posture became a kind of inner emigration, problematic because, if from the point of view of the individual, political abstinence was a kind of mute contradiction to the Hitler regime, as a whole the totalitarian system was able to disenfranchise their voices, if not actually coopt them altogether. Schröder's work represents a consistent effort to preserve the Western cultural heritage. He had a keenly developed sense for form, which he applied to his humanistic religious poetry. Carossa strived in his verse for harmony and moderation; his artistic perspective was that of a pious humanist, his models Goethe and Stifter. Carossa's conservatism and classicism were manipulated to the advantage of Nazi ideology.

The Nazi regime

Poetry written in accordance with the ideology of National Socialism largely eschewed the principles of precise objectivity. Characterized by the frequent use of archaic words and phrases, it shied away from formal innovation. Josef Weinheber (1892-

1945) studied the example of the classics and was concerned primarily with questions of form and aesthetics. He became well known with the volume *Adel und Untergang* (1932, 1934; nobility and decline) and was supported at the time of its publication by the Nazis. Some of his later writings reciprocated this support, and toward the end of the war, suffering from severe depression after having acknowledged his misguided affiliation with National Socialism, he took his own life.

The most significant party-line poet was Erwin Guido Kolbenheyer (1878-1962). The stylistic diversity of his work reveals its fundamental confusion. He greeted the rise of National Socialism as a historical necessity, explaining its emergence through digressions on philosophy, politics, history, economics, biology, religion, and culture. The appeal of his work is utterly totalitarian. Party slogans and verse become indistinguishable in his monumental panegyric to the supremacy of the German spirit in all of its manifestations. As a member of the Prussian Academy of Poets and as the recipient of several distinctions, Kolbenheyer was one of the most forceful poetic voices on the literary scene of the Third Reich. Other party-line poets included Hanns Johst (1890-1978) and Gerhard Schumann (1911-1995).

Postwar poetry and modernism

The situation for poetry after 1945 was at first ambivalent. On one hand, historical conditions presented German writers with an enormous challenge. On the other hand, the devastation, frustration, and overwhelming loss of orientation made a direct confrontation with the immediate past something to be avoided. Poets inherited a language corrupted in the Nazi era, and they recognized the need to replace it with a new idiom.

Under these circumstances, it is not hard to understand that, initially at least, issues of content mattered more than issues of form. The immediate task of assessing the relation of the present to the past rendered aesthetic considerations secondary. Historically, this phase was probably necessary, because postwar German poetry could become credible once again only after having expunged its affiliation with National Socialism. Gradually, however, aesthetic considerations emerged from the background. A critical factor in this development was the influence of foreign literatures, in particular the force of modernism.

One could therefore consider postwar German poetry along two lines: the political-social, and the linguistic-formal. Progressive experimentation in poetry was impeded by the presence of hackneyed lyric phrases and the failure to confront sociopolitical reality. Formal traditionalism and a social isolation resulting in escapism and indifference toward politics coexisted. It is significant that the most important mode of expression for the immediate postwar years was not poetry but narrative prose, above all the short story. Here, authors pursued the necessary confrontation with contemporary sociopolitical issues, while poetry continued its preoccupation with the vestiges of Surrealism, on the one hand, and the tradition of nature poetry, on the other. These coexisting trends can be visualized as four principal constellations dominating the postwar poetry scene. One of these was a political conscience combined with formal traditionalism. A second resided as well within traditional poetic forms but shied away from political commentary. The other two possibilities were a combination of formal modernism with either a political or an apolitical attitude. While such a scheme is helpful, it should be noted that a distinction between "political poetry" and "poetic escapism" can be misleading. One need only read the works of Hans Magnus Enzensberger (born 1929) to realize that these two descriptions are not mutually exclusive.

Poem after poem of the postwar years revealed that poetry in the service of spiritual and ethical rejuvenation could afford little room for new aesthetic solutions. In this regard, the poetics of Benn—namely, the rejection of everything contextual in the attempt to approximate the "absolute poem"—appears as a historically necessary step in the development of postwar German poetry. Theodor Adorno (1903-1969) pronounced that, after Auschwitz, it was no longer possible to write a poem, necessitating a reconsideration of the content, the form, and the function of poetry.

Postwar poetry can be said to have begun not in 1945 but in 1948, for it was in the latter year that the first postwar poems of Benn, Eich, Huchel, and Karl Krolow (1915-1999) appeared, not to mention the first volume by Celan (1920-1970). These poets are all identified with the tradition of Hermetic poetry, and they represent the primary avenues through which postwar German poetry drew upon the traditions of modernism. In a sense, then, German postwar modernist poetry represents no really new beginning, but instead the realization, continuation, and extension of established modernist movements. The resonance with which modernism appeared on the postwar German literary scene suggested something radically new; the war obscured lines of development reaching back into the 1930's and earlier.

The overwhelming presence of this obscured tradition was best articulated not by a poet but by a scholar. In 1956, Hugo Friedrich published *The Structure of Modern Poetry*, an attempt to reveal the unity of European-American poetry since the mid-nineteenth century through a study of its genesis and its various typologies. His work dominated scholarly discussions of poetry in Germany for some time. Tracking the development of modern poetry from its origins in Mallarmé, Friedrich isolated its more significant features, such as the rejection of old taboos, a preoccupation with darkness, an overwhelming sense of isolation and anxiety, and an insistence on the logic of discontinuity. Friedrich's book has much in common with the spirit of postwar German poetry, for he neglects the sociohistorical constituents of modern poetry and highlights instead its phenomenological-existential dimensions. Benn epitomizes this orientation among poets.

Karl Krolow

Karl Krolow once wrote that metaphor determines "the economy of the single poem." Krolow's imagery reveals the development of his poetry as a whole, as well as the shift in poetics which marked the postwar years. Krolow's first metaphors belong to the category of "traditional nature." Later, he moved to more aggressive, expressionistic, and even surrealistic metaphors. Then, he focused on decidedly intellectual images, gradually relying less and less on rhyme or regular strophes while developing a laconic style.

INGEBORG BACHMANN

Ingeborg Bachmann (1926-1973) published her first volume of poems, *Die gestundete Zeit* (borrowed time), in 1953 and immediately established her reputation as a poet with a keen ability to articulate her doubts about the meaning of history and her anticipation of catastrophe, an anxiety shared by many Western European intellectuals during the Cold War. The specific accomplishment of this volume lies in its suggestive interrelation of societal perplexity and individual despair. Several of her poems combine poetic diction and utopian thought, while others suggest their ultimate irreconcilability. In the tension between "superfluous objects" and words "for the lowest classes," Bachmann exposes as illegitimate the traditional mode of poetic speech and in its place suggests the possibility of a documentary, didactic literature.

PAUL CELAN

The difficulty in understanding the poetry of Paul Celan results less from the allusions embedded in his texts than from his concentration on the expressive possibilities and limits of language. This problem is often the central preoccupation of his poems. The "incontrovertible testimony" of the poet can be achieved only after the utmost exertion, where language is pressed to its limits. Celan's poems are always "under way," in search of a partner in conversation.

HANS MAGNUS ENZENSBERGER

By the late 1950's, the tradition of nature poetry had run its course. Already during the mid-1950's, West German poetry was becoming more explicitly political. A fundamental problem thus emerged: that of achieving the aesthetic political poem, of articulating both literary and political progressiveness. The new politicized poetry displayed a certain disenchantment with the state of things, preferred sobriety to ceremony, and, in a sense—because of its basic distrust of any "magical powers" residing in the poetic word—depoeticized poetic diction and renounced the traditional notion of "lyrical" by presenting primarily a cerebral appeal.

The successful articulation of both aesthetic and political progressiveness is perhaps best illustrated in the work of Hans Magnus Enzensberger. Initially, Enzensberger relied on Edgar Allan Poe's "Philosophy of Composition" for the theoretical basis of his work but soon incorporated the philosophy of Adorno. In the 1950's, Enzensberger conceived experimental poetry and social criticism as mutually dependent. The background of his early poetry is the Cold War, the atomic threat, the rearmament of West Germany, and in particular, the economic recovery of the Konrad Adenauer era, a process which Enzensberger viewed as threatening to the integrity of the individual. In the 1960's, Enzensberger turned increasingly toward political writings. He remains impatient with the cheap (commodified) utopias of would-be reformists. A socialist by choice, a skeptic by nature, and a realist through practice of acute observation, Enzensberger always imbued his poetry with his unmistakable mark. The work of Erich Fried (1921-1988) is likewise politically keen. Fried's poetry achieved recognition in the turbulent decade of the 1960's and is noted for its laconic style, coupled with Brechtian techniques of paradox, antithesis, and dialectic reversal.

Mid- to late twentieth century

A significant experimental phase of West German poetry, one which shared a skepticism of traditional metaphoric expression and poetic diction, was concrete poetry, best represented by Eugen Gomringer (born 1925), Franz Mon (born 1926), and Ernst Jandl (1925-2000). The term was introduced by Gomringer in analogy to concrete art, and by it he meant to distinguish a linguistically experimental literature which reflected and thematized its own raw material—that is, language. Applying the principles of functionality, clarity, simplicity, communicability, objectivity, and play, concrete poetry sought to reintegrate literature into social life. Using techniques of reduction and permutation, concrete poetry focused on the presentation of language and linguistic elements and not on the representation of reality beyond language. Ultimately, however, the experimentalism of concrete poetry soon rigidified into rather predictable patterns. Challenging (and entertaining) material was written by Jandl, whose keen wit and linguistic sensitivity inform the foreground of his work. While focusing on the acoustic and optical valences of language, Jandl at the same time recognized the social implications of his work, for language as the material of his art was also the material of his thought and speech and, as such, material shared by a significant portion of Western society.

In 1965, Walter Höllerer (1922-2003) presented a call for the "long poem," understood as an alternative to the then predominant Hermetic poem. This reformulation of poetic diction was carried out by Günter Herburger (born 1932), Rolf Dieter Brinkmann (1940-1975), and Nicolas Born (1937-1979), among others, who advocated a new subjective realism in the 1970's. For Jürgen Theobaldy (born 1944), a significant representative of the youngest poets, the long poem of the late 1960's gave way to the "new poem" of the 1970's, when several younger poets tried to relocate the self, rearticulating the individual as socially and politically relevant. This renewed emphasis on the self becomes most comprehensible when viewed as a reaction to the agitprop poetry of the late 1960's and the disillusionment of the intellectual Left in the early 1970's.

Poets of this New Subjectivity movement flourished throughout the 1970's, and their concern with personal experience and the intricacies of daily life struck a chord with the public. Theobaldy's "Schnee im Büro" (snow at the office) details the daydreams of an office worker for whom the evenings and vacations with his lover barely compensate for his mundane eight-hour workday, during which he feels "imprisoned" and a mere "number."

More women poets saw publication of their works, and gained prominence and attention to their poetry, which often defied categorization and invigorated the poetic scene. Elisabeth Borchers (born 1926) displays an acute awareness for the nuances of language, and the poems of her *Gedichte* (1976; poems) use startlingly ironic imagery such as "solid" ruins, and are infused with her personal experience, as in "Das Begräbnis in Bollschweil" (the funeral in Bollschweil). Here, memory fails the poet to compose a proper eulogy, and the death of a close one leaves behind nothing but "small, slow ghosts" scurrying between the mourners.

Hilde Domin (1909-2006) similarly includes allusions to her personal life in her poetry, which is also concerned with the play of language, and occasionally conjures up Surrealist images and associations. In "Mauern Sortieren" (sorting walls), in her *Gesammelte Gedichte* (1987; collected poems), a look at "textile patterns" in a mail-order catalog reminds the persona of "patterns of walls," which later form the alliterative "Mauern aus Menschenfleisch" (walls of human flesh) to crescendo in the paradoxical coupling of "Mutter/Mauer" (mother/wall) which lies "zwischen Geschwistern/ jeder auf seiner Seite/ Berlin" (between siblings/ each on his own side/ Berlin), bringing the poem to a personal conclusion.

The 1980's saw a surprising return to formal poetry, with rhymes and meters replacing the ubiquitous free verse of the preceding two decades. Poets such as Krolow returned to rhymed lines, and Ulla Hahn (born 1946) abandoned her earlier, political poetry in exchange for poems following traditional forms, and quite surprised her readers. Enzensberger and Jandl returned to traditional reflections on the meaning of being, and even love poetry was read by a serious audience again.

On the other hand, the political issues of the decade, most noticeably environmentalism and the squatter movement in some of the larger cities like Hamburg and Berlin, spawned a flurry of poetic activities, often arising out of the alternative scene. Concerns over America's stationing of short-range nuclear missiles in Germany briefly brought back political passions in poetry. In 1989, the momentous changes in the Soviet Union and in Eastern Europe caught quite a few German poets in the West by surprise. By October 3, 1990, before one year had passed after East Germany allowed the breaching of the Berlin Wall in November, 1989, Germany became reunified. German poets in the West and the East now had to grapple with the challenges brought forth by the reintegration of two quite different societies.

Bibliography

Appleby, Carol. *German Romantic Poetry: Goethe, Novalis, Heine, Hölderlin*. Maidstone, Kent, England: Crescent Moon, 2008. Contains a discussion of the themes that were basic to the literature of Romanticism, along with critical studies of the major poets and philosophers of the period.

Baird, Jay W. *Hitler's War Poets: Literature and Politics in the Third Reich*. New York: Cambridge University Press, 2008. An analysis of the ideas that motivated Germany's Nazi poets, including their interpretation of history and their hopes for the future. Also includes their life stories and assesses the influence of what are now recognized as inferior works. Bibliographical references and index.

Bohm, Arnd. *Goethe's Faust and European Epic: Forgetting the Future*. Rochester, N.Y.: Camden House, 2007. By placing *Faust: Eine Tragödie* (pb. 1808, 1833; *The Tragedy of Faust*, 1823, 1838) within the context of earlier works in the genre, the author supports his belief that the work should be viewed as a Christian epic. An important new study by a highly respected scholar. Bibliography and index.

Boland, Eavan, ed. and trans. *After Every War: Twentieth-Century Women Poets*. Princeton, N.J.: Princeton University Press, 2004. One of Ireland's major woman poets has collected poems by German women who survived the war, some of them well known for their literary works, others obscure. The German and English versions of the poems are on facing pages. Illustrated. Bibliography and index.

Donahue, Neil H., ed. *A Companion to the Literature of German Expressionism*. Rochester, N.Y.: Camden House, 2005. Essays on the philosophical background of expressionism, as well as on specific writers, including all the major poets involved in the movement. Also contains critical overviews and textual analyses.

Fachinger, Petra. *Rewriting Germany from the Margins: "Other" German Literature of the 1980's and 1990's*. Montreal: McGill-Queen's University Press, 2001. Looks at the views expressed in the writings of German minorities, including immigrants from other countries, German Jews, and Germans who grew up in the German Democratic Republic. A much-needed study. Bibliography and index.

Harper, Anthony, and Margaret C. Ives. *Sappho in the Shadows: Essays on the Work of German Women Poets of the Age of Goethe, 1749-1832*. New York: Peter Lang, 2000. Includes translations of the poems into English and further bibliographical references. Highlights a freshly emerging aspect of German Romanticism from a mostly feminist perspective.

Hofmann, Michael, ed. *Twentieth-Century German Poetry: An Anthology*. New York: Farrar, Straus and Giroux, 2008. A collection of superb translations of the works of major German poets, assembled by a noted poet and translator. Bilingual format.

Koelb, Clayton, and Eric Downing, eds. *German Literature of the Nineteenth Century, 1832-1899*. Rochester, N.Y.: Camden House, 2005. Volume 9 in the Camden House History of German Literature series. Sums up the political, cultural, and literary movements of the period and discusses important writers in detail. Includes list of primary and secondary sources.

Nader, Andrés José, ed. *Traumatic Verses: On Poetry in German from the Concentration Camps, 1933-1945*. Rochester, N.Y.: Camden House, 2007. Combines a study of the motivations that impelled inmates of the camps to write poetry with the poems that survived, presented both in the original and in translation. A valuable contribution to Holocaust studies and to the history of German poetry.

Vanchena, Lorie A. *Political Poetry in Periodicals and the Shaping of German National Consciousness in the Nineteenth Century*. New York: Peter Lang, 2000. An innovative approach to the subject, with detailed bibliographical references and index. Shows how some poets were quite ardent German Nationalists, and illustrates how popular periodicals helped disseminate nationalistic ideas among educated citizens.

Richard Spuler
Updated by R. C. Lutz

ROSE AUSLÄNDER

Born: Czernowitz, Bukovina (now Chernivtsi, Ukraine); May 11, 1901
Died: Düsseldorf, Germany; January 3, 1988

PRINCIPAL POETRY
Der Regenbogen, 1939
Blinder Sommer, 1965
36 Gerechte, 1967
Inventar, 1972
Ohne Visum, 1974
Andere Zeichen, 1975
Gesammelte Gedichte, 1976 (expanded 1977)
Noch ist Raum, 1976
Doppelspiel, 1977
Es ist alles anders, 1977
Selected Poems, 1977
Aschensommer, 1978
Es bleibt noch viel zu sagen, 1978
Mutterland, 1978
Ein Stück weiter, 1979
Einverständnis, 1980
Einen Drachen reiten, 1981
Im Atemhaus wohnen, 1981
Mein Atem heisst jetzt, 1981
Schatten im Spiegel, 1981 (in Hebrew)
Mein Venedig versinkt nicht, 1982
Südlich wartet ein wärmeres Land, 1982
So sicher atmet nur Tod, 1983
Gesammelte Werke in sieben Bänden und einen Nachtragsband, 1984-1990
    (8 volumes)
Festtage in Manhattan, 1985
Ich zähl die Sterne meiner Worte, 1985
Brief aus Rosen, 1994
Mother Tongue, 1995
Schattenwald, 1995
The Forbidden Tree: Englische Gedichte, 1995

Other literary forms

The reputation of Rose Ausländer (OWS-lehn- dehr) is based solely on her poetry. Volume 3 of her collected works, containing her writings from 1966 to 1975, includes several short prose pieces; volume 4, containing her writings from the year 1976, comprises, aside from her poetry, only one short autobiographical piece.

Achievements

In 1957, the highly acclaimed poet Marianne Moore awarded Rose Ausländer the poetry prize of the Wagner College in New York. In 1967, Ausländer received the Meersburger Droste Prize; in 1977, the Ida Dehmel Prize and the Andreas Gryphius Prize; in 1978, the prize of the Federation of German Industry; and in 1980, the Roswitha Medal of the city of Bad Gandersheim.

Biography

Rose Ausländer was born Rosalie Beatrice Ruth Scherzer on May 11, 1901, to Jewish parents in Czernowitz, the capital of Bukovina. Her mother's name was Etie Binder and her father's, Sigmund Scherzer. Originally her father was supposed to become a rabbi, but later he decided to become a businessman. Until 1918, Bukovina was the easternmost part of the Habsburg Empire. The population of Czernowitz was about 110,000 and consisted of Germans, Romanians, Ukranians, Poles, and a large proportion of Jews. The Jewish population had assumed the role of preserving the German culture and of being an intermediary between it and the Slavic culture. As a child, Ausländer was educated in the German-Austrian school system, but she also learned Hebrew and Yiddish. Through her schooling she became acquainted with the German literary classics, especially those by Johann Wolfgang von Goethe, Friedrich Schiller, and Heinrich Heine. She enjoyed a harmonious childhood, which was filled with love toward her parents and her native country. With the advent of World War I and the Russian occupation of Czernowitz, however, this peaceful existence was abruptly terminated. Ausländer's family fled first to Bucharest and later to Vienna. There they led a life full of suffering and misery. As a result of the Treaty of Versailles, Bukovina became a part of Romania. The family returned to their hometown, where Ausländer finished her secondary education and subsequently attended the University of Czernowitz, majoring in literature and philosophy. At the university, she became especially interested in Plato, Baruch Spinoza, and Constantin Brunner, a follower of Spinoza who lived in Berlin at that time. Later the teachings of Brunner were to become an integral part of her poetry.

Ausländer's studies and her active membership in literary circles exposed her to the poetry of Friedrich Hölderlin, Franz Kafka, Georg Trakl, Rainer Maria Rilke, Else Lasker-Schüler, and Gottfried Benn. Despite their distance from Vienna, the Jewish literary circles in Czernowitz had adopted the Viennese Karl Kraus as mentor. With the publication of the journal *Die Fackel* (the torch), Kraus had assumed the role of the "high priest of truth," the herald of an ethical humanism and poetry against nationalist chauvinism and the corruption of bureaucracy and politics.

In 1921, as a result of the worsening of the family's already dire financial situation following her father's death, Ausländer decided to emigrate to the United States. She emigrated with her childhood friend Ignaz Ausländer. After failing to establish themselves in Minneapolis-St. Paul, Minnesota, they settled in New York City, where they were married in 1923. Ausländer had a position in a bank, and her husband worked as a mechanic. The marriage was not to last; they separated in 1926 and were finally divorced in 1930. In 1924, Ausländer met Alfred Margul-Sperber, who later became the major sponsor of her poetry after her return to Czernowitz. In 1926, she became a U.S. citizen and in 1927 visited Constantin Brunner in Berlin. She returned to New York in 1928, where she lived with Helios Hecht, a graphologist, a writer, and an editor of several periodicals. She published her first poems in the *Westlicher Herold-Kalender*, a Minneapolis publication, and later published a few poems in the *New Yorker Volkszeitung*. In 1931, she returned to Czernowitz with Hecht and remained there to care for her ailing mother. After her prolonged absence from the United States, her U.S. citizenship was revoked in 1934. Eventually, she and Hecht separated.

Between 1931 and the outbreak of World War II, Ausländer published poems in various periodicals. Margul-Sperber arranged for the publication of her first volume of poetry, *Der Regenbogen* (the rainbow), despite the Romanian government's policy of suppressing non-Romanian literature. In 1941, the Germans occupied Czernowitz, forced the Jews to return to the old ghetto, and periodically deported groups to concentration camps in Transnistria. Ausländer and her mother escaped almost certain death by hiding from the Gestapo in basements where friends supplied them with food and clothes. The experience of persecution and underground existence was to become the motivating force behind Ausländer's later poetry. In secret poetry-reading groups, she met Paul Antschel, who later changed his name to Paul Celan. It was during this time that she came to believe in the existential function of poetry to preserve her own identity in a hostile world.

When the Soviet Union seized Bukovina after World War II, Ausländer, together with her mother and her brother's family, left Czernowitz for Bucharest. With the help of friends in the United States, she was able to obtain an immigration visa but only for herself; her family had to stay behind. In the fall of 1946, she arrived again in New York and found work as a translator and foreign-language secretary for a large shipping company. All her attempts to obtain an immigration visa for her mother proved futile. The news of her mother's death in 1947 caused a psychological breakdown, after which for some time she wrote poetry only in English.

Although Ausländer became naturalized again in 1948, she never felt at home in New York. The American lifestyle remained alien to her. During a visit to Europe in 1957, she again saw Celan, who had emigrated to Paris. He introduced her to contemporary European poetry, which resulted in the rebirth of her poetry in German. The new poems, however, were stripped of all harmonizing prosodic elements.

In 1961, in failing health, Ausländer could not continue her job and was forced to live on her Social Security income. In 1966, she received additional support from the West German government. By that time, she had once again returned to Europe, where she attempted unsuccessfully to settle in Vienna, which was to her the cultural center of the former Habsburg Empire. Finally, she moved to Düsseldorf, West Germany, in 1965. The year 1965 was not only the date of the publication of her second volume of poetry, twenty-six years after her first one, but also the year of her belated reintroduction to a German audience. Although she could not return to her native country, she returned to her mother tongue, the only medium through which she could express her poetic message and establish a dialogue with an audience. In 1970, she moved into Nelly-Sachs-Haus, a Jewish home for the aged, which she made her permanent home. After a long illness and an increasing retreat from the outside world, she died in 1988. She left more than twenty thousand pages of manuscripts and typescripts, as well as numerous notebooks, material that was used to form much of her posthumous collections.

ANALYSIS

Rose Ausländer did not become recognized as a major poet until the late 1960's and early 1970's, when volumes of her poetry appeared in rapid succession. At the same time, various German newspapers and magazines printed some of her poems, and her work appeared in anthologies as well. Because of the outbreak of World War II and her Jewish background, her early writings had never reached a sizable audience beyond her hometown. Not until her visit with Celan in 1957, when she became acquainted with his elliptic Hermetic style and that of his European contemporaries, did she adopt the curt, laconic manner of her mature poetry. In this style, she vividly expressed the horrors of the Nazi persecution and her total desolation and despair, which continued even after the war, in her exile in the United States and later in Germany. Although the trauma of her persecution and exile was not diminished, she was able to transcend the pain of these experiences to reach a level beyond despair, a new affirmation of life and its riches—each object of which becomes the motif for a poem. Perhaps her hard-won message of consolation and redemption explains the increasing recognition of her achievements.

The titles of Ausländer's collections, such as *Blinder Sommer* (blind summer), *Ohne Visum* (without a visa), and *Aschensommer* (ash summer), like the images and motifs in the poems themselves, such as "ash," "smoke," and "dust," clearly reveal that Ausländer's poetry is directly linked to the Holocaust. She deeply identified with the suffering of her people. Even her first volume of poetry in 1939, however, reflected a troubled outlook on life. Here, nature, homeland, and love provide a refuge from a threatening reality, as the danger of national socialism loomed on the horizon. Despite their harmonizing prosodic elements, these early poems are characterized by a beginning awareness of the general crisis during these years. This awareness is put into the cosmogonic perspective of the world's fall from its original godlike state. Poetry became to Ausländer the only means of renewing this divine state. This concept is in direct accordance with Spinoza's philosophical theory of harmonizing microcosm and macrocosm. As acceptable as the harmonizing prosodic elements may be in this idealized conception, however, they are self-contradictory in the poems from the underground, appropriately titled *Ghettomotifs*. They first became available to a wider audience in volume 1 of *Gesammelte Werke*, containing the poetry from 1927 to 1956. The English poems written from 1948 to 1956 in the United States continue in this style, which Ausländer abandoned when she was confronted with the modern development of poetry during her 1957 visit to Europe.

HOLOCAUST AND PERSECUTION

Aside from the departure from rhyme and classical meters, her change in style can best be seen in the inclusion of the Holocaust into the cosmogonic process and in the reduction of the imagery to key words or constellations. The images of sun, stars, and earth lose all their divine characteristics, and references to the Holocaust are so explicit that they evoke the absolute perversion and denaturalization of the human calling. "Ash-summer," "ash-rain" or "smoke is pouring out of the eyes of the cannibals" are only a few examples. The trauma of persecution is carried into the depiction of Ausländer's experience of exile in the United States. The escape to freedom across the Atlantic resembles the never- ending search of the Flying Dutchman for a final resting place; the Nazi persecution is reenacted in the United States: "Men in Ku Klux Klan hoods, with swastikas and guns as weapons, surround you, the room smokes with danger"; the "ghetto-garb has not been discarded" despite a "fragrant" table full of food. This threat overshadows all personal relationships: "Can it be/ that I will see you again/ in April/ free of ashes?" The exile only reinforces the expulsion from paradise; the house turns into a prison, New York into a jungle, the subway into a funeral procession of war victims, and the summer heat of one hundred degrees evokes the image of the cremations in the concentration camps. Even more significant, the technology and modern civilization in New York are seen as symbols of the absolute denial of God.

YEARNING FOR HER HOMELAND

Against this background of persecution and exile, Ausländer's native country takes on the qualities of a fairy tale—it is a "once-upon-a-time home" representing a "once-upon-a-time existence"—or is mythologized as filled with the presence of God: "the Jordan river emptied into the Pruth" (the Pruth being the main river of Bukovina, the country of beech trees). Although political reality does not allow a physical return to her homeland, Ausländer's "always back to the Pruth" can only be a spiritual return to the full awareness of her cultural, religious, and family roots, to her beginnings; in its "utopian" fulfillment it would signify the unity of beginning and ending. The poet calls this state "the dwelling," in conscious or subconscious reference to the Kabbalistic *schechina*, which symbolizes the dwelling place of God's bride, or the lowest level of the sefiroth tree. She laments, "Flying on the air swing/ Europe America Europe// I do not dwell/ I only live"; her settling in Germany becomes merely another stage in her continuous exile.

The poet's desire to return to her homeland corresponds to that of the Jewish people to reestablish their homeland in Israel: "Phoenix/ my people/ cremated// risen/ among cypress and/ orange trees." To these "wandering brethren," to "Ahasver, the wandering Jew," she offers the Jewish greeting "Le Cháim": "We/ risen/ from the void/ . . . we are talking/ softly/ with risen/ brethren." Despite that bond, her social and national identity has been lost forever: "born without a visa to this world/ she never looks the other way/ people like us are always/ suspicious." For that reason poetry itself takes over the function of reestablishing a dwelling place that secures Ausländer's spiritual identity.

The redemptive process

The creative poetic process had to build upon the foundation of annihilation and exile before any redemption and transfiguration could occur. As late as 1979, Ausländer maintained, in a poem: "I do not forget// my family roots/ mother's voice/ the first kiss/ the mountains of Bukovina/ the escape in World War I/ the suffering in Vienna/ the bombs in World War II// the invasion of the Nazis/ the anguish in the basement/ the doctor who saved our lives/ the bitter sweet America// Hölderlin Trakl Celan// my agony to write/ the compulsion to write/ still." In the strictest consistency with her fate, the redemptive process begins, "retracing my steps/ in the urn of memory," and culminates in a paradoxical statement that combines trauma and bliss: "Nothing is lost/ in the urn/ the ash is breathing." The ambiguity of this statement is heightened by the middle line being grammatically linked to both the first and the third lines. This grammatical linking is employed again in these lines: "how beautiful/ ash can blossom/ in the blood." Only by "losing herself in the jungle of words" can Ausländer "find herself again in the miracle of the word," ultimately God's Word, "my word/ born out of despair// out of the desperate hope/ that poetry/ is still possible." Only poetry can grant this renewed existence: "mother tongue is putting me together// mosaic of people" in a space "free of ashes/ among verses." Poetry offers renewed life, the divine breath of life that links past and future in a timeless present: "The past/ has composed me/ I have/ inherited the future// My breath is called/ NOW."

Such stances became more frequent in Ausländer's old age, possibly because the poet, being bedridden, had only poetry left as a means of self-affirmation: "My fatherland is dead/ they have buried it/ in fire// I live/ in my motherland/ the word"—an obvious play on the word "mother tongue," which has taken on the extreme existential function of being the only guarantor of Ausländer's identity. Even then, this process does not entail an escape from reality but rather builds upon "professing to the earth and its dangerous secrets... to man I profess myself with all the words that create me." It is a reciprocal act which grants poetic identity by giving meaning to both humankind and life. For that reason, Ausländer can arrive at an otherwise unbelievable statement affirming the poetic process out of the annihilation of humanity: "Magnificent despite all/ dust of flesh// This light-birth/ in an eyelash womb/ Lips/ yes/ much remains/ to be said."

Ausländer has called the specific mode of this poetic process "this dual play/ flower words/ war stammering." It is a play of mediation or reconciliation between language and reality that might result in simplistic affirmation if the never forgotten point of departure were not to forbid such a reduction. On the contrary, this play takes on mystical proportions, striving for the redemption of the world by making it transparent to manifest its divine destiny. This interdependence between language and reality culminates in the image of the crystal, in which microcosm and macrocosm meet, in reverence to Spinoza, who was a lens maker as well as a philosopher: "My saint/ is called Benedict// He has/ polished/ the universe// Infinite crystal/ out of whose heart/ the light radiates."

Although the later poems, especially those after 1981, reduce the poetic process to such a degree that they can become manneristic, Ausländer's total poetic production clearly shows her to be among the most significant post-World War II poets. She has been able to find meaning in life despite the traumas she has experienced. Her "self-portrait" lists all the conditions that denied her the status of a regular member of society and at the same time testifies to poetry's power to transcend personal tragedy: "Jewish gypsy/ raised/ in the German language/ under the black and yellow flag// Borders pushed me/ to Latins Slavs/ Americans Germanic people// Europe/ in your womb/ I dream/ my next birth."

Bibliography

Boase-Beier, Jean. "Translating Repetition." *Journal of European Studies* 24, no. 96 (December, 1994): 403. Any literary translation must involve a careful stylistic analysis of the source text, particularly the translation of poetry. Includes an English translation of her poem "Damit kein Licht uns liebe."

Bower, Kathrin M. *Ethics and Remembrance in the Poetry of Nelly Sachs and Rose Ausländer*. Rochester, N.Y.: Camden House, 2000. Critical interpretation of the poetry of Nelly Sachs and Ausländer relating to the Holocaust during World War II. Includes extensive bibliographic references and an index.

———. "Rose Ausländer." In *Women Writers in German-Speaking Countries: A Bio-Bibliographical Critical Sourcebook*, edited by Elke P. Frederiksen and Elizabeth G. Ametsbichler. Westport, Conn.: Greenwood Press, 1998. Excellent overview of Ausländer's life, the main themes of her poetry, and its critical reception. English translations of German quotations. Includes bibliographies of primary and secondary works and translations.

_____. "Searching for the (M)Other: The Rhetoric of Longing in Post-Holocaust Poems by Nelly Sachs and Rose Ausländer." *Women in German Yearbook* 12 (1996): 125-147. English translations and interpretations of six of Ausländer's poems.

Frederiksen, Elke P., and Elizabeth G. Ametsbichler, eds. *Women Writers in German-Speaking Countries: A Bio-Bibliographical Critical Sourcebook*. Westport, Conn.: Greenwood Press, 1997. Includes a chapter on Ausländer and an introductory essay that examines the history of literature by women in German-speaking countries. Includes an extensive bibliography.

Glenn, Jerry. "Blumenworte/Kriegsgestammel: The Poetry of Rose Ausländer." *Modern Austrian Literature* 12, nos. 3/4 (1979). A brief critical study of selected poems by Ausländer.

Keith-Smith, Brian. "Rose Ausländer." In *Encyclopedia of German Literature*, edited by Matthias Konzett. Vol. 1. Chicago: Fitzroy Dearborn, 2000. Outlines Ausländer's poetic development, from the early influences to the final epigrammatic poems.

Klaus Weissenberger

GOTTFRIED BENN

Born: Mansfeld, Germany; May 2, 1886
Died: Berlin, East Germany (now in Germany); August 7, 1956

PRINCIPAL POETRY
Morgue, und andere Gedichte, 1912
Söhne, 1913
Fleisch, 1917
Schutt, 1924
Betäubung, 1925
Spaltung, 1925
Gesammelte Gedichte, 1927
Ausgewählte Gedichte, 1911-1936, 1936
Gedichte, 1936
Zweiundzwanzig Gedichte, 1943
Statische Gedichte, 1948
Trunkene Flut, 1949
Fragmente, 1951
Destillationen, 1953
Aprèslude, 1955
Gesammelte Gedichte, 1956
Primal Vision, 1958
Primäre Tage, Gedichte und Fragmente aus dem Nachlass, 1958
Gedichte aus dem Nachlass, 1960
Gottfried Benn: Selected Poems, 1970
Gottfried Benn: The Unreconstructed Expressionist, 1972
Sämtliche Gedichte, 1998

OTHER LITERARY FORMS

Gottfried Benn (behn) was primarily a poet, but he did write some significant works in other genres, most notably a collection of novellas, *Gehirne* (1916; *Brains*, 1972); a novel, *Roman des Phänotyp* (1944; novel of the phenotype); the essay *Goethe und die Naturwissenschaften* (1949; Goethe and the natural sciences); his autobiography, *Doppelleben* (1950; *Double Life*, 2002); and a theoretical treatise, *Probleme der Lyrik* (1951; problems of lyric poetry). His writings also include other prose and dramatic works.

Achievements

No other German poet exemplifies as fully as Gottfried Benn the emergence of the modern tradition within postwar German literature. His radical aesthetic as well as his political affiliations have made Benn a controversial figure. He was the "phenotype" of his age—that is, the exemplary representation of the intellectual and spiritual condition of his times. As such, Benn can be viewed as not only a remarkable poet but also an important figure of twentieth century German *Geistesgeschichte*.

Benn's early work (until about 1920) was known only to a relatively small circle of readers. Indeed, it was only after World War II, in the last decade of his life, that Benn achieved fame. His achievements were acknowledged in 1951, when he was awarded the Georg Büchner Prize in literature. For years prior to this time, Benn had been blacklisted, as it were, as a result of his short-lived infatuation with Nazism. Because of the public commentary to which he had been subjected, Benn was reluctant to reenter public life. He did publish again, however, and in the years before his death a generation of poets in search of a tradition flocked around him like disciples around a master.

The years of Nazi control had yielded a vast wasteland in German literature. Indeed, the historical events of the twentieth century, in particular as they affected Germany, intensified the general philosophical disorientation of the immediate postwar period. Marxism was no real alternative for the West; existentialism prevailed instead, based in large measure on the writings of Martin Heidegger and Jean-Paul Sartre. In this context, Benn's theory of art as a metaphysical act had considerable authority. For postwar poets in search of a new way of writing, Benn provided a transition from the various offshoots of French Symbolism and German expressionism to contemporary modernism.

Biography

Gottfried Benn was born on May 2, 1886, the son of a Protestant minister. He studied philosophy and theology at the University of Marburg and later studied medicine at the University of Berlin. He completed his medical degree in 1910 and was awarded first prize for his thesis on the etiology of epilepsy in puberty. Benn worked as a pathologist and serologist in Berlin, where he became friends with several expressionist poets, the most important of whom was Else Lasker-Schüler. Benn also set up medical practice in Berlin, and his first volume of poetry, *Morgue und andere Gedichte* (morgue, and other poems), clearly shows the influence of his scientific and medical training: The cold and unforgiving objectivity and precision of medical and surgical technique inform these poems, with their shocking portrayal of brutality and morbidity.

In 1914, Benn traveled briefly to the United States. Upon his return, he was drafted into the military medical corps, serving as an officer in Belgium before returning to Berlin in 1917. These years, contrary to what one might expect, were extremely productive for Benn as a writer, and he later noted that during the following years, on the whole relatively uneventful for him, he constantly drew for inspiration on his experiences in Belgium.

In 1933, Benn filled the position of which Heinrich Mann had been relieved, section president of the Prussian Academy. Later, Benn became director for the department of literature. In April of the same year, he gave a radio talk, "Der neue Staat und die Intellektuellen" ("The New State and the Intellectuals"), clearly in response to a letter from Klaus Mann, the son of Thomas Mann, who wrote from the south of France. It is true that Benn initially embraced National Socialism in 1933. He greeted the political doctrines of the Nazis as a means for overcoming the stagnation and nihilism of Western civilization, but he soon regretted his participation and withdrew into silence.

In 1935, Benn left Berlin and headed for Hannover. It was Benn's early poetry that gave rise to the debate on expressionism carried in the émigré paper *Das Wort*, printed in Moscow. In the ensuing years, Benn had a run-in with W. Willrich, a party loyalist who labeled Benn a "cultural Bolshevist" and tried to have Benn effectively "removed" from public life. Ironically, only the intervention of Heinrich Himmler himself stayed Willrich's attempts. Benn remained in the army medical service from 1935 until the end of the war. After 1948, he enjoyed a new phase of poetic creativity, and his poetry eventually achieved recognition throughout Europe.

Analysis

Both poetically and existentially, Gottfried Benn resided at the crossroads of two significant traditions. At the turn of the century, the natural sciences exercised a substantial "claim to truth" and provided influential paradigms of thought. For many of Benn's generation, however, scientific study had entered a rapid phase of entropy—it was seen no longer to answer questions meaningfully from the humanist point of view. In fact, one could even say that the "scientific approach" was seen by many to "explain" the universe inadequately, precisely because it did not pose the right questions. In Germany, the most significant manifestation of this dissatisfaction with the scientific paradigm took place under the rubric of "expressionism," which in many respects carried on the tradition of German Romanticism. The tension exemplified in the conflict between Benn's scientific training and his early intoxication with expressionism came to play an important role in the development of his aesthetic theory and poetry.

A concept basic to Benn's thought was his conviction that humankind necessarily "suffered consciousness." He attributed this suffering to modern overintellectualization: "The brain is our fate, our consignment and our curse." The modern consciousness fragments the totality of the world into its conceptual categories; reality is divided past meaningful comprehension; and the loss of humans' capacity to perceive relationships points ineluctably in the direction of nihilistic resignation. During the years from 1921 to 1932, Benn studied the works of Johann Wolfgang von Goethe, Friedrich Nietzsche, Oswald Spengler, Carl Jung, Ernst Troeltsch, and Gotthold Ephraim Lessing, and through his study of prehistory, paleontology, and myth, he developed his own notions of art, reality, and the self.

In Benn's conceptual framework, the inner space once occupied by the premodern sense of harmony and totality is now filled with a kind of nostalgic longing. By somehow penetrating and deactivating the rational consciousness, Benn hoped to return (momentarily) to archetypal, primal, and prelogical experience. Benn identified this act as "hyperemic metaphysics"—that is, an intensified state of perception (such as that induced by intoxication, dream visions, or hallucinations), which he then applied exponentially to derive his "hyperemic theory of the poetic," or primal moments of poetic creativity.

It is necessary to see how Benn viewed the creative process to understand his poetry. According to Benn, the creative process required first "an inarticulate, creative nucleus, a psychic substance"; second, words familiar to the poet that "stand at his disposal" and are "suited to him personally"; and third, a "thread of Ariadne, which leads him with absolute certainty out of this bipolar tension"—that is, the tension between the psychic substance and the "word." This amalgam constitutes the basic creative situation for Benn.

"Beautiful Youth"

One of his first poems, "Schöne Jugend" ("Beautiful Youth"), perhaps best illustrates Benn's early cynicism. The poem describes the dissection of the body of a young (and possibly at one time "beautiful") girl, whose decomposed mouth and esophagus are perfunctorily noted, as is the nest of young rats discovered beneath the diaphragm, "one little sister" of which lay dead while the others lived off the liver and kidneys—"drank the cold blood and had/ spent here a beautiful youth." A quick death awaits the rats: "They were thrown all together in the water. Ah, how their little snouts did squeal!" It becomes obvious that the "beautiful youth" to which the title refers is not that of the young girl, as the reader is intended to assume, but rather of the rats.

"One Word"

A good example of Benn's preoccupation with the capacity of language to "fascinate," and in so doing to give momentary vision to meaning within meaninglessness (form from chaos), is his poem "Ein Wort" ("One Word"). This poem is about the fact that words and sentences can be transmuted into *chiffres*, from which rise life and meaning. The effect can be such as to halt the sun and silence the spheres, as everything focuses for the moment on the primal catalyst, the single word. The word, however, is transitory, brilliant but short-lived, and already in the second and last strophe of this brief poem it is gone, leaving behind it the self and the world once again apart and distinct, alone in the dark, empty space surrounding them. Perhaps this paraphrase of Benn's poem gives an idea of how Benn viewed the magic of the poetic word, its unique ability to stand (and consequently place the reader/listener) outside the "normal" conceptual categories of time and space. It communicates truth as a bolt of lightning momentarily illuminating the sky.

"Lost Self"

The radical dissolution of meaning with the evaporation of the word's spellbinding aura aligns with Benn's view of the disintegration of reality in general. Nowhere are the consequences of this loss of reality for the individual given more poignant expression than in Benn's poem "Verlorenes Ich" ("Lost Self"). Benn applies the terminology of modern science as an explanation of the radical alienation of the modern self. The strictly scientific explanation of the universe does not adequately explain the vicissitudes of human existence. Benn does not envision a return to a previous form of existence since that is an impossibility, nor does he seek refuge in a Christian answer, positing God as the source of an otherwise incomprehensible universe. Neither, however, is his stance one of resignation or of art for art's sake, even though he is often reproached for both. Instead, his predicament always centers on the struggle for human meaning and significance. The solution to this existential dilemma, he finds, is manifested in the intellectual and spiritual acts that human beings can perform, among these the creative act of giving form. "The artist," wrote Benn, "is the only one who copes with things, who decides their destiny."

"Departure"

It is true that Benn felt that all good poetry is "addressed to no one," and that he expressly refuted the possibility of poetry having any public function. To castigate Benn for an unconscionable aestheticism, though, would not be accurate or just. He does not cast aside the question of ethical responsibility; if he did, one would not expect to find such an obsession with what constitutes the essence of humanity, above all with the existential-poetic confrontation with Being. To explore this problem further, it is illuminating to consider a highly autobiographical poem by Benn, "Abschied" ("Departure"), contained originally in a cycle of poems Benn referred to as "Biographische Gedichte" ("Biographical Poems") and first published in *Zweiundzwanzig Gedichte* (twenty-two poems). Formally, the poem is a classic example of artistic control: four strophes of eight lines each in iambic pentameter, with alternating feminine and masculine rhymes in an *ababcdcd* scheme. Structurally, the poem constitutes a tightly organized unit: Its formal principles interact with its themes—namely, the schizophrenic existence of the persona and the acknowledged taking leave from the old Self.

The topos of parting (*Abschied*) is itself an interesting one within German poetry; one may recall the significant example of Goethe's "Willkommen und Abschied" ("Welcome and Farewell"). Benn's poem, however, does not deal with the separation of two individuals—two lovers, for example. Instead, it describes a separation of the persona, a division of the Self into a former "You" and a present "I." The You represents the part of the individual that belongs to a world of the past, while the I attempts to grasp and develop within the poem the process of alienation to which it has been subjected. The first strophe outlines the relationship of the former to the present Self by employing a series of metaphors, while the second strophe probes the cause of the schism and relates the sole recourse as perceived by the persona. The link between past and present—memory—becomes the topic of the third strophe, and finally the poem moves toward a further degree of estrangement, concluding with a note of sadness and melancholy typical of Benn.

The subject of each independent clause in the first strophe is the pronoun "you," and initially it is the active subject, while the "I" remains the passive object. The relationship is established via a metaphor: "You fill me as does blood the fresh wound,/ and run down its dark path." The image of the wound operates on the physical plane to suggest impairment, disease, decay. Later, in the third strophe, this physical affliction is seen to be present on a psychological plane as well. The adjective describing the wound, "fresh," can be read two ways. On one hand, it accentuates the grotesque nature of the wound by showing it in its first moments when blood flows most freely. On the other hand, "fresh" can suggest "recent." The reader is thus made privy to the suffering of the persona as it takes place. The metaphor of the wound encompasses the first two lines of the poem. The dark trace of the blood is more than merely graphic realism; it evokes an aura of mysterious origin. Blood is the life-sustaining fluid, and its escape from the wound enacts the kind of exposure that the "deep self" of the persona endures. Its dark hue contrasts with the "day of minutiae," the "heavenly light" of the third strophe, and "a high light" in the third line of the last strophe. Its opaqueness suggests obscurity and impregnability. The persona's flight into silence at the end of the second strophe ("you must take your silence, travel downward/ to night and sorrow and the roses late") gives image to the inexpressibility of the "deep self."

The night setting maintains the motif of darkness found in the "dark path" on the second line. The hour corresponds to dusk and evinces the twilight of the former self, the You. The atmosphere of darkness surrounding the You continues to dominate, although it retreats for the moment with the appearance of roses in the following line. While this imagery is initially perplexing (because it does not seem to cooperate with the earlier metaphor of the wound), under the assumption that the You represents a former state of naïve harmony and quietude, the rose will be seen to bloom now only with difficulty, indicating the suffering connected with the memory of the persona's previous unified existence.

In the second strophe, the self-reflection intensifies, resulting in a kind of linguistic breakdown: The abstract nouns lack contact with reality and no longer illustrate the tendency toward analogous thought, as in the first five lines; no finite verb appears from lines 6 to 8, leaving the explication static and ineffective. Significantly, it is the second strophe which introduces the idea of alienation. Its cause is seen as the absence of a homogeneous reality, as a craze of pluralities (Benn speaks of "realities"). Resistance against this disembodying centrifugal force is sustained within the act of composing the poem itself, in the creative act that circles around the "deep self" in an attempt to describe it with more accuracy than simple, or even scientific, language can yield. "The form *is* the poem," Benn wrote elsewhere, stating the crux of his aesthetic.

In spite of the alienation from the "deep self," it is only this region that can satisfy the needs of the persona. This part of the Self, however, is (linguistically) impregnable, and silence represents the only alternative. The poem ends as "a last day" (Benn's own advancing age), which "plays its game, and feels its light and without/ memory goes down—everything is said." Such a poetic stance is rooted in the modernist poetic tradition. Benn acknowledges that no word or sign can now reveal that for which he searches; they are but symbols of the essential thing.

Had the persona no memory of itself, then no tension or conflict would result. The plague of consciousness is such, however, that it disrupts the fluidity of expression. This is represented throughout the poem by frequent dashes, colons, and question marks. Sentences and thoughts are left incomplete, fragmented; punctuation replaces words and becomes itself a frustrated sign or symbol of the inexpressible. The "deep self" evades all intellectualization.

In his epoch-making address, *Probleme der Lyrik*, Benn postulated that

> not one of even the great poets of our time has left behind more than six or eight complete poems. The rest may be interesting from the point of view of biography and the author's development, but only a few are content in themselves, illuminating from within themselves, full of lasting fascination—and so, for these six poems, [there are] thirty to fifty years of asceticism, suffering, and struggle.

Even according to Benn's own stringent definitions, he deserves to be acknowledged as a great poet.

Other major works

LONG FICTION: *Roman des Phänotyp*, 1944; *Die Stimme hinter dem Vorhang*, 1952 (*The Voice Behind the Screen*, 1996).

SHORT FICTION: *Gehirne*, 1916 (*Brains*, 1972); *Provoziertes Leben: Eine Auswahl aus den Prosaschriften*, 1955.

NONFICTION: *Fazit der Perspektiven*, 1930; *Nach dem Nihilismus*, 1932; *Der neue Staat und die Intellektuellen*, 1933; *Kunst und Macht*, 1943; *Goethe und die Naturwissenschaften*, 1949; *Doppelleben*, 1950 (*Double Life*, 2002); *Essays*, 1951; *Probleme der Lyrik*, 1951.

MISCELLANEOUS: *Die gesammelten Schriften*, 1922; *Gesammelte Prosa*, 1928; *Ausdruckswelt: Essays and Aphorismen*, 1949; *Frühe Prosa und Reden*, 1950; *Gesammelte Werke in vier Bänden*, 1958-1960 (4 volumes).

Bibliography

Alter, Reinhard. *Gottfried Benn: The Artist and Politics (1910-1934)*. Bern, Switzerland: Herbert Lang, 1976. A biography including the history of German politics and literature in Benn's time.

Dierick, Augustinus Petrus. *Gottfried Benn and His Critics: Major Interpretations, 1912-1992*. Columbia, S.C.: Camden House, 1992. Critical interpretation and history by an expert in German expressionist literature. Includes an exhaustive bibliography.

Donahue, Neil H., ed. *A Companion to the Literature of German Expressionism*. Rochester, N.Y.: Camden House, 2005. Chapter on expressionist poetry discusses Benn.

Powell, Larson. *The Technological Unconscious in German Modernist Literature: Nature in Rilke, Benn, Brecht, and Döblin*. Rochester, N.Y.: Camden House, 2008. Examines the works of Benn, Bertolt Brecht, Rainer Maria Rilke, and Alfred Döblin, with attention to the role of nature. Contains a chapter on Benn.

Ray, Susan. *Beyond Nihilism: Gottfried Benn's Postmodernist Poetics*. New York: P. Lang, 2003. Ray analyzes Benn's poetry, placing him with the postmodern poets.

Roche, Mark William. *Gottfried Benn's Static*. Chapel Hill: University of North Carolina Press, 1991. Intellectual and historical interpretation of Benn's poetry with bibliography and index.

Travers, Martin. *The Poetry of Gottfried Benn: Text and Selfhood*. Studies in Modern German Literature 106. New York: P. Lang, 2007. Examines the question of self in Benn's poetry.

Richard Spuler

JOHANNES BOBROWSKI

Born: Tilsit, East Prussia (now Sovetsk, Russia); April 9, 1917
Died: East Berlin, East Germany (now Berlin, Germany); September 2, 1965

PRINCIPAL POETRY
Sarmatische Zeit, 1961
Schattenland Ströme, 1962
Shadow Land: Selected Poems, 1966
Wetterzeichen, 1966
Im Windgesträuch, 1970
The White Mirror, 1993

OTHER LITERARY FORMS

Although Johannes Bobrowski (bawd-ROW-skee) is remembered primarily for his poetry, he did publish two critically acclaimed experimental novels: *Levins Mühle: 34 Sätze über meinen Grossvater* (1964; *Levin's Mill: Thirty-four Statements About My Grandfather*, 1970) and *Litauische Klaviere* (1966; Lithuanian pianos). He also wrote several short stories, which are collected in the following volumes: *Boehlendorff, und andere Erzählungen* (1965; Boehlendorff, and other stories), *Mäusefest, und andere Erzählungen* (1965; festival of the mice, and other stories), and *Der Mahner* (1967; *I Taste Bitterness*, 1970). Working as a reader at an East German publishing house, he had the opportunity to edit books by others, including collections of legends and poetry. Recordings of several of his poems are available.

ACHIEVEMENTS

Johannes Bobrowski belonged to that generation of East German poets who matured late artistically, since their creative development was interrupted by the events of World War II and the founding of a new state. When Bobrowski finally published his first slender volumes in the early 1960's, they caused a great deal of excitement in both East and West Germany, for he was recognized as a major talent. His thematic concerns were new and provocative, and his unique style, based in part on classical German modes yet stripped to the bare linguistic essentials, was rich in metaphor and allegory. For his poetic accomplishments, he was awarded the prestigious prize of the Group 47 in 1962, a prize given only to the most promising new authors in the German-speaking world. In the same year, he won the Alma-Johanna-Koenig Prize in Vienna. For his novel *Levin's Mill*, he was awarded the Heinrich Mann Prize of the East Berlin Academy of the Arts and the international Charles Veillon Prize from Switzerland, both in 1965. He was posthumously granted the East German F. C. Weiskopf Prize in 1967.

Together with Erich Arendt and Peter Huchel, Bobrowski is credited with giving a new direction and inspiration to East German poetry, which until his time was bogged down in the principles of Socialist Realism and the Brechtian tradition. Bobrowski showed his own generation and younger, emerging poets that artistic integrity and genuine creativity and diversity were possible within the framework of a socialist state. He also called attention to the great classical German heritage, which had been largely forgotten in the postwar years, and to the most recent developments in West German and foreign poetry. About ten years later, in the early 1970's, his name was again invoked by younger authors in East Germany who sought a new means of aesthetic expression. Although Bobrowski was notably absent from literary anthologies and histories in East Germany immediately after his death, he later was given a place of honor in the literary canon there and is recognized as a humanitarian author who strove for socialist ideals. In West Germany, more emphasis is placed on an appreciation of his style. He is often mentioned in connection with Günter Eich and Paul Celan, who, like Bobrowski, employed a reduced and concentrated lexical inventory, to the point of being hermetic or even opaque, and who at the same time did not shy away from combining mythological elements with autobiographical and contemporary references.

BIOGRAPHY

Johannes Bobrowski was born in a German town in East Prussia, not far from Lithuania; his father was a German railroad employee of Polish descent. Bobrowski spent his childhood in the small village of Mozischken and frequently visited his grandparents on their farm in the country. It was at this time that he learned much about the culture and history of the Slavic peoples who lived across the border. In 1928, the family moved to Königsberg (later called Kaliningrad), where Bobrowski attended a college-preparatory high school. In school, he was particularly attracted to the disciplines of music and painting; one of his teachers there was the writer Ernst Wiechert. In 1937, the family moved again, this time to Berlin, where Bobrowski began to study art history.

In 1939, Bobrowski was conscripted into military service. During World War II, he served as a soldier in France, Poland, and northern Russia, but he was also a member of the Bekennende Kirche (the Confessing Church), a Protestant resistance group. He was taken prisoner of war in 1945 and remained in Russian captivity until 1949; he was held in the regions of the Don and middle Volga Rivers and did forced labor as a coal miner. He returned to East Berlin in 1949, and in 1950, he began working as a reader at the publishing house Union Verlag, affiliated with the Lutheran Church. He remained there until his death, resulting from complications after an appendicitis operation, in 1965.

Bobrowski began writing poetry in 1941, when he was stationed at Lake Ilmen, and a few of his poems were published in the "inner emigration" magazine *Das innere Reich*. He did not write much again until the early 1950's. His first poems after the war appeared in 1954 in the East German literary magazine *Sinn und Form*, which was edited by his friend Peter Huchel. Bobrowski continued to write sporadically after this literary debut, but he did not feel that his style had matured sufficiently until the early 1960's, when he published his first two volumes of poetry. He completed work on *Wetterzeichen* (signs of the weather), but it did not appear until after his death. *Im Windgesträuch* (in the wind bushes), appeared in 1970, containing poems of lesser quality which were written between 1953 and 1964.

Analysis

Many of Johannes Bobrowski's poems, as he often stated, have as their central theme the relationship between the Germans and their neighbors to the East, the Slavic peoples. Because he grew up along the river Memel, where these two cultures merge, Bobrowski was particularly sensitive to this issue. From the days of the Order of the Teutonic Knights in the Middle Ages, the Germans had treated these people very badly, and the history of their relations is marred by war, repression, and murder. Bobrowski the poet recalls these atrocities, lest contemporary Germans forget to atone for their past misdeeds.

Sarmatia poems

To accomplish this goal, Bobrowski uses the concept of Sarmatia, a vague term applied by ancient historians and geographers to the area that he has in mind—namely, the territory between Finland and southern Russia from the Baltic to the Black Sea. He populates his Sarmatia with a host of various personages: ancient gods, legendary figures, and historical personalities. Bobrowski thus creates a mythology of sorts to come to terms with the German past, but it is not a well-defined mythology, and one can discern its full richness only by studying his poems as a totality.

Thus, when one reads about the ancient gods Perkun and Pikoll in "Pruzzische Elegie" ("Prussian Elegy"), about the great Lithuanian ruler Wilna in "Anruf" ("Appeal") or in "Wilna," about the legendary sunken city of Kiteshgorod in "Erzählung" ("Story"), or about Russian writer Isaac Babel in "Holunderblüte" ("Elderblossom"), one confronts only one aspect of Bobrowski's poetic world. History is treated as myth and myth as history. The reader must be willing to mingle and combine past and present, the real and the fictional, to form a coherent concept of the historical development Bobrowski has in mind.

Layers of history

This historical dimension of Bobrowski's poetry offers a key to understanding his works. His poems contain five intertwined temporal layers: ancient times, in which the Slavic or Sarmatian tribes were free to determine their own existence and live in close harmony with nature; past centuries of conflict with the German invaders; the horrors of World War II, which Bobrowski had personally experienced; the present time, in which one must rectify old wrongs; and a future era, in which all men will live in communion with one another. It is often difficult to separate these layers, particularly when the reader finds many confusing temporal references within a single poem, yet this very ambiguity accounts for the richness of Bobrowski's verse; the various layers illuminate one another and promote an understanding of historical and cultural processes.

Moreover, these poems transcend their historical occasion, offering profound general insights into man's inhumanity to man on a global scale and forcefully arguing the need for reconciliation and the end of barbarism. They can thus be read and appreciated by people from various cultural backgrounds and different eras. This rich philosophical content of the poems also explains how Bobrowski, as a Christian non-Marxist, was able to survive and publish in East Germany. He was seen as a seer or prophet who pointed out the errors of the past and the way to achieve the future brotherhood of all men—one of the proclaimed goals of the communist state. In a manner similar to the historical process he was describing, Bobrowski's poetry underwent a noticeable thematic development or progression: His first poems are concerned primarily with the fantastic landscape of Sarmatia; later poems include historical events and persons from the recent and distant past; and finally, Bobrowski arrives at a discussion of the problems of contemporary Berlin.

Honor and remembrance

Not all Bobrowski poems deal with Sarmatia. A few treat the themes of love and death, not with any specificity, but in general philosophical terms. Two other categories, however, must be discussed in greater detail. The first contains poems written in honor or in memory of other artists with whom Bobrowski feels some affinity, such as François Villon, Joseph Conrad, Dylan Thomas, Marc Chagall, Johann Georg Hamann, Friedrich Gottlieb Klopstock, Gertrud Kolmar, Friedrich Hölderlin, Else Lasker-Schüler, Nelly Sachs, Wolfgang Amadeus Mozart, Johann Sebastian Bach, Christian Domelaitis, and Jakob Michael Reinhold Lenz. These "portrait poems" are not biographical or artistic summaries, but rather impressions of the artists or their lives. Bobrowski merely takes one aspect or feature of the artist and explains why he admires it or considers it important for his work. Thus, in the poem "An Klopstock" ("To Klopstock"), Bobrowski praises Klopstock's notion that one must recall the past and atone for former transgressions. (Bobrowski considered Klopstock to be his "taskmaster," both stylistically and thematically.) In "Hamann," he praises the eighteenth century poet for collecting and preserving ancient tales and legends. (Bobrowski was greatly influenced by Hamann while still in school and felt that Hamann's life's goals were similar to his own. He had been collecting material for years for a monograph on Hamann but was unable to complete it because of his premature death.) In the poems "Else Lasker-Schüler" and "An Nelly Sachs" ("To Nelly Sachs"), Bobrowski points to the suffering these poets endured because they were Jewish, a suffering similar to that of the Jews living in Sarmatia. Bobrowski shared with all these artists a deep humanistic commitment to others and a concern for suffering in the world.

"ALWAYS TO BE NAMED" AND "LANGUAGE"

Another significant category of Bobrowski's poems, though by no means large, could be termed metapoetry. In these poems, Bobrowski describes his concept of poetic language and poetic communication. Two of these poems are especially paradigmatic: "Immer zu benennen" ("Always to Be Named") and "Sprache" ("Language"). Here, Bobrowski shows that he believes in an almost mystical relationship between the word and the thing named, that the word somehow captures the spirit of the thing or the person to which it refers. This idea plays an important role in Bobrowski's mythology, for objects, particularly from nature, take on a new significance: They become part of humans, part of their past and their relationships to others. Thus, to advance into the future, not only history but also words and nature are important, as words and nature enable people to communicate with one another and prepare themselves for what is to come. This is for Bobrowski the highest sense of poetry—it speaks to readers on several levels and raises their degree of consciousness. Poetry does not, Bobrowski claims, move the reader to bold political or social acts.

NATURE AS SYMBOL

Because of his emphasis on humanity's relationship to nature through language, and because he believed that humanity's harmony with nature, which was somehow lost in the past, must be regained to save the human race, Bobrowski's work has often been referred to as nature poetry. This description is valid only to a certain extent. It is true that Bobrowski does employ a great number of recurring nature motifs in his poetry, most frequently rivers, birds, trees, fish, stones, wolves, light, and darkness. These motifs, however, are not an evocation of nature per se. They do not merely conjure up the beauty of landscapes to be admired and enjoyed, but rather they function as symbols within the overriding thematics of the poem. Although they have varying connotations, Bobrowski generally uses these motifs to connect human beings to nature and to show how humans are part of the natural historical process. The objects of nature remain constant throughout historical change, says Bobrowski, and so, too, does the human soul. If people can rid themselves of the barbarous acts of war and violence and return to their primeval natural state, they will have reached their ultimate goal. This strong concern for the human and communal element is what sets Bobrowski's poems apart from traditional nature poetry.

POETIC MINIMALISM

Bobrowski's symbolic treatment of nature is only one aspect of his laconic style. The most striking feature of his poetry is the reduction of the linguistic material to an extreme minimum. Frequently, lines consist of merely a word or two each, and the length of the line is very irregular. Bobrowski often employs sentence fragments consisting of a single word, and longer syntactic units are usually broken up into several lines, interrupting the semantic flow.

The breaking of the poem into small phrases gives primacy to the individual word and lends the poetic message an aspect far different from what it would possess were it written in prose or even conventional poetic style. The free rhythms are sometimes fairly regular, so that the reader is often reminded of the odes and elegies of previous centuries. Bobrowski's concentrated and abbreviated style demands the active participation of the reader, who must fill in the missing material and make the appropriate associations and connections, a process similar to that through which one tries to remember events of the distant past. Such a difficult procedure tends at times to weaken the thematic impact of the poem, but as Fritz Minde points out in an article on Bobrowski, the poems can indeed be decoded with the help of published biographical and historical material; their difficult construction mimics the deformed and incoherent structure of reality.

STRUCTURE

In *Poetry in East Germany* (1971), John Flores suggests a method by which this decoding can be performed. He believes that most of Bobrowski's poems have three parts or stages. In the first, or introductory, part, the author relies chiefly on nouns, employed in an uncertain, staccato fashion. He is setting the mood for the poem by using the naming process described above. The reader is uncertain and somewhat confused. In the second stage, spatial and temporal connections begin to appear. The style is more reflective and narrative, and nouns are linked with verbs. The thematic thrust of the poem begins to take shape. In the final stage, the staccato mode is reintroduced, but here the verb prevails. The author unleashes his thoughts and ideas in a torrent of words. These thoughts have been building in intensity throughout the poem, and they all come together in the end in a desperate cry for recognition.

LEGACY

The difficult and cryptic nature of many of Bobrowski's poems raises the question of his place in literary history. Was he a true member of the avant-garde, a forerunner of or participant in the reductive "linguistic" movement of contemporary German poetry? No, he did not use language as a collection of building blocks devoid of meaning. Instead, he can be seen as part of the movement toward radical reduction of language that began around 1910 with the expressionists in Germany and that insisted on a language free of all Decadent cultural encrustations. Such a purification of language became all the more necessary after the abuses of the Nazi years. At the same time, however, Bobrowski went beyond this essentially negative program, offering in his verse substantive arguments in favor of a new and better world.

Other Major Works

LONG FICTION: *Levins Mühle: 34 Sätze über meinen Grossvater*, 1964 (*Levin's Mill: Thirty-four Statements About My Grandfather*, 1970); *Litauische Klaviere*, 1966.

SHORT FICTION: *Boehlendorff, und andere Erzählungen*, 1965; *Mäusefest, und andere Erzählungen*, 1965; *Der Mahner*, 1967 (*I Taste Bitterness*, 1970).

Bibliography

Bridgwater, Patrick. "The Poetry of Johannes Bobrowski." *Forum for Modern Language Studies* 2 (1966): 320-334. A critical study of Bobrowski's poetic works.

Flores, John. *Poetry in East Germany: Adjustments, Visions, and Provocations, 1945-1970*. New Haven, Conn.: Yale University Press, 1971. A history and critical analysis of poetry in postwar East Germany including the works of Bobrowski during this period. Includes bibliographic references.

Glenn, Jerry. "An Introduction to the Poetry of Johannes Bobrowski." *Germanic Review* 41 (1966): 45-56. A brief critical assessment of Bobrowski's poetic works.

Keith-Smith, Brian. *Johannes Bobrowski*. London: Wolff, 1970. Introductory biography with selected poetry and prose in English translation. Includes bibliography.

O'Doherty, Paul. *The Portrayal of Jews in GDR Prose Fiction*. Atlanta: Rodopi, 1997. Contains a short section on Bobrowski's depiction of Jews in his prose work. While it does not discuss the poetry, it does shed light on who Bobrowski was and the times in which he lived.

Scrase, David. *Understanding Johannes Bobrowski*. Columbia: University of South Carolina Press, 1995 . Critical interpretation and brief biography by a specialist in German and Austrian art and literature. Includes bibliography.

Wieczorek, John P. *Between Sarmatia and Socialism: The Life and Works of Johannes Bobrowski*. Atlanta: Rodopi, 1999. Examines the chronological development of Bobrowski's Sarmatian works and places them within the context of a biography of his career.

Robert Acker

BERTOLT BRECHT

Born: Augsburg, Germany; February 10, 1898
Died: East Berlin, East Germany (now Berlin, Germany); August 14, 1956

PRINCIPAL POETRY
Hauspostille, 1927, 1951 (*Manual of Piety*, 1966)
Lieder, Gedichte, Chöre, 1934 (*Songs, Poems, Choruses*, 1976)
Svendborger Gedichte, 1939 (*Svendborg Poems*, 1976)
Selected Poems, 1947
Hundert Gedichte, 1951 (*A Hundred Poems*, 1976)
Gedichte und Lieder, 1956 (*Poems and Songs*, 1976)
Gedichte, 1960-1965 (9 volumes)
Bertolt Brecht: Poems, 1913-1956, 1976 (includes *Buckower Elegies*)
Bad Time for Poetry: 152 Poems and Songs, 1995

OTHER LITERARY FORMS

A prolific writer, Bertolt Brecht (brehkt) experimented with several literary forms and subjected nearly everything he wrote to painstaking revision. He first became known as a dramatist when he won the distinguished Kleist Prize in 1922 for his plays *Baal* (pb. 1922; English translation, 1963), *Trommeln in der Nacht* (pr., pb. 1922; *Drums in the Night*, 1961), and *Im Dickicht der Städte* (pr. 1923; *In the Jungle of Cities*, 1961), and he remains perhaps best known for plays such as *Mutter Courage und ihre Kinder* (pr. 1941; *Mother Courage and Her Children*, 1941) and his groundbreaking operas *Die Dreigroschenoper* (pr. 1928; *The Threepenny Opera*, 1949) and *Aufstieg und Fall der Stadt Mahagonny* (pb. 1929; *Rise and Fall of the City of Mahagonny*, 1957). His longer prose works include the novels *Der Dreigroschenroman* (1934; *The Threepenny Novel*, 1937, 1956) and *Die Geschäfte des Herrn Julius Caesar* (1956; the affairs of Mr. Julius Caesar). Brecht also wrote about eighty short stories, as well as essays in his *Arbeitsjournal* (1938-1955, 1973; *Bertolt Brecht Journals*, 1993).

ACHIEVEMENTS

Just as he would have it, Bertolt Brecht remains a controversial figure. His literary works, his politics, and his biography spark disagreement, but one thing is clear: Brecht belongs among the great writers of the twentieth century and certainly among the great modern poets. When Brecht died, Lion Feuchtwanger praised him as the only originator of the German language in the twentieth century.

Brecht was a bit of a showman (he was immediately recognizable in Berlin with his leather jacket, his proletarian cap, and his nickel-rimmed glasses), but he was always more interested in what people thought of his work than in what they thought of him. Eric Bentley, for example, has called Brecht's *Manual of Piety* "one of the best of all books of modern poems." Brecht's initial success on the stage in 1922, the year in which he won the Kleist Prize, was echoed in 1928 with the sensational premiere of *The Threepenny Opera* in Berlin. He received a National Institute of Arts and Letters Award in 1948. Toward the end of his life, Brecht was awarded the East German National Prize (1951), the highest distinction conferred by the German Democratic Republic on one of its citizens. In 1954, he became vice president of the East German Academy of Arts. One year before his death, he traveled to Moscow to accept the Stalin Peace Prize.

Without a doubt, Brecht is best known for his concept of the epic theater and his staging and acting technique of *Verfremdung* (alienation). He sought the intellectual rather than the emotional engagement of the audience, and his propensity for didactic structure rather than sentimental discourse is evident in his poetry as well. Brecht embraced Karl Marx's thesis that "it is not a matter of interpreting the world, but of changing it." His anti-Aristotelian theater concentrated on the factual and sober depiction of human and social conflicts, but with humorous alienation and alienating humor. To do serious theater today without acknowledging Brecht in some way is nearly impossible.

An assessment of Brecht's achievements cannot overlook his relation to literary tradition. Brecht "borrowed" freely from his predecessors, and he frequently chose the forms of parody or satire to make his readers aware of historical change and social contradictions. His candid speech did not always win favor: Because of his antiwar poem "Legende vom toten Soldaten" ("Legend of the Dead Soldier"), which was appended to his play *Drums in the Night*, Brecht was high on the Nazis' list of undesirables. It must be ranked among Brecht's accomplishments that, with his pen, he fought doggedly against the forces of evil and injustice that he saw embodied in the figure of Adolf Hitler and in the Nazi regime. The intensity and range of Brecht's voice as an essayist and dramatist have long been recognized; in contrast, because of the publication history of his poetry, it is only since Brecht's death that the power and scope of his lyric voice have begun to be appreciated.

Biography

Eugen Bertolt Friedrich Brecht was born into a comfortable middle-class home. His father, the manager of a paper factory, was Catholic; his mother, Protestant. Brecht was reared in the Lutheran faith. Before long, he turned strongly against religion, but the language of Martin Luther's translation of the Bible continued to influence Brecht throughout his life. A local Augsburg newspaper carried his first poems and essays in 1914, under the pen name "Berthold Eugen." Brecht dropped the mask in 1916 with the publication of his poem "Das Lied der Eisenbahntruppe von Fort Donald" ("Song of the Fort Donald Railroad Gang"), in the same local paper.

A restless and arrogant student ("I did not succeed in being of any appreciable help to my teachers"), Brecht enrolled in the University of Munich in 1917. There, he claimed to study medicine (as his father wished) and learned to play the guitar (less to his father's liking, no doubt). He completed a brief term of military service in 1918 as a medical orderly in a hospital for patients suffering from venereal disease. (It was in this year that Brecht wrote the "Legend of the Dead Soldier.") In Munich, Brecht soon became more interested in the local cabarets than in the study of medicine. He especially enjoyed the comedian Karl Valentin, who, along with Frank Wedekind, became an important influence on Brecht's literary development. He turned increasingly to literature and began taking seminars at the university with Professor Arthur Kutscher in 1918; he wrote the first version of *Baal* between March and June of the same year. Brecht traveled to Berlin in 1920; the city impressed him, but he returned to Munich after failing to make substantial literary contacts.

Brecht was to make one more trip to Berlin before finally moving there in 1924. From then until 1933, he spent his time in the capital and cultural center of Germany. In 1926, he first became acquainted with the writings of Marx; in its profound impact on his work, Brecht's discovery of Marx could be compared to Friedrich Schiller's reading of Immanuel Kant. At the time, Brecht was working on the play "Wheat" (to be staged by Erwin Piscator), and he wanted to understand how the exchange market worked. In the short run, his effort proved futile: "From every point of view," he wrote, "the grain market remained one impenetrable jungle." The consequences of his study, however, were far-reaching. His planned drama was never completed. Instead, he began to read Marx intensely: "It was only then that my own jumbled practical experiences and impressions came clearly into focus." Brecht's conversion to the principles of communism had begun. What followed in its literary wake were the operas and several strongly didactic plays in the early 1930's. Brecht, the eminent political poet, wisely left Germany on February 28, 1933, the day after the burning of the Reichstag. Several years of exile ensued.

"Changing countries more often than shoes," as Brecht reflected once, he eventually found his way to a place near Svendborg in Denmark, after traveling through Prague, Zurich, Lugano, and Paris. In Denmark, Brecht was—for the time being, anyway—relatively settled. Still, he remained acutely sensitive toward "escape routes" (images of doors are frequent in the poetry of his exile). He traveled to Moscow and New York in 1935, to London in 1936, and to Paris in the next year. With the threat of Nazi invasion looming large, Brecht left Denmark for Sweden in 1939 and settled near Stockholm. Before long, this sanctuary, too, appeared endangered by the Nazis. Brecht fled to the United States in 1941.

Brecht's life in exile, coupled with his fascination for the exotic, drew him in particular to the Chinese poet, Bai Juyi (Po Chü-i), whose work he had come to know through the translation of Arthur Waley. In the United States, Brecht was particularly conscious of his displacement; having settled in Santa Monica near Hollywood, he never felt comfortable in the "tinsel town." His productivity slackened somewhat during his American years, though he collaborated with artists of the stature of Fritz Lang and Charles Laughton. On October 30, 1947, the day after he appeared before the House Un-American Activities Committee, Brecht flew to Paris and shortly thereafter moved to Switzerland.

Brecht's second wife, the accomplished actress Helene Weigel, was an Austrian citizen, and it is most likely for this reason that Brecht acquired Austrian citizenship as well, even though he finally settled in East Berlin in 1949. There, until his death in 1956, Brecht worked with the Berlin Ensemble. Meanwhile, his Austrian citizenship allowed his work to remain accessible to all the German-speaking countries (Brecht was also shrewd about the business and politics of publication). As he wished, Brecht's death was noted with a quiet ceremony. He lies buried in an old cemetery not far from his apartment, near the graves of Georg Wilhelm Friedrich Hegel and Johann Gottlieb Fichte.

Analysis

It is important to note that Bertolt Brecht's creativity as a poet resulted less from any inclination toward introspection than from his desire to communicate with others. Against the prevailing tone of German poetry in the 1920's, at least as it was represented by Rainer Maria Rilke, Hugo von Hofmannsthal, and Stefan George, Brecht's poetic voice startled and shocked his readers. "These poems [of Rilke and others] tell ordinary people nothing, sometimes comprehensibly, sometimes incomprehensibly," he wrote in his youth. One of Brecht's main objections to this style of poetry was that its sense of artistic order hid rather than disclosed the chaos he saw in modern life. For this reason, Brecht eventually came to see rhyme and rhythm as obstructive and to prefer "Rhymeless Verse with Irregular Rhythms," as the title of an essay in 1939 reads. As basic to Brecht's poems as their consideration of the reader is his notion of functionality. He first articulated this concept in 1927 when asked to judge a poetry contest that had brought more than four hundred entries. Brecht read them all and awarded no prize. Instead, he acknowledged an unsubmitted poem from a little-known writer, appreciating its simplicity, its engaging choice of topics, its melodiousness, and its documentary value. The notion that "all great poems have the value of documents" was central to Brecht's thought. Writing poetry was, for Brecht, no "mere expression," but a "social function of a wholly contradictory and alterable kind, conditioned by history and in turn conditioning it."

Brecht wrote his poems in, as he called it, "a kind of Basic German." His sensitivity for the "gestic" power of language was nurtured by his fondness for Luther's Bible (the term Brecht uses, *Gestus*, is difficult to render adequately in English: John Willet identifies it with "gesture" and "gist," attitude and point). At the root of Brecht's poetry, indeed all his work, are the notions of clarity ("The truth is concrete" was Brecht's favorite maxim from Hegel) and functionality. Form, of which Brecht was a master and not a slave, was a means toward an end, that being enlightenment. In tracing Brecht's poetic development, one can see how the forms and motifs change against the backdrop of these guiding concepts.

One attribute of the term "gestic" is that of performance. Brecht was always concerned with delivery (it is central to his theory of the epic theater), and his early poetry is characterized by its close links with song. Indeed, most of Brecht's early poems were written to be accompanied by the guitar. Verse and melody often came about simultaneously, the rhythm of the words combining with the flow of the song. It is not surprising that Brecht's early poems acknowledge such traditional forms as legends, ballads, and chronicles. He was aware that no poet who considered himself important was composing ballads at that time, and this fact, too, may have intrigued the young iconoclast. What drew Brecht to these older poetic forms was their attention to adventure, to nature, and to the role of the heroic individual. Brecht rejuvenated a tired literary tradition by turning to the works of François Villon and Rudyard Kipling. Brecht's ballads mark a decisive turning point in the history of that genre.

"Song of the Fort Donald Railroad Gang"

"Song of the Fort Donald Railroad Gang," written in 1916, exhibits Brecht's youthful keenness for the frontier spirit. It relates the struggle and demise of a railroad crew laying track in the wilderness of Ohio. The portrayal of nature as rugged and indifferent marks a distinct switch for Brecht from the mediocre war poems he had been writing earlier. A common denominator, however, was the element of destructive force. This poem leads, step by inevitable step, through six strophes toward the culminating catastrophe. Initially, nature tolerates the intruders, who can be seen as pilgrims of modern progress pitted against the dense forests, "forever soulless." With the onset of torrential rains, the tolerance of nature becomes indifference, but the railroad gang forges on. Striking up a song within a song, they take to singing in the night to keep themselves awake and posted of the dangers posed by the downpour and the swelling waters. For them, escape is not an option. Death simply comes, and comes simply, leaving only the echo of their melody: "The trains scream rushing over them alongside Lake Erie/ And the wind at that spot sings a stupid melody." A stupid melody? What has happened to these modern "heroes"? There are no modern heroes, Brecht answers—and this in the poetic form that traditionally extols them. Brecht debunks their melody, uses the ballad to put an end to the balladesque hero. Death and nature prevail.

"Remembering Marie A."

Death and nature, along with murder and love, are the elemental themes distinguishing Brecht's early poems. He was wont to treat these perennial subjects, though, in nontraditional ways. He does this with great effect in what is ostensibly a love poem, "Erinnerung an die Maria A." ("Remembering Marie A."), written in 1920 and later included in *Manual of Piety*. It is more lyrical than the balladesque forms Brecht had already mastered, but it does not get lost in sentimentality. Instead, Brecht achieves a parody of the melancholy youth remembering an early love, and in its attitude it is quintessential Brecht. What the speaker in the poem actually recalls is less his "love so pale and silent/ As if she were a dream that must not fade," than it is "a cloud my eyes dwelt long upon/ It was quite white and very high above us/ Then I looked up, and found that it had gone." Not even the woman's face remains present for Brecht's persona, only her kiss, and "As for the kiss, I'd long ago forgot it/ But for the cloud that floated in the sky." The idyllic atmosphere of the first strophe turns out to be nothing but cliché.

What Brecht does with the element of time in this poem is essential to its overall effect. He establishes an internal relationship on three levels: first, the love affair, located in the past; second, the passage of time, the forgetting that wastes all memory; and third, the making present, by means of the cloud, that September day long ago. The tension Brecht succeeds in creating between these different levels has ironic consequences. For one, his use of verb tenses renders as present what is actually narrated in the past tense, while the grammatical past tense functions on the level of present time. The hierarchy of experiences is also switched: the backdrop of nature, the embodiment of everything transitory, can be remembered, while the primary experience (or what convention dictates should be the primary experience)—namely, the relationship between the lovers—falls prey to bad memory. Ultimately, it is a poem about the inconstancy of feeling and the mistrust between people that renders meaningful and lasting relationships problematic. It treats an old theme originally; where others write poems directed toward those lovers in the present, those passed away, those absent, or even those expected in the future, Brecht writes of the lover forgotten.

"Of Poor B. B."

"I, Bertolt Brecht, came out of the black forests." So begins Brecht's famous autobiographical poem, "Vom armen B. B." ("Of Poor B. B."), first written in 1922 and later revised when he was preparing *Manual of Piety* for publication. It was composed when Brecht's feet were mostly in Augsburg and Munich, but his mind was mostly in Berlin. The poem marks a turning point for Brecht. He leaves behind the ballad form and takes up the theme of the city. Nature in the raw yields to the irrepressible life of the big city, although neither locus is ever idealized. Written literally while under way (apparently on a train to Berlin), the poem is about where one feels at home, "one" in this instance being no one but Brecht himself. "In the asphalt city I'm at home," he admits, and he goes on to describe the daily routine of city dwellers, situating himself in their midst: "I put on/ A hard hat because that's what they do./ I say: they are animals with a quite peculiar smell/ And I say: does it matter? I am too." The poem is full of cynicism and despair. The poet admits that he is undependable and remains convinced that all that will remain of the cities is what passed through them—that is, the wind: "And after us there will come: nothing worth talking about." Thematically, the change of emphasis in "Of Poor B. B." prepares the way for later poems. Formally, the delivery of the poem depends less on melody (song) and relies instead on the premise of conversation between poet and reader.

"In Dark Times"

Brecht's poems of the 1930's reveal a heightened awareness of the function of the poet with regard to his readership. He had made this point quite polemically already in 1927 as the judge of the poetry contest noted above. The poem, he claimed, had functional value. Looking for the functional lyric caused Brecht to seek a new style and idiom. The often-quoted poem "In finsteren Zeiten" ("In Dark Times"), written in 1937 during Brecht's exile in Denmark, attests his self-conscious task as responsible poet. Brecht imagines what people will later say about these "dark times." "They won't say: when the child skimmed a flat stone across the rapids/ But: when the great wars were being prepared for." History, in other words, will ride along on the backs of the little people—as Brecht makes clear in "Fragen eines lesenden Arbeiters" ("Questions from a Worker Who Reads")—but what remain visible are only the "great powers." In the face of this adversity, Brecht remarks with chagrin: "However, they won't say: the times were dark/ Rather: why were their poets silent?"

"Bad Time for Poetry"

Brecht refused to be silent. His "Schlechte Zeit für Lyrik" ("Bad Time for Poetry"), written in 1939, is a personally revealing poem about his own internal struggle to reconcile aesthetic demands with demands of social responsibility: "In my poetry a rhyme/ Would seem to me almost insolent." Still, as Brecht wrote in his essay on poetry and logic, also from the 1930's, "we cannot get along without the concept of beauty." The poem "Bad Time for Poetry" thus concludes:

> Inside me contend
> Delight at the apple tree in blossom
> And horror at the house-painter's speeches.
> But only the second
> Drives me to my desk.

Brecht seldom mentioned Hitler by name, preferring to call him only "the house-painter," ridiculing Hitler's artistic pretentions.

"Legend of the Origin of the Book Tao-Tê-Ching on Lao-tzû's Road into Exile"

To appreciate Brecht's aesthetic sensitivities, one must realize that he saw the felicitous poem as one in which "feeling and reason work together in total harmony." For Brecht, too, there was no distinction between learning and pleasure, and thus a didactic poem was also cause for aesthetic pleasure. The sensual pleasure derived from knowledge is an important aspect of the title figure of Brecht's play *Leben des Galilei* (pr. 1943; *The Life of Galileo*, 1960). What to do with knowledge and wisdom was another question that, for Brecht, followed inevitably. He answered it in his poem "Legende von der Entstehung des Buches Taoteking" ("Legend of the Origin of the Book Tao-Tê-Ching on Lao-tzû's Road into Exile") written in 1938 and included in the *Svendborg Poems*.

This poem is a highly successful combination of Brecht's earlier fascination with legends, the balladesque narrative, and the aesthetics of functional poetry. It relates the journey of Laozi (Lao Tzu), "seventy and getting brittle," from his country, where "goodness had been weakening a little/ And the wickedness was gaining ground anew" (a topic of immediate interest to the exile Brecht). Brecht does not puzzle over Laozi's decision to leave; it is not even an issue. He states simply, "So he buckled his shoe." (One recalls Brecht's line that he had "changed countries more often than shoes.") Laozi needs little for the journey: books, pipe, and bread (note here the relation between knowledge and sensual pleasure). After four days, he and the boy accompanying him come across a customs official at the border: "'What valuables have you to declare here?'/ And the boy leading the ox explained: 'The old man taught'/ Nothing at all, in short." The customs official, however, is intrigued by the boy's modest assertion that the old man "'learned how quite soft water, by attrition/ Over the years will grind strong rocks away./ In other words, that hardness must lose the day.'" The official shouts to them before they are able to move on and requires them to dictate what it was the old man had to say about the water: "'I'm not at all important/ Who wins or loses interests me, though./ If you've found out, say so.'" The old man obliges him ("'Those who ask questions deserve answers'"), and he and the boy settle down for a week, the customs man providing them with food. When the dictation is finally done, "the boy handed over what they'd written./ Eighty-one sayings." This is the wisdom of Laozi, for which posterity has been grateful, but Brecht is quick to point out that "the honor should not be restricted/ To the sage whose name is clearly writ./ For a wise man's wisdom needs to be extracted./ So the customs man deserves his bit./ It was he who called for it."

Brecht's return to rhyme in this poem is consistent with its ballad form. Where rhyme no longer sufficed for what was to be said, Brecht applied his theory of rhymeless verse with irregular rhythms. He had already used this style occasionally in the 1920's but mastered it fully in the poetry of the 1930's and 1940's; the form corresponded to Brecht's perception of a society at odds with itself, and it dominated his later lyrical writings.

BUCKOWER ELEGIES

Brecht's later poetry tends to be at once more intimate and more epigrammatic than his earlier work. This late style is best illustrated in his last group of poems, the *Buckower Elegien* (*Buckower Elegies*), written in 1953. The poems are concise evidence of Brecht's fascination with the fragmentary nature of the lyric, which he viewed as an appeal to the reader. Many of the poems mimic the open form of the riddle, with a strong central image, as in "Der Radwechsel" ("Changing the Wheel"). In six brief lines, Brecht observes how a driver changes a wheel. He voices his own dissatisfaction with his course in life ("I do not like the place I have come from./ I do not like the place I am going to"). Brecht characteristically leaves this poem open toward the future: "Why with impatience do I/ Watch him changing the wheel?"

The critic Joachim Müller has written that

> In all its phases and in all its forms, Brecht's poetry is neither exclusively subjective confession, nor simply an agitator's call to arms; every confession becomes an appeal to human activity, and every appeal, however it may alienate us by its satire or its polemics, springs from the deep emotion of a rational heart that sees all conditions in the world dialectically and that always sides with what is human against every inhumanity.

Other major works

LONG FICTION: *Der Dreigroschenroman*, 1934 (*The Threepenny Novel*, 1937, 1956); *Die Geschäfte des Herrn Julius Caesar*, 1956.

SHORT FICTION: *Geschichten vom Herrn Keuner*, 1930, 1958 (*Stories of Mr. Keuner*, 2001); *Kalendergeschichten*, 1948 (*Tales from the Calendar*, 1961); *Me-ti: Buch der Wendungen*, 1965; *Prosa*, 1965 (5 volumes); *Bertolt Brecht Short Stories, 1921-1946*, 1983 (translation of *Geschichten*, volume 11 of *Gesammelte Werke*); *Collected Stories*, 1998.

PLAYS: *Baal*, pb. 1922 (English translation, 1963); *Trommeln in der Nacht*, pr., pb. 1922 (wr. 1919-1920; *Drums in the Night*, 1961); *Im Dickicht der Städte*, pr. 1923 (*In the Jungle of Cities*, 1960); *Leben Eduards des Zweiten von England*, pr., pb. 1924 (with Lion Feuchtwanger; based on Christopher Marlowe's play *Edward II*; *Edward II*, 1966); *Die Hochzeit*, pr. 1926 (wr. 1919; pb. 1953 as *Die Keinbürgerhochzeit*; *The Wedding*, 1970); *Mann ist Mann*, pr. 1926 (*A Man's a Man*, 1961); *Die Dreigroschenoper*, pr. 1928 (libretto; based on John Gay's play *The Beggar's Opera*; *The Threepenny Opera*, 1949); *Aufstieg und Fall der Stadt Mahagonny*, pb. 1929 (libretto; *Rise and Fall of the City of Mahagonny*, 1957); *Das Badener Lehrstück vom Einverständnis*, pr. 1929 (*The Didactic Play of Baden: On Consent*, 1960); *Happy End*, pr. 1929 (libretto; lyrics with Elisabeth Hauptmann; English translation, 1972); *Der Jasager*, pr. 1930 (based on the Japanese Nō play *Taniko*; *He Who Said Yes*, 1946); *Die Massnahme*, pr. 1930 (libretto; *The Measures Taken*, 1960); *Die heilige Johanna der Schlachthöfe*, pb. 1931 (radio play; pr. 1959, staged; *St. Joan of the Stockyards*, 1956); *Der Neinsager*, pb. 1931 (*He Who Said No*, 1946); *Die Mutter*, pr., pb. 1932 (based on Maxim Gorky's novel *Mat*; *The Mother*, 1965); *Die Sieben Todsünden der Kleinbürger*, pr. 1933 (cantata; *The Seven Deadly Sins*, 1961); *Die Rundköpfe und die Spitzköpfe*, pr. 1935 (based on William Shakespeare's play *Measure for Measure*; *The*

Roundheads and the Peakheads, 1937); *Die Ausnahme und die Regel*, pb. 1937 (wr. 1930; *The Exception and the Rule*, 1954); *Die Gewehre der Frau Carrar*, pr., pb. 1937 (*Señora Carrar's Rifles*, 1938); *Furcht und Elend des dritten Reiches*, pr. 1938 (in French; pr. 1945, in English; pb. 1945, in German; *The Private Life of the Master Race*, 1944); *Die Horatier und die Kuriatier*, pb. 1938 (wr. 1934; *The Horatians and the Curatians*, 1947); *Mutter Courage und ihre Kinder*, pr. 1941 (based on Hans Jakob Christoffel von Grimmelshausen's *Der abenteuerliche Simplicissimus*; *Mother Courage and Her Children*, 1941); *Der gute Mensch von Sezuan*, pr. 1943 (wr. 1938-1940; *The Good Woman of Setzuan*, 1948); *Leben des Galilei*, pr. 1943 (first version wr. 1938-1939; second version, in English, wr. 1945-1947, pr. 1947; third version, in German, pr., pb. 1955, revised pb. 1957; *The Life of Galileo*, 1947; better known as *Galileo*); *Die Antigone des Sophokles*, pr., pb. 1948 (*Sophocles' Antigone*, 1990); *Herr Puntila und sein Knecht, Matti*, pr. 1948 (wr. 1940; *Mr. Puntila and His Hired Man, Matti*, 1976); *Der kaukasische Kreidekreis*, pr. 1948 (wr. 1944-1945, in English; pb. 1949 in German; based on Li Hsing-dao's play *The Circle of Chalk*; *The Caucasian Chalk Circle*, 1948); *Der Hofmeister*, pr. 1950 (adaptation of Jacob Lenz's *Der Hofmeister*; *The Tutor*, 1972); *Der Prozess der Jeanne d'Arc zu Rouen, 1431*, pr. 1952 (based on Anna Seghers' radio play; *The Trial of Jeanne d'Arc at Rouen, 1431*, 1972); *Don Juan*, pr. 1953 (adaptation of Molière's play; English translation, 1972); *Die Gesichte der Simone Machard*, pb. 1956 (wr. 1941-1943; with Feuchtwanger; *The Visions of Simone Machard*, 1961); *Pauken und Trompeten*, pb. 1956 (adaptation of George Farquhar's *The Recruiting Officer*; *Trumpets and Drums*, 1972); *Die Tage der Commune*, pr. 1956 (wr. 1948-1949; based on Nordahl Grieg's *Nederlaget*; *The Days of the Commune*, 1971); *Der aufhaltsame Aufstieg des Arturo Ui*, pb. 1957 (wr. 1941; *The Resistible Rise of Arturo Ui*, 1972); *Schweyk im zweiten Weltkrieg*, pr. 1957 (wr. 1941-1943, in Polish; pb. 1957 in German; based on Jaroslav Hašek's novel *Osudy dobrého vojáka Švejka za svetove války*; *Schweyk in the Second World War*, 1975); *Coriolan*, pb. 1959 (wr. 1952-1953; adaptation of William Shakespeare's play *Coriolanus*; *Coriolanus*, 1972); *Turandot: Oder, Der Kongress der Weisswäscher*, pr. 1970 (wr. 1950-1954).

SCREENPLAYS: *Kuhle Wampe*, 1932 (English translation, 1933); *Hangmen Also Die*, 1943; *Das Lied der Ströme*, 1954; *Herr Puntila und sein Knecht, Matti*, 1955.

RADIO PLAYS: *Der Ozeanflug*, pr., pb. 1929 (radio play; *The Flight of the Lindberghs*, 1930); *Das Verhör des Lukullus*, pr. 1940 (radio play; *The Trial of Lucullus*, 1943).

NONFICTION: *Der Messingkauf*, 1937-1951 (*The Messingkauf Dialogues*, 1965); *Arbeitsjournal*, 1938-1955, 1973 (3 volumes; *Bertolt Brecht Journals*, 1993); *Kleines Organon für das Theater*, 1948 (*A Little Organum for the Theater*, 1951); *Schriften zum Theater*, 1963-1964 (7 volumes); *Brecht on Theatre*, 1964; *Autobiographische Aufzeichnungen, 1920-1954*, 1975 (partial translation *Diaries, 1920-1922*, 1979); *Letters*, 1990; *Brecht on Film and Radio*, 2000.

MISCELLANEOUS: *Gesammelte Werke*, 1967 (20 volumes).

BIBLIOGRAPHY

Bartram, Graham, and Anthony Waine, eds. *Brecht in Perspective*. London: Longman, 1982. Thirteen excellent essays by highly qualified scholars. The topics range from German drama before Brecht through Brecht's manifold innovations to Brecht's legacy for German and English playwrights. Indispensable reading for understanding the broader context of his works.

Dickson, Keith A. *Towards Utopia: A Study of Brecht*. Oxford, England: Clarendon Press, 1978. Places Brecht's works in the context of literary, philosophical, social, and political history. German quotations are translated at the end of the book.

Giles, Steve, and Rodney Livingstone, eds. *Bertolt Brecht: Centenary Essays*. Atlanta: Rodopi, 1998. A collection of essays on Brecht written one hundred years after his birth. Bibliography.

Hayman, Ronald. *Brecht: A Biography*. London: Weidenfeld and Nicolson, 1983. A lengthy, dispassionately objective biography with many interesting details. Hayman skillfully integrates the facts of Brecht's private life with the discussion of his works. Opens with a chronology and a list of performances.

Martin, Carol, and Henry Bial. *Brecht Sourcebook*. New York: Routledge, 2000. Collection of protean essays in three sections: Brecht's key theories, his theories in practice, and, most successful, the adoption of his ideas internationally.

Mews, Siegfried, ed. *A Bertolt Brecht Reference Companion*. Westport, Conn.: Greenwood Press, 1997. An indispensable guide for the student of Brecht. Includes bibliographical references and an index.

Speirs, Ronald, ed. *Brecht's Poetry of Political Exile*. New York: Cambridge University Press, 2000. A collection of essays that examine the poetry Brecht wrote while in exile from Germany during World War II.

Thomson, Peter, and Glendyr Sacks, eds. *The Cambridge Companion to Brecht*. New York: Cambridge University Press, 1994. This extensive reference work contains a wealth of information on Brecht. Part of the Cambridge Companions to Literature series. Bibliography and index.

Willett, John. *Brecht in Context: Comparative Approaches*. Rev. ed. London: Methuen, 1998. A comparative analysis of the works of Brecht. Bibliography and index.

Richard Spuler

JOSEPH VON EICHENDORFF

Born: Near Ratibor, Silesia (now Racibórz, Poland); March 10, 1788
Died: Neisse, Silesia (now Nysa, Poland); November 26, 1857

PRINCIPAL POETRY
Gedichte, 1837 (*Happy Wanderer, and Other Poems*, 1925)
Neue Gesamtausgabe der Werke und Schriften in vier Bänden, 1957-1958

OTHER LITERARY FORMS

Although the reputation of Joseph von Eichendorff (I-kuhn-dawrf) is based almost exclusively on the lyrical talents which both his poetry and novellas attest, his poems themselves compose but a small portion of his entire literary production. Epic poems such as "Robert Guiscard" and "Julian" are included among his more eloquent lyrical poems. His first prose work and the first of his two full-length novels, *Ahnung und Gegenwart* (1815; presentiment and the present), contains fifty poems that reinforce an already impressionistic, lyrical style. His second novel, *Dichter und ihre Gesellen* (1834; the word *Gesellen* is ambiguous: The title means both "poets and their companions" and "poets and their apprentices"), is more tightly constructed and reveals a writer somewhat less conditioned by his proclivities toward poetry. His nine novellas, highlighted by *Aus dem Leben eines Taugenichts* (1826; *Memoirs of a Good-for-Nothing*, 1866) and *Das Marmorbild* (1819; *The Marble Statue*, 1927), do not belie the lyricist and are strewn with some of Eichendorff's most appealing and musical verses. The strength of his narrative work lies not in plot but in allegorical content, landscape descriptions, dream content, and poetic language. Eichendorff's attempts at drama include *Krieg den Philistern* (pb. 1824; war on the Philistines), the comedy *Die Freier* (pb. 1833; the suitors), historical plays such as *Der letzte Held von Marienburg* (pb. 1830; the last hero of Marienburg), and a dramatic fairy tale. Among his translations are one-act religious dramas of Pedro Calderón de la Barca, some of the farces of Miguel de Cervantes, and Don Juan Manuel's *Conde Lucanor* (1335). Eichendorff is recognized also for his accomplishments as a critical historian of German literature and Romanticism, particularly in *Geschichte der poetischen Literatur Deutschlands* (1857; history of the poetic literature of Germany). He also wrote numerous treatises on history, politics, and religion.

ACHIEVEMENTS

Joseph von Eichendorff's reputation as a master craftsperson among German lyrical poets is beyond dispute. No literary history fails to list him in the first rank of German Romantic poets, and such noted poetic successors as Heinrich Heine, Theodor Storm, and Hugo von Hofmannsthal enthusiastically acknowledged his major contributions to the genre. Well into the twentieth century, his work continued to be acclaimed by such literary connoisseurs as Thomas Mann and Werner Bergengruen. He has been called "the last knight of German Romanticism," and his works are said to represent both the climax and the crisis of German Romanticism. The popularity of many of his lyrics has transformed them into veritable folk songs. Four of Eichendorff's most memorable poems, "Das zerbrochene Ringlein" ("The Broken Ring"), "Der frohe Wandersmann" ("The Happy Wanderer"), "Mondnacht" ("Moonlit Night"), and "Sehnsucht" ("Yearning"), were set to music by Robert Schumann; others were used by Johannes Brahms, Hugo Wolf, Felix Mendelssohn-Bartholdy, Hans Pfitzner, and Othmar Schoeck. His novella *Das Schloss Dürande* (1837; the castle Dürande) was the basis for an opera by Schoeck. *Memoirs of a Good-for-Nothing* is one of the most widely read German novellas of the nineteenth century and is often regarded as the quintessential Romantic novella.

Somewhat less generally conceded, however, is Eichendorff's status as a religious poet and his function as a pedagogue and a critic of Romanticism. The didactic intent in his poetry is often overshadowed by the very obvious accoutrements of Romanticism with which it abounds. The simple musicality of Eichendorff's verses, the frequent repetition of rhymes and images, the limited scope of his themes, the recurrent expression of a simple but sincere piety, and particularly his *Taugenichts* character sometimes earn Eichendorff the label of a naïve, unsophisticated lyricist, albeit a pleasant and refreshingly healthy one. The immediate, conspicuous beauty of his rhythms and melodies may suffice for the superficial reader. A more persistent and careful reading of his verses, however, yields the insight that beyond the aesthetically pleasing exterior of his opus there is a very tenacious and vital religious faith communicated through a rather surprisingly rich range of variations on the Christian theme. Neither a monastic mystic nor a simplistic, uncritical "true believer," Eichendorff was a decidedly world-involved applier of his faith to life and vice versa. His poems testify to his deeply held conviction of the necessary interrelationship between his poetry and his religion, aim to convince the reader of the desirability of such a union, and caution against the dangers of a too subjectively oriented Romanticism which does not permit the freedom to choose and to serve a higher ideal.

Biography

Despite the depiction of incessant wanderings and frequent allusions to "die weite Welt" (the wide world) in the writings of Joseph Freiherr von Eichendorff, the poet himself actually had limited exposure to the world beyond the reaches of his native Upper Silesia in southeastern Germany. His journeys were primarily spiritual ones; even university days in Halle and Heidelberg, a student trip to Paris and Vienna, and eventual civil service posts in Breslau, Danzig, Berlin, and Königsberg did not take him to those distant, exotic, non-German-speaking lands, the *Welschland*, which his work often evokes. His birthplace, the Castle Lubowitz near Ratibor, remained at least the physical mecca to which he periodically returned until the deteriorating financial status of his aristocratic family forced the sale of all its properties in 1822.

By the age of ten, when Eichendorff first read the New Testament and was moved by the story of Christ's Passion, he had already been introduced through the Polish and German folk songs and fairy tales of his native region to the second guiding force of his life, the power of poetry. The poet's deep commitment to the Roman Catholic faith and his love for the music and beauty of words as well as his soon proven facility with them were to sustain him for his entire life, even when professional success as a governmental official was withheld from him and external pressures were overwhelming.

Eichendorff had ample discourse with gifted representatives of the Romantic movement, first in 1807, at the University of Heidelberg, where he heard the lectures of the philosopher Joseph von Görres and where he made the acquaintance of such leading literary figures as Clemens von Brentano, Achim von Arnim, and Adam Müller, and then years later, in Berlin, with Ludwig Tieck and E. T. A. Hoffmann, and in Vienna, with Friedrich von Schlegel. He was, however, to turn eventually from Romanticism and to take it to task figuratively in his poetry and literally in his expository writings. Any tendency to succumb completely to narcissistic Romantic musings on Eichendorff's part was confined to his year in Heidelberg. His conscious awareness of the Dionysian dangers of Romanticism is evident in the larger body of his poetry and is particularly clear in the narrative *Viel Lärmen um Nichts* (1833; much ado about nothing).

After completion of his civil service examinations in Vienna in 1812 and his participation in the Wars of Liberation against Napoleon in 1813 and 1815, Eichendorff married Aloysia von Larisch in 1815. They produced four children. The poet held various bureaucratic posts as governmental councillor in several North German cities until he took an early retirement in 1844 for reasons of ill health. From approximately 1816 to 1855, few details are available about Eichendorff's personal life except for the indirect information revealed in his writing; the diaries he had kept regularly from the age of twelve were not continued into that period. His apparently ineffectual career gained him no special recognition; the sole honor bestowed upon him was the Medal for Science and Art by King Maximilian II of Bavaria.

From the poet's retirement until his death thirteen years later at the home of his daughter Therese in Neisse, he resided for only brief periods of time in various eastern German cities and in Vienna. In the latter city, his acquaintances included the composer Robert Schumann and the writers Franz Grillparzer and Adalbert Stifter.

Although Eichendorff had a surprisingly wide circle of intellectual, artistic, and politically influential friends in the course of his life, he seems never to have been an overtly influential personal force among them or a dynamic contributor to their social gatherings but was noted rather for his pleasant, unassuming manner and the quiet grace and spirituality of his personality. After his retirement, he turned to the writing of theoretical treatises and translations from Spanish. It seems that the rigors of a profession to which the poet felt no true emotional commitment had to be balanced by the more pleasant practice of poetry; after the duties of that profession no longer had to be met, he could turn from the perspective of age and experience to objective evaluations of the cultural, historical, and literary developments which he had witnessed throughout his life.

Analysis

Despite the fact that Joseph von Eichendorff is routinely classified among the German Romantic writers, his affiliation with them is primarily a superficial one. The idyllic nature descriptions, the wandering musicians and students, the nostalgic glance toward home and the glorious past, the veneration of the beloved, and an obvious acquaintance with the religious dogma of Catholicism play such a large role in his work that the temptation arises to accept such a generally accepted label without further question. Unlike many Romantics, however, Eichendorff demonstrated no utter abandonment to an introverted psyche but manifested instead a surrender to a specific, sharply focused ideal beyond the self and repeatedly warned against the perils of subjective self-indulgence. The wandering that is done so frequently in Eichendorff's work is not an aimless roaming, as it might at first appear, but a deliberately chosen pilgrimage to God. When Romanticism failed, in Eichendorff's eyes, to keep its promise to restore humanity's broken relationship with God, it ceased to have validity for the poet.

Eichendorff's poetry and his religious faith were one. Even a random reading of his verses should discourage any attempt to separate the two, despite the fact that his explicitly *geistliche Gedichte* (spiritual poems) do not make up the bulk of his poetic production and represent by no means his masterpieces. In his treatises on literature, Eichendorff himself emphasized the importance not of Christian content in poetry but rather of religious orientation and a permeation of the poetry by religious attitudes. He felt that the talent of a poet should be placed in the service of God and that the Christian atmosphere thus created would permit the concealed but higher meaning of earthly life to manifest itself. When he maintained that all poetry is but the expression or the spiritual body of the inner history of a nation and that the inner history of a nation is its religion, he very clearly established the framework in which his poetry should be read.

Since poetry was not an escape from life for Eichendorff but an indispensable manifestation of the truth and beauty that he found inherent in his religious belief, he believed that the poet himself has a special calling. As he does among the Romantics, the poet enjoys a lofty position in Eichendorff's view, but instead of having the function of awakening nature in the Romantic sense for aesthetic purposes, Eichendorff's poet has the moral task of awakening human beings themselves and of illuminating and promoting their deepest desire and loftiest aim—that is, the search for and movement toward God. He is to caution against selfish, godless pursuits, encouraging human acceptance of heavenly love. The title of one of Eichendorff's most frequently quoted poems is often overlooked; if cognizance is made of the title "Wünschelrute" ("Divining Rod"), then it becomes clear that the *Zauberwort* (magic word) that is sought in order to set the world singing pertains to the living waters hidden underground which are mentioned in the Gospel of John. The sleeping world will awaken to the everlasting life promised by Christ, if the proper word is found—that is, if the truth of that promise of everlasting life can be articulated.

THE SEARCH FOR GOD

In his poem "An die Dichter" ("To the Poets"), Eichendorff paints a very graphic picture of the ethical responsibilities of the poet: As the "Heart of the World," wandering in the footsteps of the Lord, the poet is to save his fellow men and set them free, for he has been given the power of the word that boldly names the darkness. To name the darkness is to tell the truth and to warn of the dark forces that threaten him who is caught unaware; the nature of that darkness Eichendorff discusses elsewhere. That the poet has an active role in the search for God is obvious in many poems, from the six sonnets produced early in his career, in which he speaks of various aspects of poetry and the poet, to much later ones, such as "Der Dichter" ("The Poet"), in which only the poet, in a mysterious fashion, is the recipient of the deepest beauties of life and the benefactor of the joy that God places in his heart. According to Eichendorff, the poet has special access through God to the truth and beauty of his religion, which he transforms into images and poetry which are reflections of that religion. One is reminded thereby of Friedrich Hölderlin's dictum: "That which endures is produced by poets." The poet's concern is religion within the larger context of human experience. For Eichendorff, poetry is a virtual spiritual personification and a governing spiritual principle of the life of humankind. The guidance of the poet is therefore essential for ordinary mortals; he is to use his divining rod to locate the living waters of his faith and to articulate them with his songs for the benefit of humankind.

EARTHLY INDULGENCE AND TEMPTATION

Eichendorff's frequently uttered admonition "Hüte dich, bleib wach und munter" (take care, stay awake and lively) is directed against two dangers, that of sensual and aesthetic excess, which he saw as the lure of Romanticism, and that of sterile, middle-class domesticity and the Philistine life. These two hazards are the substance of "Die zwei Gesellen" ("The Two Companions"). The first comrade succumbs to the snares of domestic bliss and is soon imprisoned by hearth and home; the second is seduced by the bewitching sirens of the deep, the enticements of abandoning oneself to eroticism and hedonistic self-indulgence. Interestingly , Eichendorff felt moved to treat the second danger at greater length; he apparently considered it the greater threat and articulated warnings against it more frequently in his poetry, most likely since it was this very indulgence which Romanticism tended to encourage. It is part of the poet's general protest against introversion of the personality. For the narrator of the poem, however, both extremes are distant from God, and he implores God that he be led to him.

Particularly during his student days in Heidelberg, where he was associated with the Romantic movement, Eichendorff concentrated on such poems as "Die Zauberin im Walde" ("The Sorceress in the Forest"), in which the demoniac power of a godless nature and physical beauty are the undoing of a naïve and undisciplined youth. The reader is introduced here to the evil charms of a sultry world where the fresh breezes of God's spirit can gain no entrance. In the poem "Zwielicht" ("Twilight"), the diminishing light of day permits a precarious state in which the usual clear contours are lost and distortions in human relationships are possible. Without the light, which for Eichendorff always means the light of the world, Christ, and consequently also his love, the world is in jeopardy and can be lost in darkness. That God provides the only refuge from earthly sorrows and temptations is clear in "Das Gebet" ("The Prayer"). The pilgrim moving through life, encountering its pleasures and enchantments, experiences through them sorrow as well as joy and has as his only recourse prayer, which overcomes all the evil bewitchments of life when it victoriously reaches God.

POEMS OF MOVEMENT

Eichendorff's poems are poems of movement; when there are no wandering musicians, there are flowing streams, moving clouds, or rustling forests, and always there is at least the flow of song. The two possibilities for movement away from God against which the poet cautions have already been discussed. If one decides to follow either of these choices, one follows, according to Eichendorff, "earthly ponderousness"; if one chooses instead to move toward God, one is reacting to "intimations of Heaven" and opens oneself to God's light and love. Eichendorff speaks about the two influences operating on humans as centrifugal and centripetal forces and sees human life as a constant battleground on which these opposing powers are raging. Centripetal force draws humans away from themselves and toward God as the true center; like the sun, which provides energy for physical life, the divine love of God reaches out to humans and promotes spiritual growth. Humans are free to accept that love and prosper or succumb to centrifugal forces and perish in the abyss of their own earthliness. The movement, then, that is always present in his work can usually be recognized as either of these choices and thus a descent into the darkness of the base individual self and spiritual death or an ascent upward toward the heavenly source of love and eternal salvation. When Eichendorff speaks of love, however, it need not be of divine love; its uplifting power may also be that of human love, which by itself has none of the redeeming features of divine love and which leads to an ever-diminishing world of the self if it is not touched by the light and love of God. Such ill-starred love is treated in poems such as "Verlorene Liebe" ("Lost Love") and particularly in the novella *The Marble Statue*.

"Moonlit Night"

One of Eichendorff's most famous and beautiful lyrics, "Mondnacht" ("Moonlit Night"), might at first glance appear to be solely a nature poem, even though it is listed among the religious poems in his collected works. Viewed within the framework of the poet's philosophy, the poem clearly appears to be an illustration of God's loving gesture toward his earthly creations. Somewhat in the Homeric manner of not directly describing physical traits of objects but rather depicting subjective reactions to them, Eichendorff here shows the effect of Heaven's kiss upon Earth and nature's response to it. If one takes the sky or Heaven (the German word *Himmel* means both) as a representation of God, then one sees the spirit of God moving across the landscape; the rustling of the forests and the gently waving grain are manifestations of that movement. God's creation, Earth, is visited by him and derives its beauty and holiness from that contact. The poem ends with the human reaction to such an association: The soul of the narrator moves through the quiet countryside in the presence of God's spirit as though it were already flying home.

That homeward journey is in ordinary Christian terms a return to heavenly origins. Eichendorff gives here an exceptionally effective poetic picture of heavenly love, the centripetal pull it exerts on God's creation, the beauty it produces in the physical world, and the spiritual reply to that love in the soul of humans. It is likewise noteworthy that this occurs on a moonlit night; especially with Eichendorff, one must assume that the title of a poem is as important as the text itself and that the moonlight is a significant addition to the poem. Here the light of the moon serves the purpose of illuminating God's moving spirit; were the night not moon-bright, the shimmer of blossoms and the billowing of the grain would not be visible to any human observer. What initially appears to be a magnificently executed nature description is thus demonstrated as being a poetic statement of God's love, symbolized by the kiss of Heaven, reaching, like the moonlight, down to his creation, which in turn renders physical as well as spiritual evidence of the efficacy of that love.

Recurring messages and imagery

Eichendorff is sometimes criticized for his repetitiousness and lack of originality, but such objections lose their force with the realization that the poet, in service to his well-defined worldview, is constantly and deliberately reiterating, rephrasing, rearranging, and recombining his relatively few basic concepts in the manner of any dedicated teacher following the tradition of *repetitio est mater studiorum*. Eichendorff is not the aesthete who expresses himself in random variety, casting up beautiful images in a kind of verbal "light show" but rather the pedagogue who is "preaching with other means" the established religious convictions to which his ego and his poetic talents are subordinated and with which they are harmonized. He is a kind of religious philosopher who has achieved an exercise in the sublimation or apotheosis of his philosophy in and through his poetry as well as vice versa. He is used by his poetry and his philosophy as a "musician" of these two muses to create living word entities which embody and transfer to the reader the essence of his philosophy. His poems are thus written "through him" and tend to transcend his personal attributes and abilities as they take on a being and order of their own, culminating in an entity apart from and beyond the poet's own manipulation of words, themes, ideas, and forms.

Since Eichendorff himself spoke of the hieroglyphic language used in his poetry, it would be most profitable to take note of some of his most frequently used words and images. A thorough analysis of the function of such concepts as spring, gardens, *das Bild* ("the image" or "picture"), song, *der Quell* ("source" or "fountain"), water, forests, woman, and light that appear so regularly in Eichendorff's poetry, as well as an investigation of the changing contexts of these motifs, would yield proof of the profundity of his often superficially read poems. Even a quick survey of Eichendorff's poems indicates how frequently light, particularly morning light, is featured in his work. The morning is his favorite time of day and Aurora a favorite allegorical figure.

It may seem surprising that a sound-oriented poet such as Eichendorff emphasizes light so frequently in his work. Although Eichendorff's talent is that of a musician, his sensitivity is not limited to the auditory world; much of the joy he chooses to articulate is that which he experiences through a visual awareness of the beauty of nature. Instead of employing words to paint the detailed splendors of the visually perceptible physical world, however, Eichendorff was better able to sing praises of them. His frequent allusion to light is therefore both his acknowledgment of the spiritual source of the light which illuminates the wonder of God's creation and a kind of reduction and simplification of multitudinous visual phenomena to one comprehensive symbol. Eichendorff's light is always from above, and when it is not the daylight produced by the sun, it is the light of the moon or the stars, which mitigates and provides relief from the undifferentiated, ambivalent night. Light is for Eichendorff a verification of the Heavenly Father who provides it and of his love for his earthly creatures; it is "des Himmels Kunden" ("tidings from Heaven"), as in the poem "Jugendandacht" ("Youthful Devotion"). In "Der himmlische Maler" ("The Heavenly Painter"), it is God and not the poet who is the painter: God's hand draws the contours of the landscape with the morning light, and as the light makes visible the colors of the countryside, his world is painted and shown in all its glory.

Because Eichendorff was so committed to the idea expressed by his contemporary Clemens von Brentano, that "In dem Lichte wohnt das Heil!" ("in light there is salvation!"), the arrival of light at dawn was an especially welcome occasion for him and the theme of a great many cheerful poems. For Eichendorff, the morning light clarifies the mysteries of the night and erases the worries, fears, and temptations that accompany the night. His morning poems are always expressions of a joyful new beginning; as in the biblical account of the Creation, light means the advent of new life. In Eichendorff's poems, the awakening of nature is heralded by the song of the birds; they seem to acknowledge the source of all light and life as they wing upward toward the heavens. Dawn often coincides with the start of the poet's frequently delineated journeys. Eichendorff was inclined also to write of the other daily transition between light and darkness, the twilight; the time of fading light exemplifies, in contrast to morning hope, an awareness of the bleakness of any diminution of God's light and love.

TECHNICAL AND STYLISTIC DEVICES

Neither in style nor in content does Eichendorff's poetry initially appear to be strikingly innovative; just as the poet's worldview has survived the test of time, so his poetic forms are well practiced and time-honored. For the quintessential poet Eichendorff, however, perhaps more than for poets generally, the poem is itself the message; the "how" of its delivery is as important as the "what" of its content and serves as an additional aspect or reinforcement of the thought contained within it. Eichendorff intimately and intricately links the structure, rhythm, and sounds of the poem to the discourse.

Eichendorff is far more than a facile technician; the standard technical devices he uses are painstakingly chosen to complement the ideas in question, but the full subtleties of such an interrelationship of form and content are exposed only after thorough analysis. With justification, one can say that much of the poet's art conceals itself. Since Eichendorff is a master of *Liedform* ("song form"), in which the entire poem is one organic, melodic unit, his sense of style has been compared to that of Schumann. The cyclical structure the poet often employs involves not only a rephrasing of the initial message at the conclusion of the poem and therefore a full-cycle realization of the essential meaning, but also a counter-reflecting of individual parts internally, so that a wheels-within-wheels effect is created throughout the entire structure. Eichendorff's sonnets and ballads as well as his songs are best rendered orally, so that the sounds of nature he so frequently uses, the liquid rhythms, and the eloquent, poignant melodies, are clearly communicated.

The strength of Eichendorff's work rests therefore not upon superficial novelty but rather upon the quality of his expression and the integrity and skill with which he executed his mission as an artist. What is unique and extraordinary in Eichendorff's writing is the fervor of his belief in the interrelationship of his poetry and his faith and the consistency and emotive power with which he demonstrated that belief in practice. The journeys into "the wide world" which feature so prominently in his work become particularly inviting when it becomes clear that they are ultimately excursions of the soul into regions that promise spiritual nourishment.

OTHER MAJOR WORKS

LONG FICTION: *Ahnung und Gegenwart*, 1815; *Das Marmorbild*, 1819 (novella; *The Marble Statue*, 1927); *Aus dem Leben eines Taugenichts*, 1826 (novella; *Memoirs of a Good-for-Nothing*, 1866); *Viel Lärmen um Nichts*, 1833 (novella); *Dichter und ihre*

Gesellen, 1834; *Eine Meerfahrt*, 1835; *Das Schloss Dürande*, 1837 (novella); *Die Entführung*, 1839; *Die Glücksritter*, 1841; *Das Incognito: Ein Puppenspiel*, 1841; *Libertas und ihre Freier*, 1849; *Julian*, 1853.

PLAYS: *Krieg den Philistern*, pb. 1824; *Ezelin von Romano*, pb. 1828; *Der letzte Held von Marienburg*, pb. 1830; *Die Freier*, pb. 1833; *Robert und Guiscard*, pb. 1855 (verse play).

NONFICTION: *Zur Kunstliteratur*, 1835; *Die Wiederherstellung des Schlosses der deutschen Ordensritter zu Marienburg*, 1844; *Zur Geschichte der neueren romantischen Poesie in Deutschland*, 1846; *Über die ethische und religiöse Bedeutung der neueren romantischen Poesie in Deutschland*, 1847; *Brentano und seine Märchen*, 1847; *Die deutsche Salonpoesie der Frauen*, 1847; *Die geistliche Poesie in Deutschland*, 1847; *Die neue Poesie Österreichs*, 1847; *Novellen von Ernst Ritter*, 1847; *Die deutschen Volksschriftsteller*, 1848; *Zu den Gedichten von Lebrecht Dreves*, 1849; *Der deutsche Roman des achtzehnten Jahrhunderts in seinem Verhältnis zum Christentum*, 1851; *Zur Geschichte des Dramas*, 1854; *Erlebtes*, 1857; *Geschichte der poetischen Literatur Deutschlands*, 1857 (2 volumes).

MISCELLANEOUS: *Neue Gesamtausgabe der Werke und Schriften in vier Bänden*, 1957-1958.

BIBLIOGRAPHY

Goebel, Robert Owen. *Eichendorff's Scholarly Reception: A Survey*. Columbia, S.C.: Camden House, 1993. A critical study of Eichendorff's work and the German academic culture of his time. Includes bibliographical references and an index.

Hachmeister, Gretchen L. *Italy in the German Literary Imagination: Goethe's "Italian Journey" and Its Reception by Eichendorff, Platen, and Heine*. Rochester, N.Y.: Camden House, 2002. Examines *Memoirs of a Good-for-Nothing*, which was in part a reaction to Johann Wolfgang von Goethe's *Italienische Reise* (1816, 1817; *Travels in Italy*, 1883), as well as German writers' treatment of Germany.

Lukács, Georg. *German Realists in the Nineteenth Century*. Translated by Jeremy Gaines and Paul Keast. Edited by Rodney Livingstone. Cambridge, Mass.: MIT Press, 1993. Seven essays on major nineteenth century figures in German literature, including Eichendorff, concerning the role of literature in history, society, and politics.

Purver, Judith. *Hindeutung auf das Höhere: A Structural Study of the Novels of Joseph von Eichendorff*. New York: Peter Lang, 1989. In this comprehensive study of Eichendorff's novels in English, Purver argues that the theological and didactic intentions in Eichendorff's work are vitally important.

Radner, Lawrence. *Eichendorff: The Spiritual Geometer*. Lafayette, Ind.: Purdue University Press, 1970. Radner provides a comprehensive critical interpretation of Eichendorff's works.

Saul, Nicholas, ed. *The Cambridge Companion to German Romanticism*. New York: Cambridge University Press, 2009. Contains many references to Eichendorff and his works, including his poems. Also provides perspective on the poet.

Schwarz, Egon. *Joseph von Eichendorff*. New York: Twayne, 1972. A short biography with a bibliography of Eichendorff's work.

Margaret T. Peischl

STEFAN GEORGE

Born: Büdesheim, Germany; July 12, 1868
Died: Minusio, Switzerland; December 4, 1933

PRINCIPAL POETRY
Hymnen, 1890
Pilgerfahrten, 1891 (*Pilgrimages*, 1949)
Algabal, 1892 (English translation, 1949)
Die Bücher der Hirten-und Preisgedichte, der Sagen und Sänge und der hängenden Gärten, 1895 (*The Books of Eclogues and Eulogies, of Legends and Lays, and of the Hanging Gardens*, 1949)
Das Jahr der Seele, 1897 (*The Year of the Soul*, 1949)
Der Teppich des Lebens und die Lieder von Traum und Tod, mit einem Vorspiel, 1899 (*Prelude, The Tapestry of Life, The Songs of Dream and Death*, 1949)
Die Fibel, 1901 (*The Primer*, 1949)
Der siebente Ring, 1907 (*The Seventh Ring*, 1949)
Der Stern des Bundes, 1914 (*The Star of the Covenant*, 1949)
Das neue Reich, 1928 (*The Kingdom Come*, 1949)
The Works of Stefan George, 1949 (includes the English translations of all titles listed above)

OTHER LITERARY FORMS

Of the books written by Stefan George (gay-AWR-guh), only *Tage und Taten* (1903; *Days and Deeds*, 1951) does not contain any poetry. The volume is a collection of miscellaneous small prose: sketches, letters, observations, aphorisms, and panegyrics. It was expanded to include the introductory essay from *Maximin, ein Gedenkbuch* (1906; memorial book for Maximin) for the eighteen-volume edition of George's complete works, *Gesamt-Ausgabe*, published between 1927 and 1934. In addition to his original works, George published five volumes of translations and adaptations: *Baudelaire, Die Blumen des Bösen* (1901; of Charles Baudelaire); *Zeitgenössische Dichter* (1905; of contemporary poets); *Shakespeare, Sonnette* (1909; of William Shakespeare) and *Dante, Die göttliche Komödie, Übertragungen* (1909; of Dante). *Zeitgenössische Dichter* contains George's translations of poetry by Algernon Charles Swinburne, Jens Peter Jacobsen, Albert Verwey, Paul Verlaine, Stéphane Mallarmé, Arthur Rimbaud, and others. Editions of George's correspondence with Hugo von Hofmannsthal and Friedrich Gundolf were published in 1938 and 1962, respectively.

Achievements

Most of Stefan George's works were consciously addressed to a carefully selected and limited readership, and until 1898, his lyric cycles were published only in private, limited editions. Poems that appeared in early issues of *Blätter für die Kunst* (leaves for art) were initially ignored in Germany because of the journal's limited circulation, the general obscurity of its contributors, and the poets' lack of connections with accepted literary circles. However, George's early poems and translations were received very favorably by poets and critics in France and Belgium. In 1898, the first public edition of *The Year of the Soul*, still his most popular cycle of poems, brought George the beginnings of broader recognition. Subsequent collections won him increasing acclaim for his originality and artistic virtuosity, until in 1927, he became the first, if reluctant, recipient of the Frankfurt/Main Goethe Prize. By 1928, when his collected works appeared, George was recognized internationally as the most gifted of the German Symbolist poets and the most influential renewer of the German language since Friedrich Nietzsche.

George's important contributions to modern German poetry resulted from his efforts to revitalize and elevate decaying artistic standards. His efforts in cultivating a new literary language took into account contemporary literary influences from other national literatures. While pursuing his goals, he actively encouraged other German poets, including Hofmannsthal, Leopold von Andrian, and Karl Wolfskehl, to strive for a new idealism focused on truth, originality, and self-examination, rejecting the identification of poetry with the personality of the poet and his experiences that had long characterized the nineteenth century imitators of Johann Wolfgang von Goethe.

In 1933, when the Nazis endeavored to distort and exploit his artistic ideals, George refused their offers of money and honor, including the presidency of the German Academy of Poets. Nevertheless, after his death, misinterpretation of his ideas and attitudes regarding artistic and intellectual elitism established a link with Nazi ideology that reduced his literary stature and for many years deprived him of his rightful place in German literary history. Above all else, George was a poet of uncompromising artistic integrity, whose attempts to give German poetry a new direction of humanism and idealism were prompted by profoundly moral and ethical motives.

Biography

Stefan Anton George was born in Büdesheim near Bingen in the Rhine district of Germany. His ancestors were farmers, millers, and merchants. When George was five years old, his father, a wine dealer, moved the family to Bingen. Bingen had a lasting impact on the poet's imagination, and its landscapes informed much of his early poetry. In 1882, George began his secondary education in Darmstadt. He received broad humanistic training and excelled in French. While in school, he taught himself Norwegian and Italian and began translating works by Henrik Ibsen, Petrarch, and Torquato Tasso.

When he was eighteen, he began writing poetry and published some of his earliest lyrics under the pseudonym Edmund Delorme in the journal *Rosen und Disteln* that he had founded in 1887.

Upon leaving school in 1888, George began the travels that later characterized his lifestyle. He went first to London, where he became acquainted with the writings of Dante Gabriel Rossetti, Swinburne, and Ernest Dowson, whose poems he later translated and published in German. In Paris, in 1889, he met the French poet Albert Saint-Paul, who introduced him into the circle of Symbolist poets surrounding Mallarmé. In this group of congenial literary artists, which included Verlaine, Francis Vielé-Griffen, the Belgian Albert Mockel, and the Polish poet Wacław Rolicz-Lieder, George found needed personal acceptance and friendship as well as important poetic models. Verlaine and Mallarmé became his acknowledged masters and provided him with a sense of his own poetic calling.

After returning to Germany, George studied Romance literature for three semesters in Berlin. During this time, he experimented with language and even developed a personal Lingua Romana that combined Spanish and Latin words with German syntactical forms. In 1890, he published his first book of poems, *Odes*, in a private edition. Two years later, with Carl August Klein, he founded *Blätter für die Kunst*, which served as an initial focus for his circle of disciples and remained a major vehicle for his ideas for twenty-seven years.

Other encounters with contemporary writers and artists, with his own disciples, and with other personal friends had decisive formative influence on George's career. In 1891, he began a productive if frequently stormy friendship with Hofmannsthal, whom he viewed as his only kindred spirit among modern German poets. When Hofmannsthal refused to commit himself exclusively to George's literary ideas, their association broke off in 1906. George's only significant relationship with a woman, a friendship with Ida Coblenz (later the wife of Richard Dehmel), began in 1892 and influenced many of the poems in *The Year of the Soul*, which he originally intended to dedicate to her. After their association ended in disappointment for George, he limited his emotional involvement to young male disciples, among whom Gundolf and Maximilian Kronberger had profound impact on his mature poetry. Although George was gay, his relations with his young disciples may have been platonic. Affection for Gundolf moved George to direct his creative attention toward molding German youth, while Kronberger, a beautiful adolescent who died of meningitis in 1904, provided him with a model for the divinely pure power of youth as an absolute force of life.

By 1920, most of George's poetic works had been completed. He spent his remaining years actively guiding his youngest disciples, working more as a master teacher than as a poet. When his health finally failed, he moved to Minusio near Locarno, Switzerland, where he died on December 4, 1933.

Analysis

In the preface to the first issue of *Blätter für die Kunst*, Stefan George defined artistic goals for the journal that gave direction to his own poetry for the rest of his career. With its high literary standards, its personally selected group of contributors, and its carefully formulated program, *Blätter für die Kunst* was intended to be a force in the creation of a new German poetry. Its express purpose, specifically reflecting George's perception of his own poetic calling, was to foster a newly refined and spiritual form of literature based on a rejuvenation of classical ideals and a revival of pure literary language. Poetry thus engendered was to be a manifestation of a new way of feeling, furthering the quest for permanent values while rejecting any idea of literature as simple diversion, political instrument, or vehicle for naturalistic social criticism. George's ultimate goal was to provide artistic leadership for a generation that would build a new humanistic society embodying Platonic ideals of goodness, truth, and beauty. Everything that George wrote was directed toward the accomplishment of these purposes.

Intimate association with the French Symbolists in Paris was the formative experience of George's career. It provided him with models for his approach and technique, ideas concerning the poet's role in life, and a starting point for the lifelong exploration of his own poetic nature and its delineation in his works. From Baudelaire, Mallarmé, and Verlaine, he learned to view poets as mediators between phenomena and literary art who describe their perceptions using symbolism that is understood completely only by the poets themselves. Through their symbolic creations, the poet thus isolate themselves in a world to which their own spiritual identity provides the key, a key that the reader must seek in the poem. In this regard, it is important to understand that George completely rejected the idea of identity between the poetic and the personal self. The progressive revelations in his lyrics of the poet's role in life are therefore idealizations rather than reflections of experience.

A clearly defined process of strengthening, refinement, and crystallization of the poet's role emerges in the cycles that document George's development. His *Odes*, which belong within the frame of traditional idealism, examine such themes as the tension between reason and feeling, change as a basic force in life, and unhappy love and death; therein is revealed a personal struggle with self-examination and doubt. In *Algabal*, however, there is a new sense of personal validity; the title figure symbolizes the exclusive artist who creates a private realm in isolation from nature. A further objectification of poetic self appears in the prologue to *The Tapestry of Life*, in the figure of an angel. This alter ego of the poet appears not as a heavenly messenger but as a representative of life, announcing the colorful fabric of the artistic yet puzzling order of existence. George's attempts to refine and perfect the revelation of his poetic identity culminate in the Maximin poems of *The Seventh Ring* and *The Star of the Covenant*, in which Maximin becomes the ultimate symbol for the desired perfect fusion of body and spirit in self-awareness.

Central to George's view of the social role of the poet was the idea that the poet enjoys the special position of "master" within a circle of devoted disciples. This principle, which he saw modeled in the salon of Mallarmé, had significant impact on his poetry and the conduct of his personal life. The relationship of the poet to his disciples is reflected in poems dedicated to close friends and associates in *The Books of Eclogues and Eulogies, of Legends and Lays, and of the Hanging Gardens* and other cycles. It is also evident in the consistent emergence of the symbolic poet as a teacher figure. This casting of the poet in the role of educator is readily visible in poems from *The Year of the Soul* and in the "Zeitgedichte" ("Time Poems") section of *The Seventh Ring*, in which the poet-teacher gives specific directions to his contemporaries, suggesting appropriate models for them to emulate. Developed to its ultimate in *The Kingdom Come*, the poet's role as teacher becomes that of a prophet who judges the age and sounds a warning.

From the standpoint of technique and approach, George considered the revitalization, refinement, and purification of literary language to be the most important aspect of his creative task. He protested against the debasement of language, advocating a revival of pure rhyme and meter with precise arrangement of vowels and consonants to achieve harmony in a distinctly musical poetic form. Creation of language became a basic principle of his writing. He followed the pattern of Mallarmé and rejected everyday words. Stressing the importance of sound and internal melody in his poems, he formed new, musically resonant words and imbued his verses with rich vowels, assonances, alliteration, and double rhymes. George's perception of the spoken and the written word as embodiments of the reality of the world extended even to a regard for the importance of the visual impression created by printed forms. To offer language that was unusual in this respect, he developed a special typeface and modified traditional orthography and punctuation for his publications. George undertook all these measures because he believed that language alone can open hidden levels of mind, soul, and meaning.

While progressively modifying French Symbolist and other external influences to suit his own purposes, George succeeded at least partially in creating the new German poetry toward which he was striving. Patterning his poems after Baudelaire's perception of the symbolic structure of existence, he created works that reflected his personal attitudes of austerity and self-denial, while celebrating the ethical supremacy of the spirit over material existence. The poetic cycle became his characteristic form, and each of his collections exhibits the basic unity that it demands. In addition to genuine originality in the coining of words and in imagery, George's poems typically feature colorful calmness of motion, sensually intense metaphors and symbols, and remarkable simplicity. The unaffected wording and ordering of lines in *The Year of the Soul*, for example, anticipate certain tendencies in Surrealism, while the smoothly flowing verses of the "Gezeiten" ("Tides") section of *The Seventh Ring* and the utter clarity and lack of ambiguity in the poems of *The Star of the Covenant* reflect the complete creative control of words that George consistently demonstrated in his poetry. It is perhaps in that rare mastery of personal poetic language that George made his greatest contribution to German literature.

Even George's earliest, less successful cycles reflect searching attempts to define his poetic self. From the exploratory *Odes*, which focus on artistic experiences and on the mission and position of the artists in the world, George moved in *Pilgrimages* toward a more distinctly personal approach to self-examination, styling himself a wanderer in a manner somewhat akin to Goethe's poetic perception of himself. Not until *Algabal*, however, did he present a clearly cohesive symbolic representation of his own special nature.

ALGABAL

As George's first highly characteristic work, *Algabal* offers vivid examples of the new kind of poetic creation for which the poet pleaded in the first issue of *Blätter für die Kunst*. The poems of *Algabal* are replete with samples of the musical language that became such a critical part of George's works as a whole. In uniquely worded verses characterized by sonorous repetition of melodic vowel combinations, the poet transforms carefully chosen elements of reality into symbols for his internal world. In so doing, he gives them a different kind of existence, creating new levels of artistic revelation. He develops the central complex of symbols from the life of Elagabalus, the youthful Roman emperor and priest of Baal whose promotion of physically beautiful favorites and open homosexual orgies brought about his assassination. Transforming his eccentric model into Algabal, the lonely king of a personally created subterranean realm, George creates a haunting symbol for his poetic identity.

The first section of the cycle, "Im Unterreich" ("In the Subterranean Kingdom"), focuses on Algabal's domain as a major symbol for a new level of creative feeling. In an overwhelming intensity of visual impression, the components of external nature are transformed into precious gems that flash in bright colors, illuminating from within an edifice to which the light of day does not penetrate. Similarly, the natural smells of outside reality are replaced by peculiar, musty fragrances of amber, incense, lemon, and almond oil that infuse the artificial world. The most profound symbols of "In the Subterranean Kingdom" are the lifeless birds and plants of Algabal's garden. Amid stems and branches made of carbon, the black flower appears as a symbol for art, a conscious contrast to Novalis's blue flower of romantic longing.

In the other sections of *Algabal*, "Tage" ("Days"), "Die Andenken" ("The Memories"), and "Vogelschau" ("View of Birds"), George tightens the symbolic focus to elucidate the unique personality of the ruler of the underground palace and garden. Verses that stress the self-examination aspect of the creative process reveal George's perception of himself as a poet whose nature compels him to return alone to an ancient age in which other values predominate. New symbols are formed to treat traditional literary themes. Juxtaposed to the black flower of artificial life, for example, are images of death in vivid reds and greens. "View of Birds," the final poem of the cycle, underscores the idea that it is only through the poet's actively formative power of perception that life is given to the artistically constructed poetic world.

THE YEAR OF THE SOUL

Among all George's collections of poetry, the most popular yet least typical is the key cycle of his middle period, *The Year of the Soul*. Two factors in particular distinguish the poems of this group from his other major works. *The Year of the Soul* is George's only book that centers on love between man and woman. It is an important document of his relationship with Coblenz. His poetic treatment of that ultimately unhappy emotional involvement contrasts markedly with the harmoniously warm and human love poems that he wrote for young men in *The Seventh Ring* and other later cycles. *The Year of the Soul* also differs from other George volumes in style and technique. The decorative stylization of diction and the boldness of ornamentation in nature imagery suggest a connection with the intentions and motifs of *Jugendstil*, whereas the pronounced simplicity of form that characterizes most of George's poetry reflects his tacit rejection of the *Jugendstil* tendency in art.

The poems of *The Year of the Soul* frame exploration of the problems of unfulfilled love in carefully controlled images of external reality. Modifying the traditional German nature poem, George symbolizes nature by a cultivated park that is organized and created by the gardener/poet. The park landscapes that he evokes offer individual natural phenomena as symbols for private experience and moods of the soul.

The first and most important of the book's three major sections presents the essence of the volume in concentrated form. It is divided into three subcycles, "Nach der Lese" ("After the Harvest"), "Waller im Schnee" ("Wanderer in the Snow"), and "Sieg des Sommers" ("Triumph of Summer"), each of which constitutes a rounded unit in its own right. Beginning with autumn, the poet employs the rhythm of the seasons to illuminate changing moods—hope, suffering, reflection, and mourning in an ever-renewing confrontation with the self. Special emphasis on color accents the varying moods evoked by the nature images, intensifying the dialogue between "I" and "you," newly perceived Faustian aspects of the poet's own soul which appear in the guise of the poet and a fictitious female object of his love. The motifs of "Wanderer in the Snow" augment the tension between the poet and the accompanying "you" as the wanderer traverses a winter of bitterness, austerity, and mourning. Sheer hopelessness radiates from the lines of the seventh poem, in which the poet declares that despite his faithful attention and patience, his love relationship will never bring him so much as a warm greeting. In "Triumph of Summer," a transition from the harsh emptiness of winter imagery to the anticipated warmth of summer promises a new approach to spiritual fulfillment. The ten poems of this segment dwell on the idea of joint creation of a "sun kingdom" with the "you" of the previous sections. The "sun kingdom," a symbol for the ideal realm for which George longed throughout his career, remains, however, a transitory vision as summer's end becomes a symbol for final parting.

The poems of the two other major parts of *The Year of the Soul*, "Überschriften und Widmungen" ("Titles and Dedications") and "Traurige Tänze" ("Sad Dances"), focus more precisely and personally on problems and themes introduced in the preceding section. In verses dedicated to friends, the poet again assumes the role of teacher, instructing his disciples concerning the inner spiritual encounter with love. Lyrics written specifically for Coblenz give additional substance to the symbolic portrayal of George's painful love affair, while the beautifully songlike stanzas of "Sad Dances" elevate the volume as a whole to a single powerful symbol for his private experience of *Weltschmerz*.

THE SEVENTH RING

In 1907, George published the richest, most ambitious, and most complex collection of his career. *The Seventh Ring* represents the high point and culmination of his poetic development. It is especially fascinating for its presentation of a significant spectrum of George's stylistic possibilities, themes, and poetic perceptions, together with its clear revelation of his ultimate goals. In addition to the ever-present poems dedicated to members of his circle, the cycle contains the most important elements of the new tendencies that appeared in George's poetry after 1900. To be sure, the two later volumes, *The Star of the Covenant* and *The Kindgom Come*, are important for what they reveal of the final perfecting of ideas that are central to *The Seventh Ring*. Nevertheless, the sometimes sterile rigidity and flatness of *The Star of the Covenant* and the lack of uniformity in *The Kingdom Come* (which encompasses all of George's lyric creations written after 1913) render those two books anticlimactic.

Although *The Seventh Ring* is somewhat uneven in form, a fresh poetic emphasis on principles of mathematical order is evident in the highly visible relationships between special numbers, internal symbolism, and the formal organization of the work. There are obvious connections among the title, the division of the poems into seven groupings, the seven biblical creative periods, and the year of publication, 1907. In addition, the number of items in each subcycle is a multiple of seven, while the constitution of individual poems and their integration into units are governed by specific numerical factors. Especially important is the placement of the "Maximin" section. Positioned fourth in conscious reference to the year of the death of Maximilian Kronberger, the verses that he inspired form the thematic as well as the structural nucleus of the symmetrical collection.

Viewed in its entirety, *The Seventh Ring* is George's most comprehensive attempt to define his own position within his age. The "Time Poems" at the beginning permanently establish the poet in the chosen roles of teacher and judge that characterize all his later writings. They attack the follies of the era, providing points of reference and standards against which to measure them as well as models for emulation in building a new, ideal, Hellenistic society. Goethe, Dante, Nietzsche, and Leo XIII are among the examples of great human beings whom George glorifies. In "Tides," which contains some of the most impressive love poetry in the German language, George reveals as nowhere else the intensity and inner meaning of his feelings for Gundolf and Robert Boehringer. Through the same lyrics, however, he comes to terms with the fact that those relationships have been replaced in importance by the more transcendent encounter with Maximin.

The so-called Maximin experience is commonly recognized as the key to George's mature poetry. In the "Maximin" section of *The Seventh Ring*, George transforms the life of his young friend into a symbol for the manner in which eternal, divine forces are manifest in the modern world. Deification of Maximin enables him to create a private religion as part of his quest for permanent values in the Hellenic tradition. The god Maximin is the embodiment of a primeval force, a universally present Eros. In lyrical celebrations of Maximin's life and death, George transforms the characteristic dialogues with self of earlier poems into conversations with divinity. In so doing, he elevates himself to the rank of prophet and seer. His prophetic calling then opens the way to new themes of chaos and destruction. While developing these themes, the poet creates the visions of Germany's fall that accompany the further revelation of Maximin's character in the other sections of *The Seventh Ring* and in *The Star of the Covenant* and *The Kingdom Come*.

OTHER MAJOR WORKS

NONFICTION: *Blätter für die Kunst*, 1892-1919 (12 volumes); *Tage und Taten*, 1903 (*Days and Deeds*, 1951); *Maximin, ein Gedenkbuch*, 1906.

TRANSLATIONS: Baudelaire, *Die Blumen des Bösen*, 1901; *Zeitgenössische Dichter*, 1905 (of contemporary poets); Dante, *Die göttliche Komödie, Übertragungen*, 1909; Shakespeare, *Sonnette*, 1909.

MISCELLANEOUS: *Gesamt-Ausgabe*, 1927-1934 (18 volumes; poetry and prose).

BIBLIOGRAPHY

Bennett, Edwin K. *Stefan George*. New Haven, Conn.: Yale University Press, 1954. A succinct critical study of George's works with a brief biographical background. Includes bibliography.

Goldsmith, Ulrich K. *Stefan George*. New York: Columbia University Press, 1970. Biographical essay with bibliographic references.

Metzger, Michael M., and Erika A. Metzger. *Stefan George*. New York: Twayne, 1972. Biography of George includes a bibliography of his works.

Norton, Robert E. *Secret Germany: Stefan George and His Circle*. Ithaca, N.Y.: Cornell University Press, 2002. This biography of George looks at him as a poet, a pedagogue, politician, and prophet. George and his circle were a very powerful political force in Germany, and he was viewed as the prophet and savior of the nation. One section is devoted to his poetry.

Rieckmann, Jens, ed. *A Companion to the Works of Stefan George*. Rochester, N.Y.: Camden House, 2005. Contains essays on George's poetics, his early works, his links to aestheticism, his relation to Friedrich Nietzsche and Nazism, his sexuality, and his literary circle. Also features a list of his works.

Underwood, Von Edward. *A History That Includes the Self: Essays on the Poetry of Stefan George, Hugo von Hofmannsthal, William Carlos Williams, and Wallace Stevens*. New York: Garland, 1988. A very useful monograph on the comparative poetics of the four poets. Bibliographical references, index.

Lowell A. Bangerter

JOHANN WOLFGANG VON GOETHE

Born: Frankfurt am Main (now in Germany); August 28, 1749
Died: Weimar, Saxe-Weimar-Eisenbach (now in Germany); March 22, 1832

PRINCIPAL POETRY
Neue Lieder, 1770 (*New Poems*, 1853)
Sesenheimer Liederbuch, 1775-1789, 1854 (*Sesenheim Songs*, 1853)
Römische Elegien, 1793 (*Roman Elegies*, 1876)
Reinecke Fuchs, 1794 (*Reynard the Fox*, 1855)
Epigramme: Venedig 1790, 1796 (*Venetian Epigrams*, 1853)
Xenien, 1796 (with Friedrich Schiller; *Epigrams*, 1853)
Hermann und Dorothea, 1797 (*Herman and Dorothea*, 1801)
Balladen, 1798 (with Schiller; *Ballads*, 1853)
Neueste Gedichte, 1800 (*Newest Poems*, 1853)
Gedichte, 1812-1815 (2 volumes; *The Poems of Goethe*, 1853)
Sonette, 1819 (*Sonnets*, 1853)
Westöstlicher Divan, 1819 (*West-Eastern Divan*, 1877)

OTHER LITERARY FORMS

The unique significance of the contribution to German letters made by Johann Wolfgang von Goethe (GUR-tuh) lies in the fact that his best creations provided models that influenced, stimulated, and gave direction to the subsequent evolution of literary endeavor in virtually every genre. Among more than twenty plays that he wrote throughout his career, several have special meaning for the history of German theater. *Götz von Berlichingen mit der eisernen Hand* (pb. 1773; *Götz von Berlichingen with the Iron Hand*, 1799) was a key production of the Storm and Stress movement, mediating especially the influence of William Shakespeare on later German dramatic form and substance. With *Iphigenie auf Tauris* (first version pr. 1779, second version pb. 1787; *Iphigenia in Tauris*, 1793), Goethe illustrated profoundly the ideals of perfected form and style, beauty of language, and humanistic education that characterized German literature of the classical period. His famous masterpiece *Faust: Eine Tragödie* (pb. 1808, 1833; *The Tragedy of Faust*, 1823, 1838), with its carefully programmed depiction of the spiritual polarities that torment the individual, rapidly became the ultimate paradigm for the portrayal of modern humanity's fragmented nature.

Goethe's major narratives, including *Die Leiden des jungen Werthers* (1774; *The Sorrows of Young Werther*, 1779), *Wilhelm Meisters Lehrjahre* (1795-1796; *Wilhelm Meister's Apprenticeship*, 1825), *Die Wahlverwandtschaften* (1809; *Elective Affinities*, 1849), and *Wilhelm Meisters Wanderjahre: Oder, Die Entsagenden* (1821, 1829; *Wil-*

Johann Wolfgang von Goethe
(Library of Congress)

helm Meister's Travels, 1827), are powerful illuminations of fundamental human problems. The monumental saga of Wilhelm Meister established the pattern for the German bildungsroman of the nineteenth century, and it also had a substantial impact on Romantic novel theory.

A large portion of Goethe's oeuvre is nonfiction. He completed more than fourteen volumes of scientific and technical writings, the most important of which are *Versuch die Metamorphose der Pflanzen zu erklären* (1790; *Essays on the Metamorphosis of Plants*, 1863) and *Zur Farbenlehre* (1810; *Theory of Colors*, 1840). His historical accounts, specifically *Campagne in Frankreich, 1792* (1822; *Campaign in France in the Year 1792*, 1849) and *Die Belagerung von Mainz, 1793* (1822; *The Siege of Mainz in the Year 1793*, 1849), are vividly readable reports of firsthand experience. Writings that reveal a great deal about Goethe himself and his perception of his artistic calling are his autobiography, *Aus meinem Leben: Dichtung und Wahrheit* (1811-1814; *The Autobiography of Goethe*, 1824; better known as *Poetry and Truth from My Own Life*), and the many published volumes of his correspondence.

Achievements

Johann Wolfgang von Goethe's overwhelming success as a lyricist was primarily the result of an extraordinary ability to interpret and transform direct, intimate experience and perception into vibrant imagery and symbols with universal import. In the process of overcoming the artificiality of Rococo literary tendencies, he created, for the first time in modern German literature, lyrics that were at once deeply personal, dynamically vital, and universally valid in what they communicated to the reader. Beginning with the poems written to Friederike Brion, and continuing through the infinitely passionate affirmations of life composed in his old age, Goethe consistently employed his art in a manner that brushed away the superficial trappings and facades of existence to lay bare the essential spirit of humankind.

In his own time, Goethe became a world figure, although his immediate acclaim derived more from his early prose and dramatic works than from his lyrical writings. Even after the turn of the nineteenth century, he was still recognized most commonly as the author of *The Sorrows of Young Werther*, the novel that had made him instantly famous throughout Europe. Nevertheless, the simple power, clear, appealing language, and compelling melodiousness of his verse moved it inexorably into the canon of the German literary heritage. Much of his poetry was set to music by the great composers of his own and subsequent generations, and the continuing popularity of such creations as "Mailied" ("Maysong") and "Heidenröslein" ("Little Rose of the Heath") is attributable at least in part to the musical interpretations of Franz Schubert and others.

The real importance of Goethe's lyric legacy is perhaps best measured in terms of what it taught other writers. Goethe established new patterns and perspectives, opened new avenues of expression, set uncommon standards of artistic and aesthetic achievement, assimilated impulses from other traditions, and mastered diverse meters, techniques, and styles as had no other German poet before him. His influence was made productive by figures as different as Heinrich Heine and Eduard Mörike, Friedrich Hölderlin and Hugo von Hofmannsthal, Stefan George and Rainer Maria Rilke. As a mediator and motivator of the literary and intellectual currents of his time, as a creator of timeless poetic archetypes, as an interpreter of humanity within its living context, Goethe has earned an undisputed place among the greatest poets of world literature.

Biography

Three aspects of Johann Wolfgang von Goethe's childhood contributed substantially to his development as a literary artist. A sheltered existence, in which he spent long hours completely alone, fostered the growth of an active imagination. A complicated attachment to his sister Cornelia colored his perceptions of male-female relationships in ways that had a profound impact on the kinds of experience from which his works were generated. Finally, contrasts between his parents in temperament and cultural attitudes gave him an early awareness of the stark polarities of life on which the central tensions of his major literary creations are based.

While studying law in Leipzig between 1765 and 1768, Goethe began to write poems and simple plays in the prevailing Anacreontic style. Although some of these productions relate to his infatuation with Kätchen Schönkopf, an innkeeper's daughter, they are more the product of his desire to become a part of the contemporary intellectual establishment than a direct outpouring of his own inner concerns. Among the important figures who influenced his education and thinking during this period were Christoph Martin Wieland, Christian Fürchtegott Gellert, and Adam Friedrich Oeser.

The experiences that resulted in Goethe's breakthrough to a distinctly individual and characteristic literary approach began when he entered the University of Strasbourg in 1770. Encounters with two very different people during the winter of 1770-1771 sharply changed his life. Johann Gottfried Herder introduced him to the concepts and ideals of the Storm and Stress movement, providing him with new models in Homer and Shakespeare and moving him in the direction of less artificial modes of expression. Of equal consequence for the immediate evolution of his lyrics was an idyllic love affair with Friederike Brion that ended in a parting, the emotional implications of which marked his writings long afterward.

On his return to Frankfurt in 1771, Goethe was admitted to the bar. During the next five years, he fell in love with at least three different women. A painful involvement with Charlotte Buff, the fiancé of his friend Johann Christian Kestner, was followed by a brief attraction to Maximiliane Laroche. In April, 1775, he became engaged to Lili Schönemann, the daughter of a wealthy Frankfurt banker. Of the three relationships, only the interlude with Maximiliane Laroche failed to have a significant impact on his art. *The Sorrows of Young Werther* derived much of its substance from Goethe's experiences with Charlotte Buff, while the powerful internal conflicts generated by his feelings for Lili gave rise to a small group of very interesting poems.

When the engagement to Lili became intolerable because of its demands and restrictions, Goethe went to Weimar, where he settled permanently in 1776. For the next ten years, he served as adviser to Carl August, duke of Weimar, whom he had met in Frankfurt in 1774. A broad variety of political and administrative responsibilities, ranging from supervision of road construction to irrigation, from military administration to direction of the court theater, left Goethe little time for serious literary endeavor. The resulting lack of personal fulfillment coupled with the prolonged frustrations of an unhappy platonic love affair with Charlotte von Stein caused him to flee to Italy in search of artistic and spiritual rejuvenation. While there, he perfected some of his most significant dramatic works.

The combination of exposure to Roman antiquity, classical Italian literature, and a uniquely satisfying love alliance with the simple, uneducated Christiane Vulpius formed the basis for renewed poetic productivity when Goethe returned to Weimar. In *Roman Elegies*, he glorified his intimate involvement with Christiane in imagery of the Eternal City. A second, more disappointing trip to Italy in 1790 provided the stimulus for the less well known *Venetian Epigrams*.

In 1794, Goethe accepted Friedrich Schiller's invitation to collaborate in the publication of a new journal. There followed one of the most fruitful creative friendships in the history of German letters. Among the famous lyrical compositions that emerged from their relationship were the terse, pointed forms of the epigram war that they waged against their critics in 1796, and the masterful ballads that were written in friendly competition in 1797. Goethe regarded Schiller's death, in 1805, as one of the major personal tragedies of his own life.

The two specific experiences of later years that provided the direction for Goethe's last great productive period were exposure to the works of the fourteenth century Persian poet Hafiz and a journey to the places of his own childhood. While in Frankfurt in 1814, Goethe fell in love with Marianne von Willemer, the wife of a friend. The Hafizlike dialogue of their intense spiritual communion is the focus of *West-Eastern Divan*, in which Goethe reached the culmination of his career as a lyricist. After it was published, only the final work on his immortal masterpiece *Faust* remained as a substantial task to be completed before his death.

Analysis

In his famous letter to Johann Wolfgang von Goethe of August 23, 1794, Schiller identified the addressee as a writer who sought to derive the essence of an individual manifestation from the totality of natural phenomena. More particularly, he saw Goethe's goal as the literary definition of humankind in terms of the organization of the living cosmos to which it belongs. Only to the extent that Goethe viewed himself as representative of humanity in general does Schiller's assessment offer a valid approach to the understanding of his friend's lyric poetry. The focus of Goethe's verse is less humankind in the abstract than it is Goethe himself as a distinct, feeling, suffering, loving, sorrowing, longing being. From the very beginning, his works assumed the character of subjective poetic interpretations of his specific place in society, the implications of direct encounters with nature and culture, and the significance of concrete interpersonal relationships. He later described his creative writings as elements of a grand confession, pinpointing the fact that a major key to them lay in the penetration of his own existence.

Goethe's development as a lyric poet is clearly a continuum in which internal and external events and circumstances contribute to sometimes subtle, sometimes obvious modifications in approach, technique, and style. It is nevertheless possible to recognize a number of well-defined stages in his career that correspond to important changes in his outward situation and his connections with specific individuals. The predominant tendency of his growth was in the direction of a poetry that reaches outward to encompass an ever-broader spectrum of universal experience.

The Anacreontic creations of Goethe's student years in Leipzig are, for the most part, time-bound, occasional verse in which realistic emotion, feeling, and perception are subordinated to the artificial conventions and devices of the time. Typical motifs and themes of the collection *New Poems* are wine, Rococo eroticism, the game of love with its hidden dangers, stylized pastoral representations of nature, and a peculiarly playful association of love and death. Individual poems often move on the border between sensuality and morality, mirroring the prevailing social patterns. Especially characteristic is the employment of language that magnifies the separation of the world of the poem from experienced reality. In their affirmation of the elegant facades, the deliberate aloofness, the uncommitted playfulness of Rococo culture, these lyrics document Goethe's early artistic attitudes, even though they reveal little of his unique poetic gift.

Strasbourg period

Under the influence of Herder in Strasbourg, Goethe began to move from the Decadent artificiality of his Leipzig songs. A new appreciation for the value of originality, immediacy of feeling, unmediated involvement in nature, and directness of approach is apparent in creations that are notable for their vivid imagery, plastic presentation of substance, force of expression, and power of language and rhythm.

Two types of utterance dominate the verse of this period. Highly personal outpourings of the soul, in which the representation of love is more passionate, serious, and captivating than in the Leipzig productions, are couched in formal stanzas that arose from Goethe's fondness for Friederike Brion. Free-verse poems that focus on Storm and Stress ideals of individuality, genius, and creativity reflect the lyrical influence of Pindar and the dramatic legacy of Shakespeare in their form and tone. In what they reveal of Goethe's worldview, the love poetry and the philosophical reflections are deeply intertwined. Without love, Goethe's perception of life is empty; without the depth of awareness of individual responsibility in creation, love loses its strength and vitality. Love forms the basis for the experience of nature, while the external surroundings with their beauties, tensions, conflicts, and potential for joy give full meaning to love.

The most important new feature of the Strasbourg poetry is the visible emphasis on existential polarities in the description of the poet's relationship to people and things. Love and suffering, defiance and submission, danger and ecstasy are juxtaposed in the portrayal of a world of change, growth, and struggle. In endless variation, Goethe offers the intimate revelation of loneliness, longing, and lack of final fulfillment that are the fundamental ingredients of life viewed as a pattern of restless wanderings. The very acts of searching, striving, creating, and loving are communicated with an energy and a spiritual intensity that carries the reader along in a rush of emotional participation in universal experience.

The Lili poems

Among Goethe's most interesting early works are the sometimes tender, often intensely painful lyric documents of his courtship of Lili Schönemann. Few in number, these writings illustrate the poet's cathartic use of his talent in a process of self-analysis and clarification of his position with respect to external events. At the same time, they underscore a growing tendency to come to grips with and master life through his art. Consisting of occasional pieces that are connected by recurring themes related to the tension between the attractions of love and the devastating torments of an accompanying loss of freedom, the Lili poems combine visions of joy with ironically biting yet dismal portraits of despair. A gem of the period is the famous "Auf dem See" ("On the Lake"), a vivid projection of both physical and spiritual flight from oppressive love, written in Switzerland, where Goethe had taken temporary refuge from the demands of life with Lili.

WEIMAR PERIOD

During Goethe's first years in Weimar, the frustrations of an unsatisfying association with Charlotte von Stein, the all-consuming responsibilities of the court, and his own inability to overcome completely the break with Lili contributed to his lyrics a new preoccupation with themes of melancholy resignation and self-denial. The heavy moods that characterize his works of this period inform short meditative poems as well as longer philosophical reflections, mournful love songs, and a few haunting ballads. Especially profound are two eight-line stanzas, each titled "Wanderers Nachtlied" ("Wanderer's Night Song"), in which the poet longs for and admonishes himself to courage, comfort, hope, belief, and patience. "Warum gabst du uns die tiefen Blicke?" ("Why Did You Give Us the Deep Glances?"), the most powerful of his poems to Charlotte von Stein, presents love as a mystical mystery. The two dramatic ballads, "Erlkönig" ("Elf King") and "Der Fischer" ("The Fisherman"), emphasize humanity's psychological subjection to the demonic power of its own impressions of nature.

ITALIAN JOURNEY

The experience of Italy completely changed Goethe's poetry. Among the most important developments that the journey inspired were the abandonment of suggestion and tone in favor of pure image, the transition from lyrical song to epic description, and the replacement of extended elaboration of worldview with terse epigrams and short didactic verse. During Goethe's classical period, his ballads achieved perfected form, while his depictions of nature attained their final goal in brightness and joyful plasticity. Where earlier poems feature colors that flow softly together, or points of color that invoke mood and an impression of the whole, the works created after 1790 are dominated by structure and the placement of objects in space. Ideas are presented in classical meters, especially hexameter, and as a result confessional poetry loses much of its melody.

ELEGIES, EPIGRAMS, AND BALLADS

Three groups of poems are particularly representative of the new directions in Goethe's lyrics: *Roman Elegies*, the epigrams, and the classical ballads. In their rich mural presentation of the poet's life in Rome, the *Roman Elegies* document the author's increasing tendency to circumscribe his own existence in verse, while their form, style, and combination of classical dignity with inner lightheartedness reflect the direct influence of Ovid, Catullus, and Propertius. The poems of *Venetian Epigrams* were similarly motivated by direct exposure to elements of classical Italian culture. They are especially notable for their rich imagery and their realism in depicting the emotional intensity of the poet's longing for Germany. In structure and style, they were models for the more famous epigrams written by Goethe and Schiller in 1796. Unlike the elegies and epigrams, Goethe's powerful ballads of 1797 arose out of materials that he had carried within him for a long time. The lyrical and melodic aspects that are absent from the other forms remain strong in rhythmic creations that emphasize passion and excitement while developing themes related to the classical ideal of pure humanity. Goethe viewed the ballad as an archetypal lyric form. His "Die Braut von Korinth" ("The Bride of Corinth") and "Der Gott und die Bajadere" ("The God and the Bayadere") are among the greatest German ballads ever written.

POETRY OF LATER YEARS

The erotic poetry of Goethe's old age had its beginnings in a group of sonnets that he wrote to Minchen Herzlieb in 1807. During the seven years that followed their creation, he wrote verse only occasionally. At last, however, the combination of stimuli from the deeply meaningful love affair with Marianne von Willemer and exposure to the works of Hafiz moved him to compose his greatest poetic accomplishment, *West-Eastern Divan*. In the framework of a fantasy journey of rejuvenation, Goethe entered a friendly competition with Hafiz while simultaneously declaring his own newly regained inner freedom. The central themes of the collection include longing for renewal of life, recognition of the need for spiritual transformation, coming to grips with Hafiz as a poet, love, wine, worldly experience, paradise, looking upward to God, and looking downward to the human condition. In some of the poems, Goethe returned to a kind of Anacreontic love poetry. In the heart of the cycle, he made of Hatem and Suleika timeless archetypal models for man and woman bound in the love relationship.

After *West-Eastern Divan*, Goethe wrote only a few poems of consequence. Among them, "Uworte, Orphisch" ("Primeval Words, Orphic"), in which he attempted to develop the core problems of human existence in five eight-line stanzas, and "Trilogie der Leidenschaft" ("Trilogy of Passion"), a tragic document of the state of being unfulfilled that was inspired by his final love experience, attained the power and stature of earlier lyrics. In these two creations, Goethe pinpointed once more the essence of his own spiritual struggle between the light and the night of human existence.

"WELCOME AND FAREWELL"

While living in Strasbourg and courting Friederike Brion, Goethe created for the first time sensitive love poetry and descriptions of nature that exude the vitality of immediate experience. Perhaps the most characteristic of these works is the famous "Willkommen und Abschied" ("Welcome and Farewell"). The substance of the poem is a night ride through the countryside to Sesenheim and a joyful reunion with Friederike, followed by a painful scene of parting when morning comes. Significant elements include a new and plastic rendering of nature, fresh and captivating imagery, and melodic language that is alive with rhythm and motion. A special power of observation is demonstrated in the poet's representation of that which cannot or can hardly be seen, yet the scenery is not portrayed merely for its own sake; rather, it is symbolic, for the uncanny aspects of the ride through the darkness are overcome by a courageous heart that is driven by love. Landscape and love thus become the two poles of the poem generating an inner tension that culminates in a peculiar equation of the beloved with the world as a whole. The portrayal of Friederike is especially notable for its psychological depth, while the expression of Goethe's own feelings of passion and eventual guilt lends the entire picture qualities of a universal experience of the heart.

"Prometheus" and "Ganymed"

Deeply personal yet broadly valid content is also typical of the so-called genius poems of Goethe's Storm and Stress period. The intensity of emotional extremes is particularly vivid in the sharply contrasting hymns "Prometheus" and "Ganymed," which reflect the poles of Goethe's own spirit even more strongly than do his dramas. In depicting the two mythological titans, the poet concentrated on the creation of dynamic archetypes. "Prometheus" is a hard, even harsh portrait of modern humanity. The speaker of the lines is loveless and alone. Emphasis is placed on "I"; the focus is inward and limiting. In his defiant rejection of Father Zeus and the attendant process of self-deification, Prometheus champions the value of individuality and independence. Important themes of his declaration of emancipation from gods who are less powerful than humans include faith in self, belief in the power of action, knowledge of the difficulty and questionability of life, and the divinity of humans' creative nature. The tone of "Ganymed" is completely different. In the soft language of a prayer, the title figure proclaims his total submission to the will of the Father and his desire to return to the divine presence. A new side of Goethe's religiosity is revealed in the transformation of his sensitivity to nature into a longing for God's love. The central concern is no longer "I" but "you"; the direction is outward toward the removal of all boundaries in a coming together of deity and humankind. In the manner in which they play off the real world against the ideal realm, "Prometheus" and "Ganymed" are especially representative of the existential polarity lyrics that Goethe wrote during the pre-Weimar years.

Roman Elegies

Roman Elegies, the major lyrical product of Goethe's first Italian journey, comprises twenty confessional hexameter poems knit tightly together in a cycle that documents the poet's love for a fictitious young widow (Christiane Vulpius in Roman disguise). Two primary thematic configurations dominate creations that are among Goethe's most beautiful, most sensuously erotic works. The story of the tender love affair with Faustine, integrated into the Italian framework, is played off against the problems associated with renewal and adaptation of antiquity by the modern poet. Within this context, love becomes the key that makes entry into the Roman world possible.

Lively, direct reflection of the writer's enthusiasm for Rome sets the tone for the cycle. At the center of the introductory elegy, which forms an overture to the love adventure, there is a longing for the beloved who gives the city its true character. This yearning is followed in the next segment by a cynical glance backward at the boredom of Weimar society, which is in turn contrasted with the first report of the developing amorous relationship. An attempt to idealize the new situation, focusing specifically on the rapidity with which Faustine gives herself, leads to the elaboration of the described experiences in the light of ancient mythological gods. Through the creation of a new goddess, "Opportunity," as a symbol for the woman he loves, Goethe effectively connects the motifs of the sequence with classical themes. The fifth elegy provides the first high point in the poetic chain with its projection of the spirit of the author's existence in Rome as a blend of antiquity, art, and the erotic, which mutually illuminate, intensify, and legitimize each other to yield a true "life of the gods." Other important sections of the cycle touch on questions of jealousy, gossip about the lovers, a Homeric idyll of the hearth, and a variety of encounters with Rome and its traditions, history, and secrets. Elegy thirteen is especially interesting for the tension that it establishes between the demands of lyric art and those of love for Faustine. A dialogue between Amor and the poet develops the idea that the former provides plenty of material for poetry but does not allow enough time for creative activity. Colorful pictures of the joys of love culminate in imagery of the couple's morning awakening together in bed. There is grand irony in the fact that the lament about not having enough time to write becomes a magnificent poem in itself.

Throughout the collection, love is the focus of polar conflicts on several levels. The intense need for unity with Faustine in the physical alliance is juxtaposed to the act of self-denial that provides the quiet enjoyment of pure observation and contemplation in the creative process. Within the social frame, the fulfilled love that is sought and attained cannot be brought into harmony with reality. Fear of discovery necessitates disguise of the beloved, deception of relatives, secret meetings, and isolation from the surrounding world. In the final elegy, however, Goethe is forced to conclude that the beautiful secret of his love cannot remain hidden for long because he himself is incapable of remaining quiet about it. The result is a many-faceted revelation of love as a timeless human situation.

Ballads

Careful examination of Goethe's most representative ballads reveals a clear progression from verse stories in which humans are at the mercy of a potentially destructive, magically powerful natural world to lyric accounts that proclaim the supremacy of the human spirit over the restrictions of mortal experience. Influenced by the popular pattern established in Gottfried August Bürger's "Lenore," Goethe's early ballads such as "Elf King" and "The Fisherman" describe the fatal resolution of inner conflicts in terms of individual surrender to seductive impressions of external reality. Later, philosophically more complex works ("The Bride of Corinth" and "The God and the Bayadere") portray death as a process of transcendence that purifies the individual while preparing the soul for joyful fulfillment on a higher plane of existence.

"Elf King" is somewhat similar to "Welcome and Farewell" in its representation of a night landscape's malevolent lure as it impresses its terror on the minds of those who encounter it. The substance of the narrative is the homeward night ride of a father and son; the darkness gives uncanny form and life to things that would appear harmless by day. The boy, who is ill with fever, believes that he hears the elf king enticing him, describes what he sees and feels to his father, and dies of fright when the older man's reassurances fail to convince him of the falseness of his delirious vision. Rhythmic language that conveys the beat of the horse's hooves through the countryside, immediacy created by dialogues involving the child, the phantom elf king, and the father, and moods evoked by contrasts between light and shadow, intimate fear and pale comfortings, all contribute to the psychological intensity of a presentation in which the poet attempted to find accurate formulation for the fantastic, indefinite problem of human destiny.

In "The God and the Bayadere," a confrontation with death is handled much differently. The legend of the prostitute who spends a night providing the pleasures of love to the god Siva in human form, only to awaken and find him dead on the bed, is a forceful lyrical statement about the redeeming properties of love. Denied her widow's rights because of her way of life, the bayadere makes good her claim by springing into the flames that arise from the funeral pyre. In response to this act of purification, Siva accepts the woman as his bride. Strong Christian overtones exist in the first stanza's emphasis on the god's humaneness and in the obvious parallels to the relationship between Christ and Mary Magdalene. The poem's thrust is that the divine spark is present even in a degraded individual and that even the lowest human being can be transformed and exalted through the cleansing influence of pure love.

West-Eastern Divan

A major key to the literary productions of Goethe's old age is found in the notion of personal fulfillment through direct sensual and spiritual enjoyment of life. The implications of that approach to experience are most thoroughly and splendidly elaborated in *West-Eastern Divan*, a carefully constructed collection of verse that attempts to blend and join the artistic legacies of East and West in a book about love in all its manifestations. Both the pinnacle of Goethe's lyric oeuvre and one of the most difficult of his creative works, *West-Eastern Divan* is a conscious declaration of the validity of humanity's unending search for joy in the world.

As revealed in the opening poem, the focal metaphor of the volume is the Hegira, which Goethe uses as an image for his flight from oppressive circumstances into the ideal realm of foreign art. Two central relationships dominate the twelve sections of his dream journey to the Orient. On one level, the individual poems are portions of a playful fantasy dialogue between Goethe and his Eastern counterpart Hafiz. The object of their interchange is a friendly competition in which the Western poet seeks to match the achievements of a revered predecessor. Conversations between two lovers, Hatem and Suleika, develop the second complex of themes, derived from elements of the love experience shared by Goethe and Marianne von Willemer.

"Buch des Sängers" ("Book of the Singer"), the most important of the first six cycles, sets the tone for the entire work. In the famous poem "Selige Sehnsucht" ("Blessed Longing"), Goethe explored the mystery of how one gains strength through the transformation that occurs as a result of sacrifice. Borrowing from a ghazel by Hafiz the motif of the soul that is consumed in the fire of love like a moth in a candle flame, he created a profound comment on the necessity of metamorphosis to eternal progress. The uniting of two people in love to generate the greatest possible joy is made to stand for the longing of the soul to be freed from the bonds of individuality through union with the infinite. The antithesis of "Blessed Longing" is presented in "Wiederfinden" ("Reunion"), a creation of extremely vivid imagery from "Buch Suleika" ("Book of Suleika"), the eighth and most beautiful section of *West-Eastern Divan*. Based on Goethe's separation from Marianne and their coming together again, the poem develops the idea that parting and rediscovery are the essence of universal existence. In a uniquely powerful projection of creation as division of light from darkness and their recombination in color, Goethe produced new and exciting symbols for love's power, rendered in lines that form a high point in German lyric poetry.

OTHER MAJOR WORKS

LONG FICTION: *Die Leiden des jungen Werthers*, 1774 (*The Sorrows of Young Werther*, 1779); *Wilhelm Meisters Lehrjahre*, 1795-1796 (4 volumes; *Wilhelm Meister's Apprenticeship*, 1825); *Die Wahlverwandtschaften*, 1809 (*Elective Affinities*, 1849); *Wilhelm Meisters Wanderjahre: Oder, Die Entsagenden*, 1821, 1829 (2 volumes; *Wilhelm Meister's Travels*, 1827).

SHORT FICTION: *Unterhaltungen deutscher Ausgewanderten*, 1795 (*Conversations of German Emigrants*, 1854); *Novelle*, 1826 (*Novel*, 1837).

PLAYS: *Götz von Berlichingen mit der eisernen Hand*, pb. 1773 (*Goetz of Berlichingen, with the Iron Hand*, 1799); *Clavigo*, pr., pb. 1774 (English translation, 1798,

1897); *Götter, Helden und Wieland*, pb. 1774; *Erwin und Elmire*, pr., pb. 1775 (libretto; music by Duchess Anna Amalia of Saxe-Weimar); *Claudine von Villa Bella*, pb. 1776 (second version pb. 1788; libretto); *Die Geschwister*, pr. 1776; *Stella*, pr., pb. 1776 (second version pr. 1806; English translation, 1798); *Iphigenie auf Tauris*, pr. 1779 (second version pb. 1787; *Iphigenia in Tauris*, 1793); *Die Laune des Verliebten*, pr. 1779 (wr. 1767; *The Wayward Lover*, 1879); *Jery und Bätely*, pr. 1780 (libretto); *Die Mitschuldigen*, pr. 1780 (first version wr. 1768, second version wr. 1769; *The Fellow-Culprits*, 1879); *Die Fischerin*, pr., pb. 1782 (libretto; music by Corona Schröter; *The Fisherwoman*, 1899); *Scherz, List und Rache*, pr. 1784 (libretto); *Der Triumph der Empfindsamkeit*, pb. 1787; *Egmont*, pb. 1788 (English translation, 1837); *Faust: Ein Fragment*, pb. 1790 (*Faust: A Fragment*, 1980); *Torquato Tasso*, pb. 1790 (English translation, 1827); *Der Gross-Cophta*, pr., pb. 1792; *Der Bürgergeneral*, pr., pb. 1793; *Was wir bringen*, pr., pb. 1802; *Die natürliche Tochter*, pr. 1803 (*The Natural Daughter*, 1885); *Pandora*, pb. 1808; *Faust: Eine Tragödie*, pb. 1808 (*The Tragedy of Faust*, 1823); *Des Epimenides Erwachen*, pb. 1814; *Faust: Eine Tragödie, zweiter Teil*, pb. 1833 (*The Tragedy of Faust, Part Two*, 1838); *Die Wette*, pb. 1837 (wr. 1812).

NONFICTION: *Von deutscher Baukunst*, 1773 (*On German Architecture*, 1921); *Versuch die Metamorphose der Pflanzen zu erklären*, 1790 (*Essays on the Metamorphosis of Plants*, 1863); *Beyträge zur Optik*, 1791, 1792 (2 volumes); *Winckelmann und sein Jahrhundert*, 1805; *Zur Farbenlehre*, 1810 (*Theory of Colors*, 1840); *Aus meinem Leben: Dichtung und Wahrheit*, 1811-1814 (3 volumes; *The Autobiography of Goethe*, 1824; better known as *Poetry and Truth from My Own Life*); *Italienische Reise*, 1816, 1817 (2 volumes; *Travels in Italy*, 1883); *Zur Naturwissenschaft überhaupt, besonders zur Morphologie*, 1817, 1824 (2 volumes); *Die Belagerung von Mainz, 1793*, 1822 (*The Siege of Mainz in the Year 1793*, 1849); *Campagne in Frankreich, 1792*, 1822 (*Campaign in France in the Year 1792*, 1849); *Essays on Art*, 1845; *Goethe's Literary Essays*, 1921.

MISCELLANEOUS: *Works*, 1848-1890 (14 volumes); *Goethes Werke*, 1887-1919 (133 volumes); *Goethe on Art*, 1980.

BIBLIOGRAPHY

Armstrong, John. *Love, Life, Goethe: Lessons of the Imagination from the Great German Poet.* New York: Farrar, Straus and Giroux, 2007. Goethe's works are analyzed and his life examined in this comprehensive volume. Armstrong discusses a wide range of Goethe's writings, including his lesser known works, and gives a close study of his personal life. Knowing German and English, he provides translations of several key passages, while keeping his writing style plain and clear. This volume offers readers a better understanding of Goethe's writing, and the circumstances that inspired it.

Atkins, Stuart. *Essays on Goethe.* Columbia, S.C.: Camden House, 1995. Essays on the apprentice novelist and other topics, by the preeminent Goethe scholar.

Boyle, Nicholas. *Goethe: The Poet and the Age, Volume I: The Poetry of Desire (1749-1790)*. Oxford, England: Clarendon Press, 1991. A monumental scholarly biography. See the index of Goethe's works.

———. *Revolution and Renunciation (1790-1803)*. Volume 2 in *Goethe: The Poet and the Age*. New York: Oxford University Press, 2000. This second volume covers only the next thirteen years of Goethe's life. Boyle's extensive discussion of the Wilhelm Meister novels and Goethe's drama *Faust* is set amid a period of radical political and social change, fallout from the French Revolution.

Kerry, Paul E. *Enlightenment Thought in the Writings of Goethe: A Contribution to the History of Ideas*. Rochester, N.Y.: Camden House, 2001. An examination of the philosophy that filled Goethe's writings. Bibliography and index.

Swales, Martin, and Erika Swales. *Reading Goethe: A Critical Introduction to the Literary Work*. Rochester, N.Y.: Camden House, 2002. A critical analysis of Goethe's literary output. Bibliography and index.

Wagner, Irmgard. *Goethe*. New York: Twayne, 1999. An excellent, updated introduction to the author and his works. Includes bibliographical references and an index.

Weisinger, Kenneth D. *The Classical Facade: A Nonclassical Reading of Goethe's Classicism*. University Park: Pennsylvania State University Press, 1988. The works covered by this interesting volume all come from the middle period of Goethe's life. In his analysis, Weisinger searches for a kinship between *Faust* and Goethe's classic works. The author asserts that all these classic works share a nonclassic common theme: the disunity of the modern world.

Williams, John R. *The Life of Goethe: A Critical Biography*. Malden, Mass.: Blackwell, 1998. An extensive examination of the major writings, including lyric poems, drama, and novels. Includes a discussion of epigrams, aphorisms, satires, libretti, and masquerades. Discusses Goethe's personal and literary reactions to historical events in Germany, his relationship with leading public figures of his day, and his influence on contemporary culture. Suggests that Goethe's creative work follows a distinct biographical profile. Includes large bibliography.

Lowell A. Bangerter

EUGEN GOMRINGER

Born: Cachuela Esperanza, Bolivia; January 20, 1925

PRINCIPAL POETRY
Konstellationen Constellations Constelaciones, 1953
33 Konstellationen, 1960
5 mal 1 Konstellation, 1960
Die Konstellationen les Constellations the Constellations los Constelaciones, 1963
Das Stundenbuch, 1965 (*The Book of Hours, and Constellations*, 1968; includes translations from *Konstellationen*)
Worte sind Schatten: Die Konstellationen, 1951-1968, 1969
Einsam Gemeinsam, 1971
Lieb, 1971
Eugen Gomringer, 1970-1972, 1973
Konstellationen, Ideogramme, Stundenbuch, 1977
Vom Rand nach innen: Die Konstellationen, 1951-1995, 1995

OTHER LITERARY FORMS

As the leading theoretician of concrete poetry in Europe, Eugen Gomringer (GAWM-rihn-gehr) has also published essays, manifestos, and lectures, including the important and provocatively titled *Poesie als Mittel der Umweltgestaltung* (1969; poetry as a means of shaping the environment). In addition, most of his theoretical texts were reprinted in his best-known collection of poems, *Worte sind Schatten*. Gomringer has also promoted the school of concrete poetry as an editor of journals and collections. In 1953, he cofounded the journal *Spirale* and served as the editor of its literary section. In 1960, he founded the Eugen Gomringer Press in Frauenfeld, Switzerland, serving as the editor for eleven issues of the journal *Konkrete Poesie/Poesia concreta*, which was published in Frauenfeld from 1960 to 1964. Gomringer has always been fascinated by nonrepresentational painters and artists whose "concrete" works he sees as being intimately connected to his own; in 1958, he edited a collection of essays in honor of the fiftieth birthday of sculptor, designer, and abstract painter Max Bill, and in 1968, he published monographs on the works of Josef Albers and Camille Graeser. He also collaborated with artists on books with "concrete" artistic themes.

ACHIEVEMENTS

In 1953, in Bern, Switzerland, Eugen Gomringer published his first concrete poems in his newly founded magazine *Spirale*, earning himself the title the "Father of Concrete Poetry." Although another group of concrete poets (the "Noigandres" group) had organized in Brazil at about the same time, Gomringer's first poems appear to have predated those of the Brazilians, and it was Gomringer's poems and theoretical texts that served as the basis for the spread of this new school in Europe. More important, Gomringer's linguistic ingenuity showed the German-speaking world that literary innovation and creativity were still possible in the aftermath of the (linguistic) destruction of the Third Reich. He demonstrated that it was perfectly legitimate, and even a matter of great urgency, to question the adequacy of the building blocks of any new literature—namely, the language itself. Gomringer was recognized for his efforts with the Punta Tragara Premio per la Poesia Concreta in 2007 and the Bavarian Order of Merit in 2008.

Gomringer's influence was enormous in Germany, Austria, and Switzerland. The experimental poet Helmut Heissenbüttel has openly admitted his indebtedness to Gomringer; indeed, the whole Stuttgart school of poets who gathered around the aesthetician Max Bense (including Heissenbüttel, Franz Mon, and Claus Bremer) would hardly have been conceivable had it not been for Gomringer's pioneering work. In Austria, the poets Friedrich Achleitner and Gerhard Rühm, who formed the nucleus of the short-lived but important neo-Dadaistic cabaret Die Wiener Gruppe (the Viennese group), were friends of Gomringer and transmitted his ideas to their own countrymen, including nonmembers of the group, such as the poets Ernst Jandl and Friederike Mayröcker. In Gomringer's own Switzerland, usually rather conservative in literary matters, his work acted as an impetus or signal for a new beginning. Although there was no Swiss concrete school as such, poetic creation, which had been in the doldrums since the end of the war, began to accelerate, and one can discern Gomringer's influence in the poems of Kurt Marti, Peter Lehner, Ernst Eggimann, Hans Schumacher, and others. Even German-speaking writers whose primary interest is prose owe a debt to Gomringer, for he taught them to experiment with language within their texts. This is not to say that any of these authors slavishly copied Gomringer's works, but they did change or alter their language so that it would more adequately confront a highly industrialized and technological society. This broad trend toward linguistic restructuring lasted about twenty years and is one of the central components of postwar German literature.

Biography

Although he was born in Bolivia, Eugen Gomringer received his secondary education in the German-speaking part of Switzerland and studied economics and art history at universities in Bern and Rome. His study of art brought him into contact with modern nonrepresentational painting, which he emulated in his first poems in the early 1950's. At a meeting in 1955 with other poets who wrote in a similar fashion, Gomringer decided to term these poems "concrete." From 1954 to 1958, he served as secretary for Bill, who was then the director of the Hochschule für Gestaltung (institute of design) in Ulm, West Germany, a descendant of the famous Bauhaus school. Bill, who was also the head of the departments of architecture and product design at the institute, was greatly affected by constructivist principles and frequently used elementary shapes with almost mathematical precision in his paintings and sculptures. Gomringer was in turn influenced by Bill's works. It was also in Ulm that Gomringer met other artists of the abstract school, such as Albers and Friedrich Vordemberge-Gildewart, as well as the influential professor of semiotics Bense and the poet Heissenbüttel.

After his stay in Ulm, Gomringer embarked on a decade of intense creative activity. He began publishing collections of the poems that he had been writing in the previous years, and he founded his own press and his own magazine, *Konkrete Poesie/Poesia concreta*, in 1960. He served as business manager for a Swiss labor organization, the Schweizerischer Werkbund, from 1962 to 1967, and he began working as a design and advertising consultant for various firms, including a large department store and (since 1967) the famous Rosenthal concern.

The 1960's marked the high point for Gomringer's creative output and for the concrete school that he had fostered. By the end of that decade, one could discern several signs indicating that the peak of the movement had passed. Instead of writing poems, Gomringer began writing monographs and essays. An *Anthology of Concrete Poetry* appeared in 1967 (edited by Emmett Williams), firmly establishing Gomringer's role in the movement, and an English translation of some of Gomringer's works appeared in 1968 (*The Book of Hours, and Constellations*, edited by Jerome Rothenberg). Gomringer published an anthology of his poems and theoretical writings in 1969 (*Worte sind Schatten*) and edited two anthologies of concrete poetry in 1972. In that same year, Gomringer made a lecture tour through South America that perhaps served as his official farewell to the concrete movement, for since then he has done little creative writing. He has devoted most of his energy to his design and advertising career and taught the theory of aesthetics at the art academy in Düsseldorf from 1976 to 1990. In 2000, he founded the Institut für Konstruktive Kunst und Konkrete Poesie in Rehau.

Analysis

Although Eugen Gomringer's principal inspiration derived from the visual arts, he was also attracted in his university years to poets who emphasized the visual aspects of their works. He admired Arno Holz, who arranged the lines of his poems symmetrically on either side of an imaginary "central axis" running down the middle of the page. He enjoyed the idiosyncratic vocabulary and typography of Stefan George, and he was fascinated by the condensed elliptical style of Stéphane Mallarmé and the typographical pictures of Guillaume Apollinaire's *Calligrammes* (1918; English translation, 1980). These affinities, along with concrete poetry's resemblance to the reductive and destructive tendencies of late expressionism and Dada, have led some scholars to see a direct link between prewar and postwar linguistic experimentation—a misleading connection, for Gomringer does not share the philosophical tenets (the search for the inner essence of humanity that lies beyond the grasp of reason) or the elements of shock and negation found in this earlier poetry. Instead, Gomringer affirms the economic recovery of postwar Europe and rejoices in technological progress. He argues that the modern industrial world requires a level of communication that is direct, simple, abbreviated, and universally intelligible. The irrationalism of the prewar years has no place in his work. In Gomringer's view, poetry today should resemble the signs in a large international airport, where travelers speaking a variety of languages must be able to find their way with a minimum of confusion. Poetry should be like contemporary advertising copy—straight to the point and easy to remember.

Gomringer chose to call his poetry "concrete" because his poems disregard the syntactical relationships of traditional verse. Isolated words are placed on a paper in such a way that the visual arrangement contributes to or even constitutes the field in which thoughts can move. The concrete poem is thus neither a statement nor a description but an assemblage of words that forms an object. That is, it is not an assertion about something, but rather its own concrete reality; it is not an abstraction from reality but a concrete object made of the reality of language. The development of this new form paralleled developments in what is generally called the "abstract" art of the first half of the twentieth century. A large group of abstract painters (Wassily Kandinsky, Paul Klee, Piet Mondrian, Hans Arp, and Kurt Schwitters, to name only a few) created aesthetic constructions that, like Gomringer's poetry, satisfy a natural desire for order. The aesthetic harmony characteristic of both the concrete poem and the abstract work of art is, however, basically different from the harmony of the natural world, and only the arrangement of the materials on the canvas or on the paper can make this harmony visible. Many of these artists claimed, too, that since they were dealing with the essential elements of reality, their paintings were not "abstract" at all but rather "concrete," much more concrete than traditional mimetic art. Theo van Doesburg wrote a manifesto in 1930 about concrete art, Bill termed an exhibit of his works in 1944 "concrete," and Kandinsky always maintained with great tenacity that his paintings were the only truly concrete works to have been created.

To call attention to the unique form of his poems, Gomringer uses the term "constellation." He defines a constellation as a grouping of a few different words on a page in such a manner that the relationship between the words does not arise through syntactic means but through the material, concrete, and spatial presence of the words themselves. Thus, the reader is permitted to select, by experimenting and playing with the text, the interpretation that suits him best. The poet establishes the field of language from which meaning will emerge, but the reader is invited—indeed, obliged—to participate in the creation of the poem. Nothing is taught, narrated, or described: The poem is an autonomous product.

Such a process points to the most radical aspect of Gomringer's oeuvre. Through a confrontation with the language of the concrete poem, Gomringer hopes, the reader will gain a new relationship to the objects of the real world, because these objects are reflected in and represented by language. These new relationships should lead to insights about the tyranny of language over thought—that is, the reader should realize that inherited language systems are no longer adequate to communicate ideas in a highly technological age and that a new universal language must be developed in order to facilitate the understanding of complex, specialized data. Concrete poetry promotes the development of this language by designing models from various languages and testing their efficacy on the global community. In this search for a universal language, he anticipated later developments in the science of linguistics, such as generative-transformational grammar and theories of universals.

Worte sind Schatten

Gomringer's most representative collection, *Worte sind Schatten*, includes examples of the four categories into which his constellations can be divided: visual constellations, or ideograms, whereby the arrangement of the words on the page constitutes the main impact of the poem; audiovisual constellations, which can be read either silently or aloud; constellations in foreign languages (Spanish, French, English, and Swiss-German); and constellations in book form, which require the reader to turn several pages to see the poem develop visually before his eyes, much like a film. The constellations in all categories generally employ a small number of words restructured or varied in the poem by means of combinations and permutations.

The visual texts have no real beginning and no real end, because words or letters are arranged on the page, not necessarily in lines, to form a linguistic picture. The eyes of the reader must roam about the page until they have grasped the poem, both words and picture, as an entity. In this category, one finds a poem that contains the numeral 4 printed several times to form the shape of the Roman numeral IV (much like some types of computer pictures), a poem in which the letters of the word "wind" are arranged in a seemingly haphazard pattern on the page, perhaps to suggest leaves being blown by the wind, and the famous "Schweigen" poem, in which the word *schweigen* (silence) is printed fourteen times to form a box on the page with a space in the middle, the "silence" of the poem. Such poems are usually tautologies, in that the "picture" is an illustration of the semantic content of the word being used.

The audiovisual constellations are for the most part printed in traditional verse form—that is, individual lines and stanzas are recognizable even though the lexicon has been greatly reduced. An example is the poem titled "Vielleicht" (perhaps):

>vielleicht baum
>baum vielleicht
>vielleicht vogel
>vogel vielleicht
>vielleicht frühling
>frühling vielleicht
>vielleicht worte
>worte vielleicht.

(The other words translate to "tree," "bird," "spring," and "words.") The poem suggests the extent to which names for things are arbitrary, imprecise, or inaccurate.

Gomringer's constellations in foreign languages are similar in structure to the audiovisual poems, leading some scholars to view both categories as only truncated imitations of traditional verse. An example is a poem in English, "You Blue," which can be interpreted, variously, as a comment on the color spectrum, on racial discrimination, or on the scale of human emotions: "you blue/ you red/ you yellow/ you black/ you white/ you."

The constellations in book form are perhaps the most innovative of Gomringer's works. An example of this type of poem is *5 mal 1 Konstellation*. Here, Gomringer prints various combinations of the words *mann* (man), *frau* (woman), *baum* (tree), *kind* (child), *hund* (dog), *vogel* (bird), *berg* (mountain), *land*, *wind*, *haus* (house), *wolke* (cloud), and *see* (sea or lake). Each word has a set position on the page, but all the words are not printed until the final page: Sometimes only an individual word appears, and at other times the words are in groups of two, three, or four. Each page is like a part of a landscape painting, and when the pages are turned, the landscape seems to come to life. In another of these book-poems, *1 Konstellation: 15*, words and letters appear and disappear within a grid of fifteen squares printed in the center of the page. When one leafs through the poem, these words and letters seem to jump and skip about, much like the figures in an animated cartoon. A final example, *The Book of Hours*, is both the most profound and the longest (forty-three pages) of the poems, and it requires the most meditation on the part of the reader. Using a minimal vocabulary of twenty-four words, such as *freude* (joy), *wort* (word), *frage* (question), *ziel* (goal), *geist* (spirit), and the possessive adjectives *mein* and *dein* (my, your), Gomringer provides the reader with a quasi dialogue consisting of almost every possible combination of these words—for example, "dein geist, mein geist"; "dein geist, mein wort"; and "dein mein geist." The poem invites religious and philosophical interpretation on many levels.

THE LIMITS OF CONCRETE POETRY

A further analysis of these and similar poems is not possible, for as Gomringer states repeatedly, his concrete poems do not make a statement about reality but are their own reality. This brings one to the central dilemma of Gomringer's work: If the concrete poem has no content or theme and reaches fruition only when the reader projects his own meaning onto it, how can the reader hope to gain new information about the technological and scientific world from it? Does not the reader only interpret the poem in the light of knowledge already present in his own consciousness? The lack of syntactic structures in the poem, which supposedly allows words to form new relationships, does not appear to be an adequate device to overcome this handicap, because the reader can never escape the traditional semantic categories assigned to the words in natural language. Thus, Harald Hartung, in his book *Experimentelle Literatur und konkrete*

Poesie, criticizes the words used in *The Book of Hours* arguing that they are but clichés taken from premodern and pretechnological nineteenth century poetry, of little value today.

Gomringer's followers (Heissenbüttel among them) recognized this predicament and attempted a more realistic solution. They reasoned that to change one's view of the world, which is filtered through language, one must change all the features of language, including syntax and morphology. Even these experiments were not successful, however, because the authors did not take into account the fact that communication must be based on some type of accepted norm. Drastic unilateral adjustments to the norm without the agreement of the other members of the language community can rarely have a tangible effect.

Gomringer's constellations have also been criticized for other reasons. It has been charged that, by avoiding social and political issues, the poems tend to affirm rather than censure the established order. Moreover, the detailed a priori theoretical matrix makes the poems elitist to a degree; the average reader, unaware of the manipulations he is "supposed to" perform, will dismiss the poems as unintelligible babblings. Finally, the reductive nature of the form is perhaps its most serious and inescapable liability: Solutions to complex contemporary problems cannot be achieved within such a simplistic format. Precisely because it offers an oversimplified aesthetic, concrete poetry still attracts a small number of practitioners, but Gomringer's more lasting legacy will be found in the work of writers who have turned his linguistic innovations to larger purposes—including writers who have no direct acquaintance with his work, who have nevertheless absorbed the critical attitude toward language that he fostered.

OTHER MAJOR WORKS

NONFICTION: *Manifeste und Darstellungen der Konkreten Poesie, 1954-1966,* 1966; *Camille Graeser,* 1968; *Josef Albers: Monographie,* 1968; *Poesie als Mittel der Umweltgestaltung,* 1969; *Der Pfeil: Spiel—Gleichnis—Kommunikation,* 1972 (with Anton and Joachim Stankowski); *Modulare und serielle Ordnungen,* 1973 (with Paul Lohse); *Konkretes von Anton Stankowski,* 1974 (with Anton Stankowski); *Theorie der konkreten Poesie,* 1997; *Zur Sache der Konkreten,* 2000.

EDITED TEXTS: *Max Bill,* 1958; *Konkrete Poesie: Deutschsprachige Autoren,* 1972; *Visuelle Poesie,* 1972.

BIBLIOGRAPHY

Dencker, Klaus Peter. "Visual Poetry, What Is It?" In *Translations: Experiments in Reading,* edited by Donald Wellman, Cola Franzen, and Irene Turner. Cambridge, Mass.: O.ARS, 1986. A comparison study of pattern poetry and concrete poetry genres, and an analysis of the theories of Gomringer.

Gumpel, Liselotte. *"Concrete" Poetry from East and West Germany.* New Haven,

Conn.: Yale University Press, 1976. A critical and historical study of experimental poetry in Germany. Includes bibliographic references and an index.

Hanson, Louise. "Is Concrete Poetry Literature?" In *Philosophy and Poetry*, edited by Peter A. French and Howard K. Wettstein. Boston, Mass.: Blackwell, 2009. Examines concrete poetry and tries to determine whether it is literature or perhaps visual art.

Linnemann, Martina E. "Concrete Poetry: A Post-War Experiment in Visual Poetry." In *Text into Image: Image into Text*, edited by Jeff Morrison and Florian Krobb. Amsterdam: Rodopi, 1997. A comparative study of the concrete poetry of Gomringer and Claus Bremer.

Melin, Charlotte, ed. *German Poetry in Transition, 1945-1990*. Hanover, N.H.: University Press of New England, 1999. This bilingual edition introduces the works of nearly one hundred poets, including Gomringer. Discusses concrete poetry and Gomringer in the introduction and presents his poem "Worte sind Schatten."

Robert Acker

GOTTFRIED VON STRASSBURG

Born: Alsace(?), Holy Roman Empire (now Alsace-Lorraine, France); flourished c. 1210
Died: Place and date unknown
Also known as: Godfrey of Strawbourg

PRINCIPAL POETRY
Tristan und Isolde, c. 1210 (*Tristan and Isolde*, 1899)

OTHER LITERARY FORMS

The only surviving works attributable to Gottfried von Strassburg (GOT-freed vawn STROS-boorg) are poems. Scholars believe Gottfried composed other poetry besides *Tristan and Isolde*, but they disagree about which surviving poems can be attributed to him. It is thought, however, that he composed several shorter works in the tradition of the *Minnesänger*, German lyric poets whose principal subject was love.

ACHIEVEMENTS

Gottfried von Strassburg is known for a single poem, but that work is one of the most significant among surviving poetry of the Middle Ages. *Tristan and Isolde* has been called the greatest courtly love poem extant. Written in an intricate style filled with irony and allusion, the poem celebrates the virtues of human love and cautions against its perils. What is particularly noteworthy is Gottfried's ability to graft onto the story of Tristan and Isolde a sophisticated commentary on the influence of love; his observations display a keen psychological insight into the nature of this human drive. Furthermore, his recurring critique of the literature of his own day suggests something about the nature of literary practice at the end of the twelfth century.

BIOGRAPHY

Little is known about Gottfried von Strassburg's life, although there is no doubt about his authorship of *Tristan and Isolde*. Contemporary sources mention "Gottfried" as the poem's author, often referring to him as "Meister" and appending "von Strassburg" to his given name. These scant details, as well as internal evidence from *Tristan and Isolde*, make it possible to reconstruct a sketch of his career. The date of Gottfried's birth is unknown, but it is thought that he was probably born in Alsace. The wide array of learning he displays in *Tristan and Isolde* suggests he was educated in the classics, rhetoric, literature, music, and possibly law and theology. He was probably not a nobleman, but instead was a member of the patrician class of bureaucrats that handled administrative tasks in the city of Strassburg, which in the twelfth century was a growing urban center on the Rhine River. The date of Gottfried's death is also uncertain, but scholars have been able to determine the date of composition of *Tristan and Isolde* to be around 1210. Because the poem remained unfinished—all of the thirty surviving manuscript versions break off in the middle of the tale—consensus among scholars is that Gottfried died before he could complete it.

Analysis

Like most medieval poets, Gottfried von Strassburg chose to adapt existing works rather than invent new ones. Whether a poem was composed for oral recitation or reading, it was considered good form for poets to take a story already familiar to their audience as their subject and embellish it, demonstrating their artistry by rhetorical flourish or new thematic interpretations. For example, the "matter of Britain"—largely stories dealing with King Arthur—was retold and reinterpreted frequently. Similarly, the story of Tristan and Isolde had existed in many versions for hundreds of years before Gottfried decided to make it the subject of his long romance. The tale has its origins in Celtic folklore and became part of the medieval romance tradition sometime during the eleventh or twelfth centuries. As is evident in Gottfried's *Tristan and Isolde* and other versions of the story, details of Tristan's life and adventures have parallels in the Arthurian tradition; later writers, especially Sir Thomas Malory in *Le Morte d'Arthur* (1485), go to great lengths to integrate the story into the Arthurian cycle. The story of Tristan and Isolde is emblematic of the courtly love tradition: A handsome, noble, highly skilled knight falls hopelessly in love with a woman he can never marry, and she often returns his affection. What might in other ages be considered either tragic or immoral becomes, in the hands of skilled medieval poets such as Gottfried, a noble passion that, in extreme cases, is held up as an ideal with religious overtones.

Tristan and Isolde

Relying principally on the version of the legend presented in the work of Thomas of Britain (twelfth century), Gottfried re-creates the story of Tristan in Middle High German, using rhyming couplets as his basic poetic form. His unfinished work extends for approximately twenty thousand lines. A prologue written in quatrains provides a moralizing commentary on human behavior that also serves to recognize Gottfried's patron, Dieterich, whose name is spelled out in the first letters of a succession of stanzas. Gottfried begins the narrative proper with the story of Tristan's parents, relates Tristan's life as an orphan, and describes the exploits that eventually take him to the court where Isolde resides. His lengthy description of the effect of a love potion drunk by Tristan and Isolde on their way to the court of Tristan's uncle King Mark, where Isolde is to become Mark's bride, is followed by episodes describing the lovers' efforts to pursue their passion without discovery, their brief interlude of undisturbed bliss in the Cave of Lovers, and Tristan's banishment from Mark's court.

Despite his reliance on previous versions of the Tristan legend for details of his story, the originality of Gottfried's work is undeniable. Even a cursory reading reveals his familiarity with matters of law, hunting, poetry, and classical literature. Gottfried uses his wide knowledge to invest his poem with gravitas. Furthermore, a significant difference between Gottfried's account of the Tristan legend and those of Thomas of Britain and other poets is his focus on the interior lives of the characters. Although the poem shares with other romances a certain episodic quality and contains sections of narrative describing the actions of the hero in combat, most of Gottfried's work concentrates on the feelings of the lovers as they try to understand what is happening to them. Additionally, the poet uses the structure of his work to reinforce his thematic aims: Scenes and characters are carefully balanced so that readers are able to see Gottfried's commentary on love unfold in all its complexity. The sense of cause and effect generated by the poem gives it affinities to modern fiction.

Thematically the poem can be described as an extended commentary on the conflict between love and duty. Tristan and Isolde share a perfect love, but one that cannot be enjoyed openly, since both have other obligations—Tristan as Mark's vassal and kinsman, Isolde as Mark's wife. The poem explores in great detail the nature of passionate, human love, finding it to be filled with conflicts that can drive a devoted lover to the brink of madness. The strange coexistence of pleasure and pain in the love relationship is what intrigues Gottfried most, and throughout the poem, he gives numerous examples of the way love makes Tristan and Isolde alternately blissful or despondent. The contrasting emotions generated by love are paralleled in the poem by a number of other contrasts. For example, Tristan is both a loyal knight and an inveterate liar, while Isolde is a paean of virtue and a continual source of temptation (both for her husband and her lover). *Tristan and Isolde* celebrates courtly love as superior to the knightly virtues that the hero also possesses. Gottfried emphasizes this distinction by the relative length of his accounts of Tristan's exploits as a lover and a fighter: The scenes of love are described in detail and often interrupted with more generalized commentary on the nature of love itself, while those in which Tristan demonstrates his skills as a fighter are often glossed over.

Gottfried uses a number of literary devices to call attention to his principal themes. Notable among them is his use of irony. Often what seems to be a good act has unintended consequences. Sometimes Tristan and Isolde are the beneficiaries of these ironic occurrences, at other times they suffer from them. Several critics have suggested that Gottfried is ahead of his time in employing symbolism in his tale, for example in using light and dark imagery to suggest the contrast between the purity of his fated lovers with the sordid behavior of those who would expose them to King Mark. Gottfried makes frequent use of reification, describing human emotions and actions such as love, jealousy, deceit, or surveillance as if they were active agents working on behalf of or against the interests of his protagonists. Most notable among these is his depiction of Love, which is frequently described as a huntsman, a falconer, or a physician. There is a strong implication that Love is capable of conquering men and women and holding them in thrall, much as a medieval lord might control his subjects who have no power to escape his clutches.

Gottfried also employs allegory, a common medieval device, most notably in his lengthy allegorical description of the Cave of Lovers, the sylvan grotto where the lovers retreat after Mark banishes them both from court. For a brief time, Tristan and Isolde live in this ideal retreat, needing only each other's company for sustenance. The physical properties of the cave—its ceiling, windows, door, and bedchamber—are equated to the properties of love—constancy, integrity, simplicity, kindness, good breeding, humility, and, above all, honor. In some ways the Cave of Lovers is like the Garden of Eden, where innocence prevails. Such a reading helps justify Gottfried's evident approval of Tristan and Isolde and his condemnation of the world outside the cave, where everyone is intent on destroying their happiness. This notion is reinforced by his portrayal of Mark's passion for his wife as purely sensual, while Tristan's seems to rise above the purely physical level.

Certainly the most important literary device used in the poem, and the one that has generated the most critical controversy, is the love potion. Gottfried makes no attempt to deny the literal power of the potion to imbue Tristan and Isolde with undying passion. Once they drink the potion, they are powerless to escape its effects. A more modern reading of the poem would suggest that the potion is intended as a visible symbol of the emotion it engenders. This reading seems to be borne out by the fact that Gottfried centers his interest on the lovers' feelings and takes great pains to describe their interior lives. When he does recount their efforts to deceive King Mark or others, he almost always includes some description of the inner drive that motivates their deception.

Finally, Gottfried inserts a number of digressions or "excursions" in which he builds up a special relationship with his readers. On more than one occasion, he mentions that his work is intended for those discerning readers who can understand the curious and complex nature of love—that is, those who would appreciate the courtly love tradition that he celebrates in the poem. In extended comments on the nature of literature, he offers a critique of contemporary writers in which he praises a number of them and demeans his chief rival, Wolfram von Eschenbach, author of the highly popular romance *Parzival* (c. 1200-1210; English translation, 1894). Gottfried's recurrent comments are a veiled argument that he should be regarded as a major literary figure, a claim that history has certainly accorded him.

Bibliography
Batts, Michael S. *Gottfried von Strassburg*. New York: Twayne, 1971. Provides an overview of the Tristan legend, a critical reading of Gottfried's poem, analysis of his style, and a synopsis of other interpretations of the work.

Bekker, Hugo. *Gottfried von Strassburg's "Tristan": Journey Through the Realms of Eros.* Rochester, N.Y.: Camden House, 1987. Detailed reading of the poem, focusing on the narrator's asides, interruptions, and excursions, which Bekker argues help focus on one of Gottfried's main purposes, to illustrate the journey through the various aspects of human love.

Chinca, Mark. *Gottfried von Strassburg: "Tristan."* New York: Cambridge University Press, 1997. Provides a summary of the poem, commentary on its structure and relationship to the Tristan tradition, critical analysis, and details about the original manuscript and scholarly editions.

Hasty, Will, ed. *A Companion to Gottfried von Strassburg's "Tristan."* Rochester, N.Y.: Camden House, 2003. Twelve essays discussing the artistry, themes, and critical reception of the poem; several examine the poem's relationship to other medieval literary works.

Hatto, A. T. "Introduction." *Gottfried von Strassburg: "Tristan."* Rev. ed. New York: Penguin Books, 1967. Discusses the major themes of the work and problems involved in translating Gottfried's medieval German into English; this volume includes the best modern English translation of the poem.

Jackson, W. T. H. *The Anatomy of Love: The "Tristan" of Gottfried von Strassburg.* New York: Columbia University Press, 1971. Extended analysis discussing the intellectual background, poetic structure, and use of language in conveying what Jackson believes is a countercultural view of love for Gottfried's age.

MacDonald, William C. *Arthur and Tristan: On the Intersection of Legends in German Medieval Literature.* Lewiston, N.Y.: Edwin Mellen, 1991. Explores parallels between the Tristan story and Arthurian legends in the work of Gottfried and other medieval German writers.

Sneeringer, Kristine. *Honor, Love, and Isolde in Gottfried's "Tristan."* New York: Peter Lang, 2002. Examines the concept of honor as it was understood by Gottfried's audience; explains how the poet uses structural devices to highlight the transcendent quality of love.

Laurence W. Mazzeno

HARTMANN VON AUE

Born: Swabia (now in Germany); c. 1160-1165
Died: Swabia (now in Germany); c. 1210-1220
Also known as: Hartmann von Ouwe

PRINCIPAL POETRY
Die Klage, c. 1180 (*The Lament*, 2001)
Erek, c. 1190 (*Erec*, 1982)
Gregorius, c. 1190-1197 (English translation, 1955, 1966)
Iwein, c. 1190-1205 (*Iwein: The Knight with the Lion*, 1979)
Der arme Heinrich, c. 1195 (English translation, 1931)
Arthurian Romances, Tales, and Lyric Poetry: The Complete Works of Hartmann von Aue, 2001

OTHER LITERARY FORMS

Although all extant works by Hartmann von Aue (HORT-mon vawn OW-uh) are in verse form, scholars have been tempted to consider the courtly epics *Erec*, *Iwein*, *Gregorius*, and *Der arme Heinrich* as prototypes of modern prose forms such as the novella and the novel. Nevertheless, Hartmann is first and foremost an epic poet. Because he and his contemporaries drew no such generic distinctions, neither shall this survey.

ACHIEVEMENTS

In *The Emergence of German as a Literary Language* (2d ed., 1978), Eric Blackall describes the development of "an uncouth language into one of the most subtle literary media of modern Europe," attaining respectability, however, only after 1700. Blackall implies here that until the eighteenth century, German literature was essentially derivative, struggling to define itself in the presence of other, highly developed European languages and literatures. Seen in this light, the modest oeuvre of Hartmann von Aue—often topically repetitive and linguistically naïve by modern standards—can be appreciated for its true worth: as a giant stride toward vernacular poetry of the highest stature.

Hartmann's language is a model of consistency and moderation. His sentences are clearly constructed, his rhymes are natural and unaffected, and his mastery of various verse forms is assured. His was a poetry of reflection and reason, and he frequently employed devices that clarified the theme for his audience, particularly parallelism and contrasting imagery. In his verse, he presented problematic situations that would be of interest and application to a broad audience, avoiding bizarre plots that would defeat his didactic purposes. The same concerns are reflected in his language: Hartmann pruned outdated expressions, dialect words, and foreign phrases in favor of a language accessible to a broader geographical audience. In this respect, Hartmann anticipated Martin Luther's efforts to promote a standard German language. Finally, Hartmann is credited with introducing the Arthurian romance in Germany.

For his innovations in style, form, and language, Hartmann was respected by his contemporaries, honored by patron and audience alike, and frequently imitated by his colleagues. With Wolfram von Eschenbach and Gottfried von Strassburg, Hartmann is regarded as one of the three literary trendsetters of his age—at once exemplary and inimitable.

Perhaps of greater significance than his stylistic innovations, however, was the attitude that Hartmann brought to his works. His personal experiences and reflections are presented in a serious, contemplative mood, ennobling both the man and his writing. Furthermore, an earnest involvement with the social and moral issues of his society are hallmarks of his poetry. Hartmann's thoughtful treatment of the tensions existing between society and religious devotion illuminated one of the most enduring concerns for German culture, a concern mirrored in works of later authors as diverse as Hans Jakob Christoffel von Grimmelshausen, the Brothers Grimm, and Thomas Mann.

Hartmann's popularity and literary success resulted in part from his attempts to unify form and content. He constantly strove to make his language appropriate to the experiences and emotions described in the text. The tales themselves, of Erec and Iwein, of Gregorius and Heinrich, were certainly not extraordinary for his time; many of his contemporaries created more adventurous, more bizarre stories to captivate their audiences. Hartmann, however, was able to engage his listeners in a more intellectual fashion, by stating problems inherent in his society and by examining them thoughtfully and intelligently, so that the listener understood their import for his or her own life.

Biography

As is the case with many medieval poets, documentary evidence attesting the life and deeds of Hartmann von Aue is sparse. The few tantalizing clues that have survived have become the topic of continuing scholarly debate and controversy. From brief statements within the works of Hartmann and his fellow courtly poets, from contemporary events, and from astute speculation, a plausible biography has been established. Hartmann's birth date, for example, can be surmised only by backdating—that is, by assuming that his earliest work was composed at approximately the age of twenty. Thus, since the first work attributable to Hartmann appeared around 1180, he was probably born between 1160 and 1165. His noble appellation "von Aue" indicates that he lived in the German territory known as Swabia, located in present-day Germany. From the introduction to *Der arme Heinrich*, in which Hartmann describes himself as "learned"—that is, able to read Latin (and presumably French)—one can assume that he enjoyed an education, most likely in a monastery school. As an adult, Hartmann became an unpropertied knight in the administrative service of a noble lord.

Hartmann's earliest works convey his involvement in courtly society and its chivalric conventions, but his failure at *Minne* (courtly love), the death of his beloved lord and patron, and his eventual participation in a Crusade reflect a gradual but fundamental change in his life. Hartmann forsook the conventions of *Minne* and his role as *Minnesinger*, placing himself in the service of Christ and composing instead songs of the Crusades and of renunciation. Although *Iwein* appears to have been the last secular work that Hartmann wrote, scholars now believe that this work was merely the completion of an earlier commission and thus does not accurately reflect Hartmann's mature stance. There is no evidence that Hartmann wrote anything during the last ten or more years of his life. The date and circumstances of his death remain a mystery to this day. Poets of the time implied that Hartmann was still living in 1210, but by 1220 he was mentioned as being among the deceased.

Analysis

The period of courtly love poetry presents several insoluble problems for the modern reader. Little is known of the poets as individuals, of the circumstances in which their songs were created and performed, or of the melodies that accompanied the songs. Few manuscripts survive, and these were often copied down generations after the fact; by the time individual songs were committed to parchment, deviations from the original text were inevitable. These factors impose limits on any analysis of Hartmann von Aue's poetry. Although his surviving works are few in number—sixteen songs and five works of substantial length—they are rich in variety, reflecting his changing concerns and the gradual refinement of his style.

The Lament

The earliest work attributable to Hartmann is *The Lament*, a relatively youthful attempt at conventional courtly poetry. The title is somewhat misleading, for the content clearly represents disputation or rational debate. Here a young knight, unsuccessful in courtly love, engages the service of his "body" and "heart" to clarify their roles in this delicate struggle. This didactic piece, clearly a product of reflection and not of immediate personal suffering, recommends traditional chivalric qualities such as discipline, loyalty, and dependability; moderation and modesty; striving and denial. In spite of its relative superficiality and clumsy logic, *The Lament* represents the first rational clarification of the redemptive and civilizing qualities required by courtly society. Hartmann's goal here was no less than to determine those qualities that allow the individual to find favor in the eyes of God and of other people. This question and the contemplative search for an appropriate answer characterize Hartmann's entire oeuvre.

In the same period in which he wrote *The Lament*, Hartmann composed the first of his courtly love songs. These earliest poems also uncritically propagated the chivalric qualities necessary for attaining the favor of a noble lady, though Hartmann soon demonstrated his unwillingness to feign joy over the pains of unrequited love. Later poems reflected a greater sorrow that had befallen Hartmann—the death of his lord and patron. The poet had mentioned his failure to win the favor of a particular lady, but that was only a temporary disappointment when compared to the loss of his lord. (Although more recent scholarship questions the sincerity of the singer-patron relationship, suggesting that the poet's expression of gratitude was purely conventional, Hartmann was doubtless loyal and grateful to his patron. Obviously, the death of his lord had a lasting effect on Hartmann's life and thus on his poetry.)

In any case, Hartmann's failure in love prompted him to assess his position. While not questioning the conventions of courtly society in general or of courtly love in particular, Hartmann did come to the realization that he himself was not suited to such *Minne* service. As he wrote at the time: "True joy is never having loved." He was too honorable to place blame on the lady in question, reserving all culpability for himself. In truth, Hartmann was not made for such a contest. The protest against his personal suffering eventually grew into a denial of courtly love, couched in a typically objective critique. Hartmann no longer praised this idealized, unrequited love, celebrating instead a mutually harmonious relationship with a woman of less than noble stature beyond the stifling bounds of the court. At the same time, this shift in Hartmann's attitude toward courtly love was motivated by an intense spiritual reorientation: For the salvation of his and his patron's souls, Hartmann joined a Crusade, creating songs of dignified devotion as a religious stimulus to others of his class. These changes in Hartmann's outlook took place only gradually, and their development can be traced in his works.

Erec

Hartmann's *Erec* is German literature's first Arthurian romance, a genre that has retained its popularity to this day. Though Hartmann relied on an earlier work by Chrétien de Troyes for his source, he should not be accused of plagiarism: In the Middle Ages, it was assumed that authors would choose their themes from an established collection of plots; true *inventio*, or originality, appeared in the manner of presentation. One noticeable innovation in Hartmann's version is the role of the narrator; actual dialogue is subordinated to the third-person narrative, in which an objective distance from event and character is achieved.

While Chrétien had described the successes of a mature hero, Hartmann's story begins with an impetuous youth. Overwhelmed by his passion for the beautiful Enite, Erec ignores his obligations as knight and ruler, thus bringing dishonor on himself, his court, and his land. He can regain his honor only by renewed, mature striving within the dictates of courtly society; by doing precisely that, he, too, gains personally through a more mature and balanced relationship with his wife. Their love nurtures the well-being that now permeates their entire sphere of influence.

Hartmann's young Erec has failed abysmally and must undergo a lengthy and painful process of maturation, until he can prove himself worthy of being the leader of a court and the ruler of a kingdom. The major tension in this work is provided by the concepts of personal and social love. Personal, possessive love (that is, passion) must not prove destructive to the greater good represented by a harmonious, integrated society. The prevailing motif of beauty is subtly compared and contrasted to substantiate this point: Sensual beauty is destructive, for it lures the knight to thoughts and deeds of sexual excess, but beauty can also be the outward manifestation of inner harmony, as exemplified by Enite and the lovely ladies at King Arthur's court. Hartmann explores these conflicts to demonstrate how the individual can enjoy his personal life while remaining a constructive member of society.

Symmetrically placed episodes reinforce this theme: Erec's immature adventures at the outset of the work are paralleled by his mature successes at the conclusion. In tracing the development of the titular hero from a self-centered youth to a responsible ruler, Hartmann reminded his contemporaries of the responsibilities of the individual knight to others and to society as a whole; Hartmann saw the courtly social code calcifying into a set of rules for membership in an exclusive club.

IWEIN

Hartmann's *Iwein*, based on yet another tale by Chrétien, examines the responsibilities of the knight from a different point of view. Unlike Erec, Iwein is overly concerned with acquiring honor and, from a sense of rampant egoism, neglects equally important chivalric imperatives. Iwein is persuaded to leave his wife for a year (lest he end like Erec) to participate in jousting tournaments and adventures and thereby accumulate more honor. Iwein becomes so self-centered that he fails to return home at the end of the year's time and is consequently condemned before Arthur's court as unfaithful, having betrayed his wife's and society's trust. The accusation strikes Iwein so forcefully that he goes mad and lives in the wilderness as a wild man. Only through a number of painful learning experiences does he gradually regain his senses, his honor, his wife, and his position in society. The lion mentioned in the subtitle serves to accent the importance of loyalty; Iwein rescues a lion, which then becomes his faithful companion, truly a "noble" beast. The errant Iwein is also treated with kindness by others until he can learn to reciprocate their goodness unselfishly. In stages, Iwein learns loyalty, kindness, and consideration for others, and his selfless service is rewarded with honor and salvation.

From the large number of surviving manuscripts, it is evident that *Iwein* was Hartmann's most popular work. In recognition of its important theme and stylistic excellence, modern scholars have frequently referred to it as the classical work of the high courtly period. Nevertheless, *Iwein* is a problematic work, for it appears to have been written at widely separated intervals. The first one thousand lines exhibit characteristics of Hartmann's middle period, around 1190, while the remainder of the work is composed in a mature yet detached style. Scholars speculate that the work was commissioned while Hartmann was still involved in courtly service and attempting to accommodate himself to its demands; after a lengthy interruption, during which time Hartmann had disengaged himself from *Minne* conventions, he returned to the manuscript to fulfill, albeit mechanically, the commission. Since *Iwein* still accepts the precepts of courtly society unquestioningly, one can scarcely consider it as Hartmann's definitive statement on the subject, especially in the light of his mature personal convictions and the discrepancy in style. It is a tribute to Hartmann's artistry that he could complete such a work "mechanically" yet produce one of the most popular epics of the High Middle Ages.

Gregorius

Gregorius, Hartmann's courtly legend of the life of a fictive pope, was based on a contemporary French source, *Vie du Pape Gregoire*. Despite its explicit references to Sophocles' *Oidipous Tyrannos* (c. 429 B.C.E.; *Oedipus Tyrannus*, 1715), *Gregorius* is an ingenious mixture of Asian and Occidental mythology and folklore, although Hartmann's version features a distinctly Christian accent with its traditional progression of innocence, sin and downfall, contrition, penance, and salvation. The plot itself is at once fascinating and convoluted. The devil succeeds in blinding two noble children, so that the brother seduces his own sister. The brother then dies on a pilgrimage, while the sister secretly nurses the child of the incestuous relationship. The child is set adrift at sea, accompanied only by a tablet on which is inscribed a message that explains his origin and begs that he pray for his parents' salvation. The foundling is raised by foster parents, educated at a monastery school, and named after the local abbot, Gregorius. All goes well until an argument reveals to the young man his parents' shame. Despite the Abbot's insistence that his namesake is predestined for the priesthood, young Gregorius flees to take up an adventuresome life as a knight. In his first encounter with the outside world, Gregorius frees a beleaguered city and claims the widowed queen as his bride. In all innocence, Gregorius has married his own mother, thus heaping incest upon incest. He now flees again, in complete despair. Taken to a remote island, he is chained to a rock, and the key to his bonds is thrown into the sea; thus, Gregorius spends the next seventeen years in bondage and isolation. In the meantime, a successor to the deceased pope is sought. The name of Gregorius appears in a dream to the electors, and two papal legates are dispatched to locate this holy man; they are led to the island, where, miraculously, the key to Gregorius's chains is found in the belly of a fish. Soon, the fame of the new pope draws the incestuous queen to Rome, in the hope of gaining absolution from her sins. Gregorius and his mother immediately recognize each other and are reunited and absolved of their mutual burden. The tale closes with an epilogue reminding the audience that all sins can be expiated through contrition and penance.

Aside from the titillating motif of incest, this work offers its audience several moral considerations to ponder: Is Gregorius somehow responsible for the sins of his parents?

Should he be punished for unwittingly and unwillingly becoming a participant in incest himself? Despite the folklore surrounding such "sins," the Church of Hartmann's day would have considered neither of these sins to be culpable. As several scholars have indicated, Gregorius's actual transgression is against himself and his God. In agreement with the mother's original request, the Abbot had insisted that the youth devote his life to prayer for his parents' salvation; Gregorius's defection was thus a betrayal of his sacred duty. In choosing to sally forth as a knight in search of adventure, courtly love, and honor—duties required of the chivalric class—he was placing personal gratification and *superbia* (ego or self) before his obligation to others and to his God.

In criticizing Gregorius for his blind devotion to *Minne* and honor, Hartmann was in fact questioning the entire structure of courtly society. He showed that the arch virtues mentioned above could lead to sin and downfall, and could be expiated only through a long and horrible penance such as that which Gregorius suffered, chained to his island rock. To be sure, Hartmann did not completely undermine the values inherent in the courtly system, but he did expose them as less than absolutes. Even supposedly courtly virtues can be tools of the devil to tempt innocents from their divinely chosen paths. It is significant that a story that begins badly in worldly society can end happily in the religious seclusion of Rome. This qualified renunciation of the profane in favor of the sacred was the most pronounced development in Hartmann's life and found its poetic culmination in the songs he composed for the Crusades.

DER ARME HEINRICH

Der arme Heinrich, in its own time perhaps the least appreciated of Hartmann's works (if the small number of surviving manuscripts is any indication), has ironically become the most popular. Scarcely fifteen hundred lines in length, it has been considered the prototype of the modern German novella. It was the poem's treatment of its theme, however, and not its formal aspect, that made it revolutionary in Hartmann's day. Heinrich is the epitome of a medieval nobleman. He possesses all the knightly virtues; he enjoys riches and honor, power and fame. Suddenly and inexplicably, he is struck down by leprosy, the most odious illness imaginable. The man who was once the ideal of social virtue is now cast out by that very society, for his beauty has turned to ugliness, his honor to dishonor, his fame to infamy. In search of a medical cure for his affliction, Heinrich travels first to Montpellier and then to Salerno, but he learns that he can be saved only by the blood from the heart of a pure maiden. In despair, Heinrich retires to the country, where he is welcomed and nursed by a family of loyal tenants. The daughter is especially drawn to Heinrich and asks why he has been so cursed. His answer is that he had been a worldly fool, accepting happiness and success as his just reward and not as a sign of God's grace.

Just as Heinrich had been obsessed with his worldly possessions, the daughter becomes equally fanatic in her desire to die for his salvation. In extended discussions with her parents, the girl proclaims her desire to depart this life. Eventually, Heinrich accedes to her wishes, and they leave for Salerno, but at the moment the doctor is about to make the initial incision, Heinrich glimpses the beautiful girl and experiences a change of heart. He releases the girl unharmed, knowing that he cannot accept such a sacrifice and must reconcile himself to living the remainder of his life as a leper. The girl, however, is in despair and curses Heinrich for depriving her of escape from this world. At this point, both are miraculously "cured" through God's mercy: Heinrich is restored to a youthful state of good health and beauty, while the girl regains a healthy desire to live out her life on Earth, as Heinrich's wife. Together, they live a full and happy life before entering Heaven.

In this didactic tale, Hartmann again warned of the dangers of *superbia*, of selfishly living only for worldly goals or of selfishly desiring a premature death. Both Heinrich and the girl must learn to live in this world while still recognizing the divine scheme of things. This moral was directly aimed at the courtly society of which Heinrich is representative. With his unrestrained and unquestioning appreciation for worldly values, Heinrich fails to realize that all things come from God: Heinrich's successes, his suffering, and his ultimate salvation are all the result of God's grace. That Heinrich must overcome the courtly values as limitations, that he marries a girl beneath his social standing, that he lives out the remainder of his life far from court—these developments would have seemed foreign to a courtly audience and as such were obviously viewed as unwelcome provocations. This would account for the contemporary reception of Hartmann's text.

BIBLIOGRAPHY

Fiddy, Andrea. *The Presentation of the Female Characters in Hartmann's "Gregorius" and "Der arme Heinrich."* Göppingen, Germany: Kümmerle, 2004 . Fiddy's work provides a feminist analysis through its examination of women characters in *Gregorius* and *Der arme Heinrich*.

Gentry, Francis G., ed. *A Companion to the Works of Hartmann von Aue*. Rochester, N.Y.: Camden House, 2005. A scholarly collection of essays covering a wide range of topics on Hartmann von Aue's works. Includes bibliography and index.

Hasty, Will. *Adventures in Interpretation: The Works of Hartmann von Aue and Their Critical Reception*. Columbia, S.C.: Camden House, 1996. A survey of criticism of Hartmann von Aue's work from the Enlightenment to postmodernism, which concludes that the interpretations by modern readers have been shaped mainly by critical trends.

Jackson, W. H. *Chivalry in Twelfth-Century Germany: The Works of Hartmann von Aue*. Rochester, N.Y.: D. S. Brewer, 1994. A study of Hartmann von Aue's poetic representation of knighthood and chivalric values with consideration of historical, literary, and linguistic influences.

Jackson, W. H., and S. A. Ranawake, eds. *The Arthur of the Germans: The Arthurian Legend in Medieval German and Dutch Literature.* Cardiff: University of Wales Press, 2000. A group of essays includes chapters on the emergence of the German Arthurian romance.

Pincikowski, Scott E. *Bodies of Pain: Suffering in the Works of Hartmann von Aue.* New York: Routledge, 2002. Pincikowski argues that the ideological system that informs courtly life causes suffering in both the physical body and the social body of the court.

Resler, Michael. Introduction to *Hartmann von Aue: "Erec."* Philadelphia: University of Pennsylvania Press, 1987. An extensive introduction including general historical and cultural background, specific information on the life of Hartmann, a discussion of Arthurian romance, and a full consideration of the sources, structure, and thematic issues of this work. This volume also contains a translation of *Erec* plus explanatory endnotes. Includes helpful selected bibliography, although the majority of the references are to sources in German.

Sullivan, Robert G. *Justice and the Social Context of Early Middle High German Literature.* New York: Routledge, 2001. A history of the Holy Roman Empire hinging on an examination of High German literature and its authors' focus on social, political, and spiritual issues during a time of transformation. Bibliographical references, index.

Thomas, J. W. Introduction to *Hartmann von Aue: "Erec."* Lincoln: University of Nebraska Press, 1982. Includes information on Hartmann's life and works, as well as the theme, plot structure, motifs, and style of the translated work. Explanatory notes at the end provide bibliographical information on each of these topics. A readable translation of the text follows.

———. Introduction to *Hartmann von Aue: "Iwein."* Lincoln: University of Nebraska Press, 1979. An informative introduction with an overview of Hartmann's works and discussions of the theme of *Iwein*, structure and motifs, and the narrative style. Notes include important bibliographical references as well as helpful information. The translation included in this volume is very readable.

Todd C. Hanlin

HEINRICH HEINE

Born: Düsseldorf, Prussia (now in Germany); December 13, 1797
Died: Paris, France; February 17, 1856
Also known as: Christian Johann Heinrich Heine

PRINCIPAL POETRY
Gedichte, 1822 (*Poems*, 1937)
Tragödien, nebst einem lyrischen Intermezzo, 1823 (*Tragedies, Together with Lyric Intermezzo*, 1905)
Buch der Lieder, 1827 (*Book of Songs*, 1856)
Deutschland: Ein Wintermärchen, 1844 (*Germany: A Winter's Tale*, 1892)
Neue Gedichte, 1844 (8 volumes; *New Poems*, 1858)
Atta Troll, 1847 (English translation, 1876)
Ein Sommernachtstraum, 1847 (*A Midsummer Night's Dream*, 1876)
Romanzero, 1851 (English translation, 1859)
Gedichte, 1851-1857 (4 volumes; *Poems*, 1937)
Letzte Gedichte und Gedanken, 1869 (*Last Poems and Thoughts*, 1937)
Atta Troll, and Other Poems, 1876 (includes *Atta Troll* and *A Midsummer Night's Dream*)
Heinrich Heine: The Poems, 1937
The Complete Poems of Heinrich Heine, 1982

OTHER LITERARY FORMS

Although Heinrich Heine (HI-nuh) is best remembered for his verse, he also made significant contributions to the development of the feuilleton and the political essay in Germany. Experiments with prose accelerated his rise to fame as a writer. Among the most important of his nonfiction works are *Reisebilder* (1826-1831; *Pictures of Travel*, 1855), a series of witty essays that are spiced with poetic imagination and penetrating social commentary; *Zur Geschichte der neueren schönen Litteratur in Deutschland* (1833; *Letters Auxiliary to the History of Modern Polite Literature in Germany*, 1836), which was later republished and expanded as *Die romantische Schule* (1836; *The Romantic School*, 1876) and constitutes Heine's personal settlement with German Romanticism; *Französische Zustände* (1833; *French Affairs*, 1889), a collection of sensitive newspaper articles about the contemporary political situation in France; and *Vermischte Schriften* (1854), a group of primarily political essays.

Heine's attempts to create in other genres were unsuccessful. During his student years in Berlin, he began a novel, *Der Rabbi von Bacherach* (1887; *The Rabbi of Bacherach*, 1891), but it remained a fragment. Two dramas, *Almansor* and *William*

Heinrich Heine
(Library of Congress)

Ratliff, published in *Tragedies, Together with Lyric Intermezzo*, failed on the stage, although *William Ratliff* was later employed by Pietro Mascagni as the basis of an opera.

Achievements

Second only to Johann Wolfgang von Goethe in impact on the history of German lyric poetry in the nineteenth century, Heinrich Heine was unquestionably the most controversial poet of his time. He was a major representative of the post-Romantic literary crisis and became the most renowned love poet in Europe after Petrarch, yet for decades he was more celebrated abroad than in Germany. Anti-Semitism and negative reactions to his biting satire, to his radical inclinations, and to his seemingly unpatriotic love of France combined to prevent any consistent approbation in Heine's homeland. Nevertheless, he became the first Jewish author to break into the mainstream of German literature in modern times.

Heine's poetic reputation is based primarily on *Book of Songs*, which went through twelve editions during his lifetime. The collection achieved immediate popularity with the public and was well received by critics; since 1827, it has been translated into more than fifty languages. Lyrics that became part of the *Book of Songs* were set to music as early as 1822, and within a year after the book appeared, Franz Schubert used six poems from the "Heimkehr" ("Homecoming") section in his famous cycle *Schwanengesang* (1828; "Swan Song"). Robert Schumann's *Dichterliebe* (1840; love poems) features musical settings for sixteen poems from *Tragedies, Together with Lyric Intermezzo*. By 1840, Heine's works had become prime texts for German songs. In all, more than three thousand pieces of music have been written for the creations of Heine's early period.

In 1835, four years after he went into self-imposed exile in France, Heine's works were banned in Germany, along with the writings of the social reform and literary movement Junges Deutschland (Young Germany). The critics rejected him as a bad influence on Germany's youth. His immediate popularity waned as conflicts with government censors increased. In the late nineteenth century, attempts to reclaim his works for German literature touched off riots, yet by then his enchanting lyrics had become so ingrained in German culture that it was impossible to expel them. The measure of Heine's undying significance for German poetry is perhaps the fact that even the Nazis, who formally prohibited his works once again, could not exclude his poems completely from their anthologies of songs.

Biography

Heinrich Heine was born Chaim Harry Heine, the son of a Jewish merchant. He spent his early years working toward goals set for him by his family. His secondary education ended in 1814 when he left the Düsseldorf Lyceum without being graduated. After failing in two apprenticeships in Frankfurt, he was sent to Hamburg to prepare for a career in commerce under the direction of a wealthy uncle. While there, he fell in love with his cousin Amalie. This unfulfilled relationship was a stimulus for verse that the young poet published in a local periodical. In 1818, his uncle set him up in a retailing enterprise, but within a year Harry Heine and Co. was bankrupt. Acknowledging that his nephew was unsuited for business, Uncle Salomon at last agreed to underwrite his further education.

Between 1819 and 1825, Heine studied in Bonn, Berlin, and Göttingen. His university years were very important for his development as a poet. While in Bonn, he attended lectures given by August Wilhelm von Schlegel, whose interest in his work stimulated Heine's creativity. In the fall of 1820, he moved to Göttingen. Besides law, he studied German history and philology until January, 1821, when he challenged another student to a duel and was expelled from the university. He continued his studies in Berlin and was rapidly accepted into prominent literary circles. Included among the writers with whom he associated were Adelbert von Chamisso, Friedrich Schleiermacher, and Christian Dietrich Grabbe. Rahel von Varnhagen helped in the publication of Heine's first collection of poems in 1822, and he quickly became known as a promising talent.

During a visit to Hamburg in 1823, he met Julius Campe, who afterward published all Heine's works except a few commissioned essays that he wrote in Paris. Literary success persuaded him away from the study of law, but at his uncle's request Heine returned to Göttingen to complete work toward his degree. In the summer of 1825, he passed his examinations, though not with distinction. To facilitate a public career, he was baptized a Protestant, at which time he changed his name to Heinrich.

Travel was a significantly formative experience for Heine. Vacations in Cuxhaven and Norderney provided initial powerful impressions of the sea that informed the two North Sea cycles of the *Book of Songs*. Journeys through the Harz Mountains in 1824, to England in 1827, and to Italy the following year provided material for the *Pictures of Travel* series that elevated him to the literary mainstream of his time. Exposure to foreign points of view also aroused his interest in current political questions and led to a brief involvement as coeditor of Johann Friedrich von Cotta's *Politische Annalen* in Munich in 1827 and 1828.

When continued efforts to obtain permission to practice law in Hamburg failed, Heine moved to Paris in 1831, where he began to write articles for French and German newspapers and journals. Heine loved Paris, and during the next few years friendships with Honoré de Balzac, Victor Hugo, George Sand, Giacomo Meyerbeer, and other writers, artists, and composers contributed to his sense of well-being. When the German Federal Diet banned his writings, making it impossible for him to continue contributing to German periodicals, the French government granted him a modest pension.

The 1840's were a stormy period in Heine's life. In 1841, he married Cresence Eugénie Mirat (whom he called Mathilde), his mistress of seven years. Her lack of education and understanding of his writings placed a strain on their relationship and later contributed to the poet's increasing isolation from his friends. After returning from Hamburg in 1843, Heine met Karl Marx. Their association sharpened Heine's political attitudes and increased his aggressive activism. Salomon Heine's death in 1844 unleashed between the writer and his cousins a struggle for the inheritance. Eventually they reached an accommodation that guaranteed an annuity in exchange for Heine's promise not to criticize family members in his writings.

After a collapse in 1848, Heine spent his remaining years in unceasing pain. An apparent venereal disease attacked his nervous system, leaving him paralyzed. Physical infirmities, however, did not stifle his creative spirit, and from the torment and loneliness of his "mattress grave," he wrote some of the best poetry of his career.

Analysis

Unlike many poets, Heinrich Heine never stated a formal theory of poetry that could serve as a basis for interpreting his works and measuring his creative development. For that reason, confusion and critical controversy have clouded the picture of his oeuvre, resulting in misunderstandings of his literary orientation and intentions. The general concept that he was a poet of experience is, at the very least, an oversimplification. To be sure, immediate personal observations of life were a consistent stimulus for Heine's writing, yet his product is not simply a stylized reproduction of individual encounters with reality. Each poem reveals a reflective processing of unique perceptions of people, milieus, and events that transforms seemingly specific descriptions into generally valid representations of humankind's confrontation with the times. The poet's ability to convey, with penetrating exactitude, feelings, existential problems, and elements of the human condition that correspond to the concerns and apperceptions of a broad readership enabled him to generate lyrics that belong more to the poetry of ideas than to the poetry of experience.

A characteristic of Heine's thought and verse is a purposeful poetic tension between the individual and the world. The dissonance between the artistic sensibility and reality is presented in unified constructs that represent qualities that were missing from the poet's era: unity, form, constancy, and continuity. By emphasizing condition rather than event, Heine was able to offer meaningful illustrations in the juxtaposition of antithetical concepts: sunny milieu and melancholy mood, pain and witticism, affirmation and negation, enchantment of feeling and practical wisdom of experience, enthusiasm and pessimism, love and hate, spirit and reality, tradition and anticipation of the future. The magic and power of his verse arise from his ability to clothe these dynamic conflicts in deceptively simple, compact forms, pure melodic sounds and rhythms, and playfully witty treatments of theme, substance, motif, and detail.

More than anything else, Heine was a poet of mood. His greatest strengths were his sensitivity and his capacity to analyze, create, and manipulate feeling. A colorful interchange of disillusionment, scorn, cynicism, rebellion, blasphemy, playful mockery, longing, and melancholy is the essence of his appeal to the reader's spirit. The goal, however, is not the arousal of emotion but rather the intensification of awareness, achieved by drawing the audience into a desired frame of feeling, then shattering the illusion in a breach of mood that typifies Heine's poetry.

Although he was not a true representative of any single German literary movement, Heine wrote poems that reflect clear relationships to definite intellectual and artistic traditions. Both the German Enlightenment and German Romanticism provided him with important models. In matters of form, attitude, and style, he was a child of the Enlightenment. Especially visible are his epigrammatic technique and the tendency toward didactic exemplification and pointed representation. Gotthold Ephraim Lessing was his favorite among Enlightenment authors. Heine combined the technical aspects of Enlightenment literary approach with a pronounced Romantic subjectivity in the handling of substance, theme, and motif, particularly in the examination of self, pain, experience, and condition. The absolute status of the self is a prominent characteristic of his works. In the emancipation of self, however, he carried the thoughtful exploration of personal individuality a step beyond that of the early Romantics and in so doing separated himself from them. Other Romantic traits in his lyrics include a dreamy fantasy of feeling and a pronounced element of irony. Where Friedrich Schlegel employed irony to transcend the restrictive material world and unite humankind with a spiritual cosmos, Heine used it to expand the self to encompass the cosmos. The feature of Romanticism with which Heine most consciously identified was the inclination of Joseph von Eichendorff and others toward simple musical poems modeled on the German folk song. Heine specifically acknowledged the influence of Wilhelm Müller, whose cultivation of pure sound and clear simplicity most closely approximated his own poetic ideal.

In many respects, the polish of language and form that marked Heine's *Book of Songs* was never surpassed in later collections. At most a strengthening of intonation, an increase in wit, a maturing of the intellect subtly and gradually enhanced his writings with the passing years. Nevertheless, his literary career can be divided into four distinct phases with regard to material focus and poetic concern.

EARLY YEARS

Heine's initial creative period encompassed his university years and reached its peak in the mid-1820's. In *Poems*, the cycle of verse in *Tragedies, Together with Lyric Intermezzo*, and, finally, *Book of Songs*, the young poet opened a world of personal subjectivity at the center of which is a self that undergoes unceasing examination. Consciousness of the self, its suffering and loneliness, is the essence of melodic compositions that include poems of unrequited love, lyrical mood pictures, satires, romances, confessions, and parodies. Lines and stanzas deftly reflect Heine's ability to feel his way into nature, the magic of legend, and the spiritual substance of humankind, while the poetic world remains a fragmentary manifestation of the subjective truthfulness of the moment.

THE SELF AS A MIRROR OF THE TIMES

A major change in orientation coincided with Heine's move to Paris. The political upheaval in France and the death of Goethe signaled the end of an artistic era, and Heine looked forward to the possibility of a different literature that would replace the subjectivity of Romanticism with a new stress on life, time, and reality. He was especially attracted to the Saint-Simonian religion, which inspired within him a hope for a modern doctrine that would offer a new balance between Judeo-Christian ideals and those of classical antiquity. The lyrics in *New Poems*, the major document of this period, reveal a shift in emphasis from the self per se to the self as a mirror of the times. Heine's poetry of the 1830's is shallower than his earlier creations, yet it effectively presents the inner turmoil, confusion, and splintering of the era as Heine experienced it. Accompanying a slightly faded reprise of earlier themes is a new view of the poet as a heathen cosmopolitan who affirms material reality and champions the moment as having eternal value.

POLITICAL RADICALIZATION

The third stage in Heine's career is best described as a period of political radicalization. It most visibly affected his poetry during the mid-1840's, the time of his friendship with Marx. In the aggressively satirical epics *Atta Troll* and *Germany: A Winter's Tale*, he paired sharp criticism of contemporary conditions with revelations of his love for Germany, specifically attacking his own critics, radical literature, militant nationalism, student organizations, the German hatred of the French, the fragmented condition of the German nation, and almost everything else that was valued by the establishment.

LAST OF THE ROMANTICS

Profound isolation and intense physical pain provided the catalyst for a final poetic reorientation after Heine's physical collapse in 1848. Some of the poems that he wrote in his "mattress grave" are among his greatest masterpieces; they reflect a new religiosity in spiritual penetration of the self. In *Romanzero* and other late poems, the poet becomes a kind of martyr, experiencing the world's illness in his own heart. The act of suffering generates a poetry of bleak glosses of the human condition, heartrending laments, and songs about death unequaled in German literature.

Although Heine styled himself the last of the Romantics, a significant difference in approach to substance distinguishes his early poems from those of the Romantic movement. Where Clemens Maria Brentano and Eichendorff celebrated existence as it opened itself to them, Heine sang of a life that had closed its doors, shutting him out. The dominant themes of his *Book of Songs* are longing and suffering as aspects of the experience of disappointed love. Combining the sentimental pessimism of Lord Byron with the objective portrayal of tangible reality, he succeeded in exploring love's frustrations and pain more effectively, more impressively, and more imaginatively than any of his forerunners and contemporaries had done. In dream images, songs, romances, and sonnets that employ Romantic materials yet remain suspicious of the feelings that they symbolize, the poet transformed the barrier that he felt existed between himself and the world into deceptively simple, profoundly valid treatments of universal problems.

BOOK OF SONGS

The poems of *Book of Songs* are extraordinarily flexible, self-contained productions that derive their charm from the combination of supple form and seemingly directly experienced and personally felt content. Colorful sketches of lime trees, an ancient bastion, a city pond, a whistling boy, gardens, people, fields, forests, a mill wheel, and an old tower contribute to a world of great fascination and sensual seduction. The verse is often bittersweet, however, focusing not on the sunny summer landscape but on the sadness of the poet who does not participate in a beauty that mocks him. The forceful presentation of the individual's isolation and conflict with the times represented a fresh direction in poetry that contributed greatly to Heine's early popularity. At the same time, the carefully constructed tension between the poet and his surroundings established a pattern that became characteristic of all his works.

An extremely important feature of these early lyrics is the break in mood that typically occurs at several levels, including tone, setting, and the lyricist's subjective interpretation of his situation. The tone frequently shifts from emotional to conversational, from delicate to blunt, while the settings of the imagination are shattered by the banal reality of modern society. As the poet analyzes his position vis-à-vis his milieu, his positive feeling is broken by frustration and defeat, his hope collapses beneath the awareness of his delusion, and his attraction to his beloved is marred by her unthinking cruelty. There is never any resolution of these conflicts, and the poem itself provides the only mediation between the writer and a hostile world.

Among the most exquisite compositions in *Book of Songs* are the rustically simple lyric paintings from "Die Harzreise" ("The Journey to the Harz") and the rhythmically powerful, almost mystical studies from the two cycles of "Die Nordsee" ("The North Sea"). Filled with the fairy-tale atmosphere of the Rhine and the Harz Mountains, "The Journey to the Harz" poems exemplify Heine's ability to capture the compelling musicality and inner tone of the folk song and to combine these elements with an overwhelming power of feeling in the formation of an intense poetry of mood. In "The North Sea," he cultivated a new kind of language, anticipating twentieth century verse in free rhythms that sounded the depths of elemental human experience. Constant motion, changing patterns of light, play of wind, and movement of ships and fish combine as parts of a unified basic form. Heine pinpointed the individuality of the ocean in a given moment, reproducing atmosphere with precision and intensifying impact through mythological or human ornamentation. The rolling flow of impression is a consistent product of Heine's poetic art in its finest form.

NEW POEMS

Two years after moving to Paris, Heine published *Letters Auxiliary to the History of Modern Polite Literature in Germany*, his most significant theoretical treatise on literature and a work that marked his formal break with Romanticism. The major poetic document of this transition to a more realistic brand of expression is *New Poems*, a less integrated collection than *Book of Songs*, containing both echoes of early themes and the first fruits of his increased political commitment of the 1840's. *New Poems* attests strongly a shift in approach and creative concern from poetry as an absolute to the demand for contemporary relevance.

The first cycle of *New Poems*, "Neuer Frühling" ("New Spring"), returns to the motifs that dominate the "Lyric Intermezzo" and "Homecoming" segments of *Book of Songs* yet presents them with greater polish and distance. New variations portray love as a distraction, a nuisance that causes emotional turmoil in the inherent knowledge of its transitoriness. The tone and direction of the entire volume are established in the prologue to "New Spring," in which the poet contrasts his own subjection to the hindering influence of love with the strivings of others in "the great struggle of the times."

Among the other sections of the book, "Verschiedene" ("Variae"), with its short cycles of rather acidic poems about the girls of Paris, its legendary ballad "Der Tannhäuser" ("Tannhäuser"), and its "Schöpfungslieder" ("Songs of Creation"), is the least coherent, most disturbing group of poems that Heine ever wrote. Campe, his publisher, decried the lyricist's creation of what he called "whore and chamber-pot stories" and was extremely reluctant to publish them. Nothing that Heine wrote, however, is without artistic value, and there are nuggets of brilliance even here. Despite its artificiality and seeming inconsistency with Heine's true poetic nature, "Tannhäuser," for example, must be regarded as one of his greatest masterpieces. The deeply psychological rejuvenation of the old folk epic, which served as the stimulus for Richard Wagner's opera, reflects the poet's all-encompassing and penetrating knowledge of the human heart.

"Zeitgedichte" ("Poems of the Times"), the concluding cycle in *New Poems*, sets the pattern for Heine's harsh political satire of the 1840's. Some of the lyrics were written expressly for Karl Marx's newspaper *Vorwärts*. Most of them are informed by homesickness, longing, and the bitter disappointment that Heine felt as the expected dawn of spiritual freedom in Germany failed to materialize in the evolution of a more cosmopolitan relationship with the rest of Europe. Powerful poems directed against cultural, social, and political dilettantes anticipate the incisively masterful tones of his most successful epics of the period, *Atta Troll* and *Germany: A Winter's Tale*; irreverent assaults on cherished institutions, superficial political activism, and his own critics accent his peculiar love-hate relationship with his homeland.

Romanzero

Regarded by many critics as Heine's finest collection of poems, *Romanzero* presents his final attempts to come to grips with his own mortality. Rich in their sophistication, more coherent in tone than the lyrics of *New Poems* or even the *Book of Songs*, the romances, laments, and melodies of *Romanzero* reveal the wit, irony, and epigrammatic style for which Heine is famous in the service of a new, peculiarly transparent penetration of the self. Dominant in the poems is the theme of death, which confronts the individual in many forms. A new religiosity is present in the acknowledgment of a personal God with whom the poet quarrels about a divine justice that is out of phase with humankind's needs. Individual creations pass through the spectrum of human and religious history and into the future in the expectation of a new social order. Bitter pessimism unmasks the dreams of life, pointing to the defeat of that which is noble and beautiful and the triumph of the worse human being over the better as the derisive law of the world. Voicing the mourning and bitter resistance of the tormented soul, Heine transforms personal confrontation with suffering and death into a timeless statement of universal experience.

Romanzero is divided into three main parts, each of which projects a substantial array of feeling: seriousness, despair, goodness, compassion, a longing for faith, bitterness, and mature composure. The first section, "Historien" ("Stories"), is composed of discursive, sometimes rambling narrative ballads and romances dealing with the tragedies of kings, heroes, and poets. Some of them process through a temporal distance such typical Heine themes as the yearning for love, clothing them in historical trappings. Others, such as the cruel poem "Vitzliputzli" that ends the cycle, are profound discourses on humans' inhumanity toward their own kind. The poems of "Lamentationen" ("Lamentations"), the second major section, are directly confessional in form: deeply moving cries of anguish, sublime expressions of horror, statements of longing for home. The "Lazarus" poems that conclude this portion of *Romanzero* are especially vivid documents of the poet's individual suffering in a world where God seems to be indifferent. In "Hebräische Melodien" ("Hebrew Melodies"), the last segment of the collection, Heine presented the essence of his reidentification with Judaism. Three long poems explore the broad dimensions of Jewish culture, history, and tradition, ending with an almost sinister medieval disputation between Christian and Jew that evolves into a tragicomic anticlerical satire. Thumbing his nose at irrational action, intolerance, and superstition, the poet offers a dying plea for humanism.

No other volume presents Heine so thoroughly in all his heights and depths, perfection and error, wit and seriousness. Captivating for the directness of despairing and contrite confession, repelling for its boastful, sometimes vicious cynicism, *Romanzero*, as perhaps no other work in the history of German lyric poetry, reveals the hubris of the problematic individual and penetrates the facade of the bright fool's drama that is life.

OTHER MAJOR WORKS
LONG FICTION: *Der Rabbi von Bacherach*, 1887 (*The Rabbi of Bacherach*, 1891).
SHORT FICTION: *Aus den Memoiren des Herrn von Schnabelewopsky*, 1910 (*The Memoirs of Herr von Schnabelewopski*, 1876).
PLAYS: *Almansor*, pb. 1821 (English translation, 1905); *Der Doktor Faust*, pb. 1851 (libretto; *Doktor Faust*, 1952).
NONFICTION: *Briefe aus Berlin*, 1822; *Reisebilder*, 1826-1831 (4 volumes; *Pictures of Travel*, 1855); *Die Bäder von Lucca*, 1829 (*The Baths of Lucca*, 1855); *Französische Zustände*, 1833 (*French Affairs*, 1889); *Zur Geschichte der neueren schönen Literatur in Deutschland*, 1833 (*Letters Auxiliary to the History of Modern Polite Literature in Germany*, 1836); *Der Salon*, 1834-1840 (4 volumes; *The Salon*, 1893); *Zur Geschichte der Religion und Philosophie in Deutschland*, 1835 (*On the History of Religion and Philosophy in Germany*, 1876); *Die romantische Schule*, 1836 (expansion of *Zur Geschichte der Religion und Philosophie in Deutschland*; *The Romantic School*, 1876); *Über die französische Bühne*, 1837 (*Concerning the French Stage*, 1891-1905); *Shakespeares Mädchen und Frauen*, 1838 (*Shakespeare's Maidens and Ladies*, 1891);

Ludwig Börne: Eine Denkschrift von H. Heine, 1840 (*Ludwig Börne: Recollections of a Revolutionist*, 1881); *Les Dieux en exil*, 1853 (*Gods in Exile*, 1962); *Lutetia: Berichte über Politik, Kunst, und Volksleben*, 1854 (*Lutetia: Reports on Politics, Art, and Popular Life*, 1891-1905); *Vermischte Schriften*, 1854 (3 volumes); *De l'Allemagne*, 1855 (2 volumes).

MISCELLANEOUS: *The Works of Heinrich Heine*, 1891-1905 (12 volumes).

BIBLIOGRAPHY

Cook, Roger F., ed. *A Companion to the Works of Heinrich Heine*. Rochester, N.Y.: Camden House, 2002. A collection of essays that examine Heine's work; topics include the eroticism, Jewish culture, mythology, and modernity in his poems.

Heady, Katy. *Literature and Censorship in Restoration Germany: Repression and Rhetoric*. Rochester, N.Y.: Camden House, 2009. This work on the censorship of literature that occurred in Restoration Germany examines how the intellectual and political climate affected Heine.

Hermand, Jost, and Robert C. Holub, eds. *Heinrich Heine's Contested Identities: Politics, Religion, and Nationalism in Nineteenth-Century Germany*. New York: Peter Lang, 1999. A collection of essays concerning Heine's identity, which was formed and reformed, revised and modified, in relationship to the politics, religion, and nationalism of his era. The essays offer an understanding of Heine's predicaments and choices as well as the parameters placed on him by the exigencies of the time.

Justis, Diana Lynn. *The Feminine in Heine's Life and Oeuvre: Self and Other*. New York: Peter Lang, 1997. Heine's literary representations of women and interactions with women vividly demonstrate his position as a marginal German-Jewish writer of the nineteenth century. Heine, like many Jews of that era, internalized the European cultural stereotype of the Jew as "woman," that is, as essentially inferior and marginal.

Pawel, Ernst. *The Poet Dying: Heinrich Heine's Last Years in Paris*. New York: Farrar, Straus and Giroux, 1995. In this biography of Heine, Pawel portrays a poet at the height of his creativity in the last eight years of his life, when he was confined to his bed with a mysterious ailment.

Phelan, Anthony. *Reading Heinrich Heine*. New York: Cambridge University Press, 2007. Examines Heine's poetry from the earliest to his last, and argues that Heine is a major contributor to the articulation of modernity.

Lowell A. Bangerter

HERMANN HESSE

Born: Calw, Germany; July 2, 1877
Died: Montagnola, Switzerland; August 9, 1962

PRINCIPAL POETRY
Romantische Lieder, 1899
Hinterlassene Schriften und Gedichte von Hermann Lauscher, 1901
Gedichte, 1902
Unterwegs: Gedichte, 1911
Aus Indien, 1913
Musik des Einsamen: Neue Gedichte, 1915
Gedichte des Malers, 1920
Ausgewählte Gedichte, 1921
Verse im Krankenbett, 1927
Krisis, 1928 (*Crisis: Pages from a Diary*, 1975)
Trost der Nacht: Neue Gedichte, 1929
Jahreszeiten: Zen Gedichte mit Bildern, 1931
Besinnung, 1934
Leben einer Blume, 1934
Vom Baum des Lebens, 1934
Das Haus der Träume, 1936
Jahreslauf: Ein Zyklus Gedichte, 1936
Stunden im Garten: Eine Idylle, 1936
Chinesisch, 1937
Der lahme Knabe: Eine Erinnerung aus der Kindheit, 1937
Neue Gedichte, 1937
Orgelspiel, 1937
Ein Traum Josef Knechts, 1937
Föhnige Nacht, 1938
Der letzte Glasperlenspieler, 1939
Zehn Gedichte, 1939
Fünf Gedichte, 1942
Die Gedichte, 1942
Krankennacht, 1942
Stufen: Noch ein Gedichte Josef Knechts, 1943
Der Blütenzweig, 1945
Friede 1914; dem Feieden, 1945
Späte Gedichte, 1946
In Sand geschrieben, 1947

Drei Gedichte, 1948
Jugend-Gedichte, 1950
Zwei Gedichte, 1951
Rückblick, 1952
Zwei Idyllen, 1952
Alter Maler in der Werkstatt, 1954
Klage und Trost, 1954
Wanderer im Spätherbst, 1956
Zum Frieden, 1956
Das Lied von Abels Tod, 1957
Gedichte, 1958
Treue Begleiter, 1958
Freund Peter, 1959 (also known as *Bericht an die Freunde: Letzte Gedichte*)
Vier späte Gedichte, 1959
Stufen: Alte und neue Gediochte in Auswahl, 1961
Die späten Gedichte, 1963
Buchstaben, 1965
Poems, 1970
Stufen: Ausgewählte, 1972
Poems by Hermann Hesse, 1974

Other literary forms

Though Hermann Hesse (HEHS-uh) is best known among English-speakers for his novels—especially *Demian* (1919; English translation, 1923), *Der Steppenwolf* (1927; *Steppenwolf*, 1929), *Siddhartha* (1922; English translation, 1951); *Narziss und Goldmund* (1930; *Death and the Lover*, 1932; also known as *Narcissus and Goldmund*, 1968), and *Das Glasperlenspiel: Versuch einer Lebensbeschreibung des Magister Ludi Josef Knecht samt Knechts hinterlassenen Schriften* (1943; *Magister Ludi*, 1949; also known as *The Glass Bead Game*, 1969)—he wrote a significant volume of work in other genres. He began composing poems as a child, and despite his output in other literary forms, he continued writing verse throughout his long life. Many of his novels, in fact, contain rhymes, and since the 1950's much of his poetry has been adapted for musical pieces, especially in Europe. In addition to numerous collections of poems, Hesse wrote volumes of short stories, fairy tales, essays, articles, lectures and other nonfiction. He also edited several periodicals and served as editor for dozens of books, particularly from 1910 to 1926.

Achievements

Hermann Hesse authored millions of words including hundreds, perhaps thousands, of poems. Much of his verse from the mid-1930's onward was self-published in small private editions featuring his hand-painted watercolors as gifts for friends and remains

Hermann Hesse
(©The Nobel Foundation)

uncollected. Hesse first achieved recognition in 1904, winning the Wiener Bauernfeld Prize for his novel *Peter Camenzind* (English translation, 1961). He received the Fontane Prize for *Demian* in 1920, but returned it because the award was intended for new writers. In 1936, he was honored with Zurich's Gottfried-Keller Prize for Literature. In 1946, he received both the Nobel Prize in Literature and the Goethe Prize. He added the Wilhelm Raabe Prize (1950) and the Peace Prize of the German Book Trade (1955) to his laurels and was made a Knight of the Order of Merit in 1955. More than forty years after his death and eighty years since he adopted Swiss citizenry, Hesse continues to be one of the best-selling German-language authors in the country of his birth.

Biography

Hermann Hesse was born in Calw, a picturesque village in the Black Forest. He was the grandson of a publisher of religious tracts and the son of devout missionaries from the Pietists, an evangelical Protestant sect. His father, Johannes Hesse, was a German, born the son of a physician in Estonia (then part of the Russian Empire), and his mother Marie Gundert Hesse, a widow with two sons, was also of German heritage, though she had been born in India, where her father Hermann Gundert, a scholarly linguist, had preached.

A precocious child, young Hesse was difficult to handle and particularly acted out during the five years (1881-1886) when the Hesse family lived in Basle, Switzerland. After they returned to Calw, Hesse attended preparatory Latin school in Göppingen and did well in his studies. However, when his parents enrolled him in the Maulbronn Seminary, assuming he would follow them into the religious life, he rebelled and ran away. He contemplated suicide for the first but not the last time. He briefly attended a series of other schools before enrolling at the gymnasium at Cannstadt, but he was expelled in 1893, effectively ending his formal education at the age of sixteen.

Hesse apprenticed at a steeple clock factory before working in a bookshop in Tübingen, where he published his first collection of poetry in 1899. For four years thereafter, he worked in a bookshop in Basle. In 1904, he achieved his first literary success with the publication of *Peter Camenzind*, which convinced him to become a full-time freelance writer. That same year, he married Maria Bernoulli and fathered three children—Bruno, Heiner, and Martin—between 1905 and 1911 while living in Gaienhofen, Germany. Hesse frequently contributed to literary journals; regularly published fiction, nonfiction, and poetry; and traveled often, lecturing in Italy, Switzerland, Germany, and India.

In 1912, Hesse moved with his family to Berne, Switzerland. When World War I broke out, he attempted to enlist in the German military but was turned away because of vision problems, so he worked through the German consulate in Switzerland, editing journals and books for German prisoners of war. In 1916, Hesse underwent Jungian psychoanalysis, and during the 1920's, he visited spas for his health. In 1919, the same year that he published *Demian*—he left his family to live alone in Montagnola, where he would reside for the rest of his life. When he became a Swiss citizen in 1923, he divorced his first wife, and the following year, he married Ruth Wenger. They would divorce in 1927, the same year that *Steppenwolf* was published.

Hesse wed for a third time in 1931, to Ninon Ausländer Dolbin, and this marriage lasted. The author continued to publish collections of poetry until the end of his life, although he did not write another novel after *The Glass Bead Game*, considered his fictional masterpiece. During his final years, he divided his time between writing poetry and conscientiously answering the hundreds of letters he received daily. Afflicted with leukemia, he died of a brain hemorrhage shortly after his eighty-fifth birthday.

Analysis

Virtually all of Hermann Hesse's fiction and poetry is autobiographical, even confessional to some degree. Although his major novels have been translated into English and many other languages—and to this day are the primary focus of study and critique—much of his nonfiction, short fiction, and poetry remains available only in German.

Hesse's early poems are lyrical. Regular in meter and rhyme, they revolve around typical subjects of youthful inspiration: expressions of longing for women, insightful studies of nature, observations made while traveling, considerations of the self, and as might be expected from someone of his religious upbringing, reflections on the meaning of spirituality, faith, and belief. His charming hometown of Calw comes under frequent scrutiny; such poems are replete with realistic, telling details surrounding the honest, cheerful burghers who struggle for survival, and lines are crowded with fond memories. Hesse's career as a poet was given a boost at the turn of the twentieth century by a sympathetic critique of his *Romantische Lieder* (romantic songs) from fellow poet Rainer Maria Rilke, who, while praising his contemporary's use of metallic imagery, complained that Hesse's verbiage was too abstract. Rilke pronounced the collection "unliterary," which was considered a compliment, a contrast to the usual poetry of the time.

Even from the beginning, Hesse's poetry is more downbeat than exuberant. From an early age, he considered himself an outsider, an observer rather than a participant in the stream of life; a loner, he never felt he belonged anywhere. *Romantische Lieder*, although demonstrating conscious control of rhythm, rhyme, and the acoustic effect produced by combinations of words, is laden with images of unhappiness, depression, and uneasiness. Although Hesse would move between rhyme and free verse throughout his career, he would continually revisit these themes in his poems.

CRISIS

Crisis, an aptly named collection of poems, evolved when Hesse was writing *Steppenwolf*, one of his most influential novels. The poems reflect the latest and most catastrophic in a series of major turning points in his life. Individual pieces revolve around the mid-life crisis many aging men experience. They incorporate his feelings about the breakup of his first marriage, his realization that his second marriage was doomed, bouts of illness and insomnia and extreme depression, and a complete change in his philosophical outlook. Tired of life, out of balance physically and psychologically, weary of pursuing spiritual answers in his quest for self-knowledge, and fed up with his usual preoccupation with asceticism and intellectuality, he immersed himself completely in the sensual and emotional. For two years in the mid-1920's, Hesse caroused nightly, drinking himself into oblivion, experimenting with drugs, consorting with prostitutes, and visiting nightclubs to listen to live jazz.

The poems of *Crisis*, written mostly in straightforward rhyming quatrains, are brutally frank. They speak of the author—the lone wolf of the steppes, as depicted in *Steppenwolf*—saturating himself with whiskey, dancing the shimmy, cavorting with girls named Fanny and Adelaide, waking up alone with painful hangovers, and feeling overwhelming self-pity. The titles alone of many of the forty-five verses indicate his mood and temperament: "Poet's Death Song," "Growing Old," "After an Evening at the Stag," "To John the Baptist from Hermann the Drunkard," "The Seducer," "Schizophrenia," "The Debauchee," "Still Tipsy," "The Drunken Poet," and "Poor Devil on the Morning After the Masked Ball." However, despite sinking into the depths for a time, the experience had a cathartic effect on Hesse's psyche. His mind and body cleansed, he was able to resume a productive and satisfying career, using the insight gained from his exploration of the vulgar side of his nature.

POEMS

One of the first collections of Hesse's poems in English, *Poems* presents translator James Wright's selections, in both German and English, from the poet's earlier work, published between 1899 and 1921. The seventy-eight mostly brief rhyming poems are linked by a common thread: the theme of longing for home. This was an important consideration for Hesse at the time that he wrote these poems because he was alienated from his religious parents, physically removed from his birthplace, and as a nonparticipant in the military efforts of Germany during World War I, an outcast in his own country. The selections in *Poems*—particularly "I Know, You Walk," "Lonesome Night," "The Poet," "At Night on the High Seas," "Ode to Hölderlin," and "In a Collection of Egyptian Sculptures"—provide a good introduction to Hesse's recurring subject matter: loneliness, the inevitability of death for all living things, and the exploration of the self and the soul.

OTHER MAJOR WORKS

LONG FICTION: *Peter Camenzind*, 1904 (English translation, 1961); *Unterm Rad*, 1906 (*The Prodigy*, 1957; also known as *Beneath the Wheel*, 1968); *Gertrud*, 1910 (*Gertrude and I*, 1915; also known as *Gertrude*, 1955); *Rosshalde*, 1914 (English translation, 1970); *Knulp: Drei Geschichten aus dem Leben Knulps*, 1915 (*Knulp: Three Tales from the Life of Knulp*, 1971); *Demian*, 1919 (English translation, 1923 ; also known as *Demian: The Story of Eric Sinclair's Youth*, 1965); *Klingsors letzter Sommer*, 1920 (*Klingsor's Last Summer*, 1970; includes the three novellas *Klein und Wagner*, *Kinderseele*, and *Klingsors letzter Sommer*); *Siddhartha*, 1922 (English translation, 1951); *Aufzeichnungen eines Herrn im Sanatorium*, 1925 (also known as *Haus zum Frieden: Aufzeichnungen eines Herrn im Sanatorium*, 1947); *Der Steppenwolf*, 1927 (*Steppenwolf*, 1929); *Narziss und Goldmund*, 1930 (*Death and the Lover*, 1932; also known as *Narcissus and Goldmund*, 1968); *Die Morgenlandfahrt*, 1932 (*The Journey to the East*, 1956); *Das Glasperlenspiel: Versuch einer Lebensbeschreibung des Magister Ludi Josef Knecht samt Knechts hinterlassenen Schriften*, 1943 (*Magister Ludi*, 1949; best known as *The Glass Bead Game*, 1969; also known as *Magister Ludi: The Glass Bead Game*, 1970).

SHORT FICTION: *Eine Stunde hinter Mitternacht,* 1899; *Diesseits: Erzählungen,* 1907; *Nachbarn: Erzählungen,* 1908; *Umwege: Erzählungen,* 1912; *Aus Indien,* 1913; *Anton Schievelbeyns ohn-freiwillige Reiss nachher ost-Indien,* 1914; *Der Hausierer,* 1914; *Am Weg,* 1915 (also known as *Am Weg: Erzählungen;* also known as *Am Weg Frühe Erzählungen); Hans Dierlamms Lehrzeit,* 1916; *Schön ist die Jugend,* 1916; *Alte Geschichten: Zwei Erzählungen,* 1918; *Zwei Märchen,* 1918; *Märchen,* 1919 (*Strange News from Another Star, and Other Tales,* 1972); *Im Presselschen Gartenhaus: Eine Erzählung dem alten Tübingen,* 1920; *In der alten Sonne,* 1921; *Die Officina Bodoni in Montagnola,* 1923 (English translation, 1976); *Psychologia balnearia oder Glossen eines Badener Kurgastes,* 1924 (also known as *Kurgast: Aufzeichnungen von einer Badener Kur,* 1925); *Die Verlobung: Erzählungen,* 1924; *Piktors Verwandlungen: Ein Märchen,* 1925; *Die Nürnberger Reise,* 1927; *Der Zyklon und andere Erzählungen,* 1929; *Weg nach Innen,* 1931; *Hermann Hesse,* 1932; *Kleine Welt: Erzählungen,* 1933; *Fabulierbuch,* 1935; *Stunden im Garten: Eine Idylle,* 1936; *Tragisch,* 1936; *Der Lateinschüler,* 1943; *Der Pfirsichbaum: Und andere Erzählungen,* 1945; *Traumfährte: Neue Erzählungen und Märchen,* 1945 (*The War Goes On,* 1971); *Kurgast; die Nuernberger Reise: Zwei Erzählungen,* 1946; *Geheimnisse,* 1947 (also known as *Geheimnisse: Letzte Erzählungen,* 1955); *Heumond; aus nach Innen: Vier Erzählungen,* 1947; *Weg nach Innen: Vier Erzählungen,* 1947; *Der Zwerg,* 1947; *Frühe Prosa,* 1948; *Kinderseele,* 1948; *Kinderseele und Ladidel,* 1948; *Zwei Erzählungen: Der Novalis; Der Zwerg,* 1948; *Der Bettler,* 1949; *Hermann Hesse,* 1949; *Bericht aus Normalien,* 1951; *Späte Prosa,* 1951; *Die Verlobung und andere Erzählungen,* 1951; *Weihnacht mit zwei Kinidergeschichten,* 1951; *Diesseits, Kleine Welt, Fabulierbuch,* 1954; *Beschwörungen: Späte Prosa, Neu Folge,* 1955; *Der Dichter: Eine Märchen,* 1955; *Flötentraum,* 1955; *Der Wolf und andere Erzählungen,* 1955; *Zwei jugendliche Erzählungen,* 1956; *Augustus, Der Dichter; ein Mensch mit Namen Ziegler,* 1957 (also known as *Drei Erzählungen: Sugustus, Der Dichter; ein Mensch mit Namen Ziegler,* 1960); *Gesammelte Schriften,* 1957; *Klein und Wagner,* 1958 (also known as *Klein und Wagner: Novelle,* 1973); *Tessiner Erzählungen,* 1962; *Tractat vom Steppenwolf,* 1964 (*Treatise on the Steppenwolf,* 1975); *Prosa aus dem Nachlass,* 1965; *Der vierte Lebenslauf Josef Knechts,* 1966; *Aus Kinderzeiten und andere Erzählungen,* 1968; *Stories of Five Decades,* 1972; *Iris: Ausgewählt Märchen,* 1973; *Tales of Student Life,* 1976.

PLAY: *Heimkehr,* pr. 1958 (wr. 1919).

NONFICTION: *Boccaccio,* 1904; *Franz von Assisi,* 1904; *Faust und Zarathustra,* 1909; *Kriegslektüre,* 1915; *Zum Sieg,* 1915; *Lektüre fur Kriegsgefangene,* 1916; *Zarathustras Wiederkehr: Ein Wort an die deutsche Jugend von einem Deutschen,* 1919; *Blick ins Chaos,* 1920 (*In Sight of Chaos,* 1923); *Wanderung, Aufzeichnungen: Mit farbigen Bildern vom Verfasser,* 1920 (*Wandering: Notes and Sketches,* 1972); *Elf Aquarelle aus dem Tessin,* 1921; *Erinnerung an Lektüre,* 1925; *Betrachtungen,* 1928;

Eine Bibliothek der Weltliteratur, 1929; *Magie des Buches,* 1930; *Zum Gedächtnis unseres Vatres,* 1930; *Beim Einzug ins neue Haus,* 1931; *Gedenkblätter,* 1937; *Der Novalis,* 1940; *Kleine Betrachtungen,* 1941; *Gedenkblatt für Franz Schall,* 1943; *Erinnerung an Klingsors Sommer,* 1944; *Nachruf auf Christoph Schrempf,* 1944; *Zwischen Sommer und Herbst,* 1944; *Zwei Aufsätze,* 1945; *Ansprache in der ersten Stunde des Jahres 1946,* 1946; *Dank an Goethe,* 1946; *Danksagung und moralisierende Bertrachtungen,* 1946; *Der Europaeer,* 1946; *Feuerwerk,* 1946; *Krieg und Frieden: Betrachtungen zu Krieg und Politik seit dem Jahr 1914,* 1946, 1949 (*If the War Goes On . . . Reflections on War and Politics,* 1971); *Statt eines Briefes,* 1946; *Antwort auf Bittbriefe,* 1947; *Eine Konzertpause,* 1947; *Stufen der Menschwerdung,* 1947; *Berg und See: Zwei Landschaftsstudien,* 1948; *Traumtheater: Aufzeichnungen,* 1948; *Über Romain Rolland,* 1948; *Begegnungen mit Vergagenem,* 1949; *Gedenkblatt für Adele,* 1949; *Gedenkblatt für Martin,* 1949; *Stunden am Schreibitisch,* 1949; *Wege zu Hermann Hesse,* 1949; *Erinnerung an Andre Gide,* 1951; *Gedanken über Gottfried Keller,* 1951; *Über "Peter Camenzind,"* 1951; *Herbstliche Erlebnisse,* 1952; *Lektüre für Minuten: Ein paar Gedanken aus meinen Büchern und Briefen,* 1952; *Kaminfegerchen,* 1953; *Nachruf für Marulla,* 1953; *Die Dohle,* 1954; *Notizblätter um Ostern,* 1954; *Über das Alter,* 1954; *Abendwolken: Zwei Aufsätze,* 1956; *Hilfsmaterial für den Literaturunterrich,* 1956; *Der Trauermarsch: Gedenkblatt für einen Jugendfreund,* 1957; *Eine Bodensee-Erinnirung,* 1961; *Ärzte: Ein paar Erinnerungen,* 1963; *Ein Blatt von meinem Baum,* 1964; *Neue deutsche Bücher: Literaturberichte für Bonniers Letterära Magasin, 1933-1936,* 1965; *Hermann Hesse: Essays,* 1970; *Politische Betrachtungen,* 1970; *Mein Glaube: Eine Dokumentation,* 1971; *Autobiographical Writings,* 1972; *Eigensinn: Autobiographische Schristen,* 1972; *Mein Glaube,* 1972; *Schriften zur Literatur,* 1972; *Die Kunst des Mussiggangs: Kurze Prosa aus dem Nachlass,* 1973; *My Belief: Essays on Life and Art,* 1974; *Reflections,* 1974.

EDITED TEXTS: *Der Lindenbaum: Deutsche Volkslieder,* 1910 (with Emil Strauss); *Eichendorffs Gedichte und Novellen,* 1913; *Gedichte,* 1913 (by Christian Wagner); *Des Knaben Wunderhorn,* 1913 (with Ludwig Achim von Arnim and Clemens Bretano); *Morgenländische Erzählungen,* 1913; *Der Zauberbrunnen,* 1913; *Lieder deutscher Dichter,* 1914; *Gesta Romanorum,* 1915; *Der Wandsbeker Bote: Eine Auswahl aus den Werken von Matthias Claudius,* 1915; *Alemannenbuch,* 1919; *Ein Schwabenbuch für die deutschen Kriegsgefangenen,* 1919; *Ein Luzerner Junker vor hundert Jahren,* 1920 (by Xaver Schnyder von Wartensee); *Dichtungen,* 1922 (by Salomon Gessner); *Märchen und Legenden aus der Gesta Romanorum,* 1926; *Dreissig Gedichte,* 1932 (by Johann Wolfgang von Goethe); *Geschichten aus dem Mittelalter,* 1976 (with others).

MISCELLANEOUS: *Der Junge Dichter: Ein Brief an Viele,* 1910 (also known as *An einen jungen Dichter,* 1932); *Kleiner Garten: Erlebnisse und Dichtungen,* 1919; *Aus dem "Tagebuch eines Entgleisten,"* 1922; *Sinclairs Notizbuch,* 1923 (by Emil Sinclair); *Bilderbuch,* 1926; *Kurzgefasster Lebenslauf,* 1929 (Erwin Ackerknecht, editor);

Mahnung: Erzählungen und Gedichte, 1933; *Heiroglyphen*, 1943; *Bildschmuck im Eisenbahnwafen*, 1944; *Rigi-Tagebuch*, 1945; *Brief an Adele: Februar 1946*, 1946; *Ein Brief nach Deutschland*, 1946; *Indischer Lebenslauf*, 1946 (exerpts from *Das Glasperlenspiel: Versuch einer Lebensbeschreibung des Magister Ludi Josef Knecht samt Knechts hinterlassenen Schriften*, 1943); *An einen jungen Kollegen in Japan*, 1947; *Der Autor an einen Korrektor*, 1947; *Beschreibung einer Landschaf: Ein Stück tagebuch*, 1947; *Spaziergang in Würzburg*, 1947; *Zwei Briefe über das Glasperlenspiel*, 1947; *Blätter vom Tage*, 1948; *Legende von indischen König*, 1948; *Musikalische Notizen*, 1948; *Der Stimmen und der Heilige: Ein Stück Tagebuch*, 1948; *Versuch einer Rechtfertigung*, 1948 (with Max Brod); *Alle Bücher dieser Welt: Ein Almanach für Bücherfreunde*, 1949 (K. H. Silomon, editor); *An einem jungen Künstler*, 1949; *Aus vielen Jahren: Gegichte, Erzählungen und Bilder*, 1949; *Auszüge aus zwei Briefen*, 1949; *Gerbersau*, 1949; *Eine Arbeitsnacht*, 1950; *Ein Brief zu Thomas Manns 75 Geburstag*, 1950; *Das Lied des Lebens*, 1950; *Zwei Briefe: An einen jungen Künstler; das junge Genie*, 1950 (also known as *Das junge Gen ie: Brief an einen Achtzehnjährigen*, 1950); *Glückwunsch für Peter Suhrkamp*, 1951; *Eine Handvoll Briefe*, 1951; *Nörgeleien*, 1951; *Eine Sonate*, 1951; *Ahornschatten, ein Brief*, 1952; *Allerlei Post: Rundbrief an Freunde*, 1952; *Aprilbrief*, 1952; *Dank für die Briefe und Glückwünsche zum 2 Juli 1952*, 1952; *Geburstag Ein Rundbrief*, 1952; *Gesammelte Dichtungen*, 1952 (six volumes); *Letzer Gruss an Otto Hartmann*, 1952; *Das Werk von Hermann Hesse: Ein Brevier*, 1952 (Siegfried Unseld, editor); *Engadiner Erlebnisse: Ein Rundbrief*, 1953; *Regen in Herbst*, 1953; *Der Schlossergeselle*, 1953; *Doktor Knolges Ende*, 1954; *Die Nikobaren*, 1954; *Rundbrief aus Sils-Maria*, 1954; *Aquarelle aus dem Tessin*, 1955; *Knopf-Annähen*, 1955; *Ein paar Leserbriefe an Hermann Hesse*, 1955; *Tagebuchblatt: Ein Maulbronner Seminarist*, 1955; *Über Gewaltpolitik, Krieg und das Böse in der Welt*, 1955; *Cesco und der Berg*, 1956; *Gedichte und Prosa*, 1956; *Magie des Buches: Betrachtungen und Gedichte*, 1956; *Weihnachtsgaben und anderes*, 1956; *Wiederbegegnung mit zwei Jugendgedichten*, 1956; *Ein Auswahl*, 1957 (Reinhard Buchward, editor); *Gute Stunde*, 1957; *Malfreude, Malsorgen*, 1957; *Welkes Blatt*, 1957; *Antworten*, 1958; *Chinesische Legenge*, 1959; *Ein paar indische Miniaturen*, 1959; *Sommerbrief aus dem Engadin*, 1959; *An einen Musiker*, 1960; *Aus einem tagebuch des Jahres 1920*, 1960; *Ein paar Aufzeichnungen und Briefe*, 1960; *Rückgriff*, 1960; *Dichter und Weltburger*, 1961; *Schreiben und Schriften*, 1961; *Zen*, 1961; *Der Beichvater*, 1962 (selections from *Das Glasperlenspiel: Versuch einer Lebensbeschreibung des Magister Ludi Josef Knecht samt Knechts hinterlassenen Schriften*, 1943); *Prosa und Gedichte*, 1963 (Franz Baumer, editor); *Erwin*, 1965; *Hermann Hesse: Eine Auswahl, für Ausländer*, 1966 (Gerherd Kirchhoff, editor); *Kindheit und Jungend vor Neunzehnhundert: Hermann Hesse in Briefen und Lebenszeugnissen, 1877-1895*, 1966 (Ninon Hesse, editor); *Briefwechsel: Hermann Hesse—Thomas Mann*, 1968 (Anni Carlsson, editor; *The Hesse-Mann Letters: The Correspondence of Hermann Hesse and*

Thomas Mann, 1910-1955, 1975; Carlsson and Volker Michels, editors); *Briefwechsel, 1945-1959*, 1969 (with Peter Suhrkamp; Unseld, editor); *Gesammelte Werke*, 1970 (twelve volumes); *Hermann Hesse, Helene Voigt-Diederichs: Zwei Autorenporträts in Briefen, 1897 bis 1900*, 1971 (also known as *Zwei Autorenporträts in Briefen, 1897 bis 1900*, 1971); *Briefwechsel aus der Nähe*, 1972 (Magda Kerenyi, editor); *D'une rive a i'autre: Hermann Hesse et Romain Rolland*, 1972; *Lectüre für Minuten*, 1972 (Volker Michels, editor); *Die Erzählungen*, 1973 (Volker Michels, editor); *Gesammelte Briefe*, 1973 (Volker Michels and Ursula Michels, editors); *Glück, Späte Prosa: Betrachtungen*, 1973; *Reflections*, 1974.

BIBLIOGRAPHY

Cornils, Ingo. *A Companion to the Works of Hermann Hesse.* New York: Camden House, 2009. Essays from a number of different contributors, dealing with Hesse's novels and poetry. Explores the author's interest in psychoanalysis, music, and Eastern philosophy, and the influences of politics, painting, and other writers on his work.

Helt, Richard C. *". . . A Poet or Nothing At All": The Tübingen and Basel Years of Hermann Hesse.* Providence, R.I.: Berghahn, 1996. A study of Hesse's formative years as a writer, particularly the period between 1899 and 1903, when he persevered to become a poet despite the disapproval of his family, health issues, and financial woes.

Hesse, Hermann, and Thomas Mann. *The Hesse-Mann Letters: The Correspondence of Hermann Hesse and Thomas Mann, 1910-1955.* Edited by Anne Carlsson and Volker Michels. New York: Jorge Pinto Books, 2005. This book presents the correspondence between two giants of German literature—both Nobel Prize winners—who commiserate about the ravages of war and speculate about the fate of their native country.

Stelzig, Eugene L. "The Aesthetics of Confession: Hermann Hesse's *Crisis* Poems in the Context of the Steppenwolf Period." In *Hermann Hesse*, edited by Harold Bloom. Philadelphia: Chelsea House, 2002. Essay examines the poems of *Crisis* and relates them to the Steppenwolf period.

Tusken, Lewis W. *Understanding Hermann Hesse: The Man, His Myth, His Metaphor.* Columbia: University of South Carolina Press, 1998. An overview of Hesse's life and literary significance, with particular attention paid to the themes, images, and metaphors in his novels, which often also were used in his poetry.

Ziolkowski, Theodore. *Modes of Faith: Secular Surrogates for Lost Religious Beliefs.* Chicago: University of Chicago Press, 2007. An examination of how writers in the early twentieth century—including James Joyce, Hesse, Thomas Mann, and H. G. Wells—treated the erosion of religious belief and the ascent of secular philosophies in their work.

Jack Ewing

FRIEDRICH HÖLDERLIN

Born: Lauffen am Neckar, Württemberg (now in Germany); March 20, 1770
Died: Tübingen, Württemberg (now in Germany); June 7, 1843

PRINCIPAL POETRY
Nachtgesänge, 1805
Gedichte, 1826 (*Poems*, 1943)
Selected Poems, 1944
Poems and Fragments, 1966
Selected Poems and Fragments, 1998
Odes and Elegies, 2008

OTHER LITERARY FORMS

The deep love for Greek culture that marked the lyric poetry of Friedrich Hölderlin (HURL-dur-leen) also had a profound impact on his other literary endeavors. Aside from his verse, he is most remembered for the epistolary novel *Hyperion: Oder, Der Eremit in Griechenland* (1797, 1799; *Hyperion: Or, The Hermit in Greece*, 1965). In the story of a disillusioned Greek freedom fighter, the author captured in rhythmic prose much of his own inner world. The novel is especially notable for its vivid imagery and its power of thought and language. Fascination with the legend of Empedocles' death on Mount Etna moved him to attempt to re-create the spirit of the surrounding events in the drama *Der Tod des Empedokles* (pb. 1826; *The Death of Empedocles*, 1966), which exists in three fragmentary versions. After 1800, he began translations of Sophocles' *Oidipous Tyrannos* (c. 429 B.C.E.; *Oedipus Tyrannus*, 1715) and *Antigonē* (441 B.C.E.; *Antigone*, 1729); his highly successful renderings were published in 1804. Among the various essays on philosophy, aesthetics, and literature written throughout his career, his treatises on the fine arts in ancient Greece, Achilles, Homer's *Iliad* (c. 750 B.C.E.; English translation, 1611), and the plays of Sophocles are especially significant. Only a small portion of his correspondence has been preserved.

ACHIEVEMENTS

Unlike the great German lyricists with whom he is compared, Friedrich Hölderlin did not attain substantial literary recognition in his own time. This lack of recognition was in part a result of his own misperception of his audience. While he directed his poems to the broad following of the spiritual and intellectual renewal engendered by the French Revolution, his contemporaries, excepting a special few, did not penetrate beyond the surface of his particular revelation of the rebirth of idealism's golden age.

Friedrich Schiller's early patronage gave Hölderlin access to influential editors and other promoters of mainstream literature, enabling him to publish in important journals and popular collections of the time. His work appeared in Gotthold Stäudlin's *Schwäbisches Musenalmanach auf das Jahr 1792* (1792) and *Poetische Blumenlese* (1793), as well as Schiller's *Thalia* and other periodicals. Neither Schiller nor Johann Wolfgang von Goethe, however, fully recognized Hölderlin's true gifts as a writer. Eventually, they distanced themselves from him, and Hölderlin fell into obscurity.

After his death, Hölderlin remained forgotten until his work was rediscovered by Stefan George and his circle. George acclaimed him as one of the great masters of the age, pointing especially to the uniqueness of his language and the expressiveness of his style. In the modern poets whose works reflect a keen inner struggle with the meaning of existence, he at last found a receptive audience, capable of appreciating his contribution to the evolution of the German lyric. Among those whose writings give strong evidence of his productive influence are Georg Trakl, Rainer Maria Rilke, and Hugo von Hofmannsthal.

For his special mastery of form, his naturalization of classical Greek meters and rhythms in the German language, and his unique ability to clothe prophetic vision in verse, Hölderlin now stands alongside Goethe as one of the great poets of German idealism.

Biography

The untimely deaths of both his father and his stepfather determined the course of Johann Christian Friedrich Hölderlin's childhood and youth. His mother, a devoutly religious Lutheran, insisted that he prepare for a career in the clergy. While attending monastery schools at Denkendorf and Maulbronn, he began writing poetry that reflected the suffering of a sensitive spirit under the rigors of traditional discipline and an inability to reconcile the demands of practical reality with his inner sense of artistic calling. Youthful love affairs with Luise Nast (the "Stella" of his early poems) and Elise Lebret exacerbated the tension between the two poles of his existence.

In 1788, Hölderlin entered the theological seminary at the University of Tübingen. Although he completed his studies and received a master's degree that titled him to ordination, the years spent in Tübingen eased him away from any desire to become a pastor. With his friends Christian Ludwig Neuffer and Rudolf Magenau, he founded a poetry club patterned after the Göttinger Hain. He also joined a secret political organization with Georg Wilhelm Friedrich Hegel and Friedrich Schelling and openly advocated social reforms inspired by the ideals of the French Revolution. The true key to his rejection of a life of service in the church, however, was neither purely artistic inclination nor political commitment but rather deep spiritual conflict within himself. Concentrated exposure to the literature, art, and philosophy of classical antiquity caused him to develop a worldview that placed the ancient Greek gods, as vital natural forces, next to Christ in importance for the dawning of a new, humane era of enlightenment and harmony. The tension between the old pantheon and Christian dogma made it impossible for him to feel comfortable in total dedication to institutionalized religion.

Among his contemporaries, Hölderlin's most important role model was Schiller, whose poetry had a strong impact on both his early Tübingen hymns and his later classicistic creations. In 1793, Hölderlin met Schiller for the first time. Their friendship remained rather one-sided; Schiller did not reciprocate the warmth and devotion of his awestruck protégé. Through Schiller's mediation, Hölderlin obtained the first of a long series of positions as a private tutor. These situations, despite their repeated failure, enabled him to avoid the necessity of accepting an appointment as a pastor.

Hölderlin's most significant assignment as a tutor began in 1795, when he entered the service of a wealthy banker in Frankfurt. A love affair with his employer's wife, Susette Gontard, provided the stimulus for a newfound sophistication in his poetry. Much of the substance that he treated in verse while in Frankfurt was later refined and presented in more perfect form in the exquisite odes, elegies, and hymns of his late period. Susette herself became the model for Diotima in his novel *Hyperion* and the poems related to it.

After an unpleasant scene with Susette's husband in 1798, Hölderlin fled to Homburg, where he remained until 1800 with his friend Isaak von Sinclair. Hölderlin continued to see and correspond secretly with Susette, but he was unsuccessful in establishing himself in a permanently meaningful way of life. An endeavor to edit a new journal and make his living as a freelance writer foundered. Plagued by an increasing inner isolation, he was compelled to return home to his mother.

From an artistic point of view, the years immediately after 1800 were the most important of Hölderlin's career; emotionally and spiritually, they were years of progressive devastation. New tutorial positions in Switzerland and France collapsed rapidly. In 1802, Hölderlin left Bordeaux and traveled home on foot. He arrived in Nürtingen mentally and emotionally disturbed after learning of Susette's death. In 1804, temporarily recovered from his nervous breakdown, he returned to Homburg, where Sinclair arranged for him to work as a librarian. When Sinclair was arrested for subversive political activities, Hölderlin's mental condition deteriorated drastically, and he was placed in a sanatorium. In 1806, he was declared incurably ill and given into the care of a carpenter and his wife. He spent the remainder of his life living in a tower room overlooking the Neckar, where he wrote occasional, strangely simple lyrics, played the flute and the piano, and received visitors.

Analysis

In the final stanza of his famous poem "Die Heimat" ("Homeland"), Friedrich Hölderlin captured the essence of his personal artistic calling and its lyrical product. The pairing of love, the divine fire that stimulates creativity, with suffering, the holy reward that the gods give to their poet-prophet, defines the poles of existential tension that were a primary focus of his life and works. A peculiar mixture of the poetry of experience and that of ideas, his early hymns and his mature odes, elegies, and hymns in free rhythms are at once the offspring of intense adoration—of beauty, nature, Greek antiquity, an idealized world of tomorrow—and profound spiritual pain resulting from recognition of the abyss between the poet and the things that he cherishes. The result is a constant duality of mood: on one hand, deeply elegiac longing for the elements of a lost golden age; on the other, overwhelming joy in the message of love that is the joint legacy of the Greek world and the Christian tradition. Oscillating between hope and despair, anticipation and resignation, tragic darkness and powerfully prophetic vision, his verse documents the continuing struggle of a spirit that needs to belong to society yet remains alone as a priest who serves no church, a singer of a people no longer or not yet there.

Despite the concentrated projection of the deeply personal strivings of his own soul into his writings, Hölderlin's lyrics were based firmly in an age-old and broadly recognized tradition to which he gave new life. At the same time, they represent a mating of impulses from the German classical and Romantic movements that dominated the literary mainstream of his own time. His interpretation of models ranging from Plato to Spinoza, from Homer and Hesiod to Schiller and Goethe, and including Friedrich Gottlieb Klopstock, Johann Jakob Wilhelm Heinse, Christian Friedrich Daniel Schubart, and Ludwig Christoph Hölty generated a multisided literature that mixes a glowing sense of freedom with enthusiastic, unfettered pantheism and celebration of the highest human ideals with *Weltschmerz*.

INFLUENCE OF SCHILLER AND KLOPSTOCK

The influence of Schiller upon Hölderlin's early creations is especially noticeable. Scholars often point to the melancholy longing for the beauty and glory of Greece, the lost spiritual homeland, as a defining characteristic of Hölderlin's early verse. His various elaborations of this theme, particularly his emphatic presentations of the ancient gods as living elemental forces, give remarkable evidence of having been motivated directly by Schiller's well-known poem "Die Götter Griechenlands" ("The Gods of Greece"). Moreover, his acclaim of a new humanistic age in hymns to freedom, humanity, harmony, friendship, nature, and other abstract concepts was clearly inspired not only by his infatuation with the ideas of the French Revolution but also by a deep reverence for Schiller, whose treatments of those same subjects are key building blocks in the poetry of German idealism. Even the meter and syntax of Hölderlin's first lyric efforts are obvious products of his familiarity with Schiller's language and forms.

Hölderlin's Alcaic and Asclepiadean odes on nature, landscape, and love, written in Denkendorf and Maulbronn, are strongly subjective and self-oriented, weighed down by an almost oppressive intensity of reflection. The moods of Storm and Stress are clearly visible, as is Klopstock's basic tone, in which personal experience is raised into a suprapersonal religious sphere. Amid trivial occasional verse, sentimentally broad discourses on life, and curiously sad love poems written to Nast, there are already glimmerings of the elements that eventually informed Hölderlin's more characteristic lyrics. For example, "Die Unsterblichkeit der Seele" ("The Immortality of the Soul"), an ode that bears all the marks of Klopstock's manner, anticipates in direction and perception the later "Hymne an die Unsterblichkeit" ("Hymn to Immortality"), which was written in Tübingen. In the long hexameter poem "Die Teck" ("The Teck"), a glorification of a local mountain area, important themes of the late hymns appear: the Dionysian festival of the grape harvest, the sublime nature of dead heroes, the magnificence of the forested landscape saturated with the traditions of the fatherland, and the celebration of friendship.

A MISSION AND A SPIRITUAL HOMELAND

An important focus of the works created in Tübingen is Hölderlin's growing preoccupation with the awareness of a personal poetic mission. From the rejection of seminary life's inhibiting restrictions in "Zornige Sehnsucht" ("Angry Longing") to the magnification and praise of Greece, the Muses, and his personal gods in a first formal cycle of hymns, Hölderlin's formulations stress his belief in a calling to reinterpret Christian and classical ideals within the framework of his own era. He saw himself as a kind of prophet in a time of special revelation that needed poetic amplification. Accordingly, in the hymns, he presented aspects of a holy message based on the eternal example of antiquity. A pantheistic view of nature as a complex of ethical and emotional forces unified by a grand, divine essence charges the poems with living, vital myth in the creation of an ideal, harmonious realm that is the final goal of the poet's longing, both for himself and for all humankind.

The evocation of Greece as Hölderlin's spiritual homeland, which begins in earnest in the Tübingen hymns, is fleshed out, solidified, and given its ultimate direction in the verse that emerged alongside *Hyperion* in Frankfurt. Peculiarly combined with the reincarnation of the ancient Greek spirit in Diotima (Susette Gontard), the poet's priestess of love and embodiment of eternal beauty, is a new, no longer effulgent picture of Hellas that contains sorrow, suffering, and tragic elements. Intense passion is intertwined with philosophical thoughtfulness in poetry characterized by its hearty enthusiasm, expression that is still youthfully immature, and fantastic, sensitive landscapes that are painted with fine feeling. Special emphasis is placed on quiet loveliness and the constancy of nature in a worldview that perceives life as originating in and striving toward childlike harmony. The most representative poems of this period are "Diotima," the first lyric fruit of a newly gained perception of love as a power that can suspend the continuity of time and bring to pass the rebirth of man, and "Hyperions Schicksalslied" ("Hyperion's Song of Destiny"), a penetrating treatment of the fathomlessness of existence that calls to mind Plato's separation of the realm of ideas from the world of phenomena.

Dark themes of later years

To a large extent, the significant poetic works that were written prior to Hölderlin's hasty departure from Frankfurt in 1798, and even those created shortly thereafter in Homburg, served as preliminary studies in language, form, and theme for the magnificent odes, elegies, and hymns that he wrote after 1800. It is somewhat ironic that his most sublime and deeply profound poems are the darkly mythological, prophetically intuitive visions of a mind on the brink of insanity. The ever-increasing emotional strain and existential pressure of his life without Susette served as a catalyst for the final refinement of ideas and structures that are the very essence of the night ode "Chiron," the wonderful elegy "Brot und Wein" ("Bread and Wine"), and the richly mysterious hymn "Patmos." In these and other masterworks of his final productive years, Hölderlin revealed more than ever before his quiet sensitivity, his pure and free view of nature, his precise sense of landscape saturated with the spirit of a creative life force.

Despite their diversity, the mature poems are linked together in a fusion of classical and Christian traditions that places the gods of ancient Greece and Christ on nearly equal footing. The twofold experience of the proximity of the divine and humanity's difficulty in understanding it forms the core of a poetry that is remarkable for its combination of tangible and ethereal elements. Important aspects of the integral system that is perfected and presented in these late writings include a hierarchical chain of genius-beings who govern absolute existence—Christ, the gods of Olympus, biblical prophets and patriarchs, apostles, Greek Titans, heroes, philosophers, great contemporary figures, spirits of nature and love; stress on the relationship of humans with Mother Earth; a poetic landscape that is saturated with powers that point toward the divine origins of life; and constant awareness of the prophetic task of the singer's art and of the conflict between suffering and joy. All these are expressed in language and rhythms that are pregnant with expectation, careful preparation, and unspoken faith. In many respects, it is not so much the imparted vision as the clarity, musicality, and exactness of diction and the expressive perfection and beauty of form that elevate the lyric works of Hölderlin's last creative surge to the level of true greatness.

The Tübingen hymns

A mélange of the revolutionary spirit of the times and interpretation of the basic Christian humanist tradition as mediated by Klopstock and Schiller, Hölderlin's Tübingen hymns are all variations on the same feeling: an endless willingness of heart to accept eternal values. The celebration of inalienable human rights—freedom, equality, friendship, honor—is filled with the youthful impetuousness of the poet's faith blended with a certain naïve tenderness and grace. Although not especially original in vocabulary, meter, and imagery, clearly influenced by models such as Schiller's "An die Freude" ("Ode to Joy"), these early poems convey the charm of their creator's exuberant enthusiasm, the animating tension that is central to his later works, and the love-oriented metaphysical basis of his worldview.

While the hymns do not belong to the poetry of experience, they can be described only loosely as idea poems. To be sure, they are thematically abstract, but their focus is not thought and allegory, as in Schiller's philosophical lyrics. Rather, it is a kind of fundamentally religious perception of the universe in which theoretical principles are given semidivine status. Various common symbols are employed with significant frequency. The mountain typically represents freedom or pride; the eagle stands for courage. Humility and the eternal flow of life appear as valley and river respectively. All nature thus becomes a boundless ideal whole that is the object of intense longing and the source of repeated spiritual ecstasy.

In each of the hymns, the glorification of a concept that has been elevated to godhood is presented in a clearly defined structure. First, the poet approaches the chosen divinity. A central portion of the poem then elaborates the abstract deity's sphere of operation. A triumphant view of the addressed entity's power and domain is climaxed by the poet's humble retreat into recognition of his own inadequacy.

Especially representative of the Tübingen songs are "Hymn to Immortality" and "Hymne an die Freiheit" ("Hymn to Freedom"). The former begins with the flight of the prophet-singer's spirit, powered by love, to the divine realm of endless life. The first stanza evokes two of the major themes of Hölderlin's oeuvre: the poet's godly mission as a seer who penetrates the revelation of creation, and love as the driving force, sacred center, and unifying essence of the world. The joyful intoxication of the vision, however, gradually recedes, leaving in the final lines only emptiness in the realization that human mortality makes it impossible for people to grasp and describe in song the unspeakable fulfillment of the immortal soul. "Hymn to Freedom" develops the idea that people can be completely free within the context of their intended holy life only if they remain true to the blessed laws of love that govern pure existence. By falling away from these divine ideals, humans subject themselves to the shame of hell. Anticipating the hope-filled resolution of the late hymns, the poem ends with the suggestion of a final attainment of freedom in the eternity beyond death.

NACHTGESÄNGE

In 1805, Hölderlin published a small collection of nine poems under the title *Nachtgesänge*. Although this group constitutes less than a third of his mature odes, it forms the core of his late production of Alcaic and Asclepiadean forms. The individual lyric creations are carefully refined renderings of Hölderlin's characteristic themes: the eternal existence of the Greek soul that still governs human action; the glorious mission of poets as magi ordained by the gods to be mediators of divine truth; the pain of separation and the never-ending tension between humans and the deity; spiritual reconciliation of the homeless singer's sorrow; and anticipation of the dawning of a new age in the gods' return. Accentuation of formal precision dominates a presentation that varies musically between lightly melodic language and dynamically passionate rhythms with heavily resounding vowels. Although love still appears as the binding force of extended nature, the motivating principle that gives these poems their special depth and flavor is an awareness of the tragic dominance of night.

Symbolically, night is the time of God's absence. It is the predominant feature of the entire era following the decline of classical civilization and the appearance of Christ. Ordained by the gods, it is endowed with sacred meaning and purpose, yet the poet longs for it to end in a bright revelation of light and for that reason faces its darkness with feelings that fluctuate between humble resignation and profound distress and pain.

Especially notable in the development of key odes is Hölderlin's tendency to frame his ideas in less demanding works, then to allow them to evolve in more complex versions that give full substance and direction to his message. Significant examples include "Der blinde Sänger" ("The Blind Singer") and its reinterpretation in "Chiron" and "Der gefesselte Strom" ("The Chained Stream"), rewritten as "Ganymed." "The Blind Singer" is an Alcaic ode that couches the theme of night in the problem of the poet's loss of sight. In the darkness, his creations lack inspiration, regained only when the gods restore his vision in new revelation. In "Chiron," the sightless singer-seer is transformed into a different symbol, the centaur Chiron, a healer who is struck by the arrow of the gods. The product of his wound is at once torment and ecstasy in apocalyptic visions of the cosmos. Like the blind poet, he is visited by the gods in a storm and sees a strong light break forth that gives everything order and harmony. "The Chained Stream," one of Hölderlin's most powerful celebrations of natural forces, is comparable to Goethe's "Mahomets Gesang" ("Mahomet's Song") in its vibrant imagery and pure musicality. The icebound stream, awakened from the night of winter by spring, arouses all nature to joy-filled life. In "Ganymed," the stream evolves into a symbol for the poet's feeling of aloneness in the world of mortals. It becomes the half-divine stranger Ganymed, whose only place of fulfillment and belonging lies in reconciliation with the gods in the arms of Zeus.

Mournful elegies

Hölderlin's most pronounced merging of classical Greek and Christian elements occurs in mournful elegies that combine lament for the passing of the golden age with deeply felt disappointment at the hollowness of contemporary reality. Overwhelming resignation is only partially offset by hope for the spiritual regeneration of humans. In tone, these poems are closely related to the mature odes, especially in their emphasis on night as the bridge between past and future. Their main thrust is to justify the poetic act in a dark age that destroys the very foundation of lyric art. Employing various approaches to the problem, Hölderlin examines the violent spiritual conflicts that characterize the situation of the modern lyricist. He is presented as being kept from fulfilling his divinely appointed mission by a cold era that needs his uplifting mediation more than ever. Notable is the acute awareness of the poet's homelessness in his own time; this condition is caused at least in part by his inability to forsake the Greek tradition in favor of pure belief in Christ as the only redeeming force in the world.

Two elegies stand out as representative examples of Hölderlin's mastery of this particular verse form. The most famous is "Menons Klagen um Diotima" ("Menon's Laments for Diotima"), a creation that is dominated by the experience of the author's separation from Susette Gontard. Equally powerful is the intensely mysterious "Bread and Wine," in which the figure of Christ is merged with elements of Greek gods and heroes and transformed into the wine god Bacchus at the center of a Dionysian vision of ancient Greece.

"Menon's Laments for Diotima" is a cyclical drama of the soul that begins with the separation of lovers, vacillates between the poet's resigned acceptance of the situation and longing for reunion, and ends with a prayer of thanksgiving for the hope of fulfillment in a new union beyond death. As the poem crescendos in the third section, the music of total isolation and loneliness gives way to harmonies of belief in an indissoluble relationship. The mystical conception that within the absolute context of existence true lovers can never lose each other leads in the final segments to the victory of a faith whose eternal beacon is Diotima.

In "Bread and Wine," Hölderlin comes to grips with night and emptiness in a deeply mystical revelation of the poet's role in bringing to pass the return of the gods. The invocation of darkness allows a hidden light to shine forth. From within its fire, a bright manifestation of Greece emerges, and the poet becomes a priest of Dionysus who prepares the way for a new encounter between humans and the divine. Special power arises from those parts of the poem in which concrete reality (images of evening in a small town) merges with images reflecting the fulfillment of the past and the promise of the future.

The tension between classical Greek and Christian traditions that animates all Hölderlin's mature lyrics is balanced in his Pindaric hymns by a strong mood of reconciliation and striving for harmony. Written in free verse but subject to complex structural rules, these poems are triadically arranged songs of prophetic awareness and dark, mythological, symbolic language. They treat the mysteries of life, death, and the gods in apocalyptic revelations of strange majesty that touch upon all of Hölderlin's major themes. Perhaps nowhere else in his work did he couch his view of the poet's relationship to eternity in such strong imagery of commitment, obedience, and worship.

Emphasis on Christ

Especially significant in the late hymns is a more pronounced emphasis on Christ as the center of metaphysical contemplation. At this point in his life, Hölderlin's attitude toward the Messiah was extremely complex. The Savior figure of his poetic visions is therefore something of a composite of Germanic hero, Greek Titan, and embodiment of the eternal principle of love in which the everlasting presence of God is manifest anew. Particularly noticeable characteristics of the Christ who triumphs over suffering are a sensitive look of naïve piety, peaceful radiance of bearing, and a sense of mythic uniqueness.

In one of the crowning achievements of his artistic career, the profoundly beautiful hymn "Patmos," Hölderlin embarks on a haunting journey to the scene of Saint John's revelation in search of lingering evidence of the living Christ. The poem focuses on the stark tragedy of the Crucifixion as a symbol for the terror of divine absence that is overcome only in a process of sharing. The key concept is that of community, of the impossibility of grasping God alone. Musical cadences, forceful individual words, and rhythmic presentation of ideas are among the structural features that illuminate the landscape of the poet's spiritual universe.

Despite the victorious tone of most of the hymns, none of them documents total resolution of the dilemma generated by the poet's continuing allegiance to both the Greek gods and Christ. This fact is hammered home most dramatically in "Der Einzige" ("The Only One"), in which Christ's position of unique godhood clashes with the singer-prophet's desire to glorify all the gods because he cannot reconcile successfully their conflicting claims. By proclaiming Christ the brother of Bacchus and Hercules, Hölderlin attempts to make visible the painful conflict that arises from the very essence of the dual European heritage of his own origins. In so doing, he also creates a deeply personal symbol for a worldview that stands at the center of a lyric oeuvre that is matched in importance for the history of German poetry by the creations of few other writers.

OTHER MAJOR WORKS

LONG FICTION: *Hyperion: Oder, Der Eremit in Griechenland*, 1797, 1799 (*Hyperion: Or, The Hermit in Greece*, 1965).

PLAYS: *Antigone*, pb. 1804 (translation of Sophocles); *Oedipus Tyrannus*, pb. 1804 (translation of Sophocles); *Der Tod des Empedokles*, pb. 1826 (*The Death of Empedocles*, 1966).

MISCELLANEOUS: *Sämtliche Werke*, 1846 (2 volumes); *Sämtliche Werke: Grosse Stuttgarter Ausgabe*, 1943-1977 (8 volumes).

BIBLIOGRAPHY

Allen, William S. *Ellipsis: Of Poetry and the Experience of Language Ater Heidegger, Hölderlin, and Blanchot*. Albany: State University of New York, 2007. An examination of the poetry of Hölderlin, Martin Heidegger, and Maurice Blanchot with emphasis on poetic language.

Babich, Babette E. *Words in Blood, like Flowers: Philosophy and Poetry, Music and Eros in Hölderlin, Nietzsche, and Heidegger*. Albany: State University of New York

Press, 2006. Compares and contrasts the works of Hölderlin, Friedrich Nietzsche, and Martin Heidegger. Contains topics such as philosophy and the poetic essence of thought.

Constantine, David. *Hölderlin*. Oxford, England: Clarendon Press, 1988. Substantial introduction to Hölderlin's life and work. The author seeks to write about Hölderlin chronologically and in an accessible way and to explore his life as a resource in the explication of his writing. Emphasizes Hölderlin as a poet of religious longing.

Fioretos, Arts, ed. *The Solid Letter: Readings of Friedrich Hölderlin*. Stanford, Calif.: Stanford University Press, 1999. Includes essays on philosophical and theological aspects of Hölderlin's work, his theory and practice of translation, and his poetry, ranging from early poems to uncompleted late hymns.

Heidegger, Martin. *Elucidations of Holderlin's Poetry*. Translated by Keith Hoeller. Amherst, Mass.: Humanity Books, 2000. Six essays on Hölderlin by the major twentieth century philosopher Heidegger, with an introduction by the translator. The goal is to be of use to the public as well as the scholar and includes the German as well as the English versions of the four poems to which Heidegger has devoted his essays. Emphasis is on the relationship of Hölderlin's poetry to modern European philosophy.

Henrich, Dieter, ed. *The Course of Remembrance, and Other Essays on Hölderlin*. Stanford, Calif.: Stanford University Press, 1997. A collection of essays on the ideas and the works of Hölderlin offering a glimpse of the early formation of German idealism. Contains a translation of Henrich's book devoted to Hölderlin's poem, "Remembrance." A vital resource for specialists and enthusiasts of the German Enlightenment and Romantic traditions.

Laplanche, Jean. *Hölderlin and the Question of the Father*. Edited and translated by Luke Carson. Victoria, B.C.: ELS Editions, 2007. Examines the life and works of Hölderlin with respect to his mental illness.

Lernout, Geert. *The Poet as Thinker: Hölderlin in France*. Columbia, S.C.: Camden House, 1994. A comprehensive historical survey of the reception of the poet's work by French critics and writers. Includes chapters on Heidegger's reading of Hölderlin, the French Revolution in Hölderlin's thought, and psychoanalytic theories about Hölderlin's illness. Also includes a chapter on the influence of Hölderlin on such important French authors as Albert Camus, Louis Aragon, and Philippe Sollers.

Ungar, Richard. *Friedrich Hölderlin*. Boston: Twayne, 1984. A basic and useful introduction to Hölderlin. Includes summaries and paraphrases of Hölderlin's poetry together with interpretations. Intended to assist readers who are encountering Hölderlin for the first time and to provide an understanding of the texts at the most elementary level. Includes chronology and annotated bibliography.

Lowell A. Bangerter

CHRISTIAN MORGENSTERN

Born: Munich, Germany; May 6, 1871
Died: Untermais, near Meran, Austro-Hungarian Empire (now Merano, Italy); March 31, 1914

PRINCIPAL POETRY
In Phanta's Schloss, 1895
Auf vielen Wegen, 1897
Horatius travestitus, 1897
Ich und die Welt, 1897
Ein Sommer, 1900
Und aber ründet sich ein Kranz, 1902
Galgenlieder, 1905 (*The Gallows Songs*, 1963)
Melancholie: Neue Gedichte, 1906
Einkehr, 1910
Palmström, 1910
Ich und Du: Sonette, Ritornelle, Lieder, 1911
Wir fanden einen Pfad, 1914
Palma Kunkel, 1916
Der Gingganz, 1918
Stufen, 1918
Epigramme und Sprüche, 1919
Klein Irmchen, 1921
Mensch Wanderer: Gedichte aus den Jahren 1887-1914, 1927
The Moonsheep, 1953
The Daynight Lamp, and Other Poems, 1973
Gesammelte Werke in einem Band, 1974
Lullabies, Lyrics, and Gallows Songs, 1995

OTHER LITERARY FORMS

Christian Morgenstern (MAWR-guhn-shtehrn) was an active translator of Scandinavian literature. Among his translations are August Strindberg's *Inferno* in 1898; a large number of plays and poems for the German edition of Henrik Ibsen's work; and Knut Hamsun's *Aftenrøde* (1898) in 1904 as *Abendröte*, and his *Livets spil* (1896) in 1910 as *Spiel des Lebens*. Morgenstern also translated the works of Frederick the Great. There are two editions of his letters, *Ein Leben in Briefen* (1952) and *Alles um des Menschen willen* (1962). Otherwise, Morgenstern is known chiefly for his poems.

Achievements

Christian Morgenstern began to write serious and humorous verse while still in school. By 1894, he was contributing to various magazines, and in the following years, he began to travel extensively. In 1903, he became a reader for publisher Bruno Cassirer and edited *Das Theater*. The serious side of his nature was stimulated by the lectures of Rudolf Steiner, and in 1909, he became a member of the Anthroposophical Society. The German Schiller Society made him the recipient of an honorary stipend in 1912, and in November, 1913, he was honored at a Morgenstern festival in Stuttgart.

Biography

Christian Otto Josef Wolfgang Morgenstern was born just as the Franco-Prussian War ended, and he died shortly before the outbreak of World War I. His life span covers a long interval of peace in the history of modern Germany. The lack of external political problems may have been responsible in part for his attention to that which ailed the country from within, particularly the crass materialism he perceived and the callousness of the upper class with regard to the plight of the worker.

Morgenstern was the only child of Carl Ernst Morgenstern, a landscape painter, and his wife, Charlotte, née Schertel. Both parents came from artists' families. Because of the frequent changes of residence necessitated by his father's profession, Morgenstern's education was erratic. He changed schools frequently and sometimes received private tutoring. After the death of his mother in 1881 of tuberculosis—a disease from which he also suffered, requiring frequent sanatorium visits—he was sent to his uncle's family in Hamburg. This arrangement proved to be unsuitable, and when his father married again, Morgenstern was sent to a boarding school in Landshut. The strict, oppressive environment there, which included corporal punishment, was unbearable for him, and his bitter complaints to his father resulted in his removal from the school after two years. In March, 1884, he joined his parents in Breslau and attended a local *Gymnasium* for four years. Although Morgenstern's schooling was not a positive experience, he began to write poetry and became acquainted with the philosophy of Arthur Schopenhauer and medieval German mystics such as Meister Eckhart and Johannes Tauler. Shortly before entering a military academy in 1889, he met Friedrich Kayssler, who became an actor and Morgenstern's best and lifelong friend. It quickly became obvious that Morgenstern was not suited for the military life; in 1890, he entered the *Gymnasium* in Sorau, and after his graduation in 1892, he became a student of economics and political science at the University of Breslau. The following two years brought some personal upheavals that culminated in his estrangement from his father. In the summer of 1893, his tubercular condition became more severe, requiring an extensive period of rest. He began reading Friedrich Nietzsche, to whose mother he sent his first book of poetry. Meanwhile, his father had divorced his second wife, remarried, and refused to finance his son's further schooling. In the spring of 1894, Morgenstern left for Berlin.

Newly independent, Morgenstern was briefly employed at the National Gallery. He then began to contribute to a number of different journals, among them the *Neue Deutsche Rundschau* and *Der Kunstwart*. For the latter magazine, he wrote theater reviews. This activity brought him in contact with Max Reinhardt, the famous theatrical producer, who became one of Morgenstern's friends. In 1895, his first volume of poetry, *In Phanta's Schloss*, was published. Morgenstern characterized it as humorous and fantastic, but it contains lyrics with mythological and mystical elements engulfed in pathos. Even as a sixteen-year-old, he had written a poem on reincarnation, and during the winter of 1896-1897, he had several dreams that he transformed into a cycle of lyric poems. They became part of *Auf vielen Wegen*. Between 1897 and 1903, Morgenstern translated a large number of plays and poems by Ibsen, whom he met in 1898 on a journey to Oslo. Morgenstern always had a sense of urgency about his work—a conviction that his time was limited. He traveled extensively to Scandinavia, Switzerland, Italy, and within Germany, always writing, always battling his deteriorating health. While vacationing in Dreikirchen in the Tirol, he met and became engaged to Margareta Gosebruch von Liechtenstern in 1908; they were married in 1910.

At this point in his life, Morgenstern was seriously ill and had to spend considerable time in hospitals and sanatoriums. After learning of the spiritualist and occultist research being done by Rudolf Steiner, the couple attended his lecture in January, 1909, on Leo Tolstoy and Andrew Carnegie. Steiner had written studies on Johann Wolfgang von Goethe and Nietzsche as well as on mysticism in Christianity. After having outlined his philosophy in *Philosophie der Freiheit* (1894; *Philosophy of Freedom*, 1964) and in his *Theosophie* (1904; *Theosophy*, 1954), he published a work in 1909 outlining his method of attaining a knowledge of the occult. Morgenstern became a member of his Anthroposophical Society in May, 1909, and attended Steiner's lectures in Oslo, Budapest, Kassel, and Munich. During the last years of his life, Morgenstern's longing for communication with a world beyond that of his present existence took shape in a number of poems of a meditative nature. Two weeks before his death, he determined that the last collection of his lyrics was to be called *Wir fanden einen Pfad* (we found a path). Morgenstern died on March 31, 1914.

Analysis

Christian Morgenstern himself considered his serious lyrics paramount in his poetic oeuvre, although he is best known for his humorous poems. He has been compared to contemporaries such as Stefan George, Hugo von Hofmannsthal, and Rainer Maria Rilke, with whom he shared a sense of poetic mission and a certain melodiousness of verse. Morgenstern's poetry is considerably less complicated both linguistically and metaphorically than Rilke's, although it expresses emotion sincerely. Only a few of his serious poems have been translated into English, and German audiences were more receptive to his grotesque humor than to the expressions of his religious convictions or metaphysical thought. Although Morgenstern considered his light and provocative verse to be *Beiwerke* (minor efforts), it is in this area that he anticipated trends that were later exploited more extensively in Dadaism and concrete poetry. He experimented with visually and acoustically innovative techniques, presented a satirical view of a philistine society in his verse, and playfully created new and sometimes nonsensical word constellations that appear to mock both the advocates of a *poésie pure* and the efforts of those who, thirty years after his death, attempted a reconstruction of his poetry with ciphers and absolute metaphors. Satire, religious fervor, humor, and mysticism found in Morgenstern an expressive spirit.

THE GALLOWS SONGS

Morgenstern's frivolous verse is the foundation of his fame, notwithstanding his protestations. His most popular collection was *The Gallows Songs*, which ran through fourteen editions in his lifetime and by 1937 had sold 290,000 copies. Critics persisted in reading hidden meanings into these witty lyrics, so that he felt compelled to render mock explanations in *Über die Galgenlieder* (1921; about the gallows songs). The first group of these whimsical lyrics were composed when Morgenstern was in his twenties. On the occasion of an outing with some friends, they arrived at a place referred to as Gallows Hill. Being in a bantering mood, they founded the Club of the Gallows Gang, Morgenstern contributing some frivolous poems that another of the group later set to music. These poems obviously attest Morgenstern's lighter side, and no attempt should be made to imbue them with a depth that they do not have and that was not intended, yet it will not detract from the reader's pleasure if the spirit of innovation and the subtle humor that pervade them are pointed out.

Morgenstern's raw material is the sound, the structure, the form, and the idiomatic usage of the German language. The nineteenth century saw an abundance of grammarians and linguists who attempted to regulate and explain linguistic phenomena and to limit expression to precisely defined and carefully governed modes of communication. Morgenstern perceived this approach to be hopelessly dull, "middle-class safe," and philistine. A degree of arbitrariness is an essential element of language, and he proceeded to point this out by confusing the complacent and satirizing the pedants. He accomplished this on the semantic, grammatical, and formal levels in his poems. In "Gruselett" ("Scariboo"), he created what has come to be known as a nonsense poem:

> The Winglewangle phlutters
> through widowadowood,
> the crimson Fingoor splutters
> and scary screaks the Scrood.

By arranging essentially meaningless words according to a familiar syntactical pattern within the sentence and by adding a number of adjectives and verbs that stimulate lexical memory, Morgenstern coerces the reader into believing that he has grasped the sense of what has been said. It must be pointed out here that most of the translations of Morgenstern's poems have not been literal and have frequently deviated greatly from the original to preserve a semblance of the poet's intention (the use of puns, untranslatable idioms, grammatical constructions not found in English, and so on).

"THE BANSHEE"

Proper inflection, punctuation, and use of tense also come under attack by Morgenstern, who freely admitted that his teachers had bored and embittered him. His poem "Der Werwolf" ("The Banshee") reflects the eagerness, gratitude, and eventual disillusionment of the pupil, as well as the futility and uselessness of that which is taught by smug grammarians. When the banshee requests of an entombed teacher, "Inflect me, pray," the teacher responds:

> "The banSHEE, in the subject's place;
> the banHERS, the possessive case.
> The banHER, next, is what they call
> objective case—and that is all."

The banshee, delighted at first, then asks how to form the plural of "banshee":

> "While 'bans' are frequent," he advised,
> "a 'she' cannot be pluralized."
> The banshee, rising clammily,
> wailed: "What about my family?"
> Then, being not a learned creature,
> said humbly "Thanks" and left the teacher.

The teacher's wisdom is depicted as severely limited and out of touch with reality. His linguistic expertise extends only to abstractions.

"AMONG TENSES" AND "KORF'S CLOCK"

Time, that element which is "money" to the businessperson and is "of the essence" to the philistine, is only relative to Morgenstern. He satirizes the preoccupation of humanity with the temporal in several ways, one of them grammatical. In the poem "Unter Zeiten" ("Among Tenses"), past and future are on equal terms in the present: "Perfect and Past/ drank to a friendship to last./ They toasted the Future tense/ (which makes sense)./ Futureperf and Plu/ nodded too." The clock, the object that enslaves humanity because it measures every minute and every hour and restlessly reminds us that "time flies" (*tempus fugit*), is reinvented to improve on the fatal flaw. "Die Korfsche Uhr" ("Korf's Clock") not only deprives time of its sovereignty but also recalls those people who, while still existing in the present, seem to live forever in the past:

> When it's two—it's also ten;
> when it's three—it's also nine.
> You just look at it, and then
> time gets never out of line,
>   . . . .
> time itself is nullified.

A counterpart to Korf's clock, and one with yet greater flexibility and sophistication, is Palmström's clock ("Palmströms Uhr"): It heeds requests and slows or quickens its pace according to the individual's wishes. It "will never/ stick to petty rules, however," and is "a clockwork with a heart." For those who are incurably enslaved by time and who permit it to upset their equilibrium grievously, Morgenstern suggests a cure: Since time is not a matter of reality but merely of habit, it is useful to read tomorrow's paper to find out about the resolution of today's conflicts.

"The Funnels" and "Fish's Lullaby"

Morgenstern's visual verse is a forerunner of concrete poetry. It expresses graphically in the poem what is described linguistically in the choice of words. Max Knight translates the poem "Die Trichter" ("The Funnels") in the singular:

> A funnel ambles through the night.
> Within its body, moonbeams white
> converge as they
> descend upon
> its forest
> pathway
> and
> so
> on

The funnel in effect becomes its own pathfinder as it streamlines the moonlight through its neck and directs it like a flashlight on the dark path. Although this poem is meant to be humorous, it contains an element of Morgenstern's own undaunted search for cosmic (divine) direction and communication, which is very evident in his serious poetry. As a final example of Morgenstern's humorous verse, the visual poem "Fisches Nachtgesang" ("Fish's Lullaby"), may suffice:

>   -
>   ~ ~
>   - - -
>   ~ ~ ~ ~
>   - - -
>   ~ ~ ~ ~

```
         - - -
         ~ ~ ~ ~
         - - -
         ~ ~ ~ ~
         - - -
         ~ ~
          -
```

Fish, as mute creatures, can express lyrical sentiments only wordlessly, by rhythmically opening and closing their mouths. The unverbalized song is formally recorded by Morgenstern as a series of dashes that leave the content to the imagination of the reader.

"Evolution" and "The Eighteen-Year-Old"

A large part of Morgenstern's work is serious prose, much of it dealing with profound matters, such as the search for truth, and with humanity's position in the universe and in relation to God. Not only did Morgenstern write deeply religious verse in the Christian tradition, but also he developed poems involving the concepts of pantheism and reincarnation. Although his basic philosophical tenets may not have changed significantly, a change in style, a greater facility and fluency in writing, is evident in a comparison of portions of his early with his late work. This may be perceived in the opening stanzas of two poems dealing with reincarnation, one of which, "Der Achtzehnjährige" ("The Eighteen-Year-Old"), was written in 1889, while the other, "Evolution," was written shortly before Morgenstern's death. "The Eighteen-Year-Old" begins:

> How often may I already have wandered before
> on this earthly sphere of sorrow,
> how often may I have changed
> the substance, the form of life's clothing?

The formal aspects of this poem in the German are scrupulously observed: iambic meter with four feet, regular *abab* rhyme scheme. The first two strophes posit the fundamental question (rhetorically), and the last one answers it with the metaphor of the ever-changing waves of the sea. The finality of the answer is sententious. Despite the use of enjambment, the poem grinds along with the deadening regularity that is one of the pitfalls of iambic meter, and it does so because the metric stress coincides almost perfectly with the syllabic emphasis of the words.

Thus, the prosodic perfection becomes somnolent and detrimental to the poem's overall effect. The single place (in the second stanza) in which the word "order" is reversed for the sake of the rhyme causes the verse to sound contrived and strange. It may be argued that the monotony of the verse is intentional, thereby underscoring the repetitiousness of life, death, and rebirth inherent in the concept of reincarnation. While such a theory is certainly plausible, other early poems by Morgenstern with different topics show a similar emphasis on the regularity of rhyme and meter and thereby reveal the style to be a sign of poetic immaturity and inexperience.

The difference between "The Eighteen-Year-Old" and the poem "Evolution" is striking. The latter begins:

> Barely that that, which once separated itself from Thee,
> recognized itself in its special entity,
> it immediately longs to return to its element.

The excessive pathos and the sententiousness that characterized the first poem are missing here. The certainty, too, is absent: There are no answers in "Evolution," only ambiguity, longing, and the realization that this yearning cannot yet find fulfillment. The easy solutions of youth have mellowed into a peaceful submission, a quiet recognition and acceptance of the inevitable unfolding of individual and collective destiny. The formal presentation is also different. Although the poem in its entirety retains a formal meter (iambic pentameter) and a regular rhyme scheme (*aba bcb c*), there is a natural flow of rhythm akin to that inherent in prose: The monotony of the iambs is broken by the deliberate placement of semantically significant syllables on metrically unstressed ones, and vice versa. The interlocking rhymes facilitate the smooth flow of verse, and the third strophe is not a glib retort but a reduction, a one-line confrontation with an unfathomable phenomenon.

Morgenstern's serious poetry is not without beauty and merit, although it has been neglected both by the reading public and by the critics. There is a certain dogmatism, a religious and mystical undercurrent inherent in it that limits its appeal and precludes the kind of universal acceptability that, for example, the lyrics of Rainer Maria Rilke possess. Morgenstern's lighter verse, which exemplifies the cheerful side of his personality, not only requires less empathy from the reader but also stimulates the reader's intellect without engaging the personal prejudices that he might have. It is an art worthy of pursuit.

OTHER MAJOR WORKS

NONFICTION: *Ein Leben in Briefen*, 1952; *Alles um des Menschen willen*, 1962.

TRANSLATIONS: *Inferno*, 1898 (of August Strindberg's novel); *Abendröte*, 1904 (of Knut Hamsun's play *Aftenrøde*); *Spiel des Lebens*, 1910 (of Hamsun's play *Livets spil*).

MISCELLANEOUS: *Über die Galgenlieder*, 1921.

BIBLIOGRAPHY

Bauer, Michael. *Christian Morgensterns Leben und Werk.* Munich: R. Piper, 1941. The standard biography, illustrated. In German.

Forster, Leonard. *Poetry of Significant Nonsense.* New York: Cambridge University

Press, 1962. A brief treatment of Morgenstern in the context of Dada and nonsense verse.

Hofacker, Erich P. *Christian Morgenstern*. Boston: Twayne, 1978. A good English-language introduction to Morgenstern's life and works.

Knight, Max, trans. Introduction to *The Daynight Lamp, and Other Poems*, by Christian Morgenstern. Boston: Houghton Mifflin, 1973. The translator's introduction to this slim collection casts light on Morgenstern's poetics.

Scott, Robert Ian. "Metaphorical Maps of Improbable Fictions: The Semantic Parables of Christian Morgenstern." *Et Cetera* 52, no. 3 (Fall, 1995): 276. Scott argues that Morgenstern made absolute faith in words "obviously ridiculous" in demonstrating that the world does not follow human logic. He examines a number of Morgenstern's poems.

Helene M. Kastinger Riley

EDUARD MÖRIKE

Born: Ludwigsburg, Württemberg (now in Germany); September 8, 1804
Died: Stuttgart, Germany; June 4, 1875

PRINCIPAL POETRY
Gedichte, 1838, 1848, 1856, 1867 (*Poems*, 1959)
Idylle vom Bodensee oder Fischer Martin und die Glockendiebe, 1848

OTHER LITERARY FORMS

Although Eduard Mörike (MUR-ree-kuh) is famous for his poetry, and many of his poems have been set to music, he was not primarily a poet. His first publication was a three-hundred-page novella in two parts, *Maler Nolten* (1832; *Nolten the Painter: A Novella in Two Parts*, 2005). He also wrote seven shorter works; the most well-known is *Mozart auf der Reise nach Prag* (1855; *Mozart's Journey from Vienna to Prague: A Romance of His Private Life*, 1897). Of particular significance for his poetry are his translations of classical poetry that retain the stanza form of the original. His editorial work attests to his interest in the works of contemporary Swabian poets and novelists, as well as in Greek and Roman poetry.

ACHIEVEMENTS

During Eduard Mörike's lifetime, very few German literary awards were being awarded, as most awards were not established until the twentieth century. For that reason, the recognition he received carries all the more weight. In 1847, Mörike won the Tiedge Prize for his *Idylle vom Bodensee oder Fischer Martin und die Glockendiebe*. In 1852, he received an honorary doctorate from the University of Tübingen, and in 1862, the king of Bavaria awarded him the Order of Maximilian for Arts and Sciences. In 1864, Mörike was awarded the Knight's Cross First Class of the Württemberg Order of Friedrich.

BIOGRAPHY

Eduard Mörike spent his entire life in southwest Germany, in what is now the state of Baden-Württemberg. He is sometimes referred to as a Swabian poet, because Swabian is the dialect spoken in that region. The family's standard of living was severely reduced when Mörike's father, a physician, suffered a massive stroke in 1815 and died two years later. Although Mörike was not a good student, an influential uncle arranged for him to attend the theological seminar in Urach and then to study theology in Tübingen. Mörike subsequently served reluctantly as a Protestant clergyman in numerous posts. He was not convinced of the doctrine he was required to preach and was not appreciated by his parishioners. In 1834, he was appointed pastor in Cleversulzbach and brought his mother and younger sister Klara to live with him there. It was his last position with the church. In 1843, two years after his mother's death, Mörike took early retirement.

The Mörikes were a close-knit family. Eduard Mörike was devastated when his younger brother August died of a stroke in 1824 and commemorated him in the poem "To an Aeolian Harp." Three years later, his older sister Luise died at age twenty-nine, and Mörike had to take several months' leave of absence. His own health was delicate, and he was often overextended financially because he felt obliged to help his siblings. Mörike was apolitical, and was shocked by the interrogation he underwent after his brother Carl was jailed for political protest.

In 1823-1824, during Mörike's student years, he was briefly infatuated with an attractive transient, Maria Meyer. Then, believing she had deceived him, he refused to see her again, a decision that caused him considerable emotional suffering. That relationship is the subject of his five "Peregrina" poems. He was engaged to Luise Rau from 1829 to 1833 but was also working on *Nolten the Painter* at the time, and Rau left him for someone better able to provide for her. Mörike did not marry until he was forty-seven. It is indicative of his open-mindedness in intolerant times that his wife, Margarethe Speeth, was a Roman Catholic. Their two daughters, Fanny and Marie, were born in 1855 and 1857. Mörike supported his family, which still included his sister Klara, by teaching from 1851 to 1866 at the Katharinenstift, a girls' school in Stuttgart.

Throughout Mörike's life, a friend from student days, Wilhelm Hartlaub, was a constant source of companionship and support. Mörike's poem "To Wilhelm Hartlaub" describes how Hartlaub's piano playing could transport him into other worlds. Hartlaub had what Mörike longed for, a sense of fulfillment as a clergyman and a peaceful domestic life. Mörike was estranged from his wife and in financial straits during the last years of his life. He is buried in the Prague Cemetery in Stuttgart.

Analysis

A glance at Eduard Mörike's 225 poems reveals his remarkable versatility as a poet. The influence of Greek and Roman poetry is evident in his sonnets, odes, and idylls, and in his frequent use of iambic hexameter. The Germanic influence is evident in the rhymed quatrains and simple folksongs. However, Mörike was not limited by any form: Some of his poems are just two verses long; others run for pages. In most cases, he uses rhyme, meter, and stanza structures only as artistically necessary. Many of his poems are in free verse. His writing is direct, often conversational in tone. The five "Peregrina" poems are one of only two groups of poems. (The other group, "Pictures from Bebenhausen," has been only partially translated.) Otherwise, each poem stands for itself. Mörike let a friend decide on their order of appearance when his poems were published.

Nothing in Mörike's poetry indicates that he lived in a time of political unrest; nothing indicates that he was a clergyman. Some of his contemporaries criticized him for not mentioning political or historical events, but ironically, it is his refusal to be governed by current events that has made his poetry timeless. Mörike focused on personal issues, everyday life, and the inner peace he experienced in the presence of friends or when beholding a "Beautiful Beech Tree" or an object, as in "On a Lamp." He could capture the moment and infuse it with meaning. Much of his poetry, though, has an undercurrent of dissonance, a dissonance Hugo Wolf transferred well to his musical settings of fifty-seven Mörike poems in the 1880's. Mörike shows that even "At Midnight," one is constantly reminded of the affairs of the day. He was aware of conflicting beliefs, changes brought with the passage of time, and the omnipresence of death.

"Peregrina" poems

Mörike wrote his five "Peregrina" poems between 1824 and 1828 and included versions of four of them in *Nolten the Painter*. These early poems—some rhymed, some unrhymed, some in regular stanzas, and some in free verse—derive from Mörike's intense love for and then loss of the migrant or peregrine Meyer. The male poetic persona experiences heartbreak because he still loves Peregrina, indeed will always love her, yet feels he had to send her away because of his desire to remain in respectable society.

Mörike portrays a dangerous struggle between emotion and reason, between sexual attraction and societal norms. The temptation is great. In the first poem, the speaker tells Peregrina of her powerful effect on him: "To set us both on fire with wild beguiling:/ Death in the cup of sin you hand me, smiling." The wedding scene in the second poem is far removed from any Christian context. The bride is dressed in explicitly sexual colors, with her black dress and scarlet headscarf, but the reader should remember that black and red are also the colors of traditional Black Forest costumes. The turning point is the third poem, in which the speaker realizes he has been deceived. He sends Peregrina away, but cannot stop thinking of her, and he wonders how he would react if she were to reappear. The fourth poem shows how thoughts of her still intrude and move him to tears in other surroundings. The fifth poem, a sonnet, has him longing for her return, while he remains convinced that she will never come back again.

In *Nolten the Painter*, the Peregrina figure is conflated with the gypsy Elizabeth and is portrayed as truly malign, bringing death to Nolten and any women who are interested in him. This change in her character may be seen as rationalization on the part of the author, making the object of his attraction seem worse than she was to justify his rejection of her.

"On a Christmas Rose"

"On a Christmas Rose," a two-part poem, was written in 1841. Mörike wrote to his friend Hartlaub on October 29 of that year that he and his sister Klara had found the rare flower they had been seeking in a churchyard. Known in English as the Christmas rose, the plant is actually *Helleborus niger*. Mörike describes its delicate fragrance and the green tint in its white petals.

Because he found it blooming on a grave in a churchyard and because of its common name, *Christblume*, Mörike first associates the flower with Christian imagery, mentioning an angel, the Virgin Mary, and the wounds of Christ. However, the purely Christian frame of reference was never adequate for Mörike. In the last stanza of part 1, he draws on the pre-Christian, Germanic belief in spirits of the forest by having an elf tiptoe past the flower. Mörike's poetry is rich in undercurrents because for him, many things could be simultaneously present.

Part 2 is a classic example of Mörike's inclusive vision, a fanciful superimposition of summer on winter. Commenting that a summer butterfly can never feed on the nectar of a Christmas rose that blooms in winter, Mörike then wonders if the butterfly's fragile ghost, drawn by the faint fragrance, may not still be present and hovering around its petals, although invisible to him.

"A Visit to the Charterhouse"

"A Visit to the Charterhouse (epistle to Paul Heyse—1862)," a long idyll in iambic hexameter, was one of Mörike's last poems and was recognized early on as one of his best. It refers to the Carthusian charterhouse or monastery between St. Gallen and Constance that Mörike visited in 1840.

In the poem, the speaker makes a return visit to the charterhouse after fourteen years and finds that the last monks have dispersed and the monastery building is now a brewery. The traveler falls into a reverie about the hospitable prior he met on his previous visit, and by virtue of his vivid description, the prior is present again, in the same way that the butterfly hovers around the Christmas rose.

An object then links the past with the present more tangibly. The traveler recognizes the prior's clock on the mantelpiece, a pewter clock engraved with the Latin memento mori: *Una ex illis ultima* (one of these hours will be your last). The realization that death will put an end to life is one of Mörike's main themes, as in "O Soul, Remember" and "Erinna to Sappho."

In "A Visit to the Charterhouse," thoughts of death are pleasantly interrupted. The local physician entertains the traveler with the story of the clock. The prior bequeathed it to the father steward, and when the father suffered a slight stroke, the clock disappeared. Years later, the brewer's wife found the clock wrapped up behind the chimney stack, with a label bequeathing it to the brewmaster. The poem is a tribute to companionship and conversation, the best means on earth to banish mortal fears.

Other major works

LONG FICTION: *Maler Nolten*, 1832 (*Nolten the Painter: A Novella in Two Parts*, 2005); *Das Stuttgarter Hutzelmännlein*, 1853; *Mozart auf der Reise nach Prag*, 1855

(*Mozart's Journey from Vienna to Prague: A Romance of His Private Life*, 1897); *Die Historie von der Schöen Lau*, 1873 (illustrations by Moritz von Schwind).
TRANSLATION: *Theokritos, Bion und Moschos. Deutsch im Versmasse der Urschrift*, 1855 (with Friedrich Notter).
EDITED TEXTS: *Jahrbuch Schwäbischer Dichter und Novellisten*, 1836 (with Wilhelm Zimmermann); *Classische Blumenlese: Eine Auswahl von Hymnen, Oden, Liedern, Elegien, Idyllen, Gnomen und Epigrammen der Griechen und Römer*, 1840; *Gedichte von Wilhelm Waiblinger*, 1844; *Anakreon und die sogenannten Anakreontischen Lieder: Revision und Erzänzung der J. Fr. Dege'schen Übersetzung mit Erklärungen von E. Mörike*, 1864.
MISCELLANEOUS: *Iris. Eine Sammlungerzählender und dramatischer Dichtungen*, 1839; *Vier Erzählungen*, 1856.

BIBLIOGRAPHY
Adams, Jeffrey. "Eduard Mörike." In *Dictionary of Literary Biography. Nineteenth-Century German Writers to 1840*, edited by James Hardin and Siegfried Mews. Vol. 133. Detroit: Gale, 1993. A chronological overview of Mörike's life and works.
―――, ed. *Mörike's Muses. Critical Essays on Eduard Mörike*. Columbia, S.C.: Camden House, 1990. Of the eleven essays in the anthology, only seven provide English translations of the poems discussed. Mark Lehrer's interesting essay compares Mörike's implicit values with those of his contemporary Karl Marx. Contains Stern's translation of "A Visit to the Charterhouse."
Hölderlin, Friedrich, and Eduard Mörike. *Friedrich Hölderlin, Eduard Mörike. Selected Poems*. Translated by Christopher Middleton. Chicago: University of Chicago Press, 1972. Contains translations of thirty-six of Mörike's poems. Middleton has read all of Mörike's letters and has written an informative introduction and detailed notes about the poems. Includes the five "Peregrina" poems.
Mare, Margaret. *Eduard Mörike. The Man and the Poet*. London: Methuen, 1957. An excellent, classic biography with twenty illustrations consisting of art by Mörike and family portraits. Appendix 1 contains English translations of eight major poems.
Mörike, Eduard. *Mozart's Journey to Prague and a Selection of Poems*. Translated by David Luke. London: Penguin Classics, 2003. Contains translations of forty-three of Mörike's poems, a useful introduction, and notes on the poems.
―――. *Poems by Eduard Mörike*. Translated by Norah K. Cruickshank and Gilbert F. Cunningham. With an introduction by Jethro Bithell. London: Methuen, 1959. Translation includes a useful introduction and brief information about each of the forty translated poems. Includes "On a Christmas Rose."
Oxford German Studies 36, no. 1 (2007). This special issue on Mörike contains two excellent articles on his poetry. "Mörike and the Higher Criticism," by Ritchie Robertson, focuses on Mörike's combination of Christian and pagan elements in the poem

"To a Christmas Rose." "Idyll and Elegy: Mörike's 'Besuch in der Carthause,'" by Ray Ockenden, draws on Mörike's knowledge of classical verse forms to lend deeper understanding to this previously neglected late poem.

Slessarev, Helga. *Eduard Mörike*. New York: Twayne, 1970. The long, well-organized chapter on Mörike's poetry places it in the context of his classical education and the events of his life.

Jean M. Snook

LISEL MUELLER

Born: Hamburg, Germany; February 8, 1924

PRINCIPAL POETRY
Dependencies, 1965
Life of a Queen, 1970 (chapbook)
The Private Life, 1976
Voices from the Forest, 1977 (chapbook)
The Need to Hold Still, 1980
Second Language, 1986
Waving from Shore, 1989
Alive Together: New and Selected Poems, 1996

OTHER LITERARY FORMS

Drawing upon her native language, Lisel Mueller (MYEWL-ur) has published translations of the works of two German women, including *Three Daughters* (1987), a novel by Anna Mitgutsch; *Selected Later Poems of Marie Luise Kaschnitz* (1980); *Whether or Not* (1984), a prose work by Kaschnitz; and *Circe's Mountain* (1990), a collection of Kaschnitz's short stories.

Throughout her career, Mueller has also written critical articles and reviews for the magazine *Poetry* and for the *Chicago Daily News*. Her essay "Midwestern Poetry: Goodbye to All That" appears in a collection of essays *Voyages to the Inland Sea I* (1971), edited by John Judson. Also, a brief essay titled "Parentage and Good Luck" appears in *Where We Stand: Women Poets and the Literary Tradition* (1993), edited by Sharon Bryan.

ACHIEVEMENTS

Although Lisel Mueller began writing poetry in college, she did not turn to serious writing of poetry for several more years. Her first volume of poems, *Dependencies*, was published in 1965. This volume is often regarded as excessively literary, but the lead poem, "The Blind Leading the Blind," is frequently anthologized. Mueller's second full volume of poetry, *The Private Life*, won the Lamont Poetry Selection in 1975. Mueller received the National Book Award in Poetry (1981) for *The Need to Hold Still*, the Theodore Roethke Prize from *Poetry Northwest* (1985), and the Carl Sandburg Literary Award (1989). She was awarded the Pulitzer Prize in poetry in 1997 for *Alive Together* and the Ruth Lilly Poetry Prize in 2002.

Biography

Lisel Mueller was born Lisel Neumann in Hamburg, Germany, to Fritz C. Neumann and Illse Burmester Neumann, both teachers. Leaving her grandparents behind, her immediate family fled Nazi Germany in 1939 and settled in Evansville, Indiana. Mueller was blessed with a set of parents who were, according to Mueller, "wholly and blessedly gender-blind." Mueller characterizes her mother as "feminine in the sense that she was warm, outgoing, and impulsive, but she was totally ignorant of 'feminine wiles,' such as manipulation of, and deference to, men." It was only when Mueller moved to Evansville, Indiana, at the age of fifteen that she discovered the more traditional roles of women and gender discrimination.

In 1943, Lisel Neumann married Paul Mueller, an editor, and they had two daughters, Lucy and Jenny. Although Mueller would dabble in poetry while in college, preparing for a social-work career, she began to write serious poetry only after the death of her mother in 1953. Many years later she explained, in her poem "When I Am Asked," why she began writing poetry: On a beautiful June day shortly after her mother died, Mueller discovered that she had to place her grief "in the mouth of language,/ the only thing that would grieve with me."

Mueller has worked as an instructor of creative writing at Elmhurst College, Goddard College, and the Warren Wilson M.F.A. Program for Writers. She is a self-taught poet, strongly influenced by the New Critics, including T. S. Eliot, Cleanth Brooks, I. A. Richards, and John Crowe Ransom. Mueller greatly admires Wallace Stevens; although she does not believe that she writes anything like Stevens, she does allude frequently to his poems in her own work. Mueller also developed her critical skills and her awareness of contemporary poetry by writing reviews for the *Chicago Daily News*. Perhaps most important, Mueller has drawn upon her life experiences as a mother and spouse for the material of her poems.

Mueller remained almost exclusively in the Midwest after her arrival in the United States, and it is a midwestern landscape that appears most often in her poetry. However, she has never been simply midwestern in her thoughts or outlook. Of the Midwest she says,

> I am more at home here than anywhere. At the same time I am not a native; I see the culture and myself in it, through a scrim, with European eyes, and my poetry accommodates a bias toward historical determinism, no doubt the burdensome heritage of a twentieth century native German.

Analysis

Lisel Mueller's poetry is unassuming, spare, and solidly grounded in history, both public and private. Without the banners of feminism or other celebrated causes, Mueller has quietly and steadily recorded her impressions of life in the United States. Her perspective is unique, marked as it is by her immigration experience at the age of fifteen and the loss of her grandparents to the horrors of Nazi Germany. She writes of life events that are the causes for quiet celebration—a long, happy marriage, the birth and lives of her children, and the inevitable process of growing old.

DEPENDENCIES

Looking back, Mueller was not happy with most of the poems that she wrote in *Dependencies*. She said that they "seem overly decorated, too metaphorical." Most critics agree that these poems are overly literary, but this is only a mark of the New Critics that Mueller studied so closely. The lead poem, "The Blind Leading the Blind," presents the theme of interdependencies between human beings, a theme that appears often in her poetry. In this poem, Mueller uses a cave metaphor, reminiscent of Plato's cave parable, to represent the journey of two companions through major life events. The speaker, presumably female, is the guide, and she speaks with the natural authority of one who has "been here before." She knows where the ground is rock, where it is mud, where there are turn-offs. However, she reiterates her need for the other, the fact that "there are two of us here" in this cave, or on this journey through life.

Another important theme brought forth in this work is the continuity between generations of Mueller's family. She writes of her pregnancy, a means of allowing the continuation of her and her spouse's love. The birth of her child becomes part of healing the grief of her mother's death; Mueller realizes that her own ability to love her daughter is a direct result of the love that she first experienced from her mother.

THE PRIVATE LIFE

Many critics agree that in Mueller's next full volume of poetry, *The Private Life*, she reveals her most characteristic voice and themes. In an interview with Stan Sanvel Rubin and William Heyen, Mueller identifies two important "springs" for her poetry: her domestic life with her husband and daughters, and the Vietnam War, which she says made her "think of the interdependency, certainly in our age, of the public and private life." However, Mueller seldom alludes directly to the Vietnam War. The public life of World War II remains a greater immediate interest to her because of its more direct impact upon her family of origin.

"My Grandmother's Gold Pin" begins as a charming explanation from a mother to a daughter about why the mother wears a particular pin so often. Each fleur-de-lis reminds the mother-speaker of objects in her grandparents' home, their mannerisms, the music. When the mother comes to the center pearl in the pin, she is bitterly reminded of her grandparents' death by starvation in an animal shed. Through this poem, Mueller illustrates that there can be no neat, clean separation between the public and private, past and present. The mother tells her daughter that this private memento, the pin, is

> all I have left of an age when people believed the
> heart was
> an organ of goodness, and light stronger than
> darkness,
> that death came to you in your proper time:
> An age when the dream of Man nearly came true.

The value of silence, the space beyond language or our immediate perceptions, is also an important theme introduced in *The Private Life*. "What the Dog Perhaps Hears" is a playful musing on all that people do not hear—the growth of a child, the unfurling of a snake, the birth of a baby bird pushing its way out of the shell. The final line "and we heard nothing when the world changed," reminds us that so much takes place beyond the perception of the five senses.

The poem "The Private Life" begins with a flat statement: "What happens, happens in silence." Things that happen in silence include what goes on inside other people's heads, the death of an aspen in an ice storm, the rot of fruit at the market. The poet seems weary of words, especially the screaming headlines of the daily news. More important things are happening outside language: "in a red blood cell,/ a curl in the brain,/ in the ignorant ovum."

THE NEED TO HOLD STILL

In the award-winning *The Need to Hold Still*, Mueller continues to explore the limitations of language and the continuity between past and present. She chooses to speak more often in the voices of others and begins to distance herself from her more youthful self. In "Talking to Helen," Mueller speaks to Helen Keller, imagining the absence of both sight and sound in the sequence of perceptions that led to Keller's realization of what the word "water" means. In many ways, Keller's perceptions, limited as they were to the tactile world, may have been superior to the poet's own perceptions. Keller's "world was imagination/ all possible worlds, while mine/ shrinks with the speed of speed."

In "The Triumph of Life: Mary Shelley," Mueller speaks in the voice of the nineteenth century novelist and author of *Frankenstein: Or, The Modern Prometheus* (1818), Mary Wollstonecraft Shelley, a woman with an enviably feminist upbringing. Shelley's father "taught [her] to think/ to value mind over body,/ to refuse even the airiest cage." However, "None of this kept [Shelley] from bearing/ four children and losing three/ by the time [she] was twenty-two." Mueller reminds her readers through this poem that feminism is possible only through medical science. Shelley remained a victim of biology and fate. However, the contemporary age is hardly superior with its demystification of the female body and of the heart:

> You don't speak of the heart
> in your letters, your sharp-eyed poems
> You speak about your bodies
> as though they had no mystery,
> no caves, no sudden turnings.

Shelley also refuses the role of the prophet, claiming, "But I only wanted to write/ a tale to tremble by." It is only by accident that her tale predicted the potential horrors of human genetic engineering. Shelley was concerned only with the business of living and knowing what she could about her own life.

In the poem "The Need to Hold Still," Mueller begins to explore the process of aging. Here, she uses winter weeds as a metaphor for the aging woman, who is, like the weeds, "among the thin/ the trampled on/ the inarticulate." As a woman ages, she becomes less visible and demands less from life; she notices "that gray and brown/ are colors/ she disappears into// that her body/ has stopped asking/ for anything except calm." However, aging has its compensations. There is less need to cling or to try to wring the "last drop of juice." Dignity, design, cleanness of line all remain in the winter weeds as well as the aging woman.

SECOND LANGUAGE, WAVING FROM SHORE, AND ALIVE TOGETHER

A theme that unites *Second Language*, *Waving from Shore*, and *Alive Together* is the process of sorting through what is necessary, what is important, what to keep, and what to leave behind—a process more typical of one's later years. In "Necessities," Mueller examines what is necessary on her continued journey toward old age and death. One thing that is necessary is "a map of the world." This map includes both the public and the private; it is the map with the landscape of our childhood, the place where we first made love, the roads that we did and did not take, "the private alps no one knows that we have climbed." Other necessities include "the illusion of progress," "answers to questions," and "evidence that we matter." It does not matter that people do not really progress, or that the answers may be wrong, or that the things people interpret as "evidence that we matter" may only be quirks of fate. The important thing is that humans momentarily believe, at least long enough to relieve their anxieties.

Mueller continues to grieve the loss of her parents throughout her life. In "Voyager" (*Second Language*), Mueller expresses the need for the "impossible photograph," the one that would show the world the father that she remembered from her younger years. She must somehow come to terms with "the hardest knowledge:/ that no one will remember you/ when your daughters are gone." Similarly, in "Missing the Dead" (*Waving from Shore*), Mueller wishes that she had more tangible evidence of her parents' existence. She wishes that they had been musicians who left behind their musical scores or that she could believe that their bodies were transformed into stars that she could point to so that others might see "how they shimmer,/ how they keep getting brighter/ as we keep moving toward each other."

Several poems from these three volumes deal directly with Mueller's coming to terms with her own eventual death. In "Poem for My Birthday" (*Waving from Shore*), old age has brought Mueller to the point where she is no longer "the heroine of [her] bad dreams." She has left behind "the melodramas/ of betrayal and narrow escapes." She is no longer the one who takes foolish risks like "the one/ who swims too far out to sea." Rather, she has become "the one who waves from shore," a minor player in her own life. Mueller asks, "Does that mean I have solved my life?" In many ways, the answer to the question is affirmative. Language has its limitations, but the poet's access to her own language stores has become more limited. In "Aphasia," she observes that the world "no longer/ offers itself to [her]/ as an infinite dictionary." However, this aging process that Mueller presents is far from a picture of grim, unrelenting diminishment. In "Monet Refuses the Operation," the speaker (artist Claude Monet) refuses to believe that his way of seeing is simply "an aberration/ caused by old age, an affliction." He responds to the doctors:

> I tell you it has taken me all my life
> to arrive at the vision of gas lamps as angels,
> to soften and blur and finally banish
> the edges you regret I don't see.

As Monet's speech illustrates, the old can often "see" the interconnectedness of things in a way that the young can seldom "see."

Mueller refuses to romanticize her own death or even the power of her own achievements beyond death. This vision is a difficult one to achieve; perhaps it takes someone who has lived at least half of his or her own life to understand it.

OTHER MAJOR WORKS

MISCELLANEOUS: *Learning to Play by Ear: Essays and Early Poems*, 1990.

TRANSLATIONS: *The Great Salzburg Theatre of the World*, 1969 (with John Reich; of Hugo von Hofmannsthal's play *Das Salzburger grosse Welttheater*); *Selected Later Poems of Marie Luise Kaschnitz*, 1980; *Whether or Not*, 1984 (of Kaschnitz's *Steht noch dahin*); *Three Daughters*, 1987 (of Anna Mitgutsch's novel *Züchtigung*); *Circe's Mountain*, 1990 (of Kaschnitz's short stories).

BIBLIOGRAPHY

Bryan, Sharon, ed. *Stand: Women Poets and the Literary Tradition*. New York: W. W. Norton, 1993. Mueller's essay "Parentage and Good Luck" appears in this collection and casts much light on the poet's life and concerns.

Cruze, Karen DeBrulye. "Bringing It All Together." *Chicago Tribune*, December 5,

1993, pp. 1-4. This feature provides insight into Mueller's personal history through interviews with her, with her publisher at Louisiana State University Press, and with former students of Mueller.

Mueller, Lisel. "An Interview with Lisel Mueller." Interview by Nancy Bunge. In *Finding the Words: Interviews with Writers Who Teach*, edited by Nancy Bunge. Athens, Ohio: Swallow Press, 1985. Bunge's questions encourage Mueller to reflect on bilingualism, the arts of writing and teaching, and questions of ethics.

———. "The Steady Interior Hum." Interview by Stan Sanvel Rubin and William Heyden. In *The Post-confessionals: Conversations with American Poets of the Eighties*, edited by Earl G. Ingersoll, Judith Kitchen, and Rubin. Rutherford, N.J.: Fairleigh Dickinson University Press, 1989. Mueller discusses inspiration, metaphor, and translation.

Preston, Rohan B. "'Everything Is Autobiography': Pulitzer Poet Lisel Mueller." *Chicago Tribune*, April 11, 1997, p. 1. Written on the occasion of Mueller's winning the Pulitzer Prize, this article calls her poetry "focused and accessible" and notes that it draws on her own life.

Solyn, Paul. "Lisel Mueller and the Idea of Midwestern Poetry." In *Regionalism and the Female Imagination: A Collection of Essays*, edited by Emily Toth. New York: Human Sciences Press, 1985. Solyn takes issue with many points that Mueller makes in "Midwestern Poetry: Goodbye to All That." Solyn is particularly disturbed by Mueller's separation of rural and urban midwestern poets. Mueller does not believe that urban poets from large midwestern cities are distinctly different from other urban poets.

Nancy E. Sherrod

NOVALIS
Friedrich von Hardenberg

Born: Oberwiederstedt, Prussian Saxony (now in Germany); May 2, 1772
Died: Weissenfels, Saxony (now in Germany); March 25, 1801

PRINCIPAL POETRY
Hymnen an die Nacht, 1800 (*Hymns to the Night*, 1897, 1948)
Geistliche Lieder, 1802 (*Devotional Songs*, 1910)

OTHER LITERARY FORMS

The poetry alone does not even hint at the full scope of the literary activity of Novalis (noh-VOL-uhs) or his encyclopedic interest in philosophy, science, politics, religion, and aesthetics. While two seminal collections of aphorisms—*Blütenstaub* (pollen) and *Glauben und Liebe* (faith and love)—were published in 1798, the bulk of his work was published posthumously. Among these writings are six neglected dialogues and a monologue from 1798-1799; the essay *Die Christenheit oder Europa* (*Christianity or Europe*, 1844), written in 1799 but first published fully in 1826; and two fragmentary novels, *Die Lehrlinge zu Sais* (1802; *The Disciples at Sais*, 1903) and *Heinrich von Ofterdingen* (1802; *Henry of Ofterdingen*, 1842), begun in 1798 and 1799 respectively. As prototypes of the German Romantic novel, these two works comprise a variety of literary forms: didactic dialogues, poems, and literary fairy tales. Like so much of Novalis's work, these novels were first published by Ludwig Tieck and Friedrich von Schlegel in the 1802 edition of Novalis's writings. Insights into these literary works and into Novalis's poetics are provided by his theoretical notebooks and other papers, which include his philosophical and scientific studies and outlines and drafts of literary projects, as well as his letters, diaries, and professional scientific reports.

ACHIEVEMENTS

Novalis is perhaps best known as the creator of the "blue flower," the often trivialized symbol of Romantic longing, but his importance has a far more substantial basis than this. Within the German tradition, his Romanticism influenced important writers such as Joseph von Eichendorff, E. T. A. Hoffmann, and Hermann Hesse. As an innovative theorist and practitioner of the Romantic novel, Novalis prepared the way not only for the narrative strategies of Franz Kafka's prose but also for the themes and structures of Thomas Mann's major novels. As the poet of *Hymns to the Night* and as a theorist of poetic language, Novalis set the Orphic tone for German Romantic poetry and the aesthetic agenda for German Symbolists such as Rainer Maria Rilke and Stefan George.

Novalis's impact outside Germany is no less consequential. His evocative imagery, the prose poems included in *Hymns to the Night*, and his view of poetic language as musical and autonomous make him a major precursor of the French Symbolist poets. Among them, Maurice Maeterlinck was especially drawn to Novalis's philosophy of nature, and he translated *The Disciples at Sais* in 1895. Later, Novalis's imaginative poetics not only inspired André Breton, one of the founders of French Surrealism, but also had an impact, less widely known, on Chilean Surrealism via the poets Rosamel del Valle and Humberto Díaz Casanueva. In the English-speaking world, Novalis was first praised in 1829 by Thomas Carlyle, whose enthusiasm spread ultimately to writers as diverse as Ralph Waldo Emerson, George Eliot, Edgar Allan Poe, Joseph Conrad, and George MacDonald.

In the poetry anthology *News of the Universe: Poems of Twofold Consciousness* (1980), the American poet Robert Bly justly lauded Novalis as a prime shaper of modern poetic consciousness. Such an evaluation offers hope that Novalis will continue to gain recognition as an internationally important forerunner of both modern poetry and literary theory, especially as more of his literary and theoretical works become accessible in translation.

Biography

Novalis was born Georg Philipp Friedrich von Hardenberg, the first son of Heinrich Ulrich Erasmus von Hardenberg, a strict member of the pietistic *Herrnhut* sect, and Auguste Bernhardine von Bölzig. Throughout his life, Novalis attempted to reconcile the practical demands of his father with the poetic inspiration he claimed first to have received from his mother. Novalis's acquaintance with the popular poet Gottfried August Bürger in 1789 intensified his early literary aspirations, but encouraged by his father to pursue an administrative career, Novalis began the study of law at the University of Jena in 1790. Although his lyric output during his stay in Jena seems to have abated, he soon found his poetic proclivities rekindled and redirected by the poet Friedrich Schiller, who was then a professor of history at the university. Under Schiller's spell, the young Novalis became more introspective and sought a solid foundation for his life and poetry. With this new outlook, he bowed to paternal pressure and transferred to the University of Leipzig in 1791. His experience there once again only strengthened his literary and philosophical interests, however, for it was in Leipzig that he began his friendship and fruitful intellectual exchange with Schlegel, the brilliant theorist of German Romanticism. Only after taking up studies in Wittenberg did he receive his law degree, in 1794.

After several carefree months with his family in Weissenfels, Novalis was apprenticed by his father to Coelestin August Just, the district director of Thuringia, who lived in Tennstedt. It was during his first months there that Hardenberg came to know the twelve-year-old Sophie von Kühn of nearby Grüningen, who revived his active poetic imagination and became a central figure in his new poetic attempts. Within a year, they were engaged, but Sophie's serious illness led to her death in March, 1797. Sophie's death, followed by the loss of his brother Erasmus in April, shattered Novalis, and he turned inward to come to grips with the experience of death. This experience, certainly the most crucial of his life, helped him to articulate his mission to transcend the dual nature of existence through poetry. His confrontation with death did not weaken his will to live or cause him to flee from life, as is sometimes claimed; rather, it was a catalytic event that enabled him to reorient his life and focus his imaginative powers on the fusion of life and poetry.

With a new, clearly poetic mission before him, Novalis could commit himself to life; it was at this time that he assumed the pen name (meaning "preparer of new land") by which he is known. By the end of 1797, he had resumed his intense study of the Idealist philosophers Immanuel Kant and Johann Gottlieb Fichte. Novalis's interest in science grew also, and in December, he commenced studies at the Freiberg Mining Academy, which would later give him a career. In the next year, he not only published the philosophical aphorisms of *Blütenstaub* and *Glauben und Liebe*, but also attempted to articulate his own philosophical ideas in a novel, *The Disciples of Sais*. By December, 1798, his involvement in life embraced the domestic once again, and he became engaged to Julie von Charpentier.

Novalis had finally reconciled his poetic mission with the practical demands of life and career. During 1799, he not only worked on *Devotional Songs* and *Hymns to the Night*, which had grown out of the crisis of 1797, but also accepted an appointment to the directorate of the Saxon salt mines. Both his career and his literary endeavors flourished. In 1800, he worked on *Henry of Ofterdingen*, conducted a significant geological survey of Saxony, published *Hymns to the Night*, and wrote some of his best poems. However, illness had overpowered Novalis's resolve to live and fulfill his poetic mission. On March 25, 1801, Novalis died in the family home in Weissenfels. A few days before his death, he had said to his brother Carl: "When I am well again, then you will finally learn what poetry is. In my head I have magnificent poems and songs." These died with him.

Analysis

The late eighteenth century in Germany was a time of new beginnings. The gradual change from a feudal to a capitalistic society bestowed a new importance on the individual, as reflected in the philosophy of German Idealism, which emphasized the primacy of the subjective imagination. At the same time, however, the weakening of the Holy Roman Empire gave rise to a new sense of German nationalism. German writers responded to these changes by seeking to initiate a new literary tradition, a new beginning that would free them from the tyranny of foreign taste and example. Understandably, in such a dynamic age, no single, unified movement emerged, and the literary pioneers— writers as diverse as Gotthold Ephraim Lessing, Friedrich Klopstock, and Christoph

Martin Wieland—set out in many different directions. Nevertheless, by the end of the century, Schlegel would proclaim that he lived "not in hope but in the certainty of a new dawn of a new poetry."

Schlegel's optimism was based on his conviction that his contemporaries were on the verge of creating a new mythology, a new Romantic poetry in which the newly emerging self would examine its own depths and discover universal truths, ultimately achieving a synthesis of subject and object. Like the literature of the eighteenth century, the poetry of Novalis moved toward the realization of this Romantic goal. While he experimented with many styles in his early works, betraying his debt to various currents of the Enlightenment, he soon developed a personal Romantic voice and new mode of expression that marked the advent of a new poetic age. This development became more obvious after Sophie's death in 1797, but it is evident even in the poems of his literary apprenticeship (1788-1793). Indeed, many themes that preoccupied Novalis after the crisis of 1797 had already surfaced in his earliest poetry. The theme of death and the dual images of night and darkness, for example, find their initial expression in early poems, although at this stage his poetry was largely imitative. Only after his encounter with Schiller and his relationship with Sophie, which made him more introspective, did Novalis strike out on his own to record his own experiences and the changes that had taken place within himself. He was then able to create a consistent vision, a vision proclaiming the transforming power of love and raising personal experience to the level of mythology. In transforming his subjective experience into universal symbolism, Novalis created the Romantic mythology that Schlegel had proclaimed the *sine qua non* of the new poetic age. In his last poems, which envision the return to paradise brought on by the union of poetry and love, Novalis transcended his personal experience to create symbolic artifacts behind which the poet himself nearly disappears. In his lyric poetry, then, Novalis ultimately reveals himself not only as a pioneer of Romanticism but also as a precursor of Symbolism.

If Novalis's last poems are thematically consistent and anticipate the Symbolist movement, his early poems are endlessly diversified and echo the Enlightenment. In the poets of the eighteenth century, the young writer, searching for a poetic voice, found his models, limited only by his eclectic taste. Besides translations from classical poetry, Novalis composed serious political verse influenced by the work of Friedrich Stolberg and Karl Ramler, and in the bardic tradition of Klopstock; Rococo lyrics under the particular influence of Wieland; elegiac verse echoing Ludwig Christoph Heinrich Hölty and Schiller; and a spate of lyrics in the style of Bürger. The variety of these early attempts, the assorted literary models that they imitate, and the poems showing a young poet experimenting with traditional forms (such as the invented necrologues addressed to living family members) reveal a writer in quest of a suitable mode of expression.

"To a Falling Leaf"

While they do share some common concerns, many of which inform the later writings, the early poems lack the unified vision and unique perspective that would come later with Novalis's Romantic lyrics. Poems that foreshadow later developments also contrast significantly with the more mature poetry. The first version of the poem "An ein fallendes Blatt" ("To a Falling Leaf"), written in 1789, paints a melancholy scene in which the approach of winter storms is compared to the approach of death. The melancholy tone, however, is purposely undercut by a conclusion that affirms death as a joyous experience of the eternal that need not be feared. This view of death hints, perhaps, at the thanatopsis that Novalis would elaborate in *Hymns to the Night*, but it is merely a hint, for here the idea is actually no more than a common poetic cliché, and the poem as a whole lacks the visionary perspective that underlies the later works. This poem's persona, in fact, is barely visible at all, and his emotional response to death's coming at the end of the poem is expressed impersonally: "Oh happy . . ./ One need not then fear the storm/ That forbids us our earthly life." The persona and his climactic emotional exclamation vanish behind the anonymous "one," and death—which had been only indirectly introduced through a comparison—loses not only its sting, as the poet intended, but its poetic bite as well.

"Evening"

The poem "Der Abend" ("Evening"), probably written in the same year as "To a Falling Leaf" but in many ways a more suggestive and complex work, not only has a more directly involved and visible persona but also links death and night in anticipation of *Hymns to the Night*. This poem's persona, who stands in a sympathetic relationship to a thoroughly personified nature, perceives and responds to a serene evening by wishing that "the evening of my life" might be "more peaceful still than this/ Evening of the countryside." The lovely yet decidedly rational comparison of the soul to nature is still far removed from the Romantic identification of self and nature that can be found in Novalis's last poems—for example, in "Der Himmel war umzogen" ("The Heavens Were Covered"). Moreover, despite the reflective mood that nature inspires in the persona, this is not an introspective poem like those found among Novalis's first truly Romantic poems. "Evening" does not yet focus primarily on the poetic self but on the eighteenth century ideal of bucolic harmony. Similarly, the persona's final wish, that his "soul might slumber over to eternal peace" in the same way that the weary farmer "slumbers over" toward the next day, only tentatively prefigures the ideas and vocabulary of *Hymns to the Night*. The link between death and sleep remains, after all, an eighteenth century cliché, and its one-dimensional appearance here only lightly foreshadows Novalis's later and much more complex symbol of the eternal and truly visionary "holy sleep."

This poem, like "To a Falling Leaf," is still controlled by a rationalistic poetic consciousness. Simile, not symbol, is the rhetorical means of linking humanity and nature;

subject and object are linked, not synthesized. This is the overriding technique of the early poems. The transcendent vision based on deep self-reflection and the unifying power of the imagination is not found here. The poet of "Evening" is one step closer to the Romantic poet of *Hymns to the Night* than the poet of "To a Falling Leaf," but the Romantic poet whose feelings, perceptions, and very self are the basis of Romantic expression steps forward only tentatively. Before he could free himself from his Enlightenment models, focus his vision, and become the very subject of his Romantic art, Novalis would first need to know himself.

"On a Saturday Evening"

The experience of love and death in his relationship with Sophie was the catalyst that would initiate important changes in Novalis's writings, the lens through which he would ultimately bring into sharper focus the themes and images that had been hinted at in the early poems. Initially, however, the experience led to self-examination and the definition of a new, more Romantic voice. Much of the poetry from this period—and there is relatively little—records the changes that the Sophie experience caused in Novalis, and it is, consequently, largely confessional, reflective poetry in which the poet himself becomes the subject.

In the poem "Am Sonnabend Abend" ("On a Saturday Evening"), for example, the persona expresses his astonishment at the transformation that has taken place within himself since his relationship with Sophie: "Am I still the one who yesterday morning/ Sang hymns to the god of frivolity...." This confession suggests not only the changes that had affected a once frivolous university student but also those poetic changes that had occurred in the former poet of lighthearted Anacreontic verse. Earlier, in 1791, Novalis had expressed similar reservations about his lifestyle and youthful verse in "A Youth's Laments," a poem written under the maturing influence of Schiller, but it was only after Novalis had met Sophie that his inner reorientation became complete and the poet could begin anew.

"Beginning"

In the poem "Anfang" ("Beginning"), Novalis analyzes the nature of Sophie's effect on him and argues that his new state of mind is not "intoxication" (that is, illusion) but rather "higher consciousness," which Sophie as a mediator had revealed. This aptly titled poem is in several ways profoundly significant for Novalis's development as a Romantic poet. In the first place, its conclusion that higher consciousness not be mistaken for intoxication admits a new Romantic form of perception that is aggressively antirationalistic. Second, the characterization of Sophie, the embodiment of love, as a female mediator between visible and invisible worlds, not only marks the first use of this central Romantic image in Novalis's work but also signals the inception of a Romantic theory of Symbolism, which posits the fusion of the finite with the infinite. Finally, the intensely introspective persona, whose theme is his own consciousness ("the growth of a poet's mind," as William Wordsworth put it), places this poem directly into the Romantic tradition.

In "Beginning," Novalis's new vision, based on the higher consciousness inspired by Sophie, assumes a universal import transcending the initially personal experience. This is manifest in the last lines of the poem, where the private experience of the poet is superseded by a vision of humanity raised to a new level of existence:

> Someday mankind will be what Sophie
> Is to me now—perfected—moral grace—
> Then will its *higher consciousness*
> No longer be confused with the mist of wine.

THE STRANGER

The poems Novalis wrote in 1798 and 1799 in Freiberg after Sophie's death confirm this universalizing tendency. In fact, the relative paucity of poems written in the wake of the experience itself suggests that Novalis was not simply concerned with self-indulgent solipsistic effusions. (The one poem written shortly after Sophie's death in 1797, while Novalis was still in Tennstedt, is a humorous composition commemorating the Just family's purchase of a garden.) Similarly, it has been pointed out that Novalis probably chose the classical verse forms of the Freiberg poems as a more objective medium for his universal themes. One can also point to the objectifying perspective of the several poems that analyze the self from a point of view once removed. In both "Der Fremdling" ("The Stranger"), written in January, 1798, and "Der müde Fremdling ist verschwunden" ("The Weary Stranger Has Disappeared"), a fragment from one year later, Novalis—the stranger—analyzes his initial alienation after Sophie's death and then his self-rediscovery through a persona who "speaks . . . for him." This allows Novalis to remain in the introspective mode, making use of his experience, yet standing at an objective distance. As a consequence, the stranger symbolizes any individual who seeks the return of the paradise he has lost, "that heavenly land."

SELF-KNOWLEDGE

The major poems of the Freiberg period are inhabited by seekers who ultimately find themselves. Introspection leading to self-revelation is the goal and method of these poems, but the path inward does not lead to solipsism. Self-knowledge, as Novalis teaches in "Kenne dich selbst" ("Know Thyself"), results in a deep knowledge of nature's mysteries as well. Moreover, because his own path to self-knowledge, which had been prepared by the guiding spirit of love, led to higher consciousness, Novalis interprets his experience as a symbol. He imbues his introspective poems with a universal significance, as in these lines from "Letzte Liebe" ("Last Love"):

> As the mother wakes her darling from slumber with a kiss,
> As he first sees her and comes to understand himself through her:
> So love with me—through love did I first experience the world,
> Find myself, and become what as a lover one becomes.

What *one*—anyone, not just Novalis—becomes when a lover, is a poet. The successful seeker of love and self-knowledge is called, like the poet addressed in "Der sterbende Genius" ("The Dying Genius"), to "sing the song of return," the myth of the return to paradise.

Having found himself again, Novalis defined for himself a Romantic mission: to transform his personal experience through poetry into a universal vision of love, which would lead others inward along the path to self-knowledge, higher consciousness, and rebirth: "Toward the East sing then the lofty song,/ Until the sun rises and ignites/ And opens for me the gates of the primeval world."

HYMNS TO THE NIGHT

In *Hymns to the Night*, the gates of eternity are opened not by the rising sun—the conventional symbol of rebirth—but by the fall of darkness and night. This poetic work is Novalis's "lofty song," "the song of return," the clearest and most complete fulfillment of his Romantic mission. In it, Novalis transforms his personal experience of Sophie's death—to be precise, his ostensibly mystical experience at her graveside on May 13, 1797—into a universalized vision of death and night as a realm of higher consciousness and eternal love.

Hymns to the Night was not merely an immediate emotional response to Sophie's death. Although he might have begun work on an early version in the fall of 1797, Novalis resumed serious work on the cycle only in late 1799 and early 1800, when he was well over his initial grief and actively involved in life. Moreover, the textual changes that he made between setting down that version in manuscript and publishing a still later prose version in the journal *Athenäum* in 1800 show a conscious effort to rise above personal experience and indicate that his goal was not autobiography but symbolism.

Unlike the fragmentary verse epic of 1789, *Orpheus*, which uses a classical myth to examine the theme of death, *Hymns to the Night* makes personal experience the basis of a broad symbolism utilizing elements of various mythological systems (including the theme of Orpheus). Although the first three hymns describe principally the poet's own experience of "the holy, ineffable, mysterious night"—his own Orphic descent to the realm of death—the work begins significantly with a more universal reference to all living creatures in the world of light. Among these stands "the magnificent stranger" who is man himself. As in the Freiberg poems, the stranger symbolizes the universal seeker of a lost paradise. From this broad context, it becomes clear that the persona, himself a stranger in the rational world of light, is representative and his experience symbolic. This universality is reinforced in the fourth hymn when, for example, the symbol of the Cross, which at first signifies Sophie's death and links her to Christ, is finally called "the victory banner of our race." The fifth hymn continues to broaden the significance of the poet's experience by restating his subjective development toward an understanding of death in terms of humankind's changing relationship to death in history. In the sixth and final hymn, subjective experience coalesces completely with the universal. Not only is the mediating beloved explicitly identified with Christ, but also the poet's individual voice is transformed into a universal "we" singing a communal hymn of praise. The stranger, who in the Freiberg poems had given up his voice to the poet who spoke for him, here lends his voice to the chorus of humankind.

DEVOTIONAL SONGS

Devotional Songs, also written during the years 1799 through 1800, were similarly intended to raise personal experience to the level of universal—if not entirely orthodox—religious symbolism. This is evident not only from the symbols that the poems share with *Hymns to the Night*—for example, the eroticism of Christ the beloved—but also from the shared communal context and implications. Novalis had tentatively planned these songs as part of "a new, spiritual hymnal"; in them, the Sophie experience is so thoroughly transformed by virtue of the pervasive Christian imagery that many have been adopted (and sometimes adapted) for use in hymnals.

The songs, which are sometimes confessional, sometimes exhortative, are all informed by Novalis's self-conscious mission to reveal the role of love in the re-creation of the earth. The ninth song, for example, which proclaims the day of Resurrection to be "a festival of the world's rejuvenation," is more than a profession of religious faith in the coming of God's kingdom; it is a self-conscious profession of faith in the poet's mission to reveal that kingdom in humanity's midst:

> I say to each that he lives
> And has been resurrected
> That he hovers in our midst
> And is with us forever.
> I say to each and each says
> To his friends anon
> That soon everywhere
> The new kingdom of heaven will dawn.

In truly Romantic fashion, the voice of the prophet is first and foremost the voice of a poet, speaking out of his own experience but in the service of a still higher cause and announcing to all humankind the advent of a world renewed by love, which is made manifest in his words.

"THE POEM"

Novalis's last poems are almost exclusively concerned with the renewal of the universe and the return to the Golden Age; their vision is more explicitly secular and aesthetic than that which informs *Hymns to the Night* and *Devotional Songs*. Here, Novalis's belief that poetry itself can transform the world receives full expression, and many of these last works are indeed poems about poems, in which Novalis's personal experience is not the focus.

Such is the case in the significantly titled poem "Das Gedicht" ("The Poem"). The anonymous persona who speaks for humankind in its fallen state relates how "a lost page"—a poetic saga—inspires in the present a vision of the past Golden Age and keeps alive the hope for its return. Because it is able to unite past and future in the present and give form to the spirit of love, the poem itself temporarily re-creates the Golden Age. The paramount concern of "The Poem," then, is precisely what the title announces it to be: the poem—not simply the ancient saga and not even Novalis's poem in itself, but all poems, the poem per se. In its ability to unite subject and object, spirit and matter, every poem becomes a medium of higher consciousness and the salvation of the world.

"TO TIECK"

Once poetry becomes a major theme in Novalis's work, a new poetic voice emerges. The reflective persona that had spoken in the introspective poems of 1794 to 1799 is silenced. In "The Poem," for example, the reflective self is replaced by an essentially impersonal persona. This is no longer a case of a poet reflecting on himself but of poetry reflecting on itself. In the poem "An Tieck" ("To Tieck"), another anonymous persona narrates the tale of a child's discovery of an ancient book and an encounter with Jakob Boehme, which presage the coming of the Golden Age.

Despite the dedicatory title and autobiographical allusions in the poem (Tieck had introduced Novalis to Boehme's writings), the personal significance has been entirely transformed by the symbolism of the poem. The dominance of myth in these last poems precludes the need for a personal voice, as it does in the novel *Henry of Ofterdingen* of the same period. If early poems such as "To a Falling Leaf" resort to an anonymous voice because Novalis lacked experience, then the final poems do so because he succeeded in rising above his personal experience.

AUTONOMOUS LATE POEMS

The appearance of a first-person voice among the late poems does not contradict this conclusion. A number of poems in which the poet speaks in the first person were in fact intended for fictional characters in *Henry of Ofterdingen*. In some of these and in others not intended for the novel, the persona himself becomes part of an integrated mythos. Such poems are distinct from earlier reflective works such as "Beginning" and "Last Love."

Although the late poems also describe the changing consciousness of the persona, they do so in symbolic terms and not in the largely expository or intellectual manner of the earlier poems. Whereas the poet of "Beginning" simply states that Sophie has led him to higher consciousness, the speaker of "Es färbte sich die Wiese grün" ("The Meadow Turned Green") tells the story of his rebirth by narrating his experience of spring and love: During a walk deeper and deeper into the forest, the persona marvels uncomprehendingly at the transformation of nature; he then encounters a young girl and, hidden from the sun in deep shadows, suddenly understands intuitively the changes both in nature and within himself.

One can easily discern the same theme that dominated the Freiberg poems: The spirit of love, embodied by a female mediator, reveals the higher consciousness that leads to knowledge of self and of the external world. In this narrative plot, however, the theme has been thoroughly mythologized. The symbols which Novalis uses here and in all his late poems are autonomous, stripped of all but the most general personal relevance. The forest, the sun, the girl, springtime—all these derive their mythological significance from their shared archetypal context.

"The Meadow Turned Green" is autonomous, too, in that it reflects back upon itself. It is, after all, not merely a description of revelation and the path to higher consciousness; it is both the direct result of the poet's epiphany and the re-creation of it. The poem describes and mythologizes its own creation.

The process of objectifying and imbuing his personal experience with universal meaning that Novalis had begun in the poems of 1794 to 1799 was completed in his last poems, in which he totally transforms experience into myth, into symbols which have no fixed meanings outside themselves. This creation of a reflexive and fully autonomous poetry was a significant landmark on the road to nineteenth century symbolism. To reach this stage and to find his own poetic voice, it was not enough for Novalis that he free himself from Enlightenment models and create a poetry of the self. He also needed to rise above the self and to create a mythological poetry. For this, he needed a poetic voice that not only spoke from the core of his experience but also spoke in the universal language of symbolism. In achieving this goal, Novalis fulfilled the Romantic ideal of becoming like God the Creator, whose creative voice echoes eternally throughout his autonomous creation while he hovers silently above.

OTHER MAJOR WORKS

LONG FICTION: *Die Lehrlinge zu Sais*, 1802 (*The Disciples at Sais*, 1903); *Heinrich von Ofterdingen*, 1802 (*Henry of Ofterdingen*, 1842).

NONFICTION: *Blütenstaub*, 1798; *Glauben und Liebe*, 1798; *Das Allgemeine Brouillon*, 1798-1799 (*Notes for a Romantic Encyclopaedia*, 2007); *Die Christenheit oder Europa*, 1826 (*Christianity or Europe*, 1844); *Philosophical Writings*, 1997; *The Birth of Novalis: Friedrich von Hardenberg's Journal of 1797, with Selected Letters and Documents*, 2007.

MISCELLANEOUS: *Pollen and Fragments: Selected Poetry and Prose of Novalis*, 1989.

BIBLIOGRAPHY

Freeman, Veronica G. *The Poetization of Metaphors in the Work of Novalis*. New York: Peter Lang, 2006. This work examines mysticism and Romanticism in the works of Novalis and his use of metaphors.

Hodkinson, James R. *Women and Writing in the Works of Novalis: Transformation Beyond Measure?* Rochester, N.Y.: Camden House, 2007. Hodkinson examines how Novalis was affected by women, including Sophie von Kühn, and how this is evident in his writing.

Holland, Jocelyn. *German Romanticism and Science: The Procreative Poetics of Goethe, Novalis, and Ritter*. New York: Routledge, 2009. Holland compares and contrasts the works of Novalis, Johann Wolfgang von Goethe, and Johann Wilhelm Ritter, paying particular attention to the idea of procreation.

Kennedy, Clare. *Paradox, Aphorism, and Desire in Novalis and Derrida*. London: Maney, for the Modern Humanities Research Association, 2008. Kennedy examines the themes of desire and paradoxes in the aphorisms of Novalis and philosopher-critic Jacques Derrida.

Molnár, Géza von. *Romantic Vision, Ethical Context: Novalis and Artistic Autonomy*. Minneapolis: University of Minnesota Press, 1987. Highly philosophical approach to the life and work of Novalis. Discussion of his work involves detailed expositions of Novalis's interpretations of Kantian and Fichtean philosophy. Also examines Novalis's relationship with Sophie von Kühn, his novel *Henry of Ofterdingen*, and his visionary poems in *Hymns to the Night*.

Neubauer, John. *Novalis*. Boston: Twayne, 1980. Excellent general introduction to Novalis, tailored to English-speaking readers. Interweaves the life and work to show the relationship between the two and also discusses Novalis both as a visionary and as a logical thinker. Includes discussions of Novalis's contributions to science, philosophy, the novel, poetry, politics, and religion. Includes bibliography and chronology.

Newman, Gail M. *Locating the Romantic Subject*. Detroit: Wayne State University Press, 1997. Complex interpretation of the life and work of Novalis in light of the modern object-relations theory of British psychologist D. W. Winnicott. Particular emphasis on Novalis's major novel, *Henry of Ofterdingen*, as a psychoanalytic case study.

O'Brien, William Arctander. *Novalis: Signs of Revolution*. Durham, N.C.: Duke University Press, 1995. Examines both the life and the work of Novalis with the purpose of contradicting "the myth of Novalis" as a dreamy, death-obsessed mystic. Sees Novalis as the quintessential early German Romantic. A chapter called "The Making of Sophie" brings new perspectives to Novalis's profound experience with the young Sophie von Kühn.

Donald P. Haase

RAINER MARIA RILKE

Born: Prague, Bohemia, Austro-Hungarian Empire; December 4, 1875
Died: Valmont, Switzerland; December 29, 1926

PRINCIPAL POETRY
Leben und Lieder, 1894
Larenopfer, 1896
Wegwarten, 1896
Traumgekrönt, 1897
Advent, 1898
Mir zur Feier, 1899
Das Buch der Bilder, 1902, 1906 (*The Book of Images*, 1994)
Das Stundenbuch, 1905 (*Poems from the Book of Hours*, 1941)
Neue Gedichte, 1907-1908 (2 volumes; *New Poems*, 1964)
Die frühen Gedichte, 1909
Requiem, 1909 (*Requiem, and Other Poems*, 1935)
Das Marienleben, 1913 (*The Life of the Virgin Mary*, 1951)
Duineser Elegien, 1923 (*Duinese Elegies*, 1931; better known as *Duino Elegies*)
Die Sonette an Orpheus, 1923 (*Sonnets to Orpheus*, 1936)
Vergers, suivi des Quatrains Valaisans, 1926 (*Orchards*, 1982)
Gesammelte Werke, 1927
Les Fenêtres, 1927 ("The Windows" in *The Roses and the Windows*, 1979)
Les Roses, 1927 ("The Roses" in *The Roses and the Windows*, 1979)
Verse und Prosa aus dem Nachlass, 1929
Späte Gedichte, 1934 (*Late Poems*, 1938)
Poèmes français, 1935
Aus dem Nachlass des Grafen C. W.: Ein Gedichtkreis, 1950
Christus—Visionen, pb. 1950 (wr. 1896-1898)
Poems, 1906 to 1926, 1957
Poems, 1965
Uncollected Poems, 1996

OTHER LITERARY FORMS

The rich symbolic content and specific themes that characterize the famous lyrics of Rainer Maria Rilke (RIHL-kuh) also inform his narrative prose. Recollections of his boyhood and youth are given romantic, fairy-tale coloring in *Vom lieben Gott und Anderes* (1900; republished as *Geschichten vom lieben Gott*, 1904; *Stories of God*, 1931, 1963), a cycle of short tales that replace traditional Christian perceptions of God with depictions of a finically careful artist. *Die Weise von Liebe und Tod des Cornets Christoph Rilke* (1906; *The Tale of the Love and Death of Cornet Christoph Rilke*, 1932), a terse yet beautifully written story, is more like an epic poem than a prose work, especially in its emphasis on the power of the individual word and its intensely rhythmic language. The psychologically intricate novel *Die Aufzeichnungen des Malte Laurids Brigge* (1910; *The Notebooks of Malte Laurids Brigge*, 1930; also known as *The Journal of My Other Self*) is one of Rilke's most profound creations. Written from the point of view of a young Danish nobleman living in exile in Paris, it offers in random sketches a peculiar summation of the central concerns of the author's literary art.

Between 1894 and 1904, Rilke wrote more than twenty plays, many of which were lost and never published. The most important of his remaining theatrical works are either pessimistically Naturalistic or intense dramas of the soul. *Jetzt und in der Stunde unseres Absterbens* (pr., pb. 1896; *Now and in the Hour of Our Death*, 1979) and *Im Frühfrost* (pr., pb. 1897; *Early Frost*, 1979) reflect the influence of Rudolf Christoph Jenny in their materialistic determinism, while later pieces such as *Höhenluft* (pr. 1969; *Air at High Altitude*, 1979) and *Ohne Gegenwart* (pb. 1898; *Not Present*, 1979) document a development in the direction of Symbolism, motivated especially by the dramatic theories of Maurice Maeterlinck. Rilke's best-remembered play is *Die weisse Fürstin* (pb. 1929; *The White Princess*, 1979), which in its lyric depth and power illustrates his view that drama and poetry have similar goals.

Apart from his writings in other genres, Rilke also produced a few works of nonfiction. Most notable among these are the biographical study *Auguste Rodin* (1903; English translation, 1919) and the descriptive lyric essays of *Worpswede* (1903). Much of his extensive correspondence has been collected and published. Especially important for what they reveal of his artistic personality and poetic process are volumes of letters exchanged with Lou Andreas-Salomé and Princess Marie von Thurn und Taxis.

Achievements

Commonly ranked alongside Hugo von Hofmannsthal and Stefan George as a giant of twentieth century German poetry, Rainer Maria Rilke is perhaps the most controversial of the three in point of critical and popular reception of his works. Although his substantial collections published soon after the turn of the century, especially *The Book of Hours* and *New Poems*, were greeted with uniformly favorable recognition, there is wide disagreement among critics concerning the literary value of both his early poems and those of his final, major creative period. A significant key to the divided viewpoints is his boldly daring, uniquely creative use of language in strange new relationships, his peculiar departures from traditional grammar and syntax, and his unusual forms of subjective and objective expression. The pure individuality of his poetic utterances often makes them difficult to understand and repels the reader who approaches Rilke's art with anything less than full and active concentration. As a result, the most problematic of Rilke's mature poems, especially the *Duino Elegies*, are regarded by some scholars as the most important German lyric creations of the first half of the twentieth century, whereas others dismiss them as lacking substance. Regardless of these disagreements, Rilke's influence on the development of German verse is unrivaled by that of any other German-language poet of his time. His most lasting and important contribution remains the concept of the *Dinggedicht* (thing poem) introduced in *New Poems*.

BIOGRAPHY

The life of René Karl Wilhelm Johann Josef Maria Rilke can be described in its entirety as a productive, if not always successful, search for fulfillment in reaction to an inhibiting, psychologically destructive childhood. Critical elements of Rilke's early experience contributed to his development as a hypersensitive individual unsuited to the demands of practical existence. They include the rapid failure of his parents' marriage; the rape of his personality by a mother who dressed him in feminine clothing and reared him for a time as a replacement for a lost daughter; a partial education in military academies and a school of commerce to which he could never adapt; and a brief exposure to the university world in Prague. The young Rilke responded to a continuing feeling of being out of place by trying diligently to become part of active cultural and artistic circles. While still a student, he published his first lyric anthology, composed naturalistic plays, contributed literary reviews to newspapers and journals, and founded his own periodical. He also participated in cultural organizations, lecture presentations, readings of drama and poetry, and similar activities.

When Rilke left the university in 1896, he went to Munich. An incurable restlessness dictated his lifestyle from that time forward. His serious evolution as a writer began under the influence of significant figures whom he encountered in Munich; friendships with Jacob Wassermann and Wilhelm von Scholz were especially productive. Wassermann acquainted him with the writings of Jens Peter Jacobsen, which Rilke soon learned to treasure. Still more important was the relationship that he formed with Andreas-Salomé, whom he met in 1897. It was she who persuaded him to change his name from René to Rainer. After she became his mistress, she exposed him to contemporary philosophical trends and the ideas of the Italian Renaissance. He quickly followed her to Berlin and later traveled with her and her husband twice to Russia, where he was introduced to Leo Tolstoy and other authors. The vast Russian landscape and the Russian people impressed him as examples of original, elemental nature. From them, he drew ideas and perceptions that informed his verse long afterward.

Rilke's only attempt to establish a permanent family situation ended in failure. In 1902, he dissolved his household in the Worpswede artists' colony, left his wife, the sculptress Clara Westhoff, and their daughter, and moved to Paris, where he intended to write a book about Auguste Rodin. His friendship with the famous sculptor was extremely significant for the direction of his poetic development in the years between

1902 and the beginning of World War I. Rodin provided Rilke with an example of strict artistic discipline that had profound impact on his maturation as a poet.

Even more critical to his literary growth during this time was Rilke's association with Impressionist painter Paul Cézanne, whose painting technique contributed much to the evolving visual orientation of Rilke's verse. Not only special individuals but also Paris itself, the French people, and even the French language indelibly marked Rilke's subsequent creations, giving them substance and eventually, during his final years, their very medium of expression.

The atmosphere of two other locales gave peculiar flavor to Rilke's most powerful, most complex masterworks. The first was Duino Castle near Trieste; the second, the Château de Muzot in Valais. After visiting North Africa and Egypt in 1910 and 1911, he went to Duino Castle at the invitation of Princess Marie von Thurn und Taxis. There, he wrote the first two of the *Duino Elegies* before moving on to Spain and then back to Germany. The war years, which he spent primarily in Munich, constituted an unproductive interlude that was inwardly devastating to him. He found it exceedingly difficult to begin writing again when hostilities ceased. Only after moving to Switzerland and his secluded refuge at the Château de Muzot did he find inner peace sufficient to complete his finest lyric cycles. He spent most of the remainder of his life in the Rhône Valley, where he died of leukemia.

Analysis

During the course of his development as a poet, the creative task became for Rainer Maria Rilke a process of objectification and externalization of his own inner world. Couched in language that is notable for its musicality and its frequently playful moods are the peculiarities of a unique spiritual life that emerged from special responses to outside stimuli. The melody of lyrics rich in alliteration, assonance, consonance, and rhyme provides a naturally flowing framework for the presentation of the poet's feelings and reflections. Especially typical components of his verse are encounters with sorrow and pain, powerful absorption in specific objects, a strange blending of the experiences of death and love, and an overwhelming sense of isolation.

The landscape of these revelations of self is transformed and varied in direct relationship to new outward contacts with people, things, and places. Russia, Paris, Duino, and Valais provide for different works, shaping influence and substance, timeless symbols and concrete reality, worldview and microcosmic conception. Taken in sequence, Rilke's cycles and poems document his endeavors to purify the portrayal of the scenes within him, to clarify obscurities and nail down uncertainties. By its very nature, this act of poetic refinement was deeply religious, reflecting a sincere humility in the face of creation's vast mysteries. Rilke's entire oeuvre proclaims a consciousness of an artistic calling that had its basis in an existential anxiety that was translated into joyful, almost rapturous affirmation of mortality.

EARLY POEMS

Rilke's earliest published poems, which appeared in the collections *Leben und Lieder* (life and songs), *Larenopfer* (offering to the household gods), *Wegwarten* (watch posts), and *Traumgekrönt* (dream-crowned), are marked by a naïve simplicity and a degree of sentimentality that are absent from his more mature writings. Under the influence of Jens Peter Jacobsen, he created particularly sensitive lyrics centered on nature, as well as penetrating psychological portraits of people. Among his favorite subjects were women and children. Even in these youthful creations, there is already a strong emphasis on visual imagery, although the artistic focus of attention is frequently not the object that is described, but rather the spiritual stirrings that occur within the poet because of what he sees.

MIR ZUR FEIER

In *Mir zur Feier* (celebrating me), Rilke began to move from the lyric forms and approaches of his student years, adopting in the transition techniques that he later perfected in his first broadly successful cycle, *The Book of Hours*. The poems of *Mir zur Feier* present in precise detail their creator's innermost personal concerns, describing in tones of religious fervor his yearnings, prayers, and self-perceptions. Framed in language that is rich in texture yet soft in tone, the poems glorify things that cannot be comprehended through human volition. These verse productions represent a calculated justification of the poet's art as a means of celebrating that which can be revealed in its essence and fullness in no other manner.

THE BOOK OF IMAGES

The Book of Images, a collection written at about the same time as *The Book of Hours*, is in some respects poetically stronger. Under the influence of Rodin, Rilke made the transition from a poetry informed by blurred feeling to precise, objective, carefully formed verse characterized by the complete sacrifice of the poet's immanence to an emphasis upon things in themselves. The creations of *The Book of Images* reveal the writer's progress toward the establishment of a literary integration of visual impressions with sight-oriented components of language. The artistic process becomes a perfecting of the act of seeing, in which the poet organizes the elements of the visual image through subjective cognition of his external world. Although these lyrics do not attain to the plastic monumentality of Rilke's later writings, they are forerunners of the *Dinggedichte* that are collectively the most important product of Rilke's years in Paris.

THE BOOK OF HOURS

The commemoration of self is a significant aspect of *The Book of Hours*, divided into three sections that were the product of diverse influences and experiences: Rilke's impressions of Russia and Paris, his love affair with Andreas-Salomé, the dramatic writings of Maurice Maeterlinck and Henrik Ibsen, Friedrich Nietzsche's philosophical ideas, and the cultural legacy of the Italian Renaissance. The work as a whole portrays the author's movement toward an internalization of external phenomena in a poetic act of preservation and redemption. There is evident within the individual poems a new kind of friendly relationship between the poet and God's handiwork that surrounds him. Nevertheless, what is presented is definitely not a traditional Christian attitude toward life. These lyrics are the product of an aggressively demanding mind; in them, a strongly individual interpretation of the religious dimension of experience is advanced without equivocation. The thrust of *The Book of Hours* is to refine the notion that God is not static, a complete and perfect being, but rather a continually evolving artistic creation. Rilke insists that the reader accept this idea on faith, equating his poetic message with spiritual revelation. The result is a celebration of "this world" that the poet continued to elaborate and modify until his death.

The three parts of *The Book of Hours* are discrete sets of deeply intimate confessions that arose out of special relationships and encounters that shaped Rilke's artistic outlook. "Das Buch vom mönchischen Leben" ("Of the Monastic Life"), written in 1899, reflects the strong influence of the poet's attachment to Andreas-Salomé and the cultural, historical, and philosophical ideas to which she introduced him. His ecstatic love for Andreas-Salomé and their visits to Russia are the key elements that give "Das Buch von der Pilgerschaft" ("Of Pilgrimage") its specific flavor, while "Das Buch von der Armut und vom Tod" ("Of Poverty and Death ") was a product of Rilke's impressions during his first year in Paris. The individual poems of the three cycles are experiments in which Rilke tested various symbols and metaphors, metric and rhythmic possibilities, and rhyme schemes in documenting a deep worship of life as a sacred motivating force.

"Of the Monastic Life" is a series of prayerful outpourings of the spirit in which a young monk addresses God. In this context, prayer is an elemental religious act with two goals: self-discovery in the process of establishing and expanding personal modes of expression, and the "creation" of God and the growth of a sense of brotherhood with him in one's relationship to nature. The fictive prayer situations provide the setting for a portrayal of the innermost stirrings of the soul in an endless reaching outward to illuminate the divine. Melodic language and strength of visual image are brought together with rich imagination to reveal the lyricist's almost Franciscan sympathy with the world.

Specific items of the cycle "Of Pilgrimage" attain peaks of religious rapture in the glorification of the mystical union between man and woman, offered in newly intensified homage to Andreas-Salomé. Thematically, however, this portion of *The Book of Hours* focuses primarily on key aspects of the poet's Russian experience. It emphasizes especially the idea that the pious Russian people are the embodiment of humility and spirituality within a topographical frame that is the archetype of God's creation. Spatial relationships are particularly important as the vastness of the Russian countryside melts into the author's inner landscape. A few of the lyrics reveal an inclination toward things that need humans, presenting them in impressionistic trappings that show a predilection for that which is most immediate and intricate.

"Of Poverty and Death," the final segment of *The Book of Hours*, anticipates the negative, sometimes melancholy tone of Rilke's later collections. Its substance is human misery presented in variations that expose in stark coloration the world of the homeless, the infirm, the abandoned, and the afraid. Christian motifs and themes are employed to accentuate Rilke's rejection of the Christian God, while rich images establish a substantial tie to "Of the Monastic Life" in the affirmation of God as an original poetic creation.

DINGGEDICHTE

Rilke's most lasting legacy and most important contribution to German poesy is the *Dinggedicht*, an originally conceived interpretation of inner experience generated in response to encounters with external objects and phenomena that the poet transformed into symbols for the elements of human life. With *New Poems*, in which he perfected this particular form, Rilke made a breakthrough that was immeasurably far-reaching in its implications for the expansion of German poetry's expressive domain.

A reflection of Rilke's attention to impulses from Rodin's sculpture and Cézanne's paintings, the *Dinggedicht* is the product of disciplined and thorough scrutinization of its model. Outwardly, it seeks to offer the character and intrinsic constitution of an object that is described for its own sake in painstakingly refined language. On another level, however, it documents the acquisition of external things for the poet's inner domain, thereby transforming the physical phenomenon into a precise and specifically calculated symbol for a portion of his re-creation of the world for himself. Some of the poems analyze people, buildings, natural and artificial scenes, plants, animals, and even motifs from mythology and the Bible; others are lyric translations of statues and paintings. Each provides a segment of Rilke's new interpretation and clarification of existence. Unlike the earlier forms, the *Dinggedicht* renounces the commitment to melodic sound relationships and connected imagery chains. The exacting identification of the poem's external object and its reduction to its fundamental nature permitted the poet to place it into an absolute domain of pure symbol.

NEW POEMS

Rilke achieved his most representative mastery of the *Dinggedicht* in *New Poems*, a collection in which heavy stress is placed on negative moods in the explication of the view that God is the direction and not the object of love. In their extreme subtlety and refinement of language, their worldly elegance, and their moral and emotional engagement, the most representative poems of Rilke's Paris period form the center of his work as a whole. The *Dinggedichte* of *New Poems* are a detailed reflection of his view that his poetic task was the interpretation and clarification of existence for the purpose of healing the world. By accepting, recognizing, and loving things for themselves, the poet places himself in a position to trace animals, plants, works of art, human figures, and other objects back to their true nature and substance. Precise seeing and artistic transformation enable him to project in symbols the content and meaning both of his surroundings and of that which is within him.

Divided into two loosely chronological parts, the poems in *New Poems* examine in objectively plastic, precisely disciplined structures representative manifestations and individuals that belong to the world of nature and to humanity's most important cultural attainments, from the Bible to classical antiquity, from the Middle Ages to the Renaissance. Mystical inwardness is projected in carefully defined symbols that objectively externalize the events within the poet that are stimulated by the process of seeing. Gloom, absurdity, and disintegration are common moods in poems that question the possibility for everything, including humanity, to exist and thereby to become the subject of literature.

"The Panther"

The symbolic portraits of *New Poems* focus on a broad variety of models. Among the most successful are those based on impressions from the Jardin des Plantes. "Der Panther" ("The Panther"), the earliest and most famous of the *Dinggedichte*, transforms its object into a symbol of heroic existence. By the very power of its seeing, the panther, like the poet, is able to create its own inner landscape, absorbing the visual impressions of external objects into itself, where it may modify, penetrate, or even destroy them. One of Rilke's most vivid depictions of rapport with an object, achieved in the act of intense observation, is given in "Archaïscher Torso Apollos" ("Archaic Torso of Apollo"), the first work in the second volume of *New Poems*. The headless statue becomes a kind of spiritual mirror that directs the onlooker's gaze back into the self, enabling him to recognize the need for change in his own life.

Duino Elegies and Sonnets to Orpheus

An important consequence of Rilke's Paris experience was a reevaluation of his literary existence that led ultimately to a significant turning point in his career. The problem of an irreconcilable conflict between the demands of practicality and art was compounded by a philosophical crisis involving the tensions that he felt in his need to make a definitive break with Christianity and in his loathing of modern technology. Against this background, an encounter with Søren Kierkegaard's existential philosophy led eventually to Rilke's production of the mythologically exaggerated *Duino Elegies* and *Sonnets to Orpheus* as the peak of his literary endeavor. In these mature lyrics, the creative attitudes and symbolic devices of *New Poems* were refined and perfected. Rilke responded to many different stimuli—World War I, the works of Friedrich Gottlieb Klopstock, Johann Wolfgang von Goethe, and Heinrich von Kleist, Sigmund Freud's psychology, among others—in creating a culminating synthesis of his own poetic view of human life and destiny. Dactylic and iambic meters, free rhythms, questions, and exclamations provide the frame for bold images that pinpoint once again the fundamental directions of Rilke's work as a whole.

Between 1912 and 1922, Rilke created the ten Duino elegies in monumental celebration of humanity as the final, most extreme possibility of existence. The ultimate refinement of the delineation of his own calling focuses no longer on the artist as interpreter and clarifier of his surroundings, but rather ordains the poet as a prophet and savior whose task is to preserve everything that has being. He thus becomes the protagonist and representative of humanity in a new religion of life that is an expression of unchecked aestheticism. By saving the world from a collapse that seems unavoidable, the poet engages in an act of self-purification and follows the only possible course of personal redemption.

Taken together, the elegies offer a mural of Rilke's inner landscape. Internalization of travel experiences, the lonely scenery at Duino Castle, the flight of birds, mythological constructs, and other phenomena create a background of timeless "inner space" against which the author projects his coming to grips with the existential polarities of life and death. Progressing from lament to profound affirmation of mortality, the poems glorify the fulfillment of humanity's promise to maintain all things of value through a process of transformation that rescues external nature by placing it in the protected realm of the spirit. The power by which this is accomplished is love, supremely manifested by lovers, people who die young, heroes, children, and animals. By bringing together earth and space, life and death, all dimensions of reality and time into a single inward hierarchical unity, Rilke sought to ensure the continuation of humanity's outward existence.

In the first elegy, the poet states his view of the human condition: imperfection, the questionable status of humanity, the experience of transience, the pain of love. On this basis, he builds a new mythology of life. Its center is the non-Christian angel who appears in the second elegy as a symbol for the absolute and unattainable, the norm from which humans in their limitations deviate. In a valid transformation of psychoanalysis into images, Rilke pinpoints the threat that exists within the human self in the power of natural drives. Illumination of the brokenness, ambiguity, superficiality, and mechanical senselessness of human pursuits is followed in the sixth elegy by identification of the hero as a symbolic concept that contrasts with average life. The seventh poem of the cycle breaks away from the lament of human insufficiency, suddenly glorifying the here and now in hymnic language that moves to a confessional peak. Renewed expression of the idea that the difference between humans and the natural creature cannot be resolved is followed by an attempt to show that life must be accepted and made fruitful despite its limitations. The culminating elegy creates a balance between mourning and celebration that unites the antithetical problems in a grand, affirmative vision of pain and death as the destiny of humanity and the only true evidence of his existence.

LATE POEMS IN FRENCH
The verse written in French after *Duino Elegies* and *Sonnets to Orpheus* was anticlimactic for Rilke's career. It lacks the depth and profundity of earlier works, although individual poems achieve lightness and sparkle in their reflection of a new rejoicing in mortal existence.

OTHER MAJOR WORKS
LONG FICTION: *Am Leben hin*, 1889; *Die Letzten*, 1902; *Die Weise von Liebe und Tod des Cornets Christoph Rilke*, 1906 (*The Tale of the Love and Death of Cornet Christopher Rilke*, 1932); *Die Aufzeichnungen des Malte Laurids Brigge*, 1910 (*The Notebooks of Malte Laurids Brigge*, 1930; also known as *The Journal of My Other Self*).
SHORT FICTION: *Zwei Prager Geschichten*, 1899 (*Two Stories of Prague*, 1994); *Vom lieben Gott und Anderes*, 1900 (republished as *Geschichten vom lieben Gott*, 1904; *Stories of God*, 1931, 1963); *Erzählungen und Skizzen aus der Frühzeit*, 1928.
PLAYS: *Murillo*, pb. 1895 (English translation, 1979); *Jetzt und in der Stunde unseres Absterbens*, pr., pb. 1896 (*Now and in the Hour of Our Death*, 1979); *Im Frühfrost*, pr., pb. 1897 (*Early Frost*, 1979); *Vigilien*, wr. 1897 (*Vigils*, 1979); *Ohne Gegenwart*, pb. 1898 (*Not Present*, 1979); *Das tägliche Leben*, pr. 1901 (*Everyday Life*, 1979); *Waisenkinder*, pb. 1901 (*Orphans*, 1979); *Die weisse Fürstin*, pb. 1929 (*The White Princess*, 1979); *Höhenluft*, pr. 1969 (wr. 1897; *Air at High Altitude*, 1979); *Nine Plays*, 1979.
NONFICTION: *Auguste Rodin*, 1903 (English translation, 1919); *Worpswede*, 1903; *Briefe an einen jungen Dichter*, 1929 (*Letters to a Young Poet*, 1934); *Wartime Letters of Rainer Maria Rilke, 1914-1921*, 1940; *Tagebücher aus der Frühzeit*, 1942 (*Diaries of a Young Poet*, 1997); *Letters of Rainer Maria Rilke*, 1945-1948 (2 volumes); *Selected Letters of Rainer Maria Rilke, 1902-1926*, 1947; *Briefwechsel [zwischen] Rainer Maria Rilke und Marie von Thurn und Taxis*, 1951 (*The Letters of Rainer Maria Rilke and Princess Marie von Thurn und Taxis*, 1958); *Rainer Maria Rilke, Lou Andreas-Salomé: Briefwechsel*, 1952; *Rainer Maria Rilke and Lou Andreas-Salomé: The Correspondence*, 2006.
MISCELLANEOUS: *The Poet's Guide to Life: The Wisdom of Rilke*, 2005 (Ulrich Baer, editor).

BIBLIOGRAPHY
Andreas-Salomé, Lou. *You Alone Are Real to Me: Remembering Rainer Maria Rilke*. Translated by Angela von der Lippe. New York: BOA Editions, 2003. In her memoir, Andreas-Salomé describes her relationship with Rilke.
Bernstein, Michael André. *Five Portraits: Modernity and the Imagination in Twentieth-Century German Writing*. Edited by Gary Saul Morson. Evanston, Ill.: Northwestern University Press, 2000. Presents Rilke's poetry in the context of the shift among

German writers from Romanticism and aestheticism to twentieth century modernism.

Freedman, Ralph. *Life of a Poet: Rainer Maria Rilke*. New York: Farrar, Straus and Giroux, 1996. A helpful complement to Donald Prater's definitive biography, this work draws extensive parallels between Rilke's life and the content of his poetry. Also contains several photographs of Rilke and his family.

Kleinbard, David. *The Beginning of Terror: A Psychological Study of Rainer Maria Rilke's Life and Work*. New York: New York University Press, 1993 . A critical rather than comprehensive biography, attempting a psychoanalysis of Rilke and his published writing. Examines issues such as Rilke's childhood, his relationships with his parents (both biological and surrogate), and his debilitating blood disorder and its effect on his work.

Prater, Donald. *A Ringing Glass: The Life of Rainer Maria Rilke*. New York: Clarendon Press, 1993. A definitive biography of Rilke that concentrates on his European travels and correspondence with friends. Also, the bibliography is highly helpful for those who need a comprehensive, expert guide to Rilke criticism. Illustrated.

Ryan, Judith. *Rilke, Modernism, and Poetic Tradition*. New York: Cambridge University Press, 1999. Although Rilke saw himself as a more or less self-created writer, who needed extended periods of solitude in which to work, Ryan shows him in his relationship to other writers and even painters in the European culture of his day. Traces his movement from the art-for-art's-sake school of writing into modernism.

Schoolfield, George C. *Young Rilke and His Time*. Rochester, N.Y.: Camden House, 2009. A biography of Rilke that focuses on the writer as a youth and how the circumstances of his youth affected his writing.

Lowell A. Bangerter

NELLY SACHS

Born: Berlin, Germany; December 10, 1891
Died: Stockholm, Sweden; May 12, 1970

PRINCIPAL POETRY
In den Wohnungen des Todes, 1946
Sternverdunkelung, 1949
Und niemand weiss weiter, 1957
Flucht und Verwandlung, 1959
Fahrt ins Staublose, 1961
Noch feiert Tod das Leben, 1961
Glühende Rätsel, 1964 (parts 1 and 2; 1965, part 3 in *Späte Gedichte*; 1966, part 4 in the annual *Jahresring*)
Späte Gedichte, 1965
Die Suchende, 1966
O the Chimneys, 1967
The Seeker, and Other Poems, 1970
Teile dich Nacht, 1971

OTHER LITERARY FORMS

Nelly Sachs (saks) published the short play, or "scenic poem," *Eli: Ein Mysterienspiel vom Leiden Israels* (pb. 1951; *Eli: A Mystery Play of the Sufferings of Israel*, 1967). Her fiction is collected in *Legenden und Erzählungen* (1921) and her correspondence with Paul Celan in *Paul Celan, Nelly Sachs: Correspondence* (1995).

ACHIEVEMENTS

Nelly Sachs arrived at her characteristic poetic style late in life. She was heavily influenced by the German Romantic poets and did not consider her lyric poetry of the years prior to 1943 to be representative of her mature work, excluding those poems from the collection of 1961. Her first published book, a small volume of legends and tales published in 1921, was heavily indebted in style and content to the Swedish novelist Selma Lagerlöf. In the 1920's and 1930's, Sachs published lyric poetry in such respected newspapers and journals as the *Vossische Zeitung* of Berlin, the *Berliner Tageblatt*, and *Der Morgen*, the journal of the Jewish cultural federation.

Sachs's stylistic breakthrough came with the traumatic experience of her flight from Germany and exile in Sweden. The play *Eli* was written in 1943 but published privately in Sweden in 1951. It was first broadcast on Süddeutsche Rundfunk (South German Radio) in 1958 and had its theater premiere in 1962 in Dortmund. Acceptance of her poetry

Nelly Sachs
(©The Nobel Foundation)

in West Germany was equally slow, partly because her main theme (Jewish suffering during World War II) stirred painful memories. In the late 1950's and 1960's, however, she was hailed as modern Germany's greatest woman poet and received numerous literary prizes. She was accepted for membership in several academies. In 1958, she received the poetry prize of the Swedish broadcasting system and, in 1959, the Kulturpreis der Deutschen Industrie. The town of Meersburg in West Germany awarded her the Annette Droste Prize for female poets in 1960, and the city of Dortmund founded the Nelly Sachs Prize in 1961 and presented her with its first award. In the same year, friends and admirers published the first volume of a Festschrift, followed by the second volume, *Nelly Sachs zu Ehren*, on the occasion of her seventy-fifth birthday in 1966. On October 17, 1965, she received the Peace Prize of the German Book Trade Association, and on December 10, 1966, she was awarded the Nobel Prize in Literature. Berlin, the city where she was born and in which she had lived for nearly half a century, made her an honorary citizen in 1967. The city of Dortmund, Germany, and the Royal Library in

Stockholm, Sweden, have valuable collections of her letters and transcriptions of her early poems in their Nelly Sachs Archive.

Biography

Nelly Leonie Sachs was born Leonie Sachs in Berlin on December 10, 1891, the only child of William Sachs, an inventor, technical engineer, and manufacturer, and his wife, Margarete (Karger) Sachs. The family lived in very comfortable financial circumstances, and Nelly Sachs was educated in accordance with the custom for daughters of the upper-middle class. Although both of her parents were of Jewish ancestry, her family had few ties with the Jewish community and did not practice their religion. Sachs attended public schools from 1897 to 1900, but because of poor health, she was removed and received private instruction until 1903. She then attended a private secondary school for daughters of wealthy and titled families and finished her education in 1908 without any formal professional training. In the summer of that year, she fell in love with a man whose name she never revealed. That experience, which ended unhappily, escalated into a crisis, making Sachs consider suicide. The man was later killed in one of Germany's concentration camps.

For the next twenty-five years, even after the death of her father in 1930, Sachs led a sheltered and not particularly noteworthy existence. She produced some poetry, read extensively, and did watercolors, some of which have been preserved in the Nelly Sachs Archive in Stockholm. In 1906, Sachs received Lagerlöf's novel *Gösta Berling* (1891) as a birthday present. Her admiration for the writer resulted in a correspondence between the two, and Sachs sent Lagerlöf many of her own literary experiments. Through the intervention of Lagerlöf and the brother of the reigning Swedish king, Sachs and her mother received permission to emigrate to Sweden in 1939. Shortly after Lagerlöf's death in 1940, Sachs received orders from German authorities to appear for deportation to a work camp. Leaving all their possessions behind, Sachs and her mother fled Germany, arriving in Stockholm on May 16, 1940. They took up residence in a small apartment in the industrial harbor area, where Sachs remained until her death in 1970.

The imagery in Sachs's later lyric poetry draws to a large extent on influences from her youth. Her father's extensive collection of rocks, gems, and fossils was a source of inspiration to her, and she continued his hobby with a collection of her own in Stockholm; not unexpectedly, the use of the stones as a cipher is very prevalent in her work "Chor der Steine" ("Chorus of the Stones"). From her father's library, she was also familiar with the work of Maria Sibylla Merian, a seventeenth century entomologist and graphic artist who specialized in the study of butterflies. Sachs's poem "Schmetterling" ("Butterfly") exemplifies her metaphoric use of this and other insects in her work. In 1959, Sachs wrote that of all childhood influences on her later works, her father's musical talent was paramount. When he played the piano during evenings after work, she frequently danced for hours to the strains of his music. In addition to her early lyric poems, which she characterized as "dance and music poems," the motif of the dance is also important in her later work.

In 1960, Sachs returned to Germany for the first time since her exile to receive the Annette Droste Prize. Not wishing to spend a night in Germany, she stayed instead in Zurich, traveling the short distance to Meersburg only to accept the honor. Hearing the German language spoken again proved to be so traumatic, however, that she experienced a "memory trip to hell." In Zurich, she met Paul Celan, another exiled poet, who invited her to his home in Paris. The meeting resulted in a continuing correspondence, but Celan was in the midst of a personal crisis as well, and the relationship may have contributed to Sachs's difficulties. After her return to Stockholm, Sachs suffered a mental breakdown and was hospitalized with severe delusions of persecution. Although she worked feverishly during the next decade, she continued to suffer periodic attacks in which she imagined herself persecuted and threatened with death. Her cycle *Noch feiert Tod das Leben* (death still celebrates life) was written while she recovered in the hospital. Celan attempted to aid her recovery through an intensive, supportive correspondence that was also, however, an attempt at self-healing, inasmuch as he suffered from a similar ailment. Their poetry, beginning with Sachs's *Noch feiert Tod das Leben* and Celan's *Die Niemandsrose* (1963), shows their continuing "dialogue in poems." In the spring of 1970, Sachs became mortally ill and thus was not informed when Celan was reported missing early in April of that year. He was later found—an apparent suicide by drowning; his funeral services took place in the Cimetière Parisien near Orly, France, on the same day in May on which Sachs died in a Stockholm hospital.

Analysis

It is difficult to speak of development in Nelly Sachs's poetic works, inasmuch as she was well beyond fifty years old when she produced her first significant poems. It is true that she had published lyric poetry before the 1940's, but this early work has little in common with that of her mature years. Most of the poems from the 1920's and 1930's are thematically quite distinct from the later work, devoted to musicians such as Johann Sebastian Bach, Wolfgang Amadeus Mozart, Jean-Philippe Rameau, and Luigi Boccherini or dealing poetically with certain animals, such as deer, lambs, and nightingales. The Nelly Sachs archives in Dortmund and in Stockholm have copies of a substantial number of these early efforts.

In den Wohnungen des Todes

In contrast, the work of Sachs's last twenty-five years concerns itself largely with existential problems, particularly with topics related to the Holocaust and rooted in personal experiences of flight, exile, and the death of friends. Her first collection of poems, *In den Wohnungen des Todes* (in the habitations of death), refers in its title to the Nazi death camps and is dedicated to those who perished there. It is a mistake, however, to perceive her work solely in the context of these historical events. Her topic is on a larger scale, the cycle of life itself—birth, death, rebirth—and Sachs develops various metaphors and ciphers to express the agony and the hope of this cycle.

STERNVERDUNKELUNG

Although it is desirable to interpret Sachs's work separately from the context of specific historical events, it is almost impossible to analyze an individual poem without relying on information gained from a broader knowledge of her work. This difficulty is the result of her frequent use of ciphers, poetic images that can be "decoded" only by reference to other poems in which the same images occur. Such a cipher in Sachs's work is the stone. Its properties are chiefly those of inert matter: lack of emotion, or lifelessness. The cipher may depict human callousness, death, or desolation in different contexts, and it is related to similar poetic images such as sand and dust—decayed rock—which signify the mortal human condition.

The poem "Sinai," from the collection *Sternverdunkelung* (eclipse of the stars), contains entirely negative images of the stone. Sachs compares the ancient times of Moses, in which humanity was still in intimate contact with the divine and thus vibrantly alive, with the present state of lifelessness; there are only "petrified eyes of the lovers" with "their putrefied happiness." Recounting Moses's descent from Mount Sinai, Sachs asks: "Where is still a descendent/ from those who trembled? Oh, may he glow/ in the crowd of amnesiacs/ of the petrified!" The eyes of the lovers turned to stone signify the death both of sensibility and of sensuousness, and the inability to re-create or reproduce. It is ultimately a death of humankind. The call is for one perhaps still alive among the multitude of those dead in mind and body.

In "Chassidische Schriften" ("Hasidic Scriptures"), from *Sternverdunkelung*, Sachs writes: "And the heart of stones,/ filled with drifting sand,/ is the place where midnights are stored." "Drifting sand" is sand blown skyward by the wind; thus, while it is inert matter, it has lost this inertia momentarily on the wings of the wind. The dead has come to life. Midnight, on the other hand, represents the end of one day and the dawning of the next, a time of rebirth. Sachs contends that the stone, dead as it is, is imbued with the desire for rebirth and transubstantiation. Another possibility for the stone to attain a semblance of life is offered in "Golem Tod!" ("Golem Death!"), from *Sternverdunkelung*. There, "The stone sleeps itself green with moss." The suggestion that the stone is merely sleeping, not dead, and that it is capable of producing living matter (moss) is also an affirmation of the possibility of renewal of life after death.

"CHORUS OF THE STONES" AND "MELUSINE, IF YOUR WELL HAD NOT"

Scarcely less negative is the stone cipher in the poem "Wenn nicht dein Brunnen, Melusine" ("Melusine, If Your Well Had Not"), from *Und niemand weiss weiter*. If it were not for the possibility of transformation and escape, "we should long have passed away/ in the petrified resurrection/ of an Easter Island." Easter Island's petrified statues are merely reminders of an extinct civilization, not a resurrection from the dead. Still, the poem indicates that transformation is possible (the symbol for it is Melusine). In the poem "Chorus of the Stones," from *In den Wohnungen des Todes*, stones are, like the statues of Easter Island, venerable objects depicting the history of humankind. The stone is symbolic of all that has died, but it carries memories within it and thus is not entirely devoid of life. The last lines of the poem even offer the hope that the stone is only "sleeping," that it may come to life again: "Our conglomeration is transfused by breath./ It solidified in secret/ but may awaken at a kiss."

Three ideas in "Chorus of the Stones" suggest that death is not the final answer to life: The lifeless entity (the stone) contains memories; it is imbued with breath, a necessary element of life; and it may be awakened by an act of love. Transformation, resurrection, and transfiguration are therefore within the realm of possibility. Such a flight from lifelessness to a new beginning is nevertheless fraught with difficulties.

"Halleluja"

The most dramatic depiction of the rebirth of the dead is to be found in Sachs's poem "Halleluja" ("Hallelujah"), from the volume *Flucht und Verwandlung* (flight and metamorphosis). The poem describes a mountain rising from the sea by volcanic action. The rock is portrayed as a beloved child, the crowning glory of its mother, the ocean, as it thrusts forth from the womb to the light of day. While still embedded in the sea, the rock showed signs of sustaining life. As in "Golem Death!" with its stone covered with moss, this rock has been nurturing life. For the sea algae, birth of the rock means death, which the "winged longing" of the rock will bring about; although one form of life dies, another takes its place. These poems therefore encompass the cycle of life and death of living and inert matter on Earth.

"Butterfly" and "Fleeing"

In tracing the cipher of the stone, it is evident that the nihilism of the earlier cycles has given way to a guarded optimism in the later ones. A more traditional image of transfiguration is that of the butterfly. Its life cycle includes the apparent death of the homely caterpillar and its re-emergence from the cocoon as a beautiful winged creature, and thus it is readily adaptable as a symbol of the soul's resurrection after physical death. Sachs uses the image of the butterfly within this tradition. The poem "In der Flucht" ("Fleeing"), from *Flucht und Verwandlung*, compares the flight of the Jews from their persecutors with the never-ending process of transformation, mutation, and metamorphosis. There is no rest and no end (no "Amen") for that which is considered mortal (sand, dust), for it experiences endless metamorphoses. The butterfly, itself a symbol of metamorphosis, will reenter the life-giving element at its death and complete the cycle of life.

In "Butterfly," from *Sternverdunkelung*, the butterfly is depicted as a mortal creature (one made of "dust") which nevertheless mirrors the beauty of a world beyond: "What lovely hereafter/ is painted in your dust." The butterfly is a messenger of hope for those who are dying, because it is aware through its own metamorphosis that death is only sleep. The butterfly is the symbol of farewell, just as it was the symbol of the last greeting before sleep.

"Dancer" and "She Dances"

More obscure than the image of the butterfly are Sachs's ciphers of music and dance. The dancer appears to be able to defy gravity in graceful and effortless leaps and spins. A new image of man is created in the dance—that of emancipation from earthly limitations and acceptance into the sphere of the incorporeal. On this premise, Sachs bases her depiction of the dancer as a re-creator, savior, and emancipator from material limitations. In the poem "Sie tanzt" ("She Dances"), from *Noch feiert Tod das Leben*, the dancer rescues her lover from the dead. This act of rescue is not meant to save him from physical death, for he is no longer alive; metamorphosis is her aim. This she achieves, paradoxically, by her own death: "Aber plötzlich/ am Genick/ Schlaf beünt Sie hinüber" ("But suddenly/ at the neck/ sleep bends her over"). In German, the word "over" (*hinüber*) signifies "to the other side" and thus clearly suggests death; this connotation is underscored by the image of her bending at the neck (hanging) and by the word "sleep," which Sachs frequently uses as a synonym for physical, but not spiritual, death. In the act of dancing, the dancer has liberated both the dead lover and herself. The metamorphosis has released her from life and has rescued him from death. They are united in the spiritual realm. In *Flucht und Verwandlung*, a somewhat different form of creation is discussed in the poem "Tänzerin" ("Dancer"). Here the dancer becomes the vessel for the hope of the future, and Sachs depicts with physiological clarity the birth canal for a messianic prophecy: "In the branches of your limbs/ the premonitions/ build their twittering nests." The dancer's body becomes the maternal, life-giving promise of the future.

In the poem "She Dances," the beginning and the end of life are shown to coincide at the point of metamorphosis, the dancer being the agent. The medium for transfiguration is music. The poem "O-A-O-A," in *Glühende Rätsel* (glowing enigmas), describes the rhythmic "sea of vowels" as the Alpha and Omega. Music is the means of metamorphosis: "Du aber die Tasten niederdrücktest/ in ihre Gräber aus Musik/ und Tanz die verlorene Sternschnuppe/ einen Flügel erfand für dein Leiden" ("But you pressed down the keys/ into their graves of music/ and dance the lost meteor/ invented a wing for your anguish"). The English word "keys" is ambiguous, but the German *Tasten* refers solely to the keys of a piano in this context. The graves are made of music, the transforming factor, and are being played like the keys of a piano, while dance provides the wings for the flight from the corporeal.

"IN THE BLUE DISTANCE"

Finally, in the poem "In der blauen Ferne" ("In the Blue Distance"), from *Und niemand weiss weiter*, the pregnant last lines combine the ciphers of stone, dust, dance, and music in the depiction of metamorphosis: "the stone transforms its dust/ dancing into music." The lifeless element needs no mediator here but performs the ritual of transubstantiation into music (release from corporeal existence) by "dancing" as "dust"—an action functionally identical to that of the drifting sand in the poem "Hasidic Scriptures."

It has frequently been assumed that Sachs is chiefly a chronicler of Jewish destiny during World War II, a recorder of death and despair. This narrow view does not do justice to her work. Sachs's poetry has many aspects of faith, hope, and love, and need not be relegated to a specific historical event or ethnic orientation. Sachs writes about the concerns of every human being—birth, life, love, spiritual renewal, and the possibility of an existence beyond physical death. To diminish the scope of her appeal is to misunderstand her message and to misinterpret her work.

OTHER MAJOR WORKS

SHORT FICTION: *Legenden und Erzählungen*, 1921.

PLAYS: *Eli: Ein Mysterienspiel vom Leiden Israels*, pb. 1951 (*Eli: A Mystery Play of the Sufferings of Israel*, 1967); *Zeichen im Sand: Die szenischen Dichtungen*, pb. 1962.

NONFICTION: *Paul Celan, Nelly Sachs: Correspondence*, 1995.

BIBLIOGRAPHY

Bahti, Timothy, and Marilyn Sibley Fries, eds. *Jewish Writers, German Literature: The Uneasy Examples of Nelly Sachs and Walter Benjamin*. Ann Arbor: University of Michigan Press, 1995. Biographical and critical essays of Sachs's and Benjamin's lives and works. Includes bibliographical references and an index.

Bosmajian, Hamida. *Metaphors of Evil: Contemporary German Literature and the Shadow of Nazism*. Iowa City: University of Iowa Press, 1979. A historical and critical study of responses to the Holocaust in poetry and prose. Includes bibliographical references and index.

Bower, Kathrin M. *Ethics and Remembrance in the Poetry of Nelly Sachs and Rose Ausländer*. Rochester, N.Y.: Camden House, 2000. Critical interpretation of the works of Sachs and Ausländer with particular attention to their recollections of the Holocaust. Includes bibliographical references and index.

Garloff, Katja. *Words from Abroad: Trauma and Displacement in Postwar German Jewish Writers*. Detroit: Wayne State University Press, 2005. This work on German Jewish writers contains a chapter on Sachs as well as one on her friend Celan.

Langer, Lawrence L. *Versions of Survival: The Holocaust and the Human Spirit*. Albany: State University of New York Press, 1982. Brilliantly illuminates the paradoxes in Sachs's verse.

Roth, John K., ed. *Holocaust Literature*. Pasadena, Calif.: Salem Press, 2008. Contains a chapter that analyzes Sachs's "In the Blue Distance."

Rudnick, Ursula. *Post-Shoa Religious Metaphors: The Image of God in the Poetry of Nelly Sachs*. New York: Peter Lang, 1995. A biography of the poet and an in-depth interpretation of seven poems. Rudnick traces the biblical and mystical Jewish tradition that grounds Sachs's work. Includes bibliographical references.

Sachs, Nelly. *Paul Celan, Nelly Sachs: Correspondence*. Translated by Christopher Clark. Edited by Barbara Wiedemann. Riverdale-on-Hudson, N.Y.: Sheep Meadow Press, 1995. A collection of letters by two poets living outside Germany and tormented by guilt that they had escaped the Holocaust. Includes bibliographical references and index.

Soltes, Ori Z. *The Ashen Rainbow: Essays on the Arts and the Holocaust*. Washington, D.C.: Eshel Books, 2007. This work on art and the Holocaust contains a chapter that discusses Sachs.

Helene M. Kastinger Riley

FRIEDRICH SCHILLER

Born: Marbach, Württemberg (now in Germany); November 10, 1759
Died: Weimar, Saxe-Weimar (now in Germany); May 9, 1805

PRINCIPAL POETRY
Anthologie auf das Jahr 1782, 1782
Xenien, 1796 (with Johann Wolfgang von Goethe)
Gedichte, 1800, 1803
The Poems of Schiller, 1851
The Ballads and Shorter Poems of Fredrick V. Schiller, 1901

OTHER LITERARY FORMS

Although Friedrich Schiller (SHIHL-ur) wrote poetry throughout most of his life, the bulk of his oeuvre belongs to other genres. He became especially famous for his powerful dramatic works. Among the most important of his ten major plays are *Die Räuber* (pb. 1781; *The Robbers*, 1792), *Don Carlos, Infant von Spanien* (pr., pb. 1787; *Don Carlos, Infante of Spain*, 1798), *Maria Stuart* (pr. 1800; *Mary Stuart*, 1801), and *Wilhelm Tell* (pr., pb. 1804; *William Tell*, 1841). During the early part of his career, his writings brought him little income, and poverty forced him to turn to fiction for a broader audience. *Der Verbrecher aus verlorener Ehre* (1786; *The Criminal in Consequence of Lost Reputation*, 1841) and the serialized novel *Der Geisterseher* (1789; *The Ghost-Seer: Or, The Apparitionist*, 1795) were among the most successful of these endeavors. While a professor of history at the University of Jena, Schiller wrote a number of historical books and essays, and during the early 1790's, he published a variety of theoretical and philosophical studies on aesthetics, ethics, and literature. His "Über die ästhetische Erziehung des Menschen" ("On the Aesthetic Education of Man") and "Über naive und sentimentalische Dichtung" ("On Naïve and Sentimental Poetry") are among the most significant treatises on literature and art written in Germany during the second half of the eighteenth century. His extensive correspondence with Johann Wolfgang von Goethe is the high point in the several volumes of his letters that have been collected and published since his death.

ACHIEVEMENTS

Although most of Friedrich Schiller's verse was written for a highly intellectual audience, it also enjoyed popular success. His "thought poems" laid the groundwork for the ensuing development of the poetry of ideas and brought him rightful recognition as Germany's most important eighteenth century composer of philosophical lyrics. On the other hand, his didactic purpose and his capacity for evoking moods akin to those of folk

Friedrich Schiller
(Library of Congress)

literature, especially in his ballads, made Schiller also a poet of the common people.

Schiller's poems and other writings were quickly recognized for their quality by the German literary establishment and were published in the significant periodicals of the time. Supported by Christoph Martin Wieland and Johann Gottfried Herder, Schiller became an important force among the artistic giants in Weimar, even before his friendship with Goethe. During the decade of their poetic collaboration, Schiller joined Goethe in shaping literary attitudes, approaches, and forms that influenced German poets and determined the nature of German letters from that time onward.

Even in his own time, however, some of Schiller's poetic works were highly controversial. The so-called Epigram War that he and Goethe waged against their critics was evidence that his works were not universally well received. After his death, Schiller's reputation in critical circles waned in direct relationship to the increased advocacy of realism and, eventually, naturalism. Near the turn of the century, a Schiller renaissance began on two levels. Writers such as Stefan George and Hugo von Hofmannsthal, who advocated a return to classical literary values, praised Schiller for his poetic models of idealism and beauty. Among the common people, such poems as "Das Lied von der Glocke" ("The Song of the Bell") were memorized in school, exposing a new generation of German youth to Schiller's thought. Although he was overshadowed by Goethe in pure poetic endowment, Schiller's impact on the whole of German literature is such that the renowned Thomas Mann called his works the "apotheosis of art."

Biography

The early life of Johann Christoph Friedrich von Schiller was shaped by two powerful influences: the Swabian Pietism of his origins, and the "benevolent" despotism of Karl Eugen, duke of Württemberg. After serving as a lieutenant in Bavarian, French, and Swabian regiments, Schiller's father was rewarded with an appointment as superintendent of the duke's gardens and plantations. Although Schiller's parents had planned for him to enter the ministry, those intentions were frustrated when the duke insisted that he be enrolled in a military academy at Stuttgart in 1773. After a brief and inconclusive period of legal studies at the academy, Schiller left the institution to become a medical officer in Karl Eugen's army. His dislike of the school's restrictions contributed substantially to the attacks on tyranny prevalent in his early writings.

Schiller's first poem was published in a Swabian literary magazine in 1776, and others appeared there and elsewhere during the remainder of his school years. Two months after his graduation, he rented a room from a widow, Luise Vischer, whom critics long regarded as the model for his Laura odes. While still in Stuttgart, Schiller wrote his first play, *The Robbers*. It premiered in Mannheim in January, 1782, and Schiller traveled, without the duke's permission, to attend the opening performance. Following Schiller's second secret theater visit to Mannheim, Karl Eugen placed him under two weeks' arrest and forbade him to write. The arrival of the Russian czar in Stuttgart took Karl Eugen's attention away from Schiller, and the latter fled to Mannheim.

Existence in Mannheim was a constant struggle for the young Schiller. His literary efforts brought him little monetary profit, and he survived only through the help of his friends. When the manager of the Mannheim theater refused to renew his contract as house dramatist, Schiller published a literary journal in an effort to straighten out his fiscal affairs. The emotional strain caused by his precarious economic condition and his unsuccessful encounters with women during those years is reflected in the poetry that he wrote after leaving Stuttgart. Not until he was rescued from financial disaster by Gottfried Körner and other admirers in 1784 did Schiller's personal life gain stability sufficient to foster the harmonious mastery of thought and form that typifies his more mature lyric creations. The friendship with Körner was a direct stimulus for the famous poem "An die Freude" ("Ode to Joy"), which Beethoven used for the choral movement of his Ninth Symphony.

A major turning point in Schiller's life came in 1787, after he had spent two relatively carefree years in Körner's household in Dresden. Disappointed by an unrewarding relationship with Henriette von Arnim, Schiller left Dresden for Weimar. There, he renewed an acquaintance with Charlotte von Kalb, the unhappy wife of an army major. Her friendship had created emotional problems for him in Mannheim, but she now introduced him into philosophical circles in Jena that influenced his life for years. In Weimar, he also made contact with Wieland and Herder, whose favor gave him access to the court.

In 1788, Schiller met Johann Wolfgang von Goethe for the first time. Although no close relationship developed at the time, Goethe soon recommended him for a professorship in history at the University of Jena. The stable situation provided by an annual income allowed Schiller to marry Charlotte von Lengefeld in 1790. His professional involvement in the years that followed reduced his poetic activity but moved him to concern himself more extensively with the philosophy of Immanuel Kant. His philosophical studies ultimately had a major impact on his creative work. In Jena, during the winter of 1790-1791, Schiller experienced the first attacks of the tuberculosis that eventually caused his death.

The most artistically productive period of Schiller's life began in the summer of 1794 when Goethe agreed to collaborate with him in the editing of a new journal. The intimate friendship that arose between the two authors provided them with mutual stimulus and gave rise to timeless masterworks of poetry and drama. Friendly competition between them in 1797 and 1798 yielded some of the most famous ballads in German literature. Also in 1797, the last of Schiller's historical writings was completed, winning for him membership in the Swedish Academy of Sciences. During the final years of his life, Schiller was feverishly active, writing the best of his mature plays, adapting works by William Shakespeare, Louis Picard, Gotthold Ephraim Lessing, and Goethe, traveling, and gathering new dramatic materials in defiance of the malady that slowly destroyed him. Newly completed lines for "Demetrius," an unfinished play that might have become his greatest masterpiece, were found lying on his desk on the day he died.

Analysis

In his essay "On Naïve and Sentimental Poetry," written soon after he began collaborating with Goethe, Friedrich Schiller outlined and clarified the characteristics of two kinds of poetic art, attempting to defend his own creative approach in the careful justification of "sentimental" literature. In contrast to the naïve poet, whose work is an expression of nature, Schiller's modern lyricist is a reflective creator who seeks to regain in his poetry a natural state that has been lost. The naïve poet moves the reader through an artistic presentation of sensual reality, while the sentimental poet achieves his effect in the successful development of ideas. Throughout Schiller's literary career, the conceptual tension between "naïve" and "sentimental," couched variously in the polarities of nature and culture, real and ideal, ancient and modern, and substance and form, remained the key to his poetic endeavor. Each new poem represented a concerted effort to create through art a harmonious resolution of the perpetual conflict between these fundamental aspects of humanity's existence.

ANTHOLOGIE AUF DAS JAHR 1782

The poetry of Schiller's youth is especially interesting for its clear illumination of the broad spectrum of eighteenth century literary forces that molded his attitudes. In the *Anthologie auf das Jahr 1782*, which was published to counteract what Schiller saw as the smarmy bent of other Swabian collections of the time, there are poems that reflect such diverse influences as the pathos of Friedrich Klopstock's odes, the Anacreontic tendencies of the early Enlightenment, Gottfried August Bürger's massive realism, Albrecht von Haller's philosophical lyrics, the political tendentiousness of Christian Friedrich Daniel Schubart, Christoph Wieland's Rococo style, and the purposeful tastelessness of Storm and Stress. Although personal encounters provided immediate stimuli for some of the works, the calculated refinement of perceptions through the process of reflection sets the philosophical tone of Schiller's verse from the outset.

The naïve/sentimental dichotomy is visible in two characteristic forms in Schiller's early poetry. "Der Eroberer" ("The Conqueror") exemplifies Schiller's juxtaposition of political and divine order in the concept of the "noble criminal," an almost mythical figure who goes beyond the limits of conventional morality. The conquering tyrant emerges as the adversary of God and the destroyer of moral order. In the Laura odes, however, which are central to the lyrics of Schiller's youth, the focus of poetic tension is the tortuous conflict between love's physical and spiritual dimensions. By 1780, in direct response to the writings of Adam Ferguson and under the mediated influence of Francis Hutcheson and the philosopher Anthony Ashley-Cooper, the third earl of Shaftesbury, Schiller had developed a personal metaphysics in which love is the binding force that holds the world together. The Laura odes and poems such as "Der Triumph der Liebe" ("The Triumph of Love") constitute the major literary treatments of those ideas.

A TRANSITIONAL PERIOD

The years immediately following the publication of the *Anthologie auf das Jahr 1782* were a transitional period in Schiller's growth as a lyric poet. In the lines of "Der Kampf" ("The Struggle") and "Resignation," the poet broadened the basic themes of his earlier works. While exploring in depth the conflict between humanity's right to joy and the reality of a tear-filled existence, he questioned the validity of God's justice in forcing humans to choose between earthly pleasure and spiritual peace. Some of the lyrics written between 1782 and 1788 examine the possibility of achieving a harmony between the polar forces that act on humans; other poems conclude with terrible finality that the only alternatives, pleasure in this world or hope of peace in the world to come, are mutually exclusive. Only the famous "Ode to Joy," which praises the harmony between God and a glorified world in a profound affirmation of earthly existence, forms a distinct anomaly in the otherwise troubled reflection that typifies the verse produced during this period of Schiller's life.

The major poetic works of Schiller's mature years, beginning with the first version of "Die Götter Griechenlands" ("The Gods of Greece"), written in 1788, and ending with "Das Siegesfest" ("The Victory Celebration"), composed in 1803, offer a more calmly ordered, evenly balanced, and formally perfected presentation of the fundamental Schillerian dichotomies than can be found in the emotionally charged poems of the early 1780's. With increasing emphasis on natural order as an answer to the problems of civilized society, Schiller attempts to resolve the tension between the ideal and the real. Instead of seeking to establish an internal harmony between the spiritual and physical elements of humanity, he tries in the later poems to move his reader to accept an external creation of the desired metaphysical unity in art. The appropriate models for the new synthesis were to be found in the artistic and literary legacy of the ancients. Schiller's most powerful philosophical poems present the search for a golden age of accord between rational humans and nature and the need to regain that state through reflection.

From epigram to ballad to thought poem

It is important to understand that these writings are not simply versified philosophy. In Schiller's eyes, the poet differs from the philosopher in not being required to prove his assertions. Instead, the poet employs a variety of devices to convey his message on several levels of perception, at once teaching and moving the reader through his own personal enthusiasm. To achieve his purpose, Schiller masterfully cultivated a variety of poetic forms, ranging from the epigram to the ballad to the highly stylized "thought poem."

As a consciously developed form, the epigram is a special phenomenon of the collaboration between Schiller and Goethe. It is a particularly powerful genre for Schiller. His epigrams are basically of two kinds: satirical and purely philosophical. The sharply barbed satirical poems focus on poets, thinkers, and critics of his time, especially those who attacked Schiller and Goethe, as well as the literary movements and specific currents of thought that they represented. Epigrams in the other group, primarily the "Votivtafeln" ("Votive Inscriptions"), are more general in focus and didactic in purpose.

Schiller's ballads, which are also important documents of his friendship with Goethe, represent more clearly than the epigrams the general tendency of classical German poetry to seek and establish the harmony between the ideal and the real. In that regard, they are especially clear illustrations of Schiller's aesthetics. Many of them follow a pattern established in 1795 in "Das verschleierte Bild zu Sais" ("The Veiled Image at Sais") and are best described as lyrically narrated parables that resolve the poet's metaphysical conflicts by appealing to the natural nobility of the human soul. A second type of ballad, exemplified by "Die Kraniche des Ibykus" ("The Cranes of Ibycus"), addresses itself to art's ethical and moral purposes, employing the elements of legend to achieve its goals. The ballads are the most readable of Schiller's lyric works, simply because they benefit from his mastery of drama.

Among the poems of Schiller's final creative period are some of the most extraordinarily beautiful "thought poems" in German. While stressing the inherent interdependency of ethics and aesthetics, Schiller dealt with basic existential questions such as suffering, death, transience, the quest for truth, and the perception of the absolute. In poems such as the lovely "Nänie" ("Nenia"), written in 1796, he arrived at a final answer to questions posed in his early lyrics, replacing hopelessness and resignation with the achievement in art of a timeless unity of humanity's real and ideal dimensions.

THE LAURA ODES

In 1781, Schiller published "Die Entzückung an Laura" ("Rapture, to Laura") in Gotthold Stäudlin's *Schwäbischer Musenalmanach auf das Jahr 1782* (Swabian almanac of the muses for the year 1782). It was the first of six poems that have since become known as the Laura odes. The other five—"Phantasie an Laura" ("Fantasy, to Laura"), "Laura am Klavier" ("Laura at the Piano"), "Vorwurf an Laura" ("Reproach, to Laura"), "Das Geheimnis der Reminiscenz" ("The Mystery of Reminiscence"), and "Melancholie an Laura" ("Melancholy, to Laura")—appeared for the first time in Schiller's *Anthologie auf das Jahr 1782*. As a group, these poems present Schiller's metaphysics of love. They are a product of creative reflection rather than intimate experience. When Schiller left the military academy, he had in fact had few encounters with women, and all his early works reveal a lack of realistic perception of the opposite sex.

"Rapture, to Laura" sets the tone for the odes in its portrayal of love as a force that links the real world with the cosmic realm of absolutes. Schiller employs well-developed images of sight and sound as the outward manifestations of love, with visual contacts playing an especially important role in the communication of feeling. The gaze and what the poet can see in the eyes of his imagined Laura transform him, granting him the ability to move from his own reality into the ideal domain symbolized by the young woman. The last stanza of the poem defines her glances and the love that they represent as a clearly comprehended creative influence that has the power to vivify even inanimate stone.

The external tension between the physical and the spiritual receives special emphasis in the lyric structure of "Fantasy, to Laura," in which bodily and mental activities are juxtaposed in alternate stanzas and lines. As in all the Laura odes, the two realms are bonded together through the force of love, without which the world would disintegrate into mechanical chaos. This poem, however, emphasizes the unresolved parallelism between sexual love, presented in the literary formulations of Storm and Stress, and the philosophical love of Enlightenment thought, causing the concept of love as such to remain somewhat ambiguous.

In "Laura at the Piano," Schiller developed a more precise representation of love as a metaphysical phenomenon. Consistent with his ultimate goal of natural harmony, love appears not so much as a personal experience with the feminine, but as a manifestation of the creative power of the masculine through which man masters all the cosmos. The dual character of love thus comes to symbolize the opposed forces of chaos and creation that mold the universe. A key to Schiller's message in "Laura at the Piano" lies once more in Laura's ability, through her very presence, to move her lover into a unified transcendent realm. The scope of this act is divine, and her being emerges as a subtle "proof" for the existence of God.

The notion of conflicting polarities is so basic to the Laura poems that even love has its own antagonist: death. Schiller's manner of coming to grips with the latter accords the odes a distinct kinship with his early elegies, including "Elegie auf den Tod eines Jünglings" ("Elegy to the Death of a Young Man") and "Trauer- Ode" ("Ode of Mourning"). In "Melancholy, to Laura ," the death motif receives its most powerful illumination in the baroque imagery of the beloved's decay. Laura is presented here as a symbol for the entirety of earthly existence, which rests on "mouldering bones." Even her beauty is not immune to the ravages of death. In the struggle between the optimism of love and the finality of death, death triumphs, devaluating mortality as it ends all human striving for happiness. This conclusion anticipates the pessimistic mood of the famous poem "Resignation." Although not specifically dedicated to Laura, "Resignation" may be regarded as the thematic culmination of the ideas presented in the odes, a culmination that is encapsulated in a single stanza of the lengthy poem. There, in harshly vivid imagery, the poet tears his Laura bleeding from his heart and gives her to the relentless judge, eternity, in payment for the hope of peace beyond the grave.

Perhaps the most interesting symbol of death in "Resignation" appears in the poem's second stanza in the silent god who extinguishes the poet's torch. He is a precursor of more carefully refined images that Schiller based on models from Greek and Roman antiquity and employed in the powerful philosophical lyrics of his classical period. This personification of death signals a transition that occurred in the poet's creative orientation during the mid-1780's. By the time the first version of "The Gods of Greece" was printed in Wieland's periodical *Der teutsche Merkur*, Schiller had abandoned his metaphysics of love in favor of a poetic search for humankind's lost golden age. The characteristics of this new approach are a juxtapostion of the ancient and modern worlds, renewal of classical aesthetic and ethical values, and an appeal for the creation of a unity of sensual and spiritual experience in art.

"THE GODS OF GREECE"

The two variants of "The Gods of Greece," published in 1788 and 1793, respectively, have in common their focus on the concept of beauty. In the first version, Schiller presented a justification of sensual beauty, couching his arguments in a defense of ancient polytheism against modern monotheism and rationalism. The Christian God in his roles of avenger, judge, and rational defender of truth is too strict for the natural world. For that reason, Schiller advocated return to an order of existence based on feeling.

From the notion that the Greek gods symbolize divine perfection in things earthly, a kind of theophany informs the world created by the poem, although the second rendering places heavier emphasis on the timelessness of beauty.

The carefully nurtured inner tension of "The Gods of Greece" derives from its dual nature. It is at once a lament for the loss of humankind's earlier existence in nature and a song of praise for the potential immanence of the ideal within the real. In the past for which the poet longs, a closer harmony existed between the physical and spiritual realms, because the gods were more human and humans more divine. When the old gods were driven away by reason, however, they took with them everything of beauty and majesty, leaving the world colorless, empty, and devoid of spirit. The final lines of the respective versions offer two different resolutions of the problem. In the first, the poet issues a simple plea for the return of the mild goddess, beauty. The final form of the poem places the responsibility for beauty's timeless preservation squarely in the lap of the creative artist. Next to Goethe's drama *Iphigenie auf Tauris* (pr. 1779; *Iphigenia in Tauris*, 1793), "The Gods of Greece" in its two versions is the most important document of Germanized Greek mythology in classical German literature.

BALLADS

Most of Schiller's poems reflect the instructional orientation of his literary work as a whole. Early in his career, Schiller forcefully acknowledged the author's responsibility to move his reader toward personal, moral, and ethical improvement. The ballads that he wrote after 1795 are among the most successful didactic lyrics in all German literature. They are masterful combinations of simplicity and clarity with vivid, engaging sensual imagery. The parabolic ballads, among them "Der Taucher" ("The Diver"), "Der Handschuh" ("The Glove"), "Der Kampf mit dem Drachen" ("The Battle with the Dragon"), and "Die Bürgschaft" ("The Pledge"), reveal the inherent nobility of the human soul when tested in circumstances that threaten life itself. Each presents a variation on the problem of the individual's response to extraordinary challenge or temptation, laying bare the inner motivations for action and glorifying the deed that is based on ideal and principle rather than on material gain. In "The Diver," the implications and consequences of free will are central to the story of a young man who retrieves from the sea a golden chalice, its own reward for the daredevil act, then perishes in a second venture, when the prize is the king's lovely daughter. "The Battle with the Dragon" explores the dilemma of choice between noble intent and obedience. A heroic knight defies the command of his order's leader and slays a terrible monster that has ravaged the countryside. He then meekly accepts expulsion from the order as the penalty for disobedience, thereby redeeming himself. Friendship as a moral force is the primary focus of "The Pledge," Schiller's rendering of the famous Greek legend of Damon and Pythias.

Typically, the verse parables have a two-part structure that pairs an obviously rash, foolish, and dangerous act with a reasoned deed of noble sacrifice through which the central figure ascends to a higher moral plane. In the popular ballad "The Glove," the Knight Delorges is asked by Kunigunde to retrieve her glove from the arena, where she has purposely dropped it among bloodthirsty beasts of prey. Delorges demonstrates his stature as a man, not when he faces the tiger to obtain the glove, but when he subsequently rejects Kunigunde's favors. It is not physical courage but the spiritual act of overcoming self that provides the measure of personal worth in this and similar ballads.

"The Cranes of Ibycus"

Like the parable poems, "The Cranes of Ibycus" is a dramatic, didactic short story in verse form. Its orientation, however, differs markedly from that of the works that stress the importance of heroic self-mastery. In its examination and defense of art as an active moral force in society, "The Cranes of Ibycus" forms a bridge between the ballads and Schiller's more abstract philosophical lyrics, while providing a concise vindication of his own approach to the drama. The ballad describes the murder of Ibycus by two men. A flock of cranes flying overhead witnesses the crime and later reappears over an outdoor theater where the criminals sit watching a play. Caught up in the mood of the drama, the criminals forget themselves and respond to the sight of the cranes, thereby revealing themselves to the crowd. More than a simple examination of problems of guilt and atonement, the lyric work juxtaposes audience reaction to stage events with the behavior of the villain-spectators to shatter the border between theater and reality. The scene is transformed into a tribunal that has the power to bring criminals to justice, thereby influencing events in the external world.

"The Song of the Bell"

Schiller's most famous ballad, "The Song of the Bell," is also the most ambitious of his poetic works. In some 425 lines of verse, the poet projects the broad spectrum of humankind's mortal existence against the background of the magnificent bell's creation. Alternating stanzas of varying length parallel the process of casting the bell with characteristic events of life. Birth and death, joy and tragedy, accomplishment and destruction—all find their symbolic counterparts in the steps taken by the artisans to produce a flawless artifact. The imagery is vividly real, earthy, and natural, presenting the everyday world in a practical frame with which the reader readily identifies. At the same time, the stylized presentation successfully underscores the possibility of harmony between humans' physical environment and the ideal domain of the mind.

In many respects, "The Song of the Bell" represents the culmination of Schiller's poetic art. The effective integration of the poem's two threads of description and discussion is a clear realization of the creative unity that he sought to achieve in all his literary works. In his classical ballads, Schiller at last achieved the resolution of tensions caused by the opposing forces that play on humans as they search for personal meaning. Like "The Cranes of Ibycus," "The Song of the Bell" assigns to art an ultimate responsibility for humans' attainment of peace through productive interactions between their absolute and their temporal essence. The finished bell's very name, Concordia, symbolizes the final accord of material and spiritual values that was for Schiller the goal of both literature and life.

OTHER MAJOR WORKS

LONG FICTION: *Der Verbrecher aus verlorener Ehre*, 1786 (also pb. as *Der Verbrecher aus Infamie*; *The Criminal, in Consequence of Lost Reputation*, 1841); *Der Geisterseher*, 1789 (*The Ghost-Seer: Or, The Apparitionist*, 1795).

PLAYS: *Die Räuber*, pb. 1781 (*The Robbers*, 1792); *Die Verschwörung des Fiesko zu Genua*, pr., pb. 1783 (*Fiesco: Or, The Genoese Conspiracy*, 1796); *Kabale und Liebe*, pr., pb. 1784 (*Cabal and Love*, 1795); *Don Carlos, Infant von Spanien*, pr., pb. 1787 (*Don Carlos, Infante of Spain*, 1798); *Wallensteins Lager*, pr. 1798 (*The Camp of Wallenstein*, 1846); *Die Piccolomini*, pr. 1799 (*The Piccolominis*, 1800); *Wallenstein*, pr. 1799 (trilogy includes *The Camp of Wallenstein*, *The Piccolominis*, and *The Death of Wallenstein*); *Wallensteins Tod*, pr. 1799 (*The Death of Wallenstein*, 1800); *Maria Stuart*, pr. 1800 (*Mary Stuart*, 1801); *Die Jungfrau von Orleans*, pr. 1801 (*The Maid of Orleans*, 1835); *Die Braut von Messina: Oder, Die feindlichen Brüder*, pr., pb. 1803 (*The Bride of Messina*, 1837); *Wilhelm Tell*, pr., pb. 1804 (*William Tell*, 1841); *Historical Dramas*, 1847; *Early Dramas and Romances*, 1849; *Dramatic Works*, 1851.

NONFICTION: *Die Schaubühne als eine moralische Anstalt betrachtet*, 1784 (*The Theater as a Moral Institution*, 1845); *Historischer Kalender für Damen*, 1790, 1791; *Geschichte des dreissigjährigen Krieges*, 1791-1793 (3 volumes; *History of the Thirty Years War*, 1799); *Über den Grund des Vergnügens an tragischen Gegenständen*, 1792 (*On the Pleasure in Tragic Subjects*, 1845); *Über Anmut und Würde*, 1793 (*On Grace and Dignity*, 1845); *Über das Pathetische*, 1793 (*On the Pathetic*, 1845); *Briefe über die ästhetische Erziehung des Menschen*, 1795 (*On the Aesthetic Education of Man*, 1845); *Über naïve und sentimentalische Dichtung*, 1795-1796 (*On Naïve and Sentimental Poetry*, 1845); *Über das Erhabene*, 1801 (*On the Sublime*, 1845); *Briefwechsel Zwischen Schiller und Goethe*, 1829 (*The Correspondence Between Schiller and Goethe*, 1845); *Aesthetical and Philosophical Essays*, 1845; *Schillers Briefwechsel mit Körner von 1784 bis zum Tode Schillers*, 1847 (*Schiller's Correspondence with Körner*, 1849).

MISCELLANEOUS: *Sämmtliche Werke*, 1812-1815 (12 volumes; *Complete Works in English*, 1870).

BIBLIOGRAPHY

Carlyle, Thomas. *The Life of Friedrich Schiller*. 1825. Reprint. Columbia, S.C.: Camden House, 1992. A biography of Schiller by a contemporary historian and essayist. An excellent resource on Schiller's life and work. Includes bibliographical references and index. With new introduction by Jeffrey L. Sammons.

Goethe, Johann Wolfgang von. *Correspondence Between Goethe and Schiller (1794-1805)*. Translated by Liselotte Dieckmann. New York: Peter Lang, 1994. A collection of letters that offers insight into the lives and works of Schiller and Goethe. Includes bibliographical references and index.

Kerry, Paul E., ed. *Friedrich Schiller: Playwright, Poet, Philosopher, Historian*. New York: Peter Lang, 2007. This collection contains essays examining Schiller's poetry and its effect on later German poets.

Kostka, Edmund. *Schiller in Italy: Schiller's Reception in Italy—Nineteenth and Twentieth Centuries*. New York: Peter Lang, 1997. Kostka's comprehensive study expands and deepens the understanding of the German-Italian relationship during the past two centuries. The impact of Schiller's work on Italian poets, critics, musicians, and conspirators is evaluated against the history of the military upheaval in Europe.

Martinson, Steven D. *A Companion to the Works of Friedrich Schiller*. Rochester, N.Y.: Camden House, 2005. This collection of essays about Schiller includes in-depth discussions about his literary works as well as the impact he had on twentieth century Germany.

_____. *Harmonious Tensions: The Writings of Friedrich Schiller*. Newark: University of Delaware Press, 1996. A critical interpretation of selected writing by Schiller. Includes bibliographical references and index.

Pilling, Claudia. *Schiller (Life and Times)*. London: Haus Books, 2005. A biography of Schiller that uses his correspondence, along with modern records, to place him in late eighteenth century Germany, confronting a changing middle class. Includes several color and black-and-white illustrations throughout.

Reed, T. J. *Schiller*. New York: Oxford University Press, 1991. A biography of the German writer that sheds light on his writing of dramas. Bibliography and index.

Sharpe, Lesley. *Friedrich Schiller: Drama, Thought, and Politics*. New York: Cambridge University Press, 1991. Part of the Cambridge Studies in German series, this scholarly study looks at Schiller's views and how they infused his drama and other works. Bibliography and index.

Lowell A. Bangerter

WALTHER VON DER VOGELWEIDE

Born: Probably in lower Austria; c. 1170
Died: Near Würzburg, Bavaria, Holy Roman Empire (now in Germany); c. 1230

PRINCIPAL POETRY
Songs and Sayings of Walther von der Vogelweide, 1917
Poems, 1952
Die Gedichte, 1959 (Lachmann-Kraus edition)
Walther von der Vogelweide: The Single-Stanza Lyrics, 2002 (bilingual text; translated and edited by Frederick Goldin)

OTHER LITERARY FORMS

Walther von der Vogelweide (VOL-tur fawn dur FOH-guhl-vi-duh) was exclusively a lyric poet.

ACHIEVEMENTS

Walther von der Vogelweide is recognized as the single most important Middle High German lyric poet. According to Peter Wapnewski, he made two pioneering contributions to literary history. First, he moved German courtly love poetry from the sterile artificiality of conventional literature to a fresh personal expression, even inventing a corresponding lyric genre, the *Mädchenlieder* (songs to a common-class girl, sometimes also misleadingly called songs of "lower love"). Second, he gave a new nobility to didactic and political poetry. Kuno Francke goes so far as to see in Walther's love songs "the struggle for the emancipation of the individual" that eventually led to the overthrow of "the whole system of medieval hierarchy" and "an anticipation of this great emancipation movement, a protest of the individual against the dictates of society." Scholar Peter Rühmkorf deromanticizes the ultrapatriotic German image of Walther and sees him primarily in individualistic terms as a "self" struggling for personal identity and recognition in a time of social crisis.

This much is certain: Whether addressing an emperor, a pope, or a high nobleman or lady, Walther speaks with courage, authority, and clarity; he is not intimidated by any class distinctions. In his love poetry, he is not satisfied with a one-sided platonic relationship or an adulation of mere external beauty or high social status; for him, love is a shared affection, a reciprocal meeting of hearts and minds, an inner attitude, an important ennobling force in the lives of men and women. The scope of Walther's themes and the tone and manner of their treatment make it unmistakably clear that his office as a lyric poet went beyond courtly entertainment and included functions of political propaganda and ethical critique, functions that are performed today by the communications media. However, Walther, like other medieval lyric poets, composed and sang his own songs, and he was more highly praised by his contemporaries for his singing than for his lyrics.

Biography

Walther von der Vogelweide was born about 1170, possibly of the lower nobility. Because the term *Vogelweide* was a common word meaning bird sanctuary, numerous places have claimed to be the poet's birthplace, most conspicuously Vogelweidhof, near Bozen, South Tyrol, where an impressive monument in his honor has been erected; since this region did not belong to Austria at the time and the Austrian dialect was not spoken there, however, scholars speculate that Walther probably was born in lower Austria. Wherever his birthplace, the poet "learned to sing and recite in Austria," appearing at the court of Duke Frederick in Vienna about 1190 and probably learning his craft from Reinmar von Hagenau.

In 1198, Walther's patron died; Walther was forced to leave Vienna to begin the uncertain life of a wandering minstrel. The only extant historical document concerning him is a receipt showing that Wolfger, bishop of Passau, had given "to the singer Walther de Vogelweide five solidi for a fur coat on Saint Martin's Day in the year 1203." Among his many other patrons was Count Hermann of Thuringia, at whose court he met Wolfram von Eschenbach, author of *Parzival* (c. 1200-1210; English translation, 1894), and other lyric poets. Walther wrote songs for three emperors; after Philip of Swabia was murdered and his successor Otto IV allegedly did not pay the poet enough, Walther shifted his allegiance to Friedrick II, who eventually rewarded him with a small property near Würzburg in about 1220. Presumably, Walther did not participate in the Crusade of 1228 and died about 1230 near Würzburg, where his grave could still be seen in the cathedral garden half a century later. Another minstrel, Hugo von Trimberg, grieved over Walther's death with the words, "Ah Sir Walther von der Vogelweide, I would feel sorry for whomever forgot you."

Analysis

In only one generation, from 1180 to 1210, the great flowering of Middle High German courtly culture under the Hohenstaufen Dynasty produced—in addition to four great epic writers, Hartmann von Aue, Gottfried von Strassburg, Wolfram von Eschenbach, and the anonymous author of the *Nibelungenlied* (c. 1200; English translation, 1848)—numerous lyric poets, the most renowned of them being Walther von der Vogelweide. Even princes and emperors ranked among the courtly love poets. The roots of this German medieval poetry are multiple: Provençal and northern French courtly love poetry, indigenous songs and Goliardic verse such as that collected in *Carmina burana* (1847), and a variety of Latin secular and religious genres (eulogies, sequences), some dating back to antiquity. Medieval German poetry features a great variety of meters and melodies, since the minstrel was expected to compose a new meter and melody for each song.

Courtly love poetry (*Minnesäng*) was symptomatic of a new secular culture that rejected the "contempt of the world" preached for centuries by the monastic orders and that sought instead to harmonize eternal salvation with earthly happiness. The role of women in the courts and castles was to elevate and dignify life and to convey a certain *hoher muot* (joy of life), which was the crowning virtue in the knightly code. Although the love songs sometimes have a trace of the occasional in them—they often are addressed to a particular woman and reflect specific circumstances—such love poetry was not a stylized proposal for a literal love relationship, but an artistic achievement, a fictional, public musical presentation on the theme of love for the amusement and edification of the entire court (estimated as usually comprising between thirty and seventy persons). Since the idolized woman was supposed to be of high rank, married and virtuous, no erotic reciprocation was expected but, at most, a greeting or token of appreciation. Praise of the woman was not a means to an end but an ennobling activity in itself, for the lady represented the humane ideal of beauty and dignity for which this secular knightly society was striving. Her being not only was physically beautiful and charming but also encompassed a catalog of virtues such as honor, self-discipline, constancy, moderation, and loyalty—traits of a proud, aristocratic society.

Mädchenlieder

Walther regarded highly his function as a courtly love poet who could express for the men and women of his society the emotions of body and soul. Under Walther's predecessor and teacher, Reinmar, *Minnelyrik* (love poetry) had degenerated into a genre that was obsessed with the monotonous theme of the unrequited lover. Walther broke with this tradition—and from Reinmar—and introduced many new dimensions into the thematics of courtly love poetry. His *Mädchenlieder* scandalized society by directing love and the title *Frouwe* (noble lady) to a common-class girl. He also introduced into courtly poetry a mature, reciprocally fulfilled marital love, contrary to the tradition of unrequitedness. Late in life, he rejected the ribaldry and crudity that was brought into courtly love poetry under the influence of peasant dances by a new generation of minstrels, including Neidhart von Reuenthal. Finally, he turned away from "Lady World" and his "many errors" as a *Minnesänger* and addressed God himself as "you sweet true Love." Underlying this broad span of the love concept in Walther's poems is the medieval idea of "gradualism," which sees all reality as an ascending ladder of being, each rung different in degree but analogous to the ones above and below—from the various levels of earthly reality, through a person, who is both body and soul, to the heights of spirit in God.

Paul Stapf divides the love lyrics chronologically into six periods: early love songs, songs from 1198 to 1203, high courtly love, *Mädchenlieder*, new high courtly love, and late songs.

Walther's early love songs, written before leaving the Viennese court in 1198, though still quite within the conventions of the genre, already display the sharp tension created by the ambiguity of traditional love poetry. On one hand, it was supposed to represent an approved public relationship involving "conversation" with and "instruction" as well as "praise" of the woman by the poet, who was rewarded with a "greeting" or token of esteem, all strictly on a platonic level; on the other, by the very nature of love between man and woman, it sometimes involved an implicit erotic attraction that threatened to erupt into socially unacceptable amorous fulfillment. In these early poems, the poet's love is rejected; the woman is unapproachable and on the defensive; she has maintained her dignity as a woman and will hold him accountable for any violation of proper decorum. In some poems, she would like to grant his desire for a love affair, but social pressure prevents it; she has a duty to maintain her honor. With a touch of resignation, she submits to the dictates of society: "Mir tuot einer slahte wille" ("Can She Alone Be Happy When All Others Are Sad?"). Sometimes the concept of honor is deepened to a personal ethical code. She wants "to have a woman's proper qualities . . . since a beautiful body is worthless without understanding," that is, without moral responsibility.

Perhaps the very ambiguity and wide range of meaning of courtly love is what invites some poems to be highly rational and analytical: "Whoever says that love is a sin, should first reflect well, for love contains many a distinction which one can rightly enjoy, and its consequence is constancy and great happiness. . . . I am not speaking of false love, which would better be called non-love: I will always oppose it." However, the same poem also speaks from living experience: "No one knows what true joy is who did not receive it from a woman." Walther leaves no doubt as to the edifying and positive nature of love: "Love is the source of all good qualities; without love no heart can be truly happy."

Minstrel years

Walther's departure from the court at Vienna marks a sharp break in his life and poetry and begins a second stage of his creative activity, his early years as a wandering minstrel, from 1198 to 1203. His songs now show the direct influence of the vagabond poets of the *Carmina burana*. One single theme runs through them all: how summer follows winter and love chases away sadness. Their execution is smoother and the nature imagery is brighter, used economically like a kind of symbolic shorthand: In winter, the frost hurts the little birds so much that they no longer sing; in summer, the girls will be playing ball in the street again (a rare glimpse of medieval everyday life). The poet celebrates the great power of May over humans and nature. Perhaps May is a magician, he suggests; wherever his delight goes, no one is old. The winter of 1198 must have been particularly severe; the poet believed he would "never again pick red flowers in the green meadows." His death, he muses, would have been "a loss to all good men who long for joy and who like to sing and dance."

HIGH COURTLY LOVE POEMS

The poet's third period, from 1203 to 1205, was characterized by poems of "high courtly love" which were traditional, rational, and sophisticated. Most of the poems of this period are united by a single theme: constancy and reciprocity. These are two sides of the same coin: The lady demands fidelity on the poet's part and rebukes him for praising other women; the poet replies that he cannot continue praising only her if she refuses to reciprocate his love.

A highly optimistic poem called "Ir Sult sprechen" ("Speak a Welcome") illustrates the poet's praise of other women: He has seen many countries, and German ways please him the best. German men are handsome, and German women are like angels; whoever scolds any of them is mistaken (probably an allusion to the Provençal poet Peire Vidal's castigations of German manners). Whoever seeks virtue and pure love should come to Germany. "From the Elbe to the Rhein and back again as far as Hungary live the best people I have ever known in the world. If I can judge good upbringing and beauty, by God, the women are nobler here than anywhere else." Now a harsh note is struck: His lady reproaches him for praising other women and thus being guilty of inconstancy. As if enraged at the lady's rebuke, he retaliates in the song "Staet ist ein Angest und ein Nôt" ("Constancy Is Fear and Torment"), harping ironically on constancy, naming it twelve times in two short stanzas, and finally exclaiming "Lady Constancy, set me free!"

Poem after poem reflects a period of strife, for example, "Saget mir ieman, waz ist Minne?" ("What Is Loving?"), "Daz ich dich sô selten grüeze" ("That I So Seldom Praise You Is No Misdeed of Mine"), and "Mîn Frowe ist ein ungenaedic Wîp" ("My Lady Is a Cruel Woman"). Finally, in "What Is Loving?," the poet hammers out the principle that will lead to the end of his relationship with this "lady" and to his abandonment of one-sided courtly love: "Love is the joy of two hearts. If they share equally, then love is there; if this is not so, then one heart cannot receive it." The poet, however, does not conceal a sour, unchivalric remark: "If I have grown old in her service, she's not gotten any younger either." Finally, he exhorts his young rival: "Avenge me and whip her old skin with fresh switches."

LOWER LOVE SONGS

The fourth group of songs (written after 1203 and therefore somewhat overlapping the previous group) overcomes this discord and enters a new phase of fulfillment with a woman of equal or lower rank. In "Herzeliebez Frowelîn" ("Little Maid So Dear"), whatever joy the poet experienced in this world was caused "by her beauty, her goodness, and her red mouth that laughs so lovingly." He responds to those who criticize him for directing his love songs to a person of lower rank, claiming that "they don't have any idea what love is, they have never experienced true love, since they love only for wealth or external beauty. What kind of love is that?" He reiterates his reason for having changed from "high courtly love" to this more satisfying relationship: "A Lover's affection is nothing if it goes unrequited. One-sided love is worthless; it must be shared, permeating two hearts and none besides."

The most famous of Walther's songs of "lower love" is "Unter der Linden" ("Under the Linden-Tree "), in which a naïve, common-class girl rejoices in her love experience under the linden tree, the crushed flowers still showing the place where the couple had lain. What he did with her no one will ever know except he and she and the little bird that sang the refrain "Tandaradei!" Equally masterful is the poem "Die welt was gelf, rôt unde blâ" ("The World in Red and Blue Was Gay"), also called the "vowel poem" since, in German, each stanza rhymes with one of the vowels *a, e, i, o,* and *u*; it is a highly graphic poem calling for the end of winter. One wryly humorous poem, "Wer kan nû ze danke singen?" ("Who Can Please Everyone with His Song?"), lauds the poet's broad range of experience, which makes it possible for him to sing a wide variety of songs, but observes that people still are dissatisfied.

New high love

In his fifth period, that of "new high love" (from 1205 to about 1220), Walther's songs show more depth, maturity, and formal perfection. The "lady" seems to be of very high social rank, and the relationship is a conventional one. There is sadness at court, the times are unsuited for song, true love has died, and the whole world is beset with troubles. Song is tempted to wait for better times, as in "Die zwîvelaere Sprechent" ("The Doubters"). The exuberance of youth is over, and the poet articulates a positive attitude even toward the unequal relationship represented by conventional courtly love, as long as there is some reciprocation: "He is certainly also fortunate who observes her virtues precisely so that it moves his heart. An understanding woman should respond with affection." This kind of love can motivate poetry: "Just a loving look from a woman gives joy to the heart. . . . But what is like the happiness where a beloved heart is faithful, beautiful, chaste, and of good morals? The lucky man who has won this does nothing wrong to praise it before strangers." The importance of moderation is explained in "Ich hoere iu sô vil tugende jehen" ("I Hear You Speak of So Many Virtues") and "Allerwerde keit ein Füegerinne" ("Coordinator of All Values, Lady Moderation"). One of Walther's very best poems and the crown jewel of this period is "Sô die Bluomen ûz dem Grase dringent" ("When the Flowers Spring Out of the Grass"), which compares a beautiful May day with a beautiful noblewoman in all her finery. If the poet had to choose between the two, the outcome would be: "Sir May, you would have to become March before I gave up my lady."

Late songs

Three poems can adequately represent the late songs (from 1220 to 1230). "Ir reinen Wîp" ("Ye Women Pure") is a sort of literary testament: "For forty years or more I have sung of love and of how one should live" (note the educational function of the poet). In "Frô Welt" ("Lady World"), he renounces the world because, while her beauty is lovely to look at from the front, from behind she is so horridly shameful that he wishes to spurn her forever. In "Ein Meister las" ("A Wise Man"), he meditates on the transitory quality of life and says, "It is high time for penance, since I, a sick man, now fear grim death." The poem ends in a vein of religious repentance, an emphasis found in several poems, including the long *Leich*.

SPRUCH GENRE

About half of Walther's poems belong to the broad genre of *Spruch* (political or didactic) poetry. Walther's type of *Spruch* was formerly believed to have been a single-stanza spoken poem, but the melodies of some of them have been recovered, and it is now known that they were not recited but sung. Friedrich Maurer's "song-theory" brought together in a single poem stanzas of the same "tone" or melody that had been variously scattered in the manuscripts. In Maurer's view, each "tone" of a political song was invented in its own separate period, and thus stanzas belonging to one "tone" could be dated far apart in Walther's time, although some of them were written over a period of a few years. "Each tone," Maurer asserts, "has its briefly extended time of origin, but especially its own theme and subject matter." Poems with different melodies, even though thematically similar, are not contemporaneous. The advantages of Maurer's theory are that it facilitates study of the gradual evolution of Walther's stanzaic art; it enriches interpretation by retrieving the overarching meaning connecting the stanzas of one "tone"; and it elucidates stanza-internal meaning by contrast and comparison. Maurer's theory, however, has not been unanimously accepted by scholars. Stapf, editor of a fine annotated edition and modern German translation of Walther's poems, rejects Maurer's theory in favor of more accurate dating of the individual stanzas. Annette Georgi, in her study of the Latin and German *Preislied*, seems to follow Maurer.

The major controversy discussed in Walther's political poems is the struggle between the empire and the papacy during the period of turmoil following the election of two pretenders to the imperial throne in 1198. After the death of Henry VI, son of Frederick Barbarossa, the Hohenstaufen faction elected Henry's brother, Philip of Swabia, to succeed him, while the opposing Guelphs elected Otto IV of Brunswick. When Philip was murdered, Otto succeeded him with the approval of Pope Innocent III, who later shifted his support to the Hohenstaufen Frederick II. During this time, the petty princes tried to stake their own areas of power at the expense of the Crown. In these controversies, Walther supported first Philip, then Otto, and finally Frederick II, probably reflecting the successive allegiances of his princely patrons. In "Diu Krône ist elter danne der Künec Philippes sî" ("The Crown Is Older than King Philip"), Walther argues for Philip—his legitimacy based on the preestablished condition that the crown, which is older than he, fits him so well, a poetic allusion to the Hohenstaufen's possession of the real Imperial crown (while his opponent Otto IV was crowned in the proper place, Aachen, and by the right ecclesiastic, the bishop of Cologne). Another poem in the "Philip tone" parallels, with some doctoring of historical facts, a procession of Philip at Magdeburg with the birth of Christ; Philip's wife Irene (later renamed Mary), daughter of the Byzantine Emperor, is compared with the Virgin Mary, "rose without thorn, dove without gall." Again the possession of the right insignia is stressed, but an even stronger title, the link with the great Hohenstaufen predecessors, is compared with the Trinity: "There walked an Emperor's brother and an Emperor's son in one garment, though the names are three" (Frederick, Henry, and Philip). To medieval man, accustomed to thinking in terms of the "analogy of being," the impact of this poem confirming divine appointment must have been grat.

"I Was Sitting upon a Rock"

Written in the "imperial tone," the most famous of Walther's poems, "Ich saz ûf eine Steine" ("I Was Sitting upon a Rock"), depicts Walther in the pose in which he is illustrated in the *Manessische Handschrift*: sitting on a large rock with his legs crossed and his chin and one cheek supported by the palm of one hand. He was pondering very anxiously on "how one should live in the world." He could give no advice on "how one could acquire three things," so that none of the three would be ruined. The first two are honor and property, "which often are harmful to one another"; the third is God's grace, "which is worth more than the other two." The poet would like to have all three in one chest, but unfortunately it is impossible for property, worldly honor, and God's grace ever to dwell in one heart. "Paths and roads are blocked to them: Treachery lies in ambush, violence moves on the street; peace and justice are very sorely wounded. The three have no safe convoy, until these two recover." The subject of the stanza is how to order one's life correctly in this world.

The main components of the poem are seven abstract nouns; the main structuring device is a system of mathematical vectors that creates an ethical topography and conveys an impression of objective moral certainty. There are three goals that one should attempt to attain in life: honor (a), property (b), and God's favor (c), which is more valuable than property and honor and is also eternal. There are two instrumental goods: peace (d) and justice (e). Because a and b are incompatible and together endanger c, one cannot hope to attain them all. At this point, an extended metaphor is inserted: The streets are insecure for a, b, and c, since two negative abstractions, treachery (f) and violence (g), threaten. The two ancillary values d and e are sorely wounded. The solution to a, b, and c's predicament would be an extension and reversal of the metaphor "unsafe roads." This solution cannot be achieved until the two ancillary values d and e have the "remedy" that corresponds to their "ailment." A secondary rhetorical figure occurs twice, an *apo koinu* (the relation of one grammatical component to two others, one before and one after it); the clause "I could give no advice" can relate to the "how" clause before and the "how" clause after it. Similarly, "unfortunately this cannot be" negates both "I wanted to put them in one chest" and the possibility that honor, property, and God's favor might come together in one heart.

"OTTO TONE"

Of the six poems in the "Otto tone," the first in Maurer's sequence welcomes Otto IV and announces the submission of the princes, specifically of Walther s patron Dietrich von Meissen; the second alludes to the eagle and lion on Otto's coat of arms and calls on him to establish peace in Germany with "generosity" and "power" and to direct his country's power against the pagans. The third, "Hêr Keiser" ("Sir Emperor"), calls even more emphatically for a crusade: "Sir Emperor, I am an official messenger and I bring you a message from God: you govern the earth, he governs the kingdom of heaven: he has ordered me to complain to you (you are his regent) that in his Son's land the Pagans are exulting to the disgrace of you both. You should protect His rights." The fourth Otto poem, "Hêr Bâbest" ("Sir Pope"), refers to the contradiction created when the pope first endorsed Otto and then switched to support his opponent: "We heard you command Christendom as to which Emperor they were to obey.... You should not forget that you said: 'Whoever blesses you let him be blessed; whoever curses you, let him be cursed with a complete curse.' For God's sake, think that over, if the honor of the clergy means anything to you." The fifth Otto poem applies the same complaint to the clergy at large: "We laymen are puzzled by the clergy's instructions. What they taught us till a few short days ago, they now want to contradict.... One of the two instructions is false." The sixth Otto poem retells the story of Jesus with the coin, and the conclusion gains cogency because the Middle High German words for "Caesar" and "Emperor" are identical: "Render to the Emperor what is the Emperor's and to God what is God's."

ANTIPAPAL POEMS

The thread of unity in Walther's political stance is his advocacy of a strong, united empire. This explains why in a good number of his poems he opposed the papacy, blaming papal interference in the affairs of the *Reich* for the widespread disorder in Germany. In "Künc Constantin der gap sô vil" ("King Constantine Gave So Much"), an angel cries "Alas, alas, three times alas" because of Constantine's famous (forged) donation of temporal power to the papacy, which poisoned all Christendom by striking at its civil head: "All princes now live in honor except that the highest one is weakened.... The clergy want to pervert secular law." From the first, Walther had blamed the pope for appointing two Germans to one throne "so that they would destroy and devastate the realm" and had identified cupidity as the motive: "Their German silver flows into my Italian coffers." Elsewhere Walther minces no words about the negative influence of the clergy: "You bishops and noble clergy are misled. See how the Pope ties you with the devil's ropes. If you tell us he has St. Peter's keys, then tell us why he scrapes his words out of the Bible."

He then accuses the clergy of simony and of being the devil's spokesmen. Certain lines most clearly identify the evil as seen by Walther: "If [the pope] is greedy, then all are greedy with him; if he lies, all lie with him; and if he deceives, they deceive with the same deception." Walther's viewpoint is clear: Christendom is ailing because its highest religious authority, the pope, undermines the chief secular authority, the emperor; moreover, by the pope's high authority, the evil at the top contaminates all the parts.

Patronage poems

An astonishing number of Walther's poems deal with complaints about inadequate financial support or a lack of respect from one patron or another, including the Emperor Otto, whose stinginess Walther blames for his change of allegiance to Frederick. At first, the modern reader may be repelled by an impression of crass venality, but in time, he perceives the need of a poet struggling in a marginal, insecure existence for a basic livelihood and for minimal social acceptance in the feudal class system. Two poems treat of a misunderstanding with a noble patron because a subordinate official had failed to give Walther the promised clothing. Two others describe a lawsuit against a certain Gerhart Atze for shooting Walther's horse on the grounds that its "relative" had bitten off Atze's finger. Apparently, Walther's class status was at stake, but, whatever the outcome, Walther avenged himself on Atze by poetic mockery. Other poems testify to the difficulties of being a dependent, wandering, unpropertied poet. One poem summarizes Walther's weariness with the wanderer's life: "Tonight here and tomorrow there, what a juggler's life that is." The reader rejoices with Walther when he finally receives from Frederick the small property that gives him a home of his own: "I have my fief, all the world, I have my fief! Now I do not fear the frost on my toes."

"Elegie"

One of the most poignant poems Walther wrote is the famous "Elegie," consisting of three stanzas all beginning with "Alas." The second stanza deals with the sad state of the empire and the "ungentle letters" from Rome (excommunicating Frederick II in 1227); the third is a call for a crusade and contains a primitive but striking image of fallen earthly reality: "The world is beautiful on the outside, white, green and red, and within black in color, dark as death." In the first stanza, Walther looks back on his life with elegiac poignancy like a reawakening Rip van Winkle: "Alas, where have all my years vanished? Did I dream my life, or is it true? Was all I dreamed existed really nothing? . . . My former playmates are tired and old. The meadow has been plowed, the forest has been cleared: If the river didn't flow as it once did, truly my sorrow would be great."

Bibliography

Berleth, Richard J. *The Orphan Stone: The Minnesinge r Dream of Reich*. New York: Greenwood Press, 1990. Berleth uses Walther's lyrics in this study of the relationship of the German political scene and German lyric poetry. Mixes biographical, literary, and the broader political elements of Walther's career and output.

Garland, Henry, and Mary Garland. *Oxford Companion to German Literature.* 3d ed. New York: Oxford University Press, 1997. Encyclopedic reference work with a brief but informative section on Walther. Contains several important bibliographic references.

Gibbs, Marion E., and Sidney Johnson. *Medieval German Literature: A Companion.* 1997. Reprint. New York: Routledge, 2004. Contains an overview of Walther's life and works, with a few translated passages and bibliography.

Heinen, Hubert. "Lofty and Base Love in Walther von der Vogelweide's 'So die bluomen' and 'Aller werdekeit.'" *German Quarterly* 51 (1978): 465-475. Treats Walther's concept of love; includes quotations in German and English, notes, and bibliography.

Jones, George. *Walther Von der Vogelweide.* 1968. Reprint. New York: Twayne, 1970. A brief but comprehensive study of Walther's life and major works. The first monographic treatment of Walther in English.

Kaplowitt, Stephen J. *The Ennobling Power of Love in the Medieval German Lyric.* Chapel Hill: University of North Carolina Press, 1986. Studies the theme for twenty-one minnesingers in twenty-one short chapters, of which Walther's is the longest at forty-five pages. Poems are discussed and described, but only briefly quoted.

McFarland, Timothy, and Silvia Ranawake, eds. *Walther von der Vogelweide: Twelve Studies.* Oxford, England: Meeuws, 1982. A collection of essays that covers a wide range of issues regarding influences on Walther, his influences on the genre, and his works' forms and content.

Sayce, Olive. *The Medieval German Lyric, 1150-1230: The Development of Its Theme and Forms in Their European Context.* Oxford, England: Clarendon Press, 1982. A widely ranging and very readable study that places Walther and his works in both the German and broader European streams of lyric development.

Scheibe, Fred Karl. *Walther von der Vogelweide: Troubadour of the Middle Ages.* New York: Vantage Press, 1969. A good brief introduction to Walther's life and poetry that also surveys the reception of his works and lists English translations. Contains a bibliography.

Sullivan, Robert G. *Justice and the Social Context of Early Middle High German Literature.* New York: Routledge, 2001. A history of the Holy Roman Empire hinging on an examination of High German literature and its authors' focus on social, political, and spiritual issues during a time of transformation. Bibliographical references, index.

David J. Parent

WOLFRAM VON ESCHENBACH

Born: Probably Eschenbach bei Ansbach, Franconia (now in Germany); c. 1170
Died: Probably Eschenbach bei Ansbach, Franconia (now in Germany); c. 1217

PRINCIPAL POETRY
Lieder, c. 1200
Parzival, c. 1200-1210 (English translation, 1894)
Willehalm, c. 1212-1217 (English translation, 1977)
Titurel, c. 1217 (*Schionatulander and Sigune*, 1960)

OTHER LITERARY FORMS

All surviving manuscripts of works attributed to Wolfram von Eschenbach (VAWL-from fawn EHSH-uhn-bok) lead to the conclusion that he was exclusively a poet. His masterpiece, *Parzival*, is considered the founder of the bildungsroman, or novel of development. This paternity is extremely tenuous, however, resting on affinities of characterization rather than of genre; the first recognizable novel did not appear until some 450 years after *Parzival*.

ACHIEVEMENTS

Although Wolfram von Eschenbach was roundly criticized by his contemporary Gottfried von Strassburg as a "fabricator of wild tales," other poets and especially Wolfram's audience were more appreciative. The extraordinarily large number of extant manuscripts— eighty-four separate manuscripts or fragments of *Parzival* and seventy-six of *Willehalm*—attests his popularity. In comparison, other major works of the High Middle Ages would seem to have been in less demand; the *Nibelungenlied* (c. 1200; English translation, 1848) exists in thirty-four versions, Gottfried von Strassburg's *Tristan und Isolde* (c. 1210; *Tristan and Isolde*, 1899) in only twenty-three. Many modern critics also proclaim Wolfram to have been a careless poet, unrefined and unlearned; however, Wolfram's works sparkle with his own vital personality in an era of subdued conventionality. In contrast to the sophisticated stylists Gottfried and Hartmann von Aue, Wolfram wrote with color, depicting exotic scenes and exciting adventures in vibrant tones. His language is uniquely robust, studded with heroic (rather than courtly) terminology, Franconian dialect, and French loanwords, as well as a number of neologisms. Often chosen for resonance and acoustical effect, his language lends additional energy to his rhetorically crafted tales. His style is serious and humorous, insightful and charmingly frivolous. In short, Wolfram was a thoroughly delightful storyteller who constantly manipulated his audience as well as his characters.

Wolfram has not attained immortality as a result of his personality or style, however.

Because of his inferior social status as a layman, Wolfram was able to view courtly society from both within and without, to question assumptions and conventions with unusual detachment, often with humor. He fused disparate sources and traditions to form new and challenging visions of people and society which remain viable to this day. In *Parzival*, for example, he created a poem monumental in size and scope that illuminates timeless concepts such as ignorance and wisdom, grief and courage, guilt and salvation. This tale of the Holy Grail, of King Arthur's Round Table and attendant knights and ladies, transcends the realm of the courtly romance; indeed, the Arthurian circle is shown to be less than the ideal so often propagated by lesser poets. Of greater import is the development of an individual who ultimately attains the highest position on earth, a worldly king who represents the highest of spiritual values as well—a noble goal for all humankind. Wolfram's works all exhibit this critical yet hopeful attitude. Wolfram invested his poetry with vitality, humor, mystery, and a lofty purpose. These same qualities engage the reader, now as then, and will continue to command thoughtful consideration.

Biography

To possess factual information pertaining to the life of any courtly poet is a rare occurrence; the poet as professional writer and public figure is, after all, a relatively recent phenomenon. In the case of Wolfram von Eschenbach, few documented details exist. Fortunately, Wolfram was a personable poet who could not refrain from injecting his experiences and opinions into his works. From his utterances, scholars have been able to reconstruct a plausible, if sketchy, vita.

Drawing on literary references, dialect evidence, and geographical speculation, scholars have concluded that Wolfram's home was probably in Eschenbach bei Ansbach, Franconia (now in Germany). There is no record of his family, of his formative years, or of his schooling. In fact, Wolfram's innocent pronouncement in *Parzival*, "I don't know a single letter of the alphabet," has become enigmatic: Does he intend to admit his unlearned background, to boast of his literary accomplishment despite his inability to read and write, or to twit his educated principal critic, Gottfried? In any event, it is clear that he was not formally educated, for influences of classical Latin writers (a staple in the monastery schools) are absent in his poems. Significantly, Wolfram himself never mentioned having "read" from his literary sources; his frequent references to having "heard" information leads scholars to presume that source material was actually dictated to him by a succession of literate scribes. One assumes today that Wolfram was an autodidact who learned those things necessary for the background of his tales; he was certainly familiar with French literature of the day and well acquainted with the works of contemporary German authors.

Despite his fame as a poet, Wolfram considered himself to be first and foremost a knight, though it is unlikely that he ever wielded a sword. As a layman and member of the petty nobility, he was unpropertied and poor his entire life, at the mercy of his patrons and audience. One of Wolfram's patrons, at least for a time, was the fabled Landgrave Herrmann of Thuringia; the legendary *Sängerkrieg*, or troubadours' competition, at Hermann's castle, however, appears to be only that: a legend.

A definitive chronology of Wolfram's works cannot be established. His lyric poetry, of which only nine songs still exist, consists primarily of *Tagelieder*, or morning songs—some of the finest in German poetry. Since there are so few, and they are of a conventional nature, most scholars presume that they were created before Wolfram's greater epic poems. From historical references included in the work, it appears that *Parzival* was begun about the beginning of the thirteenth century and, with interruption, finally completed approximately ten years later. *Willehalm* would appear to be the most mature of Wolfram's writings in style and content, while the other fragment, *Schionatulander and Sigune*, contains a historical note that suggests that it originated well after the completion of *Parzival*. The details of Wolfram's death remain a mystery. He is thought to have died in Eschenbach bei Ansbach about 1217; one contemporary insists that he died while writing the manuscript of *Schionatulander and Sigune*.

Analysis

The small corpus of nine songs that can be safely attributed to Wolfram von Eschenbach were presumably composed early in his literary career. More than half of these can be categorized as *Tagelieder*, or morning songs, a type of courtly poem that Wolfram refined for his German audience. The typical situation depicts daybreak and the call of the watchman, announcing the day's arrival to a pair of young lovers. Obviously, the man must leave, for if he were seen, his honor and the lady's reputation would be ruined. There is a tearful farewell, a last embrace, and the man departs. Wolfram's songs develop this theme artistically, allowing each of the three figures—watchman, man, and woman—to present in turn the episode from his (or her) individual point of view. Wolfram employed rhythmic crescendos to accentuate the dramatic moments of daybreak and farewell in a sensual atmosphere.

One noteworthy variation among Wolfram's lyrics is the antimorning song. Here, the poet speaks directly to the watchman, reprimanding him for warning the waking lovers. In praise of connubial bliss, the poet extolls the security of matrimony, which requires no secrecy and no painful farewells at dawn. Although this song is not one of Wolfram's finer creations, it does highlight his witty and often mocking temperament, a trait that can be traced throughout his later works. The same parodistic tone is evident in the remaining songs. The common theme in these poems is courting the favor of a lady. Conventional and even second-rank in appearance, these works display qualities that parody the entire established tradition of courtly love poetry. By pirating famous lines from other poems and including trite love phrases, Wolfram created fanciful songs that attest the superficiality of courtly conventions.

PARZIVAL

Wolfram's greatest achievement is clearly *Parzival*. This epic romance is enormous in scope, portraying literally dozens of legendary characters who span Europe and Asia over an extended period of time. The number of questions surrounding its creation are enormous as well: Which source or sources inspired Wolfram? Is *Parzival* indebted to Chrêtien de Troyes and Robert de Boron, to a combination of various related tales, or to the mysterious "Kyot," as Wolfram insists? Was the work interrupted by war or by Wolfram's changing mood? Was it written under the auspices of one or more patrons? Was the work composed in the same chronological order in which it appears today? Were the first two books—that is, the prologue—written only after the completion of the entire manuscript and then added to the beginning of Parzival's story? These are a few of the nagging questions surrounding Wolfram's classic tale. It is certain only that *Parzival* was not written in one uninterrupted effort and that publication of separate episodes preceded the final edition of almost twenty-five thousand lines.

Though *Parzival* is an Arthurian romance, it is clearly differentiated from earlier versions by its non-Celtic preoccupation with Christianity and the Holy Grail. Artificially divided into sixteen books by the philologist Karl Lachmann, the work traces the life and development of Parzival and his Arthurian counterpart, Gawan. In a prologue, the audience learns that Parzival's father, Gahmuret, was an exemplary knight. Through a series of adventures, Gahmuret wins and marries first a heathen queen and then a Christian queen, finally to die in chivalric pursuit of further love and fame. Upon the birth of her son, Parzival, the Christian queen fears that he will end like his father; therefore, she rears the boy in complete ignorance of courtly society. One day, young Parzival encounters several knights and immediately decides that he, too, must partake of this splendid life. For his protection, his mother sends him off in fool's garb and gives misleading advice, hoping that he will soon return unharmed and chastened. After his departure, she dies of a broken heart, but young Parzival perseveres, soon joining King Arthur's knights at the Round Table. He then discovers the Grail Castle and its king, Anfortas, who suffers from a most painful affliction. Failing to "ask the question"—that is, to show compassion and inquire as to the origins of the wound and the condition of the king—Parzival is expelled from the castle for his uncharitable silence. Because of his ignorance, inexperience, and overwhelming desire to become a knight, he commits numerous sins of omission and commission. Guided only by his heart and the wise counsel of the hermit, Trevrezent, Parzival matures through years of lonely struggle, proving that he is worthy of his responsibilities as a knight and as a Christian.

As Parzival wanders off into the wilderness in search of himself, Wolfram introduces Gawan, a member in good standing of Arthur's Round Table. Gawan is the epitome of the medieval knight, at once adept in chivalric combat and skillful in the conventional graces required of all nobility. He is ever willing to fight on behalf of a worthy cause or a beautiful lady, and he fulfills his Christian duties with similar ease. During the course of the tale, Wolfram clearly distinguishes Gawan from Parzival on one crucial issue: Gawan's Christianity is the fulfillment of a chivalric vow, an obligation to which he is committed, while Parzival's spiritual quest derives from inner motivation. Whereas Gawan accepts his religion unquestioningly, Parzival must struggle with doubt, at one point even renouncing God for his apparent injustice. This difference is finally decisive; it is the reason that Parzival and not Gawan will ultimately become Grail King—that is, the personification of the highest values both in worldly society (as king) and in the spiritual realm (of the Grail). At the conclusion of the epic, Parzival is crowned King of the Grail, reunited with his wife and friends, and introduced to a stranger from India; this speckled man is his half brother, Feirefiz, the child of Gahmuret's heathen queen. Together, from Europe to India (that being the extent of the known world in Wolfram's day), the sons of Gahmuret will uphold courtly and Christian values, to the benefit of all humankind.

It is clear, then, that *Parzival* is not the shallow, disorganized composition described by Wolfram's critics. The epic can and should be considered on various levels: as a historical depiction of the encounter between East and West, evidenced by the Crusades and the Christian mission to baptize non-Christians; as an Arthurian romance in which the knight's achievements are judged by this exemplary courtly society; as a "double novel" concerning the separate exploits of both Parzival and Gawan; and, finally, as an account of the spiritual development of a worthy soul from simpleton to sage, from sin to redemption and the attainment of humility and purity.

SCHIONATULANDER AND SIGUNE

Schionatulander and Sigune, like *Willehalm*, is an epic fragment composed at the end of Wolfram's life. The 164 stanzas of the original were later expanded by an anonymous poet who added more than six thousand stanzas to form *Der jüngere Titurel* (c. 1272)—though this final version does not seem to correspond to Wolfram's intentions. In any event, most scholars believe that the work is nearly complete as it now stands. There are few possibilities for diversion; the inevitable conclusion (Schionatulander's death) clearly limits the narrative's chronological scope.

Though there is an indication that *Schionatulander and Sigune* was Wolfram's final work, most scholars would prefer to place *Willehalm* in that position, based primarily on sentimental reasons. The latter deals with major ethical and philosophical questions concerning world peace and interdenominational coexistence, while the former is a tale revolving around two minor characters from *Parzival*. The German title *Titurel* is, in fact, a misnomer, corrected in the English translation (according to medieval custom, the title was taken from the name of the first character to appear). Thus, in a prologue, old King Titurel reflects on his long and eventful life before surrendering his kingdom and the Holy Grail to his son. Years later, one of Titurel's grandchildren marries a knight, only to die in childbirth; her surviving offspring is Sigune. Already the attentive listener will recall from *Parzival* this fateful name; Sigune is shown mourning the death of her beloved Schionatulander, who died at the hand of Orilus. This fragment, then, accounts for the earlier years of their relationship and clarifies their tragic fate. In short, the two youths fall in love and must abide by courtly convention—that is, they must restrain their passion. While on a walk in the forest one day, they discover a dog wearing a jeweled collar; the collar itself is inscribed with the love story of a similar couple. Before Sigune can finish reading the story, the dog dashes off. She then declares that she will not grant her love to Schionatulander until he brings back the collar. Here the fragment ends. From episodes appearing in *Parzival*, the listener knows that this pure, youthful love can never be fulfilled and that Sigune will spend the rest of her days mourning her lost lover until they are reunited in Heaven.

The theme here is tragic, the atmosphere filled with the poet's realization that life's brief happiness must be purchased at a fearful price. Sigune does not criticize the courtly conventions by which she must act (although some critics note that her trivial demand leads to her lover's death); as mentioned above, several other couples in Wolfram's works suffer similar losses. Sigune must learn to live with her fate and accept the fact that she was destined to love Schionatulander chastely, in sublimation of their great passion for each other. Loyalty, constancy, and God's grace will ultimately purify their love.

WILLEHALM

It is generally agreed that even had Wolfram not written his *Parzival*, he would deserve lasting fame for his *Schionatulander and Sigune* and for *Willehalm*. While *Schionatulander and Sigune* depicts the beauties and sorrows of courtly love, *Willehalm* is strikingly innovative in its treatment of timeless values. Wolfram's primary source, *Bataille d'Aliscans* (late twelfth century), was provided by Landgrave Herrmann of Thuringia for a commission, though the epic Wolfram created went far beyond the original, in scope and significance. The historical Willehalm (Guillaume d'Orange) contributed to the defeat of invading Arabs with his valiant efforts in combat, yet scarcely ten years later he renounced worldly ambitions and entered a monastery. Although Wolfram does not specifically emphasize this aspect of Willehalm's spiritual development, it becomes obvious that his story is intended as a sort of *Legende*, or life of a saint.

As one would assume from the French source, war is a major theme in *Willehalm*. Willehalm, the son of Count Henry of Narbonne, is sent into the world to seek his fortune at the court of Charlemagne. After numerous adventures, Willehalm marries Gyburg, the daughter of a heathen king who then invades Willehalm's realm to reclaim his daughter. Willehalm gathers his army and engages in fierce battles with the enemy. In spite of his ferocity, Willehalm's heroic exploits are not to be misconstrued; his immediate desire is simply to protect his wife. The increasingly murderous battle scenes are twice interrupted by carefully placed interludes; in both instances, Willehalm is able to rejoin Gyburg, and the couple enjoy a brief respite from the war in each other's arms. Here, Wolfram presents conjugal love as an extension of God's love, as a means to offset the brutal reality of life and as a form of *unio mystica* through which God's grace can be anticipated. Gradually, Willehalm and Gyburg come to the realization that both heathen and Christian are children of God, that it is a great loss when so many must die. Wolfram's is the first depiction in German literature of a loving, merciful God who would protect all his children, regardless of their faith. Following the conclusive victory over the heathen army, Willehalm's newly gained tolerance is very much in evidence; he frees his prisoners, allowing the vanquished to collect their dead and transport them to their homeland, there to be honored and buried according to their own religious customs.

Knights of the Middle Ages were deeply imbued with an Augustinian worldview: Heathens were servants of the Devil, and it was the duty of all Christians to destroy the infidel, thereby achieving more quickly the Kingdom of God on Earth. If one killed a heathen, honor and fame were the reward; if one were killed fighting heathens, so much the better, for the knight was guaranteed eternal life in Heaven. The Crusades were conducted in this spirit. Willehalm, too, pronounces his support for this credo at the outset, but as the story progresses and the slaughter mounts on both sides, Willehalm undergoes a dramatic change of heart. His initial missionary zeal, reminiscent of the Crusades, is replaced by understanding and tolerance. Thus does Wolfram combine his two major themes of war and love in a strikingly innovative presentation that proved extremely popular with its audiences.

Wolfram depicts two contending armies, heathen and Christian, which nevertheless are governed by similar conventions: knights on both sides fighting on behalf of their ladies in courtly service. Though the heathens are influenced by an almost carnal love, which is raised to a religious fervor, the Christians are motivated by courtly love and spiritual devotion to God. Wolfram's critical insight here is that both sides represent poles of one great love that originates in God. This sophisticated concept of love is Wolfram's contribution to eternal respect, love, and peace.

Willehalm could have concluded with a happy ending reminiscent of fairy tales, but the older Wolfram sought a more realistic solution, one which recognized that life's brief joys are often outweighed by horrendous tragedy and sadness. Despite obvious similarities, the significant differences between *Parzival* and *Willehalm* concern the appearance of this new reality, akin to the modern concept of existential angst. These differences are partly the result of the differences in the two distinct literary forms, the romance, which calls for a reliable reassuring order, and the battle epic, which draws attention to the fragility of human existence. In *Willehalm*, Wolfram demonstrates that courtly convention is precisely that: a formality that does not protect the individual from the vicissitudes of life. Here it becomes evident how far Wolfram has strayed from the

Augustinian attitude. His literary creation, Willehalm, is no missionary zealot, possessed with exterminating the heathens. He is a defender of Christian values as embodied in the Holy Roman Empire, though his martial duties are as painful to him as his enforced separation from his wife, Gyburg. However, she, too, plays an important role in this new vision of Christian tolerance, for in this character Wolfram has created perhaps the most vivid portrait of a woman in all medieval literature. Though Gyburg, as a woman, has no recourse to such knightly philosophy, she represents in her person the admirable traits of humanity, piety, mercy, and love, which are a reflection of God's grace. Like Willehalm, Gyburg is proclaimed a saint at the story's conclusion.

Out of a desire for symmetry or the aforementioned sentimentality, most scholars would find it especially fitting if *Willehalm*—this mature, noble, and modern work—were Wolfram's last testament. His *Parzival* will continue to inspire readers with its idealism, but it is *Willehalm* which offers the most hope to humankind through its thoughtful and realistic portrayal of tolerance and universal love as antidotes to the eternal curses of prejudice, hate, and aggression.

Bibliography

Gibbs, Marion E., and Sidney M. Johnson. "Wolfram von Eschenbach." In *German Literature of the High Middle Ages*, edited by Will Hasty. Rochester, N.Y.: Camden House, 2006. Briefly discusses what is known about Wolfram and contains sections on his best-known writings, as well as his songs.

Groos, Arthur. *Romancing the Grail: Genre, Science, and Quest in Wolfram's "Parzival."* Ithaca, N.Y.: Cornell University Press, 1995. With roots in the critical theory of Russian scholar Mikhail Bakhtin, this study examines the narrative discourse of one of Wolfram's major poems. Unfortunately, Groos is not especially successful in applying a critical theory that was designed to interpret modern novels to this major work of medieval poetry. Moreover, he does not pay enough attention to Wolfram's other major works.

Hasty, Will, ed. *A Companion to Wolfram's "Parzival."* Columbia, S.C.: Camden House, 1999. Essays provide analysis of the popular vernacular work as well as social and cultural context.

Hughes, Jolyon Timothy. *Wolfram von Eschenbach's Criticism of "Minnedienst" in His Narrative Works*. Lanham, Md.: University Press of America, 2009. Examines *Parzival* and *Schionatulander and Sigune* for *Minnedienst* ("love service") and how it negatively affects female characters.

Jones, Martin, and Timothy McFarland, eds. *Wolfram's "Willehalm": Fifteen Essays*. New York: Camden House, 2001. Jones and McFarland provide fifteen essays on Wolfram's epic of the Christian-Muslim conflict, placing it in historical and literary context and elucidating the epic's main themes, characters, and techniques.

Murphy, G. Ronald. *Gemstone of Paradise: The Holy Grail in Wolfram's "Parzival."*

New York: Oxford University Press, 2006. Murphy examines the Holy Grail, which Chrétien de Troyes had described as a golden serving dish set with jewels, large enough for a fish, and linked to Celtic traditions, and which Robert de Boron had described as a chalice and associated with Christianity. Wolfram instead asserts that the grail is a green stone, with special powers.

Poag, James F. *Wolfram von Eschenbach.* New York: Twayne, 1972. A useful introduction with quotations in both English and German. Contains index and bibliography.

Sivertson, Randal. *Loyalty and Riches in Wolfram's "Parzifal."* New York: Peter Lang, 1999. A reinterpretation of *Parzival* as the presentation of a conflict in medieval knighthood between the fight for abstract ideals and service for material gain. The author argues that Wolfram's epic defends feudal values that were in a state of decline. Compares works by Chrétien de Troyes and others.

Starkey, Kathryn. *Reading the Medieval Book: Word, Image, and Performance in Wolfram von Eschenbach's "Willehalm."* Notre Dame, Ind.: University of Notre Dame Press, 2004. Starkey relates the image and performance of *Willehalm* to the written word in an attempt to further understanding of the work.

Wynn, Marianne. *Wolfram's "Parzival": On the Genesis of Its Poetry.* 2d ed. New York: Peter Lang, 2002. Examines *Parzival* as poetry, examining Wolfram's creative process.

Todd C. Hanlin

CHECKLIST FOR EXPLICATING A POEM

I. The Initial Readings

A. Before reading the poem, the reader should:
 1. Notice its form and length.
 2. Consider the title, determining, if possible, whether it might function as an allusion, symbol, or poetic image.
 3. Notice the date of composition or publication, and identify the general era of the poet.

B. The poem should be read intuitively and emotionally and be allowed to "happen" as much as possible.

C. In order to establish the rhythmic flow, the poem should be reread. A note should be made as to where the irregular spots (if any) are located.

II. Explicating the Poem

A. *Dramatic situation.* Studying the poem line by line helps the reader discover the dramatic situation. All elements of the dramatic situation are interrelated and should be viewed as reflecting and affecting one another. The dramatic situation serves a particular function in the poem, adding realism, surrealism, or absurdity; drawing attention to certain parts of the poem; and changing to reinforce other aspects of the poem. All points should be considered. The following questions are particularly helpful to ask in determining dramatic situation:
 1. What, if any, is the narrative action in the poem?
 2. How many personae appear in the poem? What part do they take in the action?
 3. What is the relationship between characters?
 4. What is the setting (time and location) of the poem?

B. *Point of view.* An understanding of the poem's point of view is a major step toward comprehending the poet's intended meaning. The reader should ask:
 1. Who is the speaker? Is he or she addressing someone else or the reader?
 2. Is the narrator able to understand or see everything happening to him or her, or does the reader know things that the narrator does not?
 3. Is the narrator reliable?
 4. Do point of view and dramatic situation seem consistent? If not, the inconsistencies may provide clues to the poem's meaning.

C. *Images and metaphors.* Images and metaphors are often the most intricately crafted vehicles of the poem for relaying the poet's message. Realizing that the images and metaphors work in harmony with the dramatic situation and point of view will help the reader to see the poem as a whole, rather than as disassociated elements.
 1. The reader should identify the concrete images (that is, those that are formed from objects that can be touched, smelled, seen, felt, or tasted). Is the image projected by the poet consistent with the physical object?
 2. If the image is abstract, or so different from natural imagery that it cannot be associated with a real object, then what are the properties of the image?
 3. To what extent is the reader asked to form his or her own images?
 4. Is any image repeated in the poem? If so, how has it been changed? Is there a controlling image?
 5. Are any images compared to each other? Do they reinforce one another?
 6. Is there any difference between the way the reader perceives the image and the way the narrator sees it?
 7. What seems to be the narrator's or persona's attitude toward the image?

D. *Words.* Every substantial word in a poem may have more than one intended meaning, as used by the author. Because of this, the reader should look up many of these words in the dictionary and:
 1. Note all definitions that have the slightest connection with the poem.
 2. Note any changes in syntactical patterns in the poem.
 3. In particular, note those words that could possibly function as symbols or allusions, and refer to any appropriate sources for further information.

E. *Meter, rhyme, structure, and tone.* In scanning the poem, all elements of prosody should be noted by the reader. These elements are often used by a poet to manipulate the reader's emotions, and therefore they should be examined closely to arrive at the poet's specific intention.
 1. Does the basic meter follow a traditional pattern such as those found in nursery rhymes or folk songs?
 2. Are there any variations in the base meter? Such changes or substitutions are important thematically and should be identified.
 3. Are the rhyme schemes traditional or innovative, and what might their form mean to the poem?
 4. What devices has the poet used to create sound patterns (such as assonance and alliteration)?
 5. Is the stanza form a traditional or innovative one?
 6. If the poem is composed of verse paragraphs rather than stanzas, how do they affect the progression of the poem?

7. After examining the above elements, is the resultant tone of the poem casual or formal, pleasant, harsh, emotional, authoritative?

F. *Historical context.* The reader should attempt to place the poem into historical context, checking on events at the time of composition. Archaic language, expressions, images, or symbols should also be looked up.

G. *Themes and motifs.* By seeing the poem as a composite of emotion, intellect, craftsmanship, and tradition, the reader should be able to determine the themes and motifs (smaller recurring ideas) presented in the work. He or she should ask the following questions to help pinpoint these main ideas:
   1. Is the poet trying to advocate social, moral, or religious change?
   2. Does the poet seem sure of his or her position?
   3. Does the poem appeal primarily to the emotions, to the intellect, or to both?
   4. Is the poem relying on any particular devices for effect (such as imagery, allusion, paradox, hyperbole, or irony)?

BIBLIOGRAPHY

GENERAL REFERENCE SOURCES

BIOGRAPHICAL SOURCES

Jackson, William T. H., ed. *European Writers*. 14 vols. New York: Scribner, 1983-1991.
Kunitz, Stanley, and Vineta Colby, eds. *European Authors, 1000-1900: A Biographical Dictionary of European Literature*. New York: Wilson, 1967.
Magill, Frank N., ed. *Critical Survey of Poetry: Foreign Language Series*. 5 vols. Englewood Cliffs, N.J.: Salem Press, 1984.
_____. *Critical Survey of Poetry: Supplement*. Englewood Cliffs, N.J.: Salem Press, 1987.
Serafin, Steven, ed. *Encyclopedia of World Literature in the Twentieth Century*. 3d ed. 4 vols. Detroit: St. James Press, 1999.

CRITICISM

Coleman, Arthur. *A Checklist of Interpretation, 1940-1973, of Classical and Continental Epics and Metrical Romances*. Vol. 2 in *Epic and Romance Criticism*. 2 vols. New York: Watermill, 1974.
Jason, Philip K., ed. *Masterplots II: Poetry Series, Revised Edition*. 8 vols. Pasadena, Calif.: Salem Press, 2002.
The Year's Work in Modern Language Studies. London: Oxford University Press, 1931.

DICTIONARIES, HISTORIES, AND HANDBOOKS

Auty, Robert, et al. *Traditions of Heroic and Epic Poetry*. 2 vols. Vol. 1, *The Traditions*; Vol. 2, *Characteristics and Techniques*. Publications of the Modern Humanities Research Association 9, 13. London: Modern Humanities Research Association, 1980, 1989.
Bede, Jean-Albert, and William B. Edgerton, eds. *Columbia Dictionary of Modern European Literature*. 2d ed. New York: Columbia University Press, 1980.
France, Peter, ed. *The Oxford Guide to Literature in English Translation*. New York: Oxford University Press, 2000.
Henderson, Lesley, ed. *Reference Guide to World Literature*. 2d ed. 2 vols. New York: St. James Press, 1995.
Oinas, Felix, ed. *Heroic Epic and Saga: An Introduction to the World's Great Folk Epics*. Bloomington: Indiana University Press, 1978.

INDEX OF PRIMARY WORKS

Hoffman, Herbert H. *Hoffman's Index to Poetry: European and Latin American Poetry in Anthologies.* Metuchen, N.J.: Scarecrow Press, 1985.

POETICS

Gasparov, M. L. *A History of European Versification.* Translated by G. S. Smith and Marina Tarlinskaja. New York: Oxford University Press, 1996.

Wimsatt, William K., ed. *Versification: Major Language Types: Sixteen Essays.* New York: Modern Language Association, 1972.

GERMAN POETRY

BIOGRAPHICAL SOURCES

Hardin, James, ed. *German Baroque Writers, 1580-1660. Dictionary of Literary Biography 164.* Detroit: Gale Research, 1996.

———. *German Baroque Writers, 1661-1730. Dictionary of Literary Biography 168.* Detroit: Gale Research, 1996.

Hardin, James, and Will Hasty, eds. *German Writers and Works of the Early Middle Ages, 800-1170. Dictionary of Literary Biography 148.* Detroit: Gale Research, 1995.

Hardin, James, and Siegfried Mews, eds. *Nineteenth-Century German Writers to 1840. Dictionary of Literary Biography 133.* Detroit: Gale Research, 1993.

———. *Nineteenth-Century German Writers, 1841-1900. Dictionary of Literary Biography 129.* Detroit: Gale Research, 1993.

Hardin, James, and Max Reinhart, eds. *German Writers and Works of the High Middle Ages, 1170-1280. Dictionary of Literary Biography 138.* Detroit: Gale Research, 1994.

———. *German Writers of the Renaissance and Reformation, 1280-1580. Dictionary of Literary Biography 179.* Detroit: Gale Group, 1997.

Hardin, James, and Christoph E. Schweitzer, eds. *German Writers from the Enlightenment to Sturm und Drang, 1720-1764. Dictionary of Literary Biography 97.* Detroit: Gale Research, 1990.

———. *German Writers in the Age of Goethe, Sturm und Drang to Classicism. Dictionary of Literary Biography 94.* Detroit: Gale Research, 1990.

———. *German Writers in the Age of Goethe, 1789-1832. Dictionary of Literary Biography 90.* Detroit: Gale Research, 1989.

DICTIONARIES, HISTORIES, AND HANDBOOKS
Appleby, Carol. *German Romantic Poetry: Goethe, Novalis, Heine, Hölderlin.* Maidstone, Kent, England: Crescent Moon, 2008.
Baird, Jay W. *Hitler's War Poets: Literature and Politics in the Third Reich.* New York: Cambridge University Press, 2008.
Browning, Robert M. *German Poetry from 1750 to 1900.* New York: Continuum, 1984.
_____. *German Poetry in the Age of the Enlightenment: From Brockes to Klopstock.* University Park: Pennsylvania State University Press, 1978.
Dobozy, Maria. *Re-membering the Present: The Medieval German Poet-Minstrel in Cultural Context.* Turnhout, Belgium: Brepois, 2005.
Faulhaber, Uwe K., and Penrith B. Goff. *German Literature: An Annotated Reference Guide.* New York: Garland, 1979.
Hanak, Miroslav John. *A Guide to Romantic Poetry in Germany.* New York: Peter Lang, 1987.
Hofmann, Michael, ed. *Twentieth-Century German Poetry: An Anthology.* New York: Farrar, Straus and Giroux, 2008.
Hutchinson, Peter, ed. *Landmarks in German Poetry.* New York: Peter Lang, 2000.
Leeder, Karen J. *Breaking Boundaries: A New Generation of Poets in the GDR, 1979-1989.* New York: Oxford University Press, 1996.
Mathiew, Gustave, and Guy Stern, eds. *Introduction to German Poetry.* New York: Dover Publications, 1991.
Nader, Andrés José, ed. *Traumatic Verses: On Poetry in German from the Concentration Camps, 1933-1945.* Rochester, N.Y.: Camden House, 2007.
Owen, Ruth J. *The Poet's Role: Lyric Responses to German Unification by Poets from the GDR.* Amsterdam: Rodopi, 2001.

WOMEN WRITERS
Boland, Eavan, ed. and trans. *After Every War: Twentieth-Century Women Poets.* Princeton, N.J.: Princeton University Press, 2004.
Classen, Albrecht, ed. and trans. *Late-Medieval German Women's Poetry: Secular and Religious Songs.* Rochester, N.Y.: D. S. Brewer, 2004.
Harper, Anthony, and Margaret C. Ives. *Sappho in the Shadows: Essays on the Work of German Women Poets of the Age of Goethe, 1749-1832.* New York: Peter Lang, 2000.

GUIDE TO ONLINE RESOURCES

WEB SITES

The following sites were visited by the editors of Salem Press in 2010. Because URLs frequently change, the accuracy of these addresses cannot be guaranteed; however, long-standing sites, such as those of colleges and universities, national organizations, and government agencies, generally maintain links when their sites are moved.

LitWeb
http://litweb.net

LitWeb provides biographies of hundreds of world authors throughout history that can be accessed through an alphabetical listing. The pages about each writer contain a list of his or her works, suggestions for further reading, and illustrations. The site also offers information about past and present winners of major literary prizes.

The Modern Word: Authors of the Libyrinth
http://www.themodernword.com/authors.html

The Modern Word site, although somewhat haphazard in its organization, provides a great deal of critical information about writers. The "Authors of the Libyrinth" page is very useful, linking author names to essays about them and other resources. The section of the page headed "The Scriptorium" presents "an index of pages featuring writers who have pushed the edges of their medium, combining literary talent with a sense of experimentation to produce some remarkable works of modern literature."

Poetry Foundation
http://www.poetryfoundation.org

The Poetry Foundation, publisher of *Poetry* magazine, is an independent literary organization. Its Web site offers links to essays; news; events; online poetry resources, such as blogs, organizations, publications, and references and research; a glossary of literary terms; and a Learning Lab that includes poem guides and essays on poetics.

Poetry in Translation
http://poetryintranslation.com

This independent resource provides modern translations of classic texts by famous poets and also provides original poetry and critical works. Visitors can choose from several languages, including English, Spanish, Chinese, Russian, Italian, and Greek. Original text is available as well. Also includes links to further literary resources.

Poetry International Web
http://international.poetryinternationalweb.org

Poetry International Web features information on poets from countries such as Indonesia, Zimbabwe, Iceland, India, Slovenia, Morocco, Albania, Afghanistan, Russia, and Brazil. The site offers news, essays, interviews and discussion, and hundreds of poems, both in their original languages and in English translation.

Poet's Corner
http://theotherpages.org/poems

The Poet's Corner, one of the oldest text resources on the Web, provides access to about seven thousand works of poetry by several hundred different poets from around the world. Indexes are arranged and searchable by title, name of poet, or subject. The site also offers its own resources, including "Faces of the Poets"—a gallery of portraits—and "Lives of the Poets"—a growing collection of biographies.

Western European Studies
http://wess.lib.byu.edu

The Western European Studies Section of the Association of College and Research Libraries maintains this collection of resources useful to students of Western European history and culture. It also is a good place to find information about non-English-language literature. The site includes separate pages about the literatures and languages of the Netherlands, France, Germany, Iberia, Italy, and Scandinavia, in which users can find links to electronic texts, association Web sites, journals, and other materials, the majority of which are written in the languages of the respective countries.

ELECTRONIC DATABASES

Electronic databases usually do not have their own URLs. Instead, public, college, and university libraries subscribe to these databases, provide links to them on their Web sites, and make them available to library card holders or other specified patrons. Readers can visit library Web sites or ask reference librarians to check on availability.

Canadian Literary Centre

Produced by EBSCO, the Canadian Literary Centre database contains full-text content from ECW Press, a Toronto-based publisher, including the titles in the publisher's Canadian fiction studies, Canadian biography, and Canadian writers and their works series; *ECW's Biographical Guide to Canadian Novelists*; and *George Woodcock's Introduction to Canadian Fiction*. Author biographies, essays and literary criticism, and book reviews are among the database's offerings.

Literary Reference Center

EBSCO's Literary Reference Center (LRC) is a comprehensive full-text database designed primarily to help high school and undergraduate students in English and the humanities with homework and research assignments about literature. The database contains massive amounts of information from reference works, books, literary journals, and other materials, including more than 31,000 plot summaries, synopses, and overviews of literary works; almost 100,000 essays and articles of literary criticism; about 140,000 author biographies; more than 605,000 book reviews; and more than 5,200 author interviews. It contains the entire contents of Salem Press's MagillOnLiterature Plus. Users can retrieve information by browsing a list of authors' names or titles of literary works; they can also use an advanced search engine to access information by numerous categories, including author name, gender, cultural identity, national identity, and the years in which he or she lived, or by literary title, character, locale, genre, and publication date. The Literary Reference Center also features a literary-historical time line, an encyclopedia of literature, and a glossary of literary terms.

MagillOnLiterature Plus

MagillOnLiterature Plus is a comprehensive, integrated literature database produced by Salem Press and available on the EBSCOhost platform. The database contains the full text of essays in Salem's many literature-related reference works, including *Masterplots*, *Cyclopedia of World Authors*, *Cyclopedia of Literary Characters*, *Cyclopedia of Literary Places*, *Critical Survey of Poetry*, *Critical Survey of Long Fiction*, *Critical Survey of Short Fiction*, *World Philosophers and Their Works*, *Magill's Literary Annual*, and *Magill's Book Reviews*. Among its contents are articles on more than 35,000 literary works and more than 8,500 poets, writers, dramatists, essayists, and philosophers; more than 1,000 images; and a glossary of more than 1,300 literary terms. The biographical essays include lists of authors' works and secondary bibliographies, and hundreds of overview essays examine and discuss literary genres, time periods, and national literatures.

Rebecca Kuzins; updated by Desiree Dreeuws

CATEGORY INDEX

AESTHETIC POETS
    George, Stefan, 92
    Goethe, Johann Wolfgang von, 102
    Schiller, Friedrich, 225

BALLADS
    Goethe, Johann Wolfgang von, 102
    Schiller, Friedrich, 225

CLASSICISM: NINETEENTH CENTURY
    Hölderlin, Friedrich, 159

CONCRETE POETRY
    Gomringer, Eugen, 116

DADAISM
    Morgenstern, Christian, 170

ELEGIES
    Brecht, Bertolt, 70
    Goethe, Johann Wolfgang von, 102
    Hölderlin, Friedrich, 159
    Mörike, Eduard, 179
    Rilke, Rainer Maria, 205

ENLIGHTENMENT
    Heine, Heinrich, 138
    Novalis, 192

EPICS
    Hartmann von Aue, 129
    Wolfram von Eschenbach, 248

EPIGRAMS
    Goethe, Johann Wolfgang von, 102
    Schiller, Friedrich, 225

EXPRESSIONISM
    Benn, Gottfried, 55
    Brecht, Bertolt, 70

GAY AND LESBIAN CULTURE
    George, Stefan, 92

GOETHE, AGE OF
    Eichendorff, Joseph von, 81
    Goethe, Johann Wolfgang von, 102
    Heine, Heinrich, 138
    Hölderlin, Friedrich, 159
    Novalis, 192
    Schiller, Friedrich, 225

GRUPPE
    Bobrowski, Johannes, 63

HYMNS
    Hölderlin, Friedrich, 159
    Novalis, 192

JEWISH CULTURE
    Ausländer, Rose, 47
    Heine, Heinrich, 138
    Sachs, Nelly, 216

JUGENDSTIL
    George, Stefan, 92
    Rilke, Rainer Maria, 205

LOVE POETRY
    Gottfried von Strassburg, 124
    Hartmann von Aue, 129
    Heine, Heinrich, 138
    Mörike, Eduard, 179
    Walther von der Vogelweide, 237

LYRIC POETRY
    Benn, Gottfried, 55
    Eichendorff, Joseph von, 81
    Goethe, Johann Wolfgang von, 102
    Hartmann von Aue, 129
    Hesse, Hermann, 149

Hölderlin, Friedrich, 159
Morgenstern, Christian, 170
Rilke, Rainer Maria, 205
Sachs, Nelly, 216
Schiller, Friedrich, 225
Walther von der Vogelweide, 237
Wolfram von Eschenbach, 248

MIDDLE HIGH GERMAN PERIOD
Gottfried von Strassburg, 124
Hartmann von Aue, 129
Walther von der Vogelweide, 237
Wolfram von Eschenbach, 248
MINIMALIST POETRY
Bobrowski, Johannes, 63
MODERNISM
Benn, Gottfried, 55
Rilke, Rainer Maria, 205

NARRATIVE POETRY
Eichendorff, Joseph von, 81
Gottfried von Strassburg, 124
Hartmann von Aue, 129
Heine, Heinrich, 138
Wolfram von Eschenbach, 248
NATURE POETRY
Bobrowski, Johannes, 63
George, Stefan, 92
NEOCLASSICAL POETS
Goethe, Johann Wolfgang von, 102
Schiller, Friedrich, 225
NEO-ROMANTICISM
Benn, Gottfried, 55

ODES
Hölderlin, Friedrich, 159
Mörike, Eduard, 179
Schiller, Friedrich, 225

POLITICAL POETS
Brecht, Bertolt, 70
Walther von der Vogelweide, 237
POSTCONFESSIONAL POETS
Mueller, Lisel, 185
POSTMODERNISM
Mueller, Lisel, 185

RELIGIOUS POETRY
Eichendorff, Joseph von, 81
Morgenstern, Christian, 170
ROMANTICISM
Eichendorff, Joseph von, 81
Goethe, Johann Wolfgang von, 102
Heine, Heinrich, 138
Hölderlin, Friedrich, 159
Mörike, Eduard, 179
Novalis, 192

SATIRIC POETRY
Heine, Heinrich, 138
Morgenstern, Christian, 170
SONGS
Goethe, Johann Wolfgang von, 102
Hartmann von Aue, 129
Heine, Heinrich, 138
Mörike, Eduard, 179
Novalis, 192
Walther von der Vogelweide, 237
SONNETS
Goethe, Johann Wolfgang von, 102
Mörike, Eduard, 179
Rilke, Rainer Maria, 205
STURM UND DRANG
Goethe, Johann Wolfgang von, 102
Schiller, Friedrich, 225
SYMBOLIST POETS
George, Stefan, 92

TOPOGRAPHICAL POETRY
    Bobrowski, Johannes, 63

VISIONARY POETRY
    Novalis, 192
    Rilke Rainer Maria, 205

WAR POEMS
    Brecht, Bertolt, 70
WOMEN POETS
    Ausländer, Rose, 47
    Mueller, Lisel, 185
    Sachs, Nelly, 216

SUBJECT INDEX

Adorno, Theodor, 41
Algabal (George), 97
Alive Together (Mueller), 189
"Always to Be Named" (Bobrowski), 67
"Among Tenses" (Morgenstern), 174
Anthologie auf das Jahr 1782 (Schiller), 229
Arme Heinrich, Der (Hartmann), 135
Arthurian legends, 6
Ausländer, Rose, 47-54

Bachmann, Ingeborg, 42
"Bad Time for Poetry" (Brecht), 76
"Banshee, The" (Morgenstern), 174
Baroque poetry, 14
"Beautiful Youth" (Benn), 58
Becher, Johannes R., 36
"Beginning" (Novalis), 197
Benn, Gottfried, 36, 55-62
    "Beautiful Youth," 58
    "Departure," 59
    "Lost Self," 59
    "One Word," 58
Biedermeier, 24
Bobrowski, Johannes, 63-69
    "Always to Be Named," 67
    "Language," 67
Bodmer, Johann Jakob, 17
Book of Hours, The (Rilke), 209
Book of Images, The (Rilke), 209
Book of Songs (Heine), 144
Borchers, Elisabeth, 44
Brant, Sebastian, 9
Brecht, Bertolt, 39, 70-80
    "Bad Time for Poetry," 76
    Buckower Elegies, 77
    "In Dark Times," 76

"Legend of the Origin of the Book Tao-Tê-Ching on Lao-tzû's Road into Exile," 76
"Of Poor B. B.," 75
"Remembering Marie A.," 74
"Song of the Fort Donald Railroad Gang," 74
Svendborg Poems, 77
Breitinger, Johann Jakob, 17
Brentano, Clemens, 23
Britting, Georg, 38
Buch der Bilder, Das. See *Book of Images, The*
Buch der Lieder. See *Book of Songs*
Buch von der deutschen Poeterey, Das (Opitz), 14
Buckower Elegies (Brecht), 77
"Butterfly" (Sachs), 221

Celan, Paul, 42, 49
"Chorus of the Stones" (Sachs), 220
Concrete poetry
    Germany, 43
    Eugen Gomringer, 116
"Cranes of Ibycus, The" (Schiller), 234
Crisis (Hesse), 153

"Dancer" (Sachs), 222
"Departure" (Benn), 59
Dependencies (Mueller), 187
Devotional Songs (Novalis), 200
Dinggedichte (Rilke), 211
Discontinuity, German expressionism, 33
Domin, Hilde, 44
Droste-Hülshoff, Annette von, 25
Duino Elegies (Rilke), 212

Eich, Günther, 38
Eichendorff, Joseph von, 24, 81-91
    "Moonlit Night," 87
"Eighteen-Year-Old, The" (Morgenstern), 176
"Elegie" (Walther), 246
Enzensberger, Hans Magnus, 42
Erec (Hartmann), 132
Erotic poetry, 15
"Evening" (Novalis), 196
"Evolution" (Morgenstern), 176
Expressionism, 33

"Fish's Lullaby" (Morgenstern), 175
"Fleeing" (Sachs), 221
Folk poetry
    Germany, 18
"Funnels, The" (Morgenstern), 175

Galgenlieder. See *Gallows Songs, The*
Gallows Songs, The (Morgenstern), 173
"Ganymed" (Goethe), 110
Geistliche Lieder. See *Devotional Songs*
George, Stefan, 31, 92-101
    Algabal, 97
    The Seventh Ring, 99
    The Year of the Soul, 98
German poetry
    origins to nineteenth century, 1-16, 18-21
    nineteenth century to Reunification, 22-46
Godfrey of Strawbourg. See Gorrfried von Strassburg
"Gods of Greece, The" (Schiller), 232
Goethe, Johann Wolfgang von, 18, 102-115
    "Ganymed," 110
    "Prometheus," 110
    Roman Elegies, 110
    "Welcome and Farewell," 109
    West-Eastern Divan, 112

Gomringer, Eugen, 116-123
    Poesie als Mittel der Umweltgestaltung, 116
    Worte sind Schatten, 120
Gottfried von Strassburg, 124-128
    Tristan and Isolde, 125
Gottsched, Johann Christoph, 16
Gregorius (Hartmann), 134
Gryphius, Andreas, 14

"Halleluja" (Sachs), 221
Hardenberg, Friedrich von. See Novalis
Hartmann von Aue, 6, 129-137
    Der Arme Heinrich, 135
    Erec, 132
    Gregorius, 134
    Iwein, 133
    The Lament, 131
Hebbel, Friedrich, 28
Heine, Heinrich, 26, 138-148
    Book of Songs, 144
    Last of the Romantics, 144
    New Poems, 145
    Romanzero, 146
Herder, Johann Gottfried, 18
Hermeticism, 41
Hesse, Hermann, 149-158
    Crisis, 153
    Poems, 154
Heym, Georg, 34
Hoddis, Jakob von, 33
Hofmannsthal, Hugo von, 31
Hofmannswaldau, Christian Hofmann von, 15
Holz, Arno, 30
Huchel, Peter, 37
Humanism, 11
Hymnen an die Nacht. See *Hymns to the Night*
Hymns, 12

Hymns to the Night (Novalis), 23, 199
Hölderlin, Friedrich, 20, 159-169
   Nachtgesänge, 165

"I Was Sitting upon a Rock" (Walther), 244
Ideology of art, 32
"In Dark Times" (Brecht), 76
In den Wohnungen des Todes (Sachs), 219
"In the Blue Distance" (Sachs), 223
Iwein (Hartmann), 133

Jahr der Seele, Das. See *Year of the Soul, The*
Jugendstil, 30

Klage, Die. See *Lament, The*
Klopstock, Friedrich Gottlieb, 17
"Korf's Clock" (Morgenstern), 174
Krisis. See *Crisis*
Krolow, Karl, 41

Lament, The (Hartmann), 131
Langgässer, Elisabeth, 38
"Language" (Bobrowski), 67
Lasker-Schüler, Else, 34
Last of the Romantics (Heine), 144
"Legend of the Origin of the Book Tao-Tê-Ching on Lao-tzû's Road into Exile" (Brecht), 76
Lehmann, Wilhelm, 38
Lenau, Nikolaus, 26
Lichtenstein, Alfred, 36
Liliencron, Detlev von, 30
Loerke, Oskar, 38
"Lost Self" (Benn), 59
Lyric poetry, 7

"Melusine, If Your Well Had Not" (Sachs), 220
Meyer, Conrad Ferdinand, 29

Minne (poetic form), 7
Mir zur Feier (Rilke), 209
Modernism, 40
"Moonlit Night" (Eichendorff), 87
Morgenstern, Christian, 170-178
   "Among Tenses," 174
   "The Banshee," 174
   "The Eighteen-Year-Old," 176
   "Evolution," 176
   "Fish's Lullaby," 175
   "The Funnels," 175
   The Gallows Songs, 173
   "Korf's Clock," 174
Mueller, Lisel, 185-191
   Alive Together, 189
   Dependencies, 187
   The Need to Hold Still, 188
   The Private Life, 187
   Second Language, 189
   Waving from Shore, 189
Mysticism, Germany, 10
Mörike, Eduard, 26, 179-184
   "On a Christmas Rose," 181
   "A Visit to the Charterhouse," 182

Nachtgesänge (Hölderlin), 165
National Socialism, 39
Naturalism, 29
Nature poetry, 37
Need to Hold Still, The (Mueller), 188
New Poems (Heine), 145
New Poems (Rilke), 211
New Subjectivity, 43
Nibelungenlied, 5
Novalis, 23, 192-204
   "Beginning," 197
   Devotional Songs, 200
   "Evening," 196
   Hymns to the Night, 23, 199
   "On a Saturday Evening," 197

"The Poem," 201
The Stranger, 198
"To Tieck," 201
"To a Falling Leaf," 196

Object poem, 32
"Of Poor B. B." (Brecht), 75
"On a Christmas Rose" (Mörike), 181
"On a Saturday Evening" (Novalis), 197
"One Word" (Benn), 58
Opitz, Martin, 14
"Otto tone" (Walther), 245

"Panther, The" (Rilke), 212
Parzival (Wolfram von Eschenbach), 6, 251
Patriotic verse, German, 24
"Poem, The" (Novalis), 201
Poems (Hesse), 154
Poesie als Mittel der Umweltgestaltung (Gomringer), 116
Poetics
    German Enlightenment, 17
    Romanticism, 22
Political poetry, 24, 42
Private Life, The (Mueller), 187
"Prometheus" (Goethe), 110

Realism, 28
"Remembering Marie A." (Brecht), 74
Rhetorical poetry, 14
Rilke, Rainer Maria, 32, 205-215
    The Book of Hours, 209
    The Book of Images, 209
    Dinggedichte, 211
    Duino Elegies, 212
    Mir zur Feier, 209
    New Poems, 211
    "The Panther," 212
    Sonnets to Orpheus, 212
Roman Elegies (Goethe), 110

Romances, 6
Romanticism, 22
Romanzero (Heine), 146

Sachs, Nelly, 216-224
    "Butterfly," 221
    "Chorus of the Stones," 220
    "Dancer," 222
    "Fleeing," 221
    "Halleluja," 221
    In den Wohnungen des Todes, 219
    "In the Blue Distance," 223
    "Melusine, If Your Well Had Not," 220
    "She Dances," 222
    Sternverdunkelung, 220
Schiller, Friedrich, 19, 225-236
    Anthologie auf das Jahr 1782, 229
    "The Cranes of Ibycus," 234
    "The Gods of Greece," 232
    "The Song of the Bell," 234
Schionatulander and Sigune (Wolfram von Eschenbach), 252
Second Language (Mueller), 189
Seventh Ring, The (George), 99
"She Dances" (Sachs), 222
Siebente Ring, Der. See *Seventh Ring, The*
Sonette an Orpheus, Die. See *Sonnets to Orpheus*
"Song of the Bell, The" (Schiller), 234
"Song of the Fort Donald Railroad Gang" (Brecht), 74
Sonnets to Orpheus (Rilke), 212
Stadler, Ernst, 35
Sternverdunkelung (Sachs), 220
Storm, Theodor, 29
Stramm, August, 37
Stranger, The (Novalis), 198
Strassburg, Gottfried von. *See* Gottfried von Strassburg
Strophe (poetic form), 23